SCATTERED JEWELS OF A WISDOM TRADITION

A Vedanta Glossary

DANIEL MCKENZIE

Broken Tusk Press

A

Adhikaritva - Qualifications required for Vedanta study *2*

Adhyaropa-Apavada - Superimposition-negation; the teaching method of provisional attribution and later retraction *5*

Adhyasa - Superimposition of the unreal on the real *9*

Advaita - Non-duality; the identity of Self and Brahman *13*

Agami Karma - Future karma created by present actions *17*

Ahankara - Ego-sense; the "I-maker" *21*

Ajata-Vada - The teaching of no-birth showing creation never truly occurred *25*

Ananda - Bliss; more precisely, limitlessness *28*

Anatma - The non-Self; all that is not consciousness *32*

Anirvachaniya - The indefinable nature of maya *35*

Antahkarana - The inner instrument: mind, intellect, ego, memory *38*

Ashtanga Yoga - The eight-limbed discipline of yoga *41*

Atman - The Self; pure consciousness *44*

Atma-Vichara - Inquiry into the nature of the Self *48*

Avarana - The veiling power of maya *51*

Avastha-Traya - Three states of existence: waking, dreaming, and deep sleep *55*

Avidya - Ignorance of the Self *58*

Avyakta - The unmanifest; the causal state of maya *62*

B

Bhakti Yoga - Discipline of devotion *65*

I

Ishvara - The Lord; maya plus consciousness *118*

J

Jagat - The world; that which is born and perishes *124*

Jagrat - Waking state; one of three states of experience *127*

Jiva - The individual; consciousness identified with body-mind *130*

Jivanmukta - One liberated while living *135*

Jnana - Knowledge of the Self *138*

Jnana Yoga - Path of Self-knowledge through inquiry *142*

Jnanendriyas - Five organs of knowledge or perception: hearing, touch, sight, taste, smell *148*

Jnani - One who knows the Self *151*

K

Kama - Desire *155*

Karana Sharira - The causal body; the seed state of ignorance and latent impressions *160*

Karma - Action and its results *166*

Karma Yoga - Offering action without attachment to results *171*

Karmendriyas - Five organs of action: speech, hands, feet, excretion, procreation *177*

Karta-Bhokta - The sense of agency and enjoyership *180*

L

Lila - Divine play; the appearance of creation *183*

Laya - Individual dissolution *186*

M

Mahavakya - Great Upanishadic statements of identity between self and Brahman *190*

Mala - Impurity; the psychological residue that burdens the mind *193*

Manana - Reflection to remove doubts *198*

Manas - Mind; the faculty of thought and doubt *200*

Maya - The power of illusion and projection *203*

Mithya - Dependent reality; apparent existence *211*

Moksha - Liberation; freedom from bondage *215*

Mumukshutva - Strong desire for liberation *220*

N

Neti Neti - "Not this, not this"; method of negation *223*

Nididhyasana - Contemplation to assimilate Self-knowledge *226*

Nirguna Brahman - Brahman without attributes *231*

Nirvikalpa Samadhi - Unbroken meditative absorption *234*

Niyati - Cosmic order *239*

O

Om - Primordial sound; symbol of Brahman *243*

P

Panchakosha - Five layers "covering" the Self: physical, vital, mental, intellectual, bliss *247*

Pancha Mahabhuta - Five basic elements: space, air, fire, water, earth *250*

Panchikarana - Quintuplication; cosmological process of gross element formation *254*

Paramarthika - Absolute reality *258*

Prajna - Waking state; one of three states of experience *261*

Prakriti - Nature; primordial matter *264*

Prakriya - Teaching method *269*

Pralaya - Cosmic dissolution *186*

Pramana - Valid means of knowledge *277*

Pranas - Vital energies; five physiological functions *280*

Prarabdha Karma - Karma responsible for present birth *283*

Pratibhasika - Illusory reality, like a dream or mirage *286*

Pratibimba-Vada - Teaching of reflection of consciousness *289*

Purnatva - Fullness, completeness *292*

Purusharthas - Four human goals: dharma, *artha, kama, moksha* *295*

R

Raga-Dvesha - Likes and dislikes *298*

Preface

Vedanta is not simply a philosophy to be studied, but a teaching tradition designed to guide the seeker toward Self-knowledge. Its methods are subtle, layered, and precise, often employing metaphor and negation to point beyond what can be objectified. Words in Vedanta rarely function as fixed definitions; they are carefully chosen pointers, meant to operate differently depending on context and readiness, guiding attention toward what is already present.

This glossary is therefore not intended as a dictionary of static meanings. Rather, it is a map of the tradition's methods and insights, offering multiple entry points into the same non-dual truth. Each entry includes not only the root and meaning of a term, but also its scriptural context, traditional role, Vedantic analysis, common misunderstandings, and the way the teaching resolves them.

Just as a teacher chooses a *prakriya* (method) according to the readiness (*adhikaritva*) of the student, this glossary allows a reader to explore according to their own inclination. Some entries point to practical discriminations (such as the three states of experience or the five sheaths), others unfold conceptual frameworks (like *mithya, vivarta-vada,* or *ajata-vada*), and still others describe the inner qualifications of the seeker. Together they form a complete picture: a set of mirrors revealing that the Self, ever-present and unborn, is already free.

Vedanta insists that no single word, analogy, or method is absolute. Each term is like a ladder rung: useful for climbing, but left behind once the view is attained. This glossary, then, is both a reference and a companion — a way of gathering the scattered jewels of the tradition into one place, so that their light can be seen in relation to each other.

adhikaritva

(adhikaritva — *uh-dhi-kuh-RIT-vuh*)

In Vedanta, not everyone is considered equally ready for the teachings. Truth may be universal, but the capacity to assimilate it is not. This preparedness of the student is called *adhikaritva* — the condition of being an *adhikari*, or qualified aspirant. The word itself comes from *adhikara*, meaning authority, fitness, or eligibility. Just as not every soil can receive a seed, not every mind can receive the knowledge of the Self without distortion.

The sages recognized that spiritual inquiry requires a particular maturity. It is not about academic intelligence, nor about devotion in the emotional sense, but about a subtle ripening of the whole personality. A student must be able to sustain attention, endure difficulty, cultivate discernment, and possess genuine yearning for liberation. Otherwise, the teaching turns into another philosophy to debate, another cultural identity to wear, or another pursuit to decorate the ego.

Tradition identifies four main qualifications (*sadhana-chatushtaya*) that together form adhikaritva: discrimination (*viveka*), dispassion (*vairagya*), discipline (*sat-sampatti*), and longing for liberation (*mumukshutva*). These are not arbitrary requirements but the natural signs of a person ready to turn inward. Just as a fruit falls when ripe, the mind of such a student becomes capable of grasping the radical vision of Vedanta — that one's very Self is limitless, already free.

The emphasis on *adhikaritva* does not imply exclusion or hierarchy. It is descriptive, not prescriptive. Everyone is, in essence, Brahman; but in practice, only certain minds are sufficiently quiet and clear to recognize it. For others, the path involves further purifications through *karma yoga, upasana,* devotion, and ethical living until that clarity arises. In this way, *adhikaritva* serves as a compassionate safeguard: it prevents premature grasping at the highest truth, which can otherwise lead to confusion, arrogance, or despair.

Ultimately, the measure of *adhikaritva* is sincerity. A mind that is humble, steady, and single-pointed — even if not outwardly accomplished — can be more qualified than one with dazzling intellect but restless attachment. Vedanta recognizes that it is not brilliance but readiness that opens the way to liberation.

—

Root & Meaning

Adhikaritva: the state of being qualified or eligible. From *adhikara* = authority, eligibility, fitness; with suffix *-tva* = "-ness" or "state of."

Scriptural References

- **Vivekachudamani of Shankara:** lays out the fourfold qualifications (*sadhana-chatushtaya*) as the basis of *adhikaritva*.
- **Bhagavad Gita (esp. Ch. 2, 4, 6):** highlights qualities such as steadiness, renunciation, and self-discipline as prerequisites for wisdom.
- **Mundaka Upanishad 1.2.12:** "Truth is not grasped by one without strength, nor by carelessness, nor without *tapas*.

Traditional View

Teachers stress that without *adhikaritva*, Vedanta is like pouring nectar into a muddy vessel. *Karma yoga*, meditation, and ethical living polish the vessel, preparing the student to assimilate the teachings without distortion.

Vedantic Analysis

Adhikaritva is an inner qualification, unrelated to caste or social standing. The Self is equally present in all, but ignorance veils it to differing degrees. Only when the mind is sufficiently quiet can the teaching be recognized as one's own truth.

Common Misunderstandings

- **Elitism:** It is not exclusionary, but descriptive of readiness.
- **Fixed status:** *Adhikaritva* is dynamic; it can ripen through practice or diminish through negligence.
- **Intellect = qualification:** Mere brilliance does not equal readiness; humility and sincerity matter more.

Vedantic Resolution

The highest knowledge requires the right vessel. *Adhikaritva* ensures that Vedanta is received not as abstract philosophy but as transformative recognition of the Self. It safeguards both the student and the teaching.

adhyaropa-apavada

(adhyāropa-apavāda — *udh-YAA-ro-puh
uh-pu-VAA-duh*)

When we first approach Vedanta, the tradition does not hand
us the highest truth all at once. To do so would be like giving
a child a book of calculus before they have learned arithmetic.
Instead, the teacher begins where the student stands. We are told
that Brahman created the world, that karma shapes our destiny,
that devotion and meditation can purify our minds. All of this is
granted provisionally, because it matches what our experience
seems to confirm. We see a world of plurality, we feel bound by
action and reaction, we long for a God who governs the order of
things.

Yet this granting is not the final word. Slowly, as the student
matures, the scaffolding is removed. What was once presented
as creation is later shown to be only appearance. What was once
taken as karma is revealed to be a provisional explanation that
vanishes when the Self is known. What was once devotion to a
distant God ripens into the recognition that there was never any
distance at all. This is the method of *adhyaropa–apavada
(adhyāropa-apavāda)* — superimposition and negation.

It is not deception, but compassion. The truth is too subtle to be
forced upon an unprepared mind. To tells a student on day one
that "All is Consciousness" would be a disservice. So the tradition
gives us steps, each one suited to the stage we are in, each one
designed to dissolve as soon as its purpose is served. Just as the
snake seen in semi-darkness gives way to the rope when light is
brought, so the world of duality gives way to non-duality when
knowledge dawns.

In this way, Vedanta does not contradict itself but unfolds itself.

First, it accepts what the student already believes; then, when the mind is ready, it gently rescinds that acceptance and points to what was always true. What remains at the end of this process is simple and luminous: there is only Brahman, untouched, actionless, whole. The rest was never more than appearance.

—

Root & Meaning

Adhyaropa: superimposition; the erroneous attribution of qualities or functions to something that does not possess them.

Apavada: negation, rescission, or withdrawal.

Together, *adhyaropa-apavada* refers to Vedanta's primary teaching methodology: first attributing or granting a provisional explanation to meet the student's current understanding, and later withdrawing it to reveal the higher truth.

Scriptural References
- **Chandogya Upanishad (6.2.3–6.2.4):** Describes Brahman "becoming many" and producing fire, water, and food—an example of provisional *adhyaropa* of creation.
- **Katha Upanishad (2.1.11):** "There is no plurality at all here." This is *apavada*, the later rescission of the earlier teaching of creation.
- **Brihadaranyaka Upanishad (2.3.6):** "Not this, not this (*neti, neti*)." The final negation of attributes projected onto Brahman.

Traditional View
Teachers begin with explanations suited to a seeker's level — granting creation, karma, and duality as real enough to work with. These provisional teachings (*karma yoga, upasana,* the acceptance of *Ishvara* as creator) refine the mind and provide security.

Only once the student is mature are these teachings rescinded. The final revelation is that Brahman neither creates nor acts, and the world is only an appearance (*mithya*).

Vedantic Analysis

The method works like scaffolding: temporary structures used until the final edifice is secure. Examples:

- The rope-snake: the snake (superimposition) is later dismissed as rope alone.
- The dream: appears real while dreaming, later negated upon waking.
- The pot–clay analogy: the pot is only name and form (*nama–rupa*), with no reality apart from clay.

Through this method, Vedanta guides the student from *shrishti–drishti vada* (creation is real) to *drishti–shrishti vada* (creation is appearance only), and finally to non-origination (*ajati vada*).

Common Misunderstandings

- **"Vedanta contradicts itself."** In truth, the teaching strategy is consistent: what is given provisionally is taken back once its utility is over.
- **"The provisional teaching was a lie."** No — it was a skillful step, like telling a child a story until they can grasp abstract truth. The intent is not deception but pedagogy.
- **"The world is utterly false."** Vedanta does not call the world non-existent (*asat*), but dependent (*mithya*), borrowing its reality from Brahman.

Vedantic Resolution

Adhyaropa–apavada is the pedagogical heartbeat of Advaita Vedanta. By provisionally granting reality to creation, karma, and duality, it provides a framework for practice and maturity. By rescinding these later, it reveals the non-dual Self as free of all action, causality, and limitation. It is not contradiction, but a compassionate unfolding of truth — step by step — until nothing remains but Brahman.

adhyasa

(adhyāsa — *uh-DHYAA-suh*)

In a dim alley at dusk, something coiled lies across your path. Your breath tightens. The heart leaps. You see a snake. But it's only a rope.

This is *adhyasa (adhyāsa)* — the error of superimposition. A false overlay of one thing onto another, born of incomplete knowledge. You saw the rope, but not clearly. So the mind filled in the rest, projecting fear where there was none. The illusion vanished when the truth was known, but not before the body had tensed, the breath had faltered, and suffering had begun.

Vedanta tells us that this is not a rare occurrence. It is our constant state. We live not in truth, but in projection. We mistake the body for the Self, the mind for identity, the world for permanence. We fear death as if we could die, grieve loss as if anything were ever ours. The Self — unchanging, unborn, untouched — is superimposed with the attributes of the body. In return, the body and mind are assumed to be conscious and real in themselves.

This mutual misidentification — between the Knower and the known (in the *Bhagavad Gita*, the *kshetrajna* and the *kshetra*) is *adhyasa*. It is not metaphor. It is the root of every thought and action in a life lived without Self-knowledge.

There are two classical forms of *adhyasa*:

- **The individual projection (pratibhasika):**
  You see a snake where there is a rope. The mind, operating under partial ignorance, fills in the missing details. When corrected by knowledge, the illusion ends. This is error by personal misapprehension, and it can be resolved by direct perception.
- **The cosmic projection (vyavaharika):**

You see the sun rise and set. The trees appear to move as the train rolls forward. These illusions persist not because you're personally mistaken, but because of the reference frame you're embedded in. The body-mind itself is a reference frame. Even when you know the truth, the world appears as before. The illusion doesn't end — but you no longer believe it.

This second kind of *adhyasa* is not your doing. It is *Ishvara srishti* — the projection of maya. You cannot stop the sunrise by knowing the sun does not rise. But you stop suffering over it.

When Arjuna lays down his bow at the start of the *Gita*, he is overwhelmed by grief. But the grief is not love. It is *moha*, delusion. He has confused *adharma* for dharma. He imagines virtue in abandoning his duty. He mistakes emotion for truth. This is *adhyasa* in action.

Arjuna is not seeing reality as it is. He is seeing through the lens of attachment — *raga* — which gives rise to sorrow — *shoka* — which clouds his judgment — *moha*. From there, all action is misaligned. Dharma bends under the weight of his projection.

Krishna doesn't fix Arjuna's grief by offering comfort. He corrects the error. He shines light on the rope.

Adhyasa is not just a concept to grasp, it is the very mechanism of suffering. To superimpose is to suffer. To misidentify is to be bound. Freedom (*moksha*) is not a change in the world — it is the removal of error.

When you know the rope, the snake disappears. But when you know the Self, the world remains but you are free of it.

Even the enlightened, the *jnani*, continues to see sunrise and sunset. But he knows what is real. He walks through the world like one in a lucid dream — not disturbed, not confused. The projection remains, but the identification is gone.

Adhyasa is where Vedanta begins. Shankara opens his commentary on the *Brahma Sutras* with this very error. Without understanding *adhyasa*, the rest of Vedanta cannot be understood. For it is not a philosophy of belief, but a path of correction — a lifting of the veil, a waking from a misperception that never was.

To see clearly is not to change what is seen. It is to know what you are — not the seen, not the body, not the mind. But That which sees.

—

Root & Meaning

Sanskrit *adhi-* ("upon") + *asa* ("to sit"); literally "to sit upon" or "superimpose."

Scriptural References

- **Bhagavad Gita (2.16, 2.22, 13.1–2):** Contrasts the perishable field (*kshetra*) with the imperishable Knower (*kshetrajna*).
- **Brahma Sutra Bhashya (Introductory Adhyasa Bhashya by Shankara):** Defines *adhyasa* as the superimposition of the Self and the not-Self.
- **Mundaka Upanishad (2.2.5):** The rope-snake metaphor as an example of ignorance-based error.
- **Mandukya Karika (3.29–31):** Describes waking life as projection due to ignorance.
- **Vivekachudamani (108–111):** Lists *adhyasa* as the fundamental cause of bondage.

Traditional View

The mechanism by which *avidya* operates, causing the confusion of Self and non-Self.

Vedantic Analysis

Adhyasa has no independent reality; it is sublated through Self-knowledge, just like the snake disappears when the rope is recognized.

Common Misunderstandings

• Believing *adhyasa* is a conscious act rather than an automatic, unconscious projection.
• Assuming it can be removed by willpower alone without Self-knowledge.

Vedantic Resolution

Discrimination (*viveka*) and sustained contemplation (*nididhyasana*) reveal the Self and dissolve *adhyasa*.

Advaita

(Advaita — *uh-dvai-tuh*)

Advaita is both the simplest and the most unsettling of truths: there is no second thing. Not you and me, not subject and object, not even God and creation. Only Brahman (pure awareness), appearing as all.

For most seekers, this is terrifying. In *dvaita* (duality), we find comfort: objects provide material security, relationships provide emotional support, and God provides a cosmic anchor. Advaita threatens to strip these away. Swami Paramarthananda notes that immature seekers often feel Advaita is unsafe — like losing every support system at once. Yet the teaching insists: you do not lose support; you discover you are the support of the entire cosmos.

This paradox — that the very security we seek in the finite can only be found by letting it go — is at the heart of Advaita. Gaudapada offers radical clarity: the world has not truly originated. Out of Brahman, changeless, no change can come. Out of nothing, nothing can come. What, then, is the world? An appearance without origin, like a dream.

Dreams offer the perfect analogy. While dreaming, the mind creates mountains, oceans, friends, and enemies, and believes them real. Only upon waking do we realize that the dream never "originated" — it was a projection of mind. So too with waking life. The world, says Vedanta, is *mithya* — empirically useful, transactionally real, but without independent substance. Its apparent solidity is a borrowed existence, lent by Brahman.

No wonder Advaita provokes resistance. As long as we mistake ourselves for limited beings — *Vishva* (waker), *Taijasa* (dreamer), or *Prajna* (deep sleeper) — we feel insecure, grasping for relationships and supports. But Advaita reveals that our true nature is *turiya*: ever free, ever secure, untouched by the play of states. To the immature, this appears as loss; to the mature, as liberation.

It is easy to dismiss such teaching as abstract. Yet in quieter moments, we may sense its truth. The boundaries we cling to — of self and other, mine and yours — waver. A glimpse of the ocean, the silence of meditation, or even the collapse of a cherished certainty can open into non-duality. For a moment, the quarrel of philosophies subsides. As Gaudapada observed, dualists argue endlessly, but the non-dualist has no quarrel.

Modern science, for all its brilliance, still assumes division as its foundation: observer vs. observed, particle vs. wave, mind vs. matter. Yet quantum physics, with its entanglements and indeterminacies, edges toward Advaita's vision — a reality where division is provisional, not absolute. The philosopher may analyze; the mystic may proclaim; the physicist may measure. But Advaita whispers a simpler truth: I am that non-dual Brahman.

Advaita is frightening because it asks us to surrender the familiar scaffolding of duality. But in that surrender lies the only real freedom. What we fear to lose was never ours; what we cannot lose is what we already are. The wave has always been ocean. The dream has always been mind. The self has always been Brahman.

—

Root & Meaning

Advaita is formed from *a* (not) + *dvaita* (duality, twoness). It literally means "not-two" or "non-dual." It points not to oneness as another concept, but to the negation of all duality — the realization that there is no second thing apart from Brahman.

Scriptural References
• **Mandukya Upanishad (7):** describes *turiya* as "advaita,"

beyond waking, dream, and deep sleep.

- **Kaivalya Upanishad (19):** "Everything is born in me alone; everything is based on me alone; everything resolves into me alone. I am that non-dual Brahman."
- **Chandogya Upanishad (6.8.7):** *tat tvam asi* — "That thou art."
- **Brhadaranyaka Upanishad (1.4.10):** *aham brahmasmi* — "I am Brahman."

Traditional View

In Advaita Vedanta, consolidated by Gaudapada and Shankaracharya, the world is understood as *mithya* — transactionally real (having empirical utility) but without independent substance. The individual self (*jiva*) is not truly separate from Brahman, but only appears so due to maya. Liberation (*moksha*) comes not through creating union, but through recognizing there was never separation.

Vedantic Analysis

Gaudapada outlined four key points:

- The origination of the world is to be negated (Brahman, being changeless, cannot be a cause).
- The factuality of the world's independent existence is to be negated.
- The appearance and experience of the world are accepted as empirical (*vyavahara*).
- The cause of the appearance is maya or *avidya*.

The world is like a dream: it appears, is experienced, and serves a role, but vanishes upon awakening.

Common Misunderstandings

- Advaita is not "monism." Monism affirms one substance;

Advaita points to that which is beyond all substance/attribute categories.

- It does not deny experience; it denies independent reality to experience.
- It is not a mere mystical state (*nirvikalpaka avastha*) but a vision (*darshana*) that redefines one's understanding of self and world.
- Many fear Advaita, mistaking it for insecurity — the loss of God, world, and relationship. But the teaching shows that the Self is the very support of all.

Vedantic Resolution

Advaita is not achieved, it is recognized. The walls of the pot may seem to divide space, but space was never divided. Similarly, the Self was never separated from Brahman. The only "obstacle" is ignorance (*avidya*), which projects the illusion of duality. Removal of ignorance is liberation.

agami karma

(āgāmi karma — *AA-gAA-mee KAR-muh*)

When we speak of karma, we often imagine a heavy past dragging us along, or a present destiny we cannot escape. But Vedanta
adds another subtle category, one that points forward: *agami*
(*āgāmi*), the karma that is not yet here but is being generated
moment by moment. The word itself means "arriving." Unlike
sanchita — the vast backlog of accumulated deeds — or *prarabdha*
— the portion already fructifying in this life — *agami* is the fresh
imprint of today's actions. Every decision, every word, every
thought that arises with the sense of "I am the doer" becomes a
seed that may ripen into tomorrow's experience.

In this sense, *agami* represents our most immediate freedom and
our most immediate bondage. Freedom, because right now I can
choose how to act, how to respond, and whether to align with
dharma or with impulse. Bondage, because if those actions spring
from ignorance and self-centeredness, they weave new threads
in the net of samsara. The present is not a clean slate; it is a loom,
and every movement of mind and hand weaves another pattern
that will either bind or release.

Yet the Vedantic teaching does not leave us in despair at this endless production of karmic fabric. It shifts the focus from the action
to the actor. For the ordinary person, karma is inescapable: the
doer acts, the results accrue, and *agami* piles on. But for the one
who has seen the truth of the Self, no *agami* arises. Why? Because
action itself is not the problem; it is the sense of doership. When
the ego dissolves in the light of knowledge, the burnt rope of
action may still move, but it cannot bind. From the standpoint of
the *jnani* (one with Self-knowledge), there is no one left to accumulate karma — no account in which to deposit new seeds.

This is why the scriptures often say: *sanchita* destroyed, *agami* neutralized, *prarabdha* alone remains. The liberated one lives out the unfolding *prarabdha* of the body but does so untouched, like the sun reflecting in a puddle yet never wet. For such a person, there is no "future karma" to be feared, because the very machinery of karma has lost its fuel.

For seekers, the concept of *agami* is both a warning and an invitation. It warns us that every careless act sows a seed we will eventually harvest. But it invites us, too, to live deliberately: to align each choice with dharma, to cultivate *sattva*, to let our daily life become a field of purification rather than entanglement. More than anything, it invites us to question the root assumption — "I am the doer" — and see through it. Because the true Self does not act, does not enjoy, and does not bind.

In that vision, the very category of *agami* collapses. What could possibly arrive for that which is timeless?

—

Root & Meaning

The word *agami* comes from the Sanskrit root *gam* ("to go"), with the prefix *a-* ("towards, approaching"). Thus *agami* means "that which is coming" or "arriving." In Vedantic terminology, *agami karma* refers to the "arriving karma," i.e., the new karmas generated in the present life that will bear fruit in the future.

Scriptural References

- **Bhagavad Gita 4.37–38 (commentaries):** Krishna speaks of how the fire of knowledge burns up accumulated karmas; commentators clarify that while *sanchita* and *agami karmas* are destroyed by knowledge, prarabdha must be lived out.
- **Yoga Vasishtha:** Defines *agami* as the results of present actions that will be added to one's store of karmas.

- **Advaita Vedanta teachers:** Swami Tejomayananda, Swami Paramarthananda, and others consistently explain *agami* as the karmic "income" that gets added to the karmic "capital" of *sanchita*.
- **Sri Ramana Maharshi:** Accepted the working of *agami* at the empirical level, but taught that once the ego dissolves in Self-realization, there is no doer left to generate new karma.

Traditional View

The threefold division of karma is often explained through analogy:

- **Sanchita** = accumulated karmas (capital account)
- **Prarabdha** = portion of karmas currently fructifying (spending account)
- **Agami** = newly created karmas in this life (income account)

Agami karma arises whenever action is performed with a sense of doership (*kartritva*) and ownership (*bhoktritva*). The results may fructify in the current life or remain in seed form to join the storehouse of *sanchita*.

Vedantic Analysis

Advaita Vedanta clarifies that karma itself does not bind; rather, identification with the ego-doer binds. For the *ajnani* (ignorant one), every action done with ego creates *agami*. For the *jnani* (knower of the Self), there is no longer a doer, and thus no new *agami* accrues.

Shankara and later teachers emphasize that self-knowledge (*atma-jnana*) burns *sanchita*, neutralizes *agami*, and allows *prarabdha* alone to play out until the body falls. Hence the *jivanmukta* is free of future birth, as no fresh karmic seeds are being sown.

Common Misunderstandings

- **"Agami means future suffering only."** Not so. *Agami* is simply the future karmic result of present actions, whether pleasant (*punya*) or painful (*papa*).
- **"All agami must be experienced immediately."** Some *agami* does fructify in this very life, but much of it is deferred, feeding into the reservoir of *sanchita*.
- **"Agami continues even after realization."** From the standpoint of non-duality, the *jnani* is not a doer; hence no new karma is generated. Post-realization actions are like the movement of a burnt rope — appearing real, but powerless to bind.

Vedantic Resolution

Agami highlights the dynamic aspect of karma: as long as one functions as a doer, the cycle perpetuates itself, and rebirth becomes inevitable. Vedanta resolves this by pointing to the falsity of the doer itself. When the ego is sublated through self-knowledge, no one remains to generate new karmas. In this way, *agami* — like the other forms of karma — belongs only to the empirical realm of ignorance and has no standing in the vision of the Self.

ahankara

(ahaṅkāra — *uh-hung-KAA-ruh*)

We walk through life with a familiar companion, so intimate that we rarely question it: the "I." This sense of self, called *ahankara (ahaṅkāra)* in Sanskrit, is more than pride or arrogance. It is the "I-maker," the principle that constructs individuality by joining the pure light of consciousness with the shifting conditions of the mind.

Vedanta says the ego is not an independent entity. It is like a reflection in a mirror — a mysterious third thing, borrowing light from the face and form from the glass. The face is the Self, ever-present and shining. The mirror is the mind, which reflects. And what we see in the mirror is the ego: an image, recognizable and experienced, yet with no substance of its own. Remove the face or the mirror and the reflection vanishes. In the same way, in deep sleep when the mind resolves, the ego disappears.

The *ahankara* borrows its "I am" from the Self — the undeniable fact of existence and awareness. But it borrows its attributes from the body and mind: "I am tall, I am old, I am happy, I am sad." These borrowed predicates change constantly, yet we cling to them as if they define us. This is the trick of maya: to mistake the impermanent reflection for the permanent reality.

The ego cannot be surrendered, destroyed, or slain, for it is not a solid object in the first place. The very thought, "I will destroy the ego," is itself the ego speaking. What Vedanta proposes instead is discrimination. By inquiring into the nature of the "I," we discover that the ego is *mithya* — dependent, provisional, a necessary fiction for functioning as a person, but not the Self. The "I" that is aware of the ego is untouched by it, like the face forever unaffected by its shifting reflections.

Even enlightened beings continue to use *ahankara*. When Krishna speaks, when Vyasa writes, when Shankara comments, the ego is functioning — but as an instrument only, no longer mistaken for the Self. This is called an enlightened ego, one that knows itself as a tool, not the truth.

In the end, the ego is like a ghost: haunting, insubstantial, kept alive by our identification with it. If we look directly at it through inquiry — "Who am I?" — the ghost vanishes, leaving only the living presence of the Self, changeless and whole.

—

Root & Meaning

The Sanskrit word *ahankara* is composed of two parts: *aham* ("I") and *kara* ("maker" or "doer"). Literally, it means the "I-maker" — the principle that fashions the sense of individuality. In Vedantic usage, it does not primarily mean pride or arrogance (though it can manifest that way), but rather the root sense of personal identity: "I am this."

Scriptural References

- **Bhagavad Gita (3.27):** *"Prakriteh kriyamanani gunaih karmani sarvashah / ahankara-vimudhatma kartaham iti manyate"* — "Actions are performed by the *gunas* of *prakriti*; but one whose mind is
deluded by ego thinks, 'I am the doer.'"
- **Mandukya Karika:** teaches that the *ahankara* is *mithya*, neither entirely real nor unreal, arising only in conjunction with mind and consciousness.
- **Upadesha Sara (Ramana Maharshi, verse 19–20):** points to the disappearance of the "I-thought" (*ahankara*) upon self-inquiry, leaving only the pure Self.

Traditional View

Ahankara is classified as part of the *antahkarana* (inner instrument), alongside *manas* (mind), *buddhi* (intellect), and *chitta* (memory). It is the principle that appropriates experiences by saying "I see," "I do," "This is mine." In this sense it functions as the owner, the doer (karta), and the interpreter of experience.

Vedantic teachers distinguish between:

- **Enlightened ahankara:** the "I-sense" of a liberated person, who still uses the functional ego for worldly interaction but no longer mistakes it as the Self.
- **Unenlightened ahankara:** the "I-sense" bound by ignorance, which takes itself to be the true self and clings to identification with body, mind, and world.

Vedantic Analysis

Ahankara has no independent reality. It is a reflected consciousness (*atma-abhasa*), a composite borrowing:

- From Atman (original consciousness) it borrows existence and awareness.
- From the mind it borrows attributes, emotions, and limitations.

Like the reflection of a face in a mirror, *ahankara* is visible, experienced, and seemingly real, yet neither belongs to the mirror (mind) nor to the face (Self). It is a dependent, in-between phenomenon — mithya, real only in a transactional sense.

In waking and dream states, *ahankara* is active. In deep sleep, when the mind resolves, it disappears. Its impermanence reveals that it is not the true "I," which remains ever-present as pure consciousness.

Common Misunderstandings

- **Ego as pride only.** While pride (*mada*) is one manifestation of ego, *ahankara* is more fundamental — it is the entire I-sense.
- **The ego must be destroyed.** Vedanta does not advocate "killing" the ego. Since *ahankara* is not an independent entity, it cannot be destroyed. It can only be understood as mithya and no longer
mistaken for the Self.
- **Surrender means removing ego.** One cannot "surrender" the ego, because the one who surrenders is the ego itself. What Vedanta means by surrender is adopting an attitude of humility and recognition that all belongs to *Ishvara*, thereby loosening identification with the ego.

Vedantic Resolution

The ego is neither to be feared nor worshipped. It is a necessary instrument for functioning as a *jiva* in the world, but bondage arises when it is taken as absolute reality. Through *atma-vichara* (self-inquiry) or systematic Vedantic study, one learns to separate the eternal subject (atman) from the impermanent I-sense (*ahankara*). What remains is the pure "I," the witnessing consciousness (*sakshi*), which is ever-free and actionless. Thus, Vedanta resolves the paradox: the *ahankara* is real enough to transact, but not real enough to define who we are.

ajata-vada

(ajāta-vāda — *uh-JAA-tuh-VAA-duh*)

Of all Vedantic standpoints, none is more uncompromising than *ajata-vada (ajāta-vāda)*: the doctrine of no-birth. It declares that the universe, the individual, and even bondage itself have never truly arisen. What we call creation is only an appearance in the changeless Self, like a dream or a mirage. In reality, there is no creation, no dissolution, no seeker, no bondage, and therefore no liberation. There is only Brahman, ever unborn (*ajata*), ever free.

This is the view most famously articulated by Gaudapada in his *Mandukya Karika*. He presents *ajata-vada* not as a speculative philosophy but as the logical conclusion of non-duality. If Brahman is absolute, infinite, and without a second, then there cannot truly be another thing called "the world" that comes into being alongside it. Birth implies duality — a "before" and "after," a cause and effect. But the Self, being limitless, cannot undergo such change.

Ajata-vada is not a denial of lived experience. It does not suggest that the world is nothing; rather, it is *mithya*—an appearance that borrows its existence from Brahman, like a reflection borrows its light from the sun. At the level of conventional reality, creation appears, seekers strive, and liberation is taught. But from the highest standpoint (*paramarthika satya*), nothing has ever happened.

This vision is profoundly liberating. The burden of becoming, of traveling from bondage to freedom, is lifted. One recognizes that freedom is not an attainment but the very nature of the Self here and now. As Gaudapada declares: "No creature is ever born. There is no one bound, no one seeking, no one liberated. This is the highest truth."

Such teaching, however, requires great maturity (*adhikaritva*).

For most, it can only be appreciated after long purification of the mind. Otherwise, it risks sounding like nihilism or apathy. Properly understood, *ajata-vada* is not a negation of reality but an unveiling of the unshakable fullness of being.

—

Root & Meaning

Ajata-vada: "the doctrine of no birth." From *a-* = not, *jata* = born, arisen; *vada* = doctrine or teaching.

Scriptural References

- **Mandukya Karika of Gaudapada (esp. 3.48):** "No creature is ever born; there is no origination of anything."
- **Upanishads: e.g. Brihadaranyaka Upanishad 4.4.19 hints at unborn reality:** "This Self is unborn, eternal, undecaying."
- **Bhagavad Gita 2.20:** "The Self is never born, nor does it ever die."

Traditional View

Ajata-vada is regarded as the *paramartha-satya* (highest truth) of Advaita. However, teachers often present it only to advanced students, since for practical instruction a graduated view of creation (*vivarta-vada or parinama-vada*) is used. *Ajata-vada* crowns the teaching.

Vedantic Analysis

Ajata-vada rests on the principle that Brahman is changeless. If Brahman alone is real, then creation cannot be an actual event. Instead, it is a superimposition, comparable to a rope mistakenly seen as a snake. The rope was never transformed; only the perception shifted. Similarly, the world is never actually "born." It is a projection upon the unborn Self.

Common Misunderstandings

- **Nihilism:** *Ajata-vada* does not deny existence; it denies independent origination. The world appears, but has no separate, absolute reality.
- **Practical Irrelevance:** It does not negate dharma, yoga, or practice. These remain valid at the empirical level. *Ajata-vada* simply clarifies the final standpoint.
- **Contradiction with devotion:** Non-origination does not negate devotion. In fact, devotion ripens the mind to appreciate this radical vision.

Vedantic Resolution

Ajata-vada reveals that liberation is not a future event but recognition of what always is. From the highest truth, nothing is ever bound, nothing is ever freed. Yet this is not a denial of life but its sanctification: the realization that every appearance shines only in the unborn light of the Self.

ananda

(ānanda — *AA-nun-duh*)

Ananda (ānanda) is often translated as "bliss," but this translation can be misleading. In Vedanta, the word refers to two very different kinds of joy — one transient and experiential, the other eternal and intrinsic to the Self.

Most spiritual seekers associate *ananda* with enlightenment, which is accurate — but only if we understand the nuances. Without this clarity, *ananda* can become yet another object we chase, rather than the nature of what we are.

Reflected Bliss (Pratibimbananda)

The first kind of *ananda* is experiential bliss — joy gained through sensory experiences or subtle states of mind. This includes:

• Sensual pleasures, such as delicious food or physical affection
• Sattvic joys, like those found in music, art, or intellectual insight
• Spiritual highs, such as those encountered in meditation or
  samadhi

All of these are undeniably pleasurable, but they are also temporary. They come and go. Because of this, we are forced to constantly seek new objects, places, relationships, or states to keep the stream of joy alive. When we can't — due to circumstances, aging, or just life's unpredictability — we may become restless, frustrated, or disillusioned.

Vedanta explains why this cycle never leads to lasting satisfaction. No object or experience contains happiness in and of itself. If it did, it would bring the same joy to everyone at all times. The fact that it doesn't proves a crucial point: The joy must be coming from me.

Vedanta calls this reflected bliss (*pratibimbananda*). It's the bliss of the Self briefly reflected in the mind when desire temporarily ceases. The moment we acquire what we want, the agitation caused by wanting subsides — and for a fleeting moment, the mind becomes still. That stillness allows the inherent fullness of the Self to shine through.

Unfortunately, we misattribute this inner stillness to the outer object. We believe the person, car, vacation, or spiritual vision made us happy, when in fact the object merely removed our inner turbulence long enough to let happiness be felt.

Original Bliss (Atmananda / Bimbananda)

The second type of *ananda* has nothing to do with objects or experiences. It is the bliss of the Self itself — limitless satisfaction, unchanging fullness, the feeling of needing nothing.

This is the ananda in the phrase *sat-chit-ananda* — "existence-consciousness-bliss." But here, bliss doesn't mean pleasure. It means limitlessness (*ananta*). In fact, *ananda* in this context is better translated as: "Existence-Consciousness-Limitlessness." These three are not separate attributes, but synonymous pointers to the non-dual Self — whole, unconditioned awareness.

Vedanta refers to this as original bliss (*bimbananda* or *atmananda*). It is not the giddy thrill of experience. It is the silent, unwavering satisfaction of knowing: I am always okay, no matter what happens. This recognition arises through Self-knowledge and sustained attention on the Self — not through spiritual highs or emotional experiences.

The Real Meaning of Bliss

True bliss isn't the thrill of buying a new car, starting a romance, traveling to a tropical island, or even reaching a spiritual peak. It's not about chasing "feelings" at all. Real *ananda* is the quiet joy of knowing I am not the doer, not the enjoyer. I am the Self: infinite, eternal, whole, free.

As long as we continue to seek bliss in the world of objects, we remain caught in cycles of longing and loss. But the moment we recognize bliss as our true nature — not something to be gained, but something to be known — the search ends.

Ananda is not a reward. It is who you are.

—

Root & Meaning

Ananda:"bliss," "fullness"; from the root *nand* ("to rejoice, to delight") with prefix *a* ("towards, near, fully").

Scriptural References

- **Taittiriya Upanishad 2.7:** "From Brahman comes *ananda*... he who knows Brahman attains *ananda*."
- Brhadaranyaka Upanishad 4.3.32: "This Self is dearer than a son, dearer than wealth... this Self is ananda."
- **Chandogya Upanishad 7.23.1:** "Where one sees nothing else... that is the infinite; that is *ananda*."

Traditional View

The intrinsic nature of Brahman; not caused, not dependent on time, place, or object.

Vedantic Analysis

Happiness from objects is only a reflected glimpse of *ananda*, revealed when mental disturbance subsides.

Common Misunderstandings

• Equating *ananda* with emotional pleasure or ecstasy
• Thinking it must be "created" or "reached" through practice

Vedantic Resolution

Recognize *ananda* as your own nature; no object or state is required.

anatma

(anātma — *uh-NAAT-muh*)

If Atman is the light of awareness, then *anatma (anātma)* is everything that appears in that light. The term literally means "not-Self" (*an* = not, *atman* = Self). It refers to all objects of experience, beginning with the body and extending outward to the entire universe.

The tradition is careful here: *anatma* is not "bad" or "illusory" in the sense of being nonexistent. It is very much present and available for transaction. What makes it "not-Self" is that it is an object of knowledge, observed by me. The body, thoughts, emotions, roles, possessions, and even the grand cosmos itself — all fall under *anatma*. None of these are constant; they change, decay, and dissolve back into their sources.

Vedanta insists that the Self can never be reduced to what is observed. The body is made of the five elements and returns to them at death. The mind is made of impressions and dissolves in deep sleep. Even subtle identifications like "I am a thinker, a feeler, a doer" are *anatma*, for they rise and fall in the witnessing awareness. The Self alone never comes or goes.

This recognition is the cornerstone of *viveka* — discrimination between atma and *anatma*. The practice is simple, though not easy: whatever is known, changing, or limited cannot be me. I am the witness of the body, the one aware of the mind, the background in which the world arises. Freedom lies not in rejecting *anatma* but in seeing it for what it is: dependent, transient, and never my essential nature.

When this clarity deepens, life's disturbances soften. The wise person remains the witness even as the play of *anatma* unfolds. Emotions may come, but their frequency, intensity, and recovery period diminish. The world still appears, but its grip loosens, because the one who knows "I am the Self" is no longer lost in what is not-Self.

—

Root & Meaning

Anatma is formed from *an* (not) + *atman* (Self). It designates all that is "not the Self," namely, the entire field of objects — body, mind, senses, and world.

Scriptural References

- **Bhagavad Gita (2.16):** *"Na'sato vidyate bhavo, na'bhavo vidyate satah"* — "The unreal (*anatma*) has no being; the real (atman) never ceases to be."
- **Vivekachudamani (verse 108):** enumerates the body, senses, and mind as *anatma*, to be clearly distinguished from the Self.
- **Mandukya Upanishad:** describes the waking, dream, and deep sleep states as *anatma*, observed by the *turiya*, the Self.

Traditional View

Vedanta classifies the following as *anatma*:

- **Gross body (sthula sharira):** the physical form, sustained by the five elements.
- **Subtle body (sukshma sharira):** mind, intellect, senses, *prana*.
- **Causal body (karana sharira):** the seed of ignorance.
- **Five sheaths (panchakosha):** food, vital, mental, intellectual, and bliss sheaths.
- **Three states (avastha-traya):** waking, dream, and deep sleep.

All of these are objects of experience, changing and perishable, and therefore *anatma*.

Vedantic Analysis

The method of Vedanta is *atma–anatma viveka* — discerning the subject (Self) from the objects (not-Self). *Anatma* is characterized by:

• Being known (an object of awareness).
• Being changeful and time-bound.
• Being composed of the elements and returning to them.

The Self, by contrast, is ever the witness, never known as an object, free of change and limitation. Thus, the true "I" is not body, mind, or world, but awareness itself.

Common Misunderstandings

• **Anatma as nonexistence:** *Anatma* is not unreal like a barren woman's son; it exists but does not define me.
• **Anatma as worthless:** Vedanta does not dismiss the world; it only places it in its proper order — transactional, not ultimate.
• **Liberation requires destroying anatma:** Freedom lies not in erasing the world or the body but in knowing they are not-Self.

Vedantic Resolution

By constant discrimination, one learns: "I am the Self, awareness; the body, mind, and world are *anatma*." With this clarity, life continues, but the burden of identification is lifted. The *jnani* (Self-realized) still interacts with *anatma* — eats, thinks, speaks, works — yet no longer mistakes any of these as the essence of who he is.

anirvachaniya

(anirvacanīya — *uh-nir-vuh-chuh-NEE-yuh*)

In Advaita Vedanta, *anirvachaniya (anirvacanīya)* means indescribable, inexpressible. The term is most often used to describe
mithya — the ontological status of the world.

When we ask, "Is the world real?" the answer is paradoxical.
From the standpoint of *vyavahara* (transactional reality), it is real
enough to live in: fire burns, water quenches, actions yield results.
But from the standpoint of *paramarthika satya* (absolute reality), the
world cannot be ultimately real, since it is changing, dependent,
and negated by knowledge. Nor can it be dismissed as completely
unreal, like a barren woman's son.

Thus, the world is *anirvachaniya* — neither absolutely real nor
unreal, but indescribable. It appears by the power of maya, like a
rope mistaken for a snake. The snake is not real, because knowledge of the rope cancels it; yet it is not entirely unreal, because the
fear it produces is experienced.

Shankara and later Advaitins highlight this term to show the limits of binary categories. The intellect demands either/or answers,
but reality as revealed in Vedanta transcends these opposites. By
declaring the world *anirvachaniya*, Advaita prevents us from abso-
lutizing appearances while still affirming their empirical role.

—

Root & Meaning

From *an* (not) + *nirvachaniya* (explainable, definable).
Anirvachaniya = indefinable, indescribable, inscrutable.

Scriptural References

- Though the exact word may not appear in the early Upanishads, it is emphasized in later Advaita works:
- Shankara's commentaries use the rope–snake example to show the *anirvachaniya* nature of the world.
- **Vivekachudamani (108–112):** speaks of the world as neither real nor unreal.
- **Panchadashi (6.18):** explicitly describes maya as *anirvachaniya*.

Traditional View

- *Anirvachaniya* is the ontological status of *mithya*.
- Applies to the world as projected by maya.
- It is real for transaction, unreal from the absolute standpoint, and thus not fully classifiable.

Vedantic Analysis

- Real (*satya*) = changeless, independent, eternal (Brahman alone).
- Unreal (*asat*) = absolutely nonexistent, like sky-flowers.
- *Mithya/anirvachaniya* = dependent, changing, provisionally real.
- The world falls into this third category — neither *satya* nor *asat*.

Common Misunderstandings

- **That anirvachaniya means mystical or vague:** It is a precise philosophical category to account for empirical reality.
- **That anirvachaniya denies the world's existence:** It does not deny appearances, only their absolute status.
- **That anirvachaniya = subjective dream only:** It includes the shared empirical order governed by *Ishvara*.

Vedantic Resolution

The world is *anirvachaniya* — not ultimately real, not

utterly unreal, but dependent, provisional, and indescribable. Recognizing this frees the seeker from both naïve realism and nihilism, orienting them toward Brahman as the only reality.

Reflection: When Logic Stops

Anirvachaniya marks the limit of logic in Vedanta. The world is neither fully real nor unreal, and ignorance (*avidya*) itself cannot be explained. Questions such as "Why does maya exist?" or "Why creation?" have no ultimate answer — because any reason presupposes something outside Brahman, which is impossible.

Here, Vedanta bows to mystery. The answer is: we need not know. What matters is not why the illusion appears, but who we are amidst it. The inquiry into "Who am I?" has a definitive resolution: the Self as pure awareness.

In this way, *anirvachaniya* prevents endless speculation, humbles the intellect, and points us back to the direct recognition of the Self.

antahkarana

(antaḥkaraṇa — *uhn-tuh-kuh-ruh-nuh*)

The sages speak of the mind as if it were one thing, but Vedanta refines the picture. What we casually call "mind" is actually a set of coordinated faculties, together called the *antahkarana* (*antaḥkaraṇa*) — the "inner instrument." Just as the body is an instrument for action in the world, the *antahkarana* is the instrument through which the Self experiences, interprets, remembers, and identifies.

The term is significant: "inner" because it belongs to the subtle body, unseen by others yet immediately available to one's own awareness; "instrument" because it is not the Self itself but a tool of transaction. The *antahkarana* does not shine on its own. Like the moon borrowing light from the sun, it derives its illumination from consciousness. Without the Self as witness, the mind would be inert, a dark mirror.

The tradition distinguishes four functions within the *antahkarana*:

- **Manas (mind):** the faculty of desire, doubt, and emotion. It vacillates, considers options, and feels.
- **Buddhi (intellect):** the faculty of determination and discrimination. It decides, reasons, and concludes.
- **Chitta (memory):** the storehouse of impressions and recollections. It retrieves the past to inform the present.
- **Ahankara (ego):** the sense of individuality and doership, the "I" that claims experience.

Though divided in function, these are not separate organs. They are different facets of a single subtle instrument, like one crystal reflecting light in many colors.

Vedanta emphasizes that the *antahkarana* is *anatma* — not the Self.

It is known, variable, and dependent, while the Self is the constant knower. Still, it plays a vital role: liberation requires a mind that is purified, steady, and prepared. *Karma yoga*, devotion, meditation, and ethical living all have as their immediate aim the refinement of the *antahkarana*. Only such a mind can reflect the knowledge of the Self clearly, like a polished mirror.

When the *antahkarana* is restless, the world seems overwhelming. When it is sattvic, quiet, and clear, it reveals the truth that the Self was ever free.

—

Root & Meaning

Antah = inner
Karana = instrument
Together, "the inner instrument," referring to the subtle functioning of mind.

Scriptural References

- **Tattvabodha**: identifies the fourfold division of *antahkarana* — *manas, buddhi, chitta*, and *antahkarana*.
- **Bhagavad Gita (6.5):** speaks of uplifting oneself by the Self, which requires mastery over the inner instrument.
- **Upanishads:** frequently refer to the mind (*manas*) and intellect (*buddhi*) as the key mediators of experience and knowledge.

Traditional View

The *antahkarana* is a central component of the subtle body (*sukshma sharira*). It coordinates perception (via the sense organs), action (via *karmendriyas*), and experience. Its four functions are:

- **Manas (mind):** doubt, desire, emotion.
- **Buddhi (intellect):** discrimination, reasoning, decision.

- **Chitta (memory):** storing and retrieving impressions.
- **Ahankara (ego):** self-identity, ownership, doership.

Vedantic Analysis

The *antahkarana* is essential for experience, yet it is not the Self. It is subtle matter, a modification of *prakriti*, and therefore inert by nature. It becomes enlivened only in proximity to consciousness. Like a mirror reflecting light, it reveals but does not generate illumination.

For Vedanta, the goal is not to destroy the *antahkarana* but to refine it. A mind disciplined by *karma yoga* and meditation becomes sattvic and clear, capable of reflecting Self-knowledge without distortion. In realization, the *antahkarana* continues to function — the *jnani* still thinks, decides, remembers, and says "I" — but without misidentification. The instrument is known as an instrument, not mistaken for the Self.

Common Misunderstandings

- **Equating antahkarana with just "mind":** In Vedanta it is a fourfold faculty, not a single undifferentiated organ.
- **Assuming it is the Self:** The *antahkarana* is known, variable, and limited — hence *anatma*.
- **Believing liberation requires killing the mind:** The *antahkarana* is not to be destroyed but purified, stabilized, and understood in its proper role.

Vedantic Resolution

The *antahkarana* is indispensable for living and for liberation. With it, the Self can transact in the world and undertake inquiry. When purified, it reflects the Self's light steadily, allowing knowledge to dawn. When mistaken as the Self, it binds. Freedom lies in discriminating between the ever-free witness and this subtle inner instrument.

ashtanga yoga

(aṣṭāṅga yoga — *ush-TAAN-guh YO-guh*)

When we hear the word "yoga" today, most think of postures and stretching. But in Patanjali's *Yoga Sutras*, *yoga* means something far more subtle: *chitta vritti nirodhah* — the quieting of the mind's movements. To achieve this mastery, Patanjali prescribes a graduated discipline known as *ashtanga yoga (aṣṭāṅga yoga)*, the "eight-limbed path."

The eight limbs are not eight separate practices but an integrated system:

1. **Yama** — ethical restraints such as non-violence and truthfulness
2. **Niyama** — personal disciplines like purity, contentment, and surrender to the Lord.
3. **Asana** — steady, comfortable postures.
4. **Pranayama** — regulation of the breath.
5. **Pratyahara** — withdrawal of the senses from external objects
6. **Dharana** — one-pointed attention.
7. **Dhyana** — sustained meditation.
8. **Samadhi** — absorption, where subject, object, and process converge.

At its heart, *ashtanga yoga* is a discipline of reclaiming ownership over the mind. Left unchecked, the mind runs on involuntary thoughts — fears, anxieties, regrets — that kidnap attention and exhaust vitality. Through deliberate practice, one snatches the mind back from these intruders and trains it to be steady, present, and luminous.

Vedanta accepts the practice of *ashtanga yoga* not as an end in itself, but as a preparation. A quiet mind is not liberation, but it is indispensable for it. A yogi may reach *nirvikalpa samadhi*, a state of thought-free absorption, but this too ends; it is still an experience within time. Self-knowledge alone reveals the timeless freedom that is not gained or lost. Thus, Vedanta honors *ashtanga yoga* as a profound *sadhana*, a discipline that refines the mind into a fit instrument for inquiry, while making clear that the final step is knowledge, not experience.

—

Root & Meaning

Ashta = eight
Anga = limb
Together, "eight limbs" — the eightfold discipline of yoga set forth in the *Yoga Sutras*.

Scriptural References

- **Yoga Sutra (2.29):** enumerates the eight limbs.
- **Bhagavad Gita (6.5–6):** emphasizes the importance of mind-discipline, resonant with the aims of *ashtanga yoga*.
- **Vedantic Commentators (Shankara, Swami Paramarthananda):** reinterpret *ashtanga yoga* as mental discipline serving Vedantic inquiry.

Traditional View

Alongside the classic eightfold structure given by Patanjali, teachers in the Vedantic tradition often treat *ashtanga yoga* as the practical basis for what is now called *upasana yoga* — meditation and contemplative practices meant to prepare the mind for knowledge. In this context, the Yoga philosophy (dualistic metaphysics) is set aside, while the discipline of the eight limbs is preserved as a powerful method of inner purification.

The eight limbs are:

1. **Yama** — universal values (*ahimsa, satya, asteya, brahmacharya,*

aparigraha).

2. **Niyama** — personal disciplines (*shauca, santosha, tapah, svad-hyaya, ishvara-pranidhana*).
3. **Asana** — posture.
4. **Pranayama** — breath regulation.
5. **Pratyahara** — sense withdrawal.
6. **Dharana** — concentration.
7. **Dhyana** — meditation.
8. **Samadhi** — absorption.

Common Misunderstandings

- **"Yoga equals posture"**: In truth, *asana* is only one limb; the goal is mastery of the mind.
- **"Samadhi is liberation"**: It is profound, but temporary. True freedom is not an altered state but recognition of what is always present.
- **"Vedanta rejects Yoga"**: Vedanta rejects Patanjali's metaphysics but accepts *ashtanga yoga* as a powerful discipline, reinterpreted in harmony with non-duality.

Vedantic Analysis

Strengths: *Ashtanga yoga* disciplines the mind, reduces emotional disturbances, and cultivates focus and serenity. It is invaluable in preparing the mind (*antahkarana shuddhi*).

Limitations: *Samadhi* is still an experience, and therefore finite. Liberation (*moksha*) in Vedanta is not experiential absorption but the recognition of the ever-free Self.

atman

(ātman — *AAT-muhn*)

Atman *(ātman)* is identical in essence to Brahman, the absolute
reality. However, the word *atman* is typically used when referring
to the Self from the standpoint of the individual. If Brahman is
like vast, undivided space, then atman is that same space appearing as if confined within a pot. Of course, the space within a pot
is not different in quality from the space outside it. And when the
pot breaks, we do not say the space merges with outer space — it
was never truly separate. Space, like awareness, is indivisible,
partless, and always whole.

Likewise, atman, as pure awareness associated with an individual, is never truly divided. When the body ends its cycle, it returns
to the material universe, but awareness remains untouched—not
as "David's awareness" or "Susan's awareness," but as the single,
universal awareness principle.

A traditional analogy compares atman to electricity: just as electricity powers various appliances without being altered by them,
awareness enlivens body-mind-sense complexes without itself
being changed or limited. Yet unlike electricity, awareness is not
perceptible, measurable, or objectifiable. Scientists continue to
be baffled by consciousness because it cannot be grasped like an
object — it is the very subject.

Etymologically, atman is also related to the root *at*, meaning "to
breathe." As breath gives life and sound to a wind instrument, so
atman breathes life into the body. The resulting expression will
vary depending on the instrument, but the breath remains one.
Similarly, awareness is one, though it appears as many through
different body-mind-sense complexes.

When we examine the nature of atman, five salient features

stand out:

- Atman is not a part, product, or property of the body. Atman is not made of the body nor located in it. It exists on a different order of reality. What affects the body does not affect atman, just as what happens to a pot does not alter the space inside. The body is born, changes, and dies, but awareness remains unchanged.
- Atman is an independent presence that enlivens the body. Just as a light bulb glows when electricity flows through it, the body appears alive in the presence of awareness. But awareness depends on nothing. It is not "inside" the body, nor is it a function of it. It simply is.
- Atman is not limited by the body's boundaries. Though awareness is seemingly associated with one body, it is never confined by it. Just as space is never truly enclosed by walls or containers, awareness remains limitless despite its apparent individuality.
- Atman remains even after the body dissolves. Awareness precedes the body and remains after it dissolves. There is a profound shift when one realizes that awareness does not emerge from the body — it is the other way around. Just as space is not created by the pot, awareness is not created by the brain.
- Atman is unborn, undying, and impersonal. There is no "my awareness" or "your awareness." These are just names and forms. Awareness is not personal — it is the one impersonal reality in which all personalities arise. As Vedanta teaches, what we call the person is simply a configuration of the five elements. We are, in a sense, walking earth animated by awareness.

Lastly, another name for atman is the Self — our true nature and the silent witness of all experience. It is not an object but the light by which all objects are known. It is attributeless, limitless, ever-present — and the greatest discovery of a human life.

Root & Meaning

Atman: "self," "essence," "soul"; possibly from the root *an* ("to breathe") or *at* ("to pervade").

Scriptural References

- **Brihadaranyaka Upanishad (3.7.3, 4.4.5)**: Declares atman as the imperishable, beyond cause and effect.
- **Chandogya Upanishad (6.8.7)**: *"Tat tvam asi"* (That thou art), equating the individual Self with Brahman.
- **Mandukya Upanishad (verse 7)**: Describes atman as non-dual, the fourth state beyond waking, dream, and deep sleep.
- **Bhagavad Gita (2.16–25)**: Teaches that atman is unborn, eternal, and indestructible.
- **Vivekachudamani (254–260)**: Explains that atman is the witness, distinct from the body, mind, and senses.

Traditional View

The unchanging, witnessing consciousness that is identical with Brahman.

Vedantic Analysis

Self is self-revealing; never becomes an object; the basis of all experience.

Common Misunderstandings

- Equating atman with the ego, personality, or soul as a finite entity.
- Thinking the Self is "inside" the body like a physical occupant.

Vedantic Resolution

Atman is limitless consciousness — not confined to space, time, or the body-mind.

atma-vichara

(ātma-vicāra — *AAT-muh vi-CHAA-ruh*)

Atma-vichara (ātma-vicāra) means "Self-inquiry" — a disciplined investigation into the true nature of the Self. In Advaita Vedanta, this inquiry is not an experiment in meditation techniques, nor an attempt to produce an experience. It is the thoughtful and systematic use of reasoning (*vichara*) in alignment with the Upanishads, guided by a teacher, to resolve the fundamental question: *Who am I?*

The ordinary answer — "I am this body, these thoughts, these roles" — is shown to be mistaken. Through inquiry, the student comes to see that the body, senses, and mind are objects of knowledge, subject to change and limitation. They cannot be the Self. What remains is the ever-present awareness, the witness of all change.

This method of inquiry is embedded in the traditional threefold process:

Shravana — listening to the teaching.
Manana — reflecting on the meaning.
Nididhyasana — deeply assimilating the vision.

Thus, *atma-vichara* is the very heart of Vedanta — not a practice aimed at manufacturing blissful states, but the reasoning process that removes ignorance and reveals that the Self is already free.

—

Root & Meaning

Atma = Self.
Vichara = inquiry, reflection, reasoning.
Atma-vichara = inquiry into the true nature of the Self.

Scriptural References

- **Vivekachudamani (11–12):** "Of all means to liberation, knowledge alone is supreme. Inquiry (*vichara*) alone leads to knowledge."
- **Shankara's Upadesha Sahasri (1.1.4):** emphasizes that liberation arises from inquiry into the Self, not from ritual or meditation alone.

Traditional View

- *Vichara* is systematic reasoning aligned with scripture (*shastra*), under the guidance of a teacher.
- It is the primary means to Self-knowledge and freedom.
- It removes misidentification with non-Self (body, senses, mind).

Vedantic Analysis

- The Self (atman) is never an object of experience; it is the subject, awareness itself.
- *Atma-vichara* reveals this by showing that all that is changeful is not-Self (*anatman*).
- The inquiry culminates in the recognition: I am pure consciousness, limitless and free.

Common Misunderstandings

- **That Self-inquiry is a meditation technique:** In Vedanta, it is reflective reasoning, not experiential absorption.
- **That it produces Self-realization:** The Self is ever-present; inquiry only removes ignorance.
- **That inquiry can be done in isolation:** In tradition, it is supported by *shravana, manana, nididhyasana,* and guidance from *shastra* and teacher.

Vedantic Resolution

Atma-vichara is the structured reasoning that removes the false identification with body and mind. It reveals that the Self is not an object to be gained or experienced, but pure awareness, ever free.

avarana

(āvaraṇa — *AA-vuh-ruh-nuh*)

There is something quietly astonishing about human perception. We live every moment in and as pure awareness, yet almost no one recognizes it. The most obvious fact — the reality of oneself — is the one thing the mind consistently overlooks. Vedanta calls this strange lapse *avarana (āvaraṇa)*: the power of concealment.

Avarana does not hide the Self the way a curtain hides a lamp. The Self cannot be obscured; it is self-revealing. What *avarana* conceals is our recognition of it. It covers not the truth, but the mind's ability to discern the truth. It is a subtle, cognitive fog, a kind of metaphysical forgetting in which the ever-present light of awareness seems absent. In this sense, *avarana* is not darkness but mis-taking — a blindness that causes the obvious to appear hidden.

When *avarana* operates, the mind overlooks its own nature and turns outward. It searches for meaning, fulfillment, and identity in the field of objects — the very field that depends on the light of consciousness for its existence. The result is an inverted life: we seek the Self while standing in the Self; we chase wholeness while already being whole.

This concealment is felt not only in ignorance but in our ordinary restlessness. Even the most intelligent person may sense that something essential is missing but be unable to name it. The experience of "I don't know what I really am" is avarana at work. And because the mind cannot remain in a vacuum, concealment inevitably pairs with projection (*vikshepa*), filling the perceived absence with desires, fears, concepts, and identities.

Vedanta's radical claim is that *avarana* is not a personal defect. It is a universal condition — the basic structure of maya functioning through the mind. The individual does not create this concealment; the individual arises because of it. Liberation, then, lies not in acquiring a new experience but in removing the covering that makes the obvious appear hidden.

When *avarana* weakens, something quiet shifts. The mind becomes available. The teachings land. Inquiry deepens. One begins to see that awareness has never been absent; only the recognition of awareness was veiled. In that clarity, the pursuit for wholeness ends not in a mystical climax but in the simple realization that the seeker was never separate from what was sought.

Avarana lifts not by force but by understanding. When the mind learns to see clearly — through *viveka, shravana,* and the steady work of refinement — the concealment dissolves like fog in the morning sun. What remains is what has always been: the light by which the fog was known.

—

Root & Meaning

From the Sanskrit root *vr* — "to cover, to veil, to conceal." *Avarana* literally means a covering or an obscuration, referring to the cognitive veil that prevents the mind from recognizing the Self.

Scriptural References

While the term itself appears more fully in later Advaita literature, the function of *avarana* is clearly described in the Upanishads and classical commentaries:

- **Katha Upanishad 2.1.1–2:** The senses turn outward and fail to perceive the inner Self.
- **Mundaka Upanishad 1.2.8:** Ignorance (*avidya*) binds beings in misunderstanding.
- **Vivekachudamani (108–115):** Shankara describes the concealing power that hides the Self and gives rise to superimposition.
- **Panchadashi (6.1–6):** Vidyaranya explicitly distinguishes

avarana (concealment) from *vikshepa* (projection).

These texts collectively articulate the idea that the Self is ever-present yet unrecognized due to a veil of ignorance.

Traditional View

Avarana is one of the two powers of maya, along with *vikshepa* (projection):

Avarana – Conceals the real.
Vikshepa – Projects the unreal.

Tradition describes *avarana* as a kind of root ignorance (*moola avidya*) responsible for the mind's failure to see its true nature. It is said to have two effects:

• Veiling the Self (*atma-avarana*)
• Creating confusion about the non-Self (*anatma-avarana*)

This concealment is universal, not personal — it belongs to maya, not to the individual mind.

Vedantic Analysis

Avarana does not hide the Self the way a wall hides an object. The Self cannot be concealed, because it is self-luminous. Instead, *avarana* hides the fact of the Self from the mind.

This concealment manifests as:

• Misidentification with body and mind
• Searching for fulfillment in external objects
• A vague existential sense of "missing something"
• The inability to grasp the teaching even when hearing it
• Mistaking the projection (*vikshepa*) for reality

The crucial point: *avarana* blocks recognition, not existence.
It explains why a person can be intelligent, disciplined, even

spiritual — and still fail to "see" the obvious truth that awareness is the nature of the Self.

When *avarana* begins to thin through inquiry and assimilation, the mind becomes available for knowledge. The teaching lands. Insight becomes possible.

Common Misunderstandings

- **"Avarana makes the Self disappear."** No. The Self cannot be hidden or revealed; it is ever-known. *Avarana* covers only the mind's recognition of it.
- **"Avarana is a personal psychological defect."** It is not personal. It is the universal condition of ignorance that gives rise to the very sense of individuality.
- **"Avarana lifts through mystical experience."** Experiences come and go; many are vivid but do not touch the root ignorance. Only knowledge (*jnana*) removes concealment.
- **"If the Self is always present, why isn't realization immediate?"** Because *avarana* creates the illusion that the Self is elsewhere, causing the mind to look outward. Vedanta resolves this through teaching, not sensation.

Vedantic Resolution

Avarana is dispelled only by understanding — the clear recognition that the Self is already free, whole, and ever-present.

The process follows a precise sequence:

Shravana – Hearing the teaching clearly.
Manana – Resolving intellectual doubts.
Nididhyasana – Steady assimilation until the mind stops slipping back into old identifications.

As the veil lifts, the seeker discovers that nothing new is gained. Rather, what was always there becomes unmistakably evident. The end of *avarana* is the end of the seeker.

avastha-traya

(avasthā-traya — *uh-vuhs-THAA-tray-uh*)

Every human being passes through three states each day: waking, dreaming, and deep sleep. To ordinary eyes, these are simply conditions of mind and body. To Vedanta, they are doorways into understanding the Self.

In the waking state (*jagrat*), the individual experiencer is called *Vishva*, and at the macrocosmic level the total is *Virat*. In the dream state (*svapna*), the experiencer is *Taijasa*, illumined by the light of consciousness within, and the corresponding total is *Hiranyagarbha*, the cosmic subtle mind. In the deep sleep state (*sushupti*), the individual is *Prajna*, merged in causal ignorance, while the macrocosmic counterpart is *Ishvara*, the total causal reality.

Vedanta emphasizes that each of these states comes and goes, but something remains constant: the witnessing Self. The waking ego disappears in dream, the dream-ego disappears in deep sleep, but I — the awareness of their arising and subsiding — never vanish. Just as day and night alternate against the unmoving backdrop of the sky, these three states alternate against the changeless Self.

This inquiry into the three states is central to the *Mandukya Upanishad*, which culminates in the teaching of a fourth: *turiya*, the ever-present reality beyond waking, dream, and sleep. *Turiya* is not another state but the very consciousness in which all states arise.

Thus the *avastha-traya* teaching serves as a powerful mirror. By examining the transience of waking, dream, and sleep, one discriminates the eternal from the ephemeral. The Self is neither the doer of the waking, nor the dreamer of the dream, nor the sleeper of the sleep. It is the light of awareness in which all three appear.

Root & Meaning

Avastha = state, condition
Traya = three
Together: "the three states" of individual experience — waking
(*jagrat*), dream (*svapna*), and deep sleep (*sushupti*).

Scriptural References

- **Mandukya Upanishad:** the primary text analyzing the three
  states and revealing *turiya,* the non-dual Self.
- **Bhagavad Gita (2.69):** uses the metaphor of waking and sleep-
  ing to distinguish the wise from the ignorant.
- **Panchadashi (Chapter 1):** elaborates on the states as aids to
  Self-inquiry.

Traditional View

The three states and their corresponding identities:

- **Waking (jagrat):** Individual *Vishva* / Cosmic *Virat* (gross total).
- **Dream (svapna):** Individual *Taijasa* / Cosmic
  Hiranyagarbha (subtle total).
- **Deep sleep (sushupti):** Individual *Prajna* / Cosmic
  Ishvara (causal total).

Vedantic Analysis

- Each state is real while it lasts, but each is temporary and negated by the next.
- The unchanging witness (*sakshi*) is the invariable factor across
  all three.
- Liberation is recognizing oneself as that witness — not confined
  to any state.
- The teaching culminates in *turiya*: the timeless awareness that is

one's true nature.

Common Misunderstandings

- **Deep sleep as liberation:** It is a state of ignorance, not freedom. Awareness remains, but without recognition.
- **Turiya as a "fourth state":** *Turiya* is not a new experience; it is the ever-present reality of awareness itself.
- **Dream as unreal, waking as real:** Both are relative appearances; Vedanta treats them equally as *mithya*.

Vedantic Resolution

By inquiring into the three states, one recognizes that the Self is not limited to any of them. Waking, dream, and sleep belong to the *jiva*; the Self transcends them. The fruit of this knowledge is freedom here and now, as *turiya* is understood to be one's true identity.

avidya

(avidyā — *uh-vid-YAA*)

In Advaita Vedanta, *avidya (avidyā)* — ignorance — is the foundational principle that explains human suffering and bondage in the cycle of birth and death (samsara). It is not mere absence of information, but a fundamental misapprehension: the failure to discriminate between the real (Self) and the unreal (non-Self). This ignorance veils our true nature and projects a world of multiplicity, creating the illusion of individuality and separation.

Yet, when asked, "Where does this ignorance come from?" Vedanta often responds that its origin is *anirvachaniya* — inexplicable. It cannot be fully classified as real, because it disappears upon knowledge. But it is not entirely unreal either, since we clearly experience its effects. Like a dream, it persists until one awakens.

Adi Shankaracharya, the great 8th-century teacher of Advaita, begins his *Brahma Sutra Bhashya* by defining *avidya* in terms of *adhyasa*, or superimposition. This refers to the projection of something unreal onto something real — like mistaking a rope for a snake. In the same way, we superimpose body, mind, gender, and personality onto the Self, and mistake that bundle for "I." This error, subtle and deep-rooted, is *avidya*.

Throughout his works, Shankara uses various Sanskrit terms for this ignorance: *viparita jnana* (erroneous cognition), *moha* (delusion), *tamas* (darkness), *mithya ajnana* (false knowledge), among others. All of them point to a single misstep —the failure to recognize that the Self (atman) is not an object, not limited, and not in need of becoming anything.

While *avidya* refers to the individual's ignorance, maya is its macrocosmic counterpart — the power that brings about the appearance of the world itself. From the standpoint of the manifest cosmos, maya is said to be under the control of *Ishvara* (the Lord), whereas *avidya* controls the *jiva* (individual) until the dawn of Self-knowledge.

Maya is composed of the three *gunas* — *sattva* (intelligence), *rajas* (activity), and *tamas* (inertia). When these mix and project form and function, the One appears as many. This is the mystery of manifestation: not a real transformation, but an apparent one, arising due to ignorance.

In this view, *avidya* and maya are not two separate forces, but two aspects of the same power — seen from the individual and cosmic perspectives.

Why Does Ignorance Exist?

This is where Vedanta departs from conventional metaphysics. Vedanta does not offer a causal origin for ignorance, because any such explanation would only reinforce duality. From the standpoint of Brahman (non-dual reality) ignorance simply does not exist. The question "Why is there ignorance?" arises only within the realm of ignorance, just as the question "Why is there a mirage?" is relevant only until one sees there is no water.

Still, seekers often speculate. One poetic answer offered in the tradition is *lila* — divine play. Ignorance makes possible the appearance of experience, variety, striving, love, loss, and transcendence. Without it, there would be no *jiva*, no effort, no liberation. But even this answer is provisional, not ultimate.

Some interpret *avidya* as arising due to the *jiva's* failure to inquire into the Self. But Vedanta clarifies: the *jiva* itself is born of ignorance — so there is no one "before" ignorance to blame. Like the chicken and the egg, *jiva* and *avidya* arise together. The *jiva* exists only so long as ignorance persists. When ignorance is absent, there is no identification with the body-mind, and therefore no *jiva*. No ignorance, no identification; no identification, no *jiva*.

Ultimately, Vedanta's purpose is not to satisfy intellectual curiosity, but to end suffering through Self-realization. It acknowledges the limits of the intellect and teaches that liberation (*moksha*) comes not by resolving every metaphysical puzzle, but by dissolving the one root error — misidentifying with what you are not.

Once the Self is known, the question "Why is there ignorance?" is revealed to be like asking, "Why was I dreaming?" once you've woken up. The dream never really happened.

In Summary:

- *Avidya* is the root misperception that gives rise to individuality and bondage. It is the failure to see the Self as non-dual, ever-free, and limitless.
- It manifests both individually (as *avidya*) and cosmically (as maya), shaping our sense of identity and the world around us.
- Its origin is inexplicable (*anirvachaniya*) — not real, not unreal — but removable through knowledge.
- Vedanta does not dwell on the "why" of ignorance, but rather shows that it can be overcome through inquiry, contemplation, and Self-knowledge.
- From the standpoint of Brahman, there is no ignorance, no seeker, and no question — only reality, whole and complete.

—

Root & Meaning

Sanskrit *a-* ("not") + *vidya* ("knowledge"); literally "non-knowledge" or "ignorance."

Scriptural References

- **Brihadaranyaka Upanishad (1.4.10):** Declares that ignorance arises from superimposition and is removed by Self-knowledge.
- **Mandukya Karika (1.16–1.18, 3.19):** Explains ignorance as the cause of duality and bondage, and its resolution through non-dual knowledge.
- **Bhagavad Gita (5.15–16, 7.14):** Describes ignorance as delusion born of the three *gunas*, overcome by the light of knowledge.
- **Vivekachudamani (108–113):** Identifies ignorance as the root of misidentification and outlines inquiry as the means to remove it.
- **Brahma Sutra Bhashya (1.1.1, Shankara's Introduction):** Defines *avidya* through the principle of *adhyasa* (superimposition) as the starting point of Vedanta.

Traditional View

The root cause of bondage and misidentification.

Vedantic Analysis

Avidya has no independent reality; it is dependent on the Self for its seeming existence.

Common Misunderstandings

- Treating *avidya* as a "thing" that exists independently.
- Thinking it can be removed by rituals or worldly learning alone.

Vedantic Resolution

Only Self-knowledge removes *avidya* completely, revealing the Self as ever free.

avyakta

(avyakta — *uh-VYUK-tuh*)

Vedanta often describes the universe as an endless cycle of manifestation and dissolution. At one moment, the world appears in countless names and forms. At another, it resolves back into a seed state, unmanifest yet pregnant with potential. That seed state is called *avyakta* — the "unmanifest."

Unlike the manifest world, *avyakta* cannot be directly perceived. It is known only through its effects: the fact that the manifest emerges from it and returns to it. In deep sleep, we have a taste of it. The world is absent, individuality is resolved, but existence continues. This "seed" condition of non-differentiation is *avyakta*.

The tradition equates *avyakta* with several other terms: *prakriti* (primordial matter), *mulavidya* (primordial ignorance), and maya (the power of appearance). Each term emphasizes a different aspect:

- As *prakriti*, it is the source of creation, the potentiality from which the elements and beings arise.
- As maya, it is the inscrutable power of projection and concealment.
- As *mulavidya*, it is the root ignorance, beginningless and without a cause.

And yet Vedanta admits a paradox: if *avyakta* is unmanifest, how can it be said to exist? If it is devoid of the *gunas*, it would seem to be Brahman itself; but if it possesses the *gunas*, it belongs to maya. Traditional commentators resolve this by saying maya and *gunas* are *anirvachaniya* — indescribable, neither absolutely real nor absolutely unreal.

For the seeker, the significance of *gunas* is not theoretical but practical. It is a reminder that the manifest universe has no independent reality; it is dependent on a prior condition. But Brahman, the Self, is beyond both manifest and unmanifest. The wise recognize themselves not as *gunas,* nor as the world that springs from it, but as the awareness in which both appear and disappear.

—

Root & Meaning

A- = not
Vyakta = manifest, expressed
Avyakta = "the unmanifest," the seed state of creation.

Scriptural References

- **Bhagavad Gita (8.18–20):** describes beings as arising from the unmanifest (*avyakta*) and returning to it, while the higher *avyakta* — Brahman — remains beyond dissolution.
- **Mandukya Karika (1.6):** distinguishes the unmanifest causal state experienced in deep sleep from the Self, which transcends it.
- Shankara's commentaries: equate *avyakta* with maya and emphasize its *anirvachaniya* nature.

Traditional View

Avyakta is used to describe:

- **The causal condition of the universe:** unmanifest potential.
- **Prakriti/maya:** the beginningless power of creation.
- **Mulavidya:** primordial ignorance, the root cause of appearance.
- It is beginningless (*anadi*), without a cause, and serves as the seed of manifestation.

Vedantic Analysis

- *Avyakta* is not Brahman, for Brahman is beyond manifest and unmanifest.
- *Avyakta* is not absolutely real, because it is experienced indirectly and depends on Brahman for existence.
- It is *mithya* — empirically real but ultimately dependent.
- In deep sleep, we glimpse the state of *avyakta*: individuality resolves, but ignorance persists.

Common Misunderstandings

- **Avyakta as liberation:** Deep sleep (a taste of *avyakta*) is not freedom, for ignorance remains. Liberation is knowledge of the Self, not absorption in the unmanifest.
- **Avyakta as Brahman:** Though sometimes described as "higher unmanifest," Brahman transcends the categories of manifest/unmanifest.
- **Avyakta as non-existence:** It is not sheer nothingness; it is potential existence, the seed of manifestation.

Vedantic Resolution

Vedanta points beyond both *vyakta* (manifest) and *avyakta* (unmanifest) to the Self. By recognizing that both world and seed-state belong to the order of maya, one dis-identifies from them and abides in Brahman, the ever-free awareness.

bhakti yoga

(bhakti yoga — *bhuhk-tee YO-guh*)

In Vedanta, *bhakti yoga* is defined as a means of devotion leading to union with God. Traditional Vedanta generally recommends three disciplines — *karma yoga, upasana yoga,* and *jnana yoga. Bhakti yoga* is not listed as a fourth, separate practice because *bhakti* is considered the attitude or approach applied to all three.

For example:

- In *karma yoga, bhakti* is dedicating all actions to God and accepting the results as grace.
- In traditional *upasana yoga,* it is worship through single-pointed meditation on the attributes and glories of God.
- In *jnana yoga, bhakti* is the discovery of the truth regarding the nature of existence, which is the same truth regarding God.

It could be argued you cannot have *karma yoga, upasana yoga,* or *jnana yoga* without *bhakti.*

This point is seldom emphasized with Western students, partly because of a general aversion toward God — let alone any devotion to God. But in Vedanta, God is not seen as a separate being with human-like qualities, as in the Biblical tradition. Instead, God is defined as both the consciousness principle and the creative principle. The first is the formless "spirit" (pure consciousness), while the second is the force that includes the intelligence, energy, and matter of the material world.

From Duality to Non-Duality

More broadly, *bhakti yoga* is the devotee's journey from *dvaita* (duality; the belief that God and I are separate) to *advaita* (non-duality; the knowledge that God and I are one). The outcome satisfies both the heart — our yearning to be in harmony with all that is — and the intellect — our desire to understand the nature of reality.

Bhakti yoga is the slow transformation from being an *arta* (from *arti*, meaning sorrow, grief, or trouble) to being a *jnani* (one who knows the Self — consciousness as the basis of reality). *Jnana yoga*, although not outwardly ritualistic, is considered the highest form of devotion because only through Self-knowledge can one realize unity with God. We were never apart from God; ignorance simply made us think so.

Another way to see *bhakti* is as the willful decision to seek security in what is unborn, unchanging, and always present. As *jivas*, it benefits us to build our foundation on what is substantial (the Self), rather than on what comes and goes — people, objects, events, and circumstances. *Bhakti* is also a way to be in harmony with a force we barely understand, even in an age of science.

Even the most resolute atheist must still ponder the how and why of existence.

The Inevitability of Worship

Writer David Foster Wallace, in a commencement address , once put it this way:

> Because here's something else that's weird but true: in the day-to-day trenches of adult life, there is actually no such thing as atheism. There is no such thing as not worshipping. Everybody worships. The only choice we get is what to worship. And the compelling reason for maybe choosing some sort of god or spiritual-type thing to worship — be it JC or Allah, be it YHWH or the Wiccan Mother Goddess, or the Four Noble Truths, or some inviolable set of ethical principles — is that pretty much anything else you worship will eat you alive. If you worship money and things, if they are where you tap real meaning in life, then

you will never have enough, never feel you have enough. It's the truth. Worship your body and beauty and sexual allure and you will always feel ugly. And when time and age start showing, you will die a million deaths before they finally grieve you. On one level, we all know this stuff already. It's been codified as myths, proverbs, clichés, epigrams, parables; the skeleton of every great story. The whole trick is keeping the truth up front in daily consciousness. Worship power — you will feel weak and afraid, and you will need ever more power over others to keep the fear at bay. Worship your intellect, being seen as smart — you will end up feeling stupid, a fraud, always on the verge of being found out. And so on.

We are all devotees. The question isn't whether we worship, but what we choose to worship.

The *Bhagavata Purana* offers a similar lesson in the form of a short parable: a wasp captures an insect and brings it to its nest. The insect, consumed with fear, can think of nothing else — until it becomes a wasp itself. The moral is simple: you become what you give your attention to. Worship money and you become greedy; worship sex and you become lecherous; worship power and you become tyrannical. All such devotions are selfish, worldly, and binding. *Bhakti* shifts attention from the small self ("me") and the objects "out there" to that which frees rather than binds.

The Roadmap of Bhakti

Unique to *bhakti yoga* is that it provides a clear roadmap to *moksha* (spiritual freedom) — beginning with belief in God and maturing into knowledge of God. Most people never see devotion as a progression; they imagine worshiping a personal God is the end. In Vedanta, it is only the beginning. Faith is important at first, but it is meant to be a bridge to knowledge, not a substitute for it.

Bhakti yoga's five stages form a continuum from dualistic to non-dual devotion:

Stage 1 – Informal devotion. Calling on God for help with security, pleasure, or emotional support. Worship is physical and extroverted: charity, *puja*, temple visits. This stage is not required for self-inquiry.

Stage 2 – Karma yoga. Offering all actions to God, accepting results as *prasad* (grace). Actions shift from selfish to selfless, often in service. Devotion remains outward.

Stage 3 – Upasana yoga (God with form). Meditation on a chosen deity such as Krishna or Rama. Life is simplified, the mind steadied. Worship turns inward.

Stage 4 – Upasana yoga (God as totality). Seeing God in all things, both "good" and "bad." Understanding God as both maker and material. Worship remains inward and mental.

Stage 5 – Jnana yoga (Self-knowledge). Worship takes the form of self-inquiry:

- *Shravana* — listening to Vedanta's teachings.
- *Manana* — reflecting until doubts are resolved.
- *Nididhyasana* — contemplating the Self as the formless essence of all.

Here, God is no longer seen as separate. Worship is the steady recognition of one's own nature.

Beyond the Stages

The first four stages are *dvaita bhakti* (dualistic worship); the last is *advaita bhakti* (non-dualistic worship). None negates the others — they simply expand the picture. A mature devotee can appreciate God as both form and formless, as personal deity and totality, as the very essence of all.

The roadmap also explains why few reach the last stage: it requires not only faith but understanding, and understanding requires preparation and the guidance of a qualified teacher.

In conclusion, *bhakti yoga* is more than emotional worship; it is the unifying spirit behind all spiritual disciplines in Vedanta. It begins with seeking from God and ends with seeing that you are not other than God. The journey transforms the heart, sharpens the intellect, and culminates in freedom — *moksha* — the recognition that the Self and the whole are one.

—

Root & Meaning

Sanskrit *bhaj* ("to share," "to partake in," "to love") + *yoga* ("discipline" or "union"); literally "the discipline of devotion/love."

Scriptural References

- **Bhagavad Gita (9.22, 9.34, 12.8–12.20):** Defines devotion, its forms, and the qualities of the true devotee; emphasizes surrender to God and constant remembrance.
- **Bhagavata Purana (11.14.21, 11.14.26):** Describes devotion as the supreme means to liberation, above all other yogas.
- **Narada Bhakti Sutras (2, 19, 27–28):** Outlines the nature of pure devotion and its stages from desire-based to desireless love for God.
- **Mundaka Upanishad (3.2.3–4):** States that the Self is attained by the one whom the Self chooses, emphasizing devotion as an essential qualification.
- **Vivekachudamani (31–32):** Identifies *bhakti* as seeking the truth of one's own Self and recognizing it as non-different from Brahman.

Traditional View

Devotion to *Ishvara* is both a path and a purifier; emotional surrender leads to mental stillness and receptivity to Self-knowledge.

Vedantic Analysis

In Advaita, *bhakti* matures into knowledge (*jnana*); the duality of "I" and "God" resolves into the non-dual vision where only Brahman is.

Common Misunderstandings

• Limiting *bhakti* to emotional worship without self-inquiry.
• Thinking devotion and knowledge are separate paths with different goals.

Vedantic Resolution

The highest *bhakti* and *jnana* are identical — both reveal the Self as limitless awareness.

Brahman

(Brahman — *bruh-muhn*)

Not to be confused with Brahma — the Hindu god of creation — Brahman literally means "great" or "the vast." It is that which is greater than the greatest — beyond all experience, accommodating all things. This greatness is not a matter of size but of being unlimited by time, space, or any object, because Brahman is the reality in which time and space themselves appear.

Brahman cannot be described in words because Brahman is not an object of experience. How is one to describe something that is attributeless, actionless and not available to the senses? Vedanta uses scripture as a "word mirror" that points to Brahman as the Self — the eternal subject.

Ultimately, Brahman can only be described using a process of negation (*neti-neti*) or by using indicators / pointers (*lakshanas*). One classic example of the latter is the analogy of the clay and the pot, where it is shown that the essence of the pot is clay and that the pot itself is just name and form.

Similarly, the essence of who / what we are is Brahman (the clay), while the body-mind (the pot) is just an object known by Brahman (pure awareness). When the pot is broken it is no longer a pot, and yet the clay (the truth of the pot) remains.

Nevertheless, it's not a question of whether or not Brahman can be known. Brahman can be known because Brahman is self-evident. Brahman is the "I am" when I say "I am a man," "I am a son," "I am an employee," etc. We needn't be taught that I exist, because "I" as the Self, is the one thing that can never be denied.

In his translation and commentary on the Upanishads, Swami Nikhilananda writes:

As Brahman is the essence of Being, so It is the essence of Consciousness or Light. Brahman needs no other light to illumine Itself. It is self-luminous. "It is pure; It is the Light of lights; It is That which they know who know the Self."..."When He shines, everything shines after Him; by His light everything is lighted."

Referring to Brahman as "Him" shows it has religious overtones. Brahman is often categorized as both God with qualities (*Saguna Brahman*) and God without qualities (*Nirguna Brahman*). The former is God as creator, sustainer and destroyer of the universe (Brahman plus maya), while the latter is God as pure, attributeless awareness — the Self. However, there is only one absolute and that is *Nirguna Brahman*. *Nirguna Brahman* is not another kind of Brahman — it's
Brahman without the superimposition of maya. Knowledge of *Nirguna Brahman* is the culmination of God knowledge and considered the highest form of devotion.

The three traditional epithets for Brahman are existence, consciousness and bliss. These are not separate attributes of Brahman but instead synonyms, such that we say Brahman is existence-consciousness-bliss, or in Sanskrit, *sat-chit-ananda*. *Sat* is existence absolute, that is, the "I am" or the is-ness of our everyday contact with objects. *Chit* is consciousness absolute and is also sometimes translated as "pure knowledge "or "knowledge as such" (but shouldn't be confused with the mind or the workings of the mind). Lastly, *ananda* is bliss absolute. "Bliss" in this case equates to perfect satisfaction as a result of the absence of any limitation. "Limitlessness" or "absence of division" is sometimes used instead of bliss in order to remove the confusion with Brahman being some kind of state of ecstasy (Brahman is not a state or a feeling). So, when Brahman is described as bliss, it's really showing that its nature is absolute freedom. All objects are of the nature to bind, only formless Brahman is of the nature to be limitless.

In summary, Brahman is not something to be attained later, in another world, or in a special state of mind. It is the limitless, unchanging reality that is your very Self — the existence by which all things are, the awareness by which all things are known, and the freedom in which all things appear and disappear.

—

Root & Meaning

From Sanskrit root *brh* ("to expand," "to grow," "the greatest") + suffix *man* (indicating the abstract). Meaning: "the vast," "the infinite."

Scriptural References

- **Taittiriya Upanishad (2.1.1):** Declares Brahman as *satyam jñānam anantam* (truth, knowledge, infinity).
- **Chandogya Upanishad (6.2.1):** States *sarvam khalvidam brahma* ("All this is Brahman").
- **Brihadaranyaka Upanishad (2.4.6, 3.8.8):** Teaches that Brahman is imperishable, infinite, and the Self of all beings.
- **Mundaka Upanishad (2.2.11):** Describes Brahman as the light by which all is illumined.
- **Bhagavad Gita (13.13, 14.27):** Presents Brahman as the highest reality, the basis of immortality and eternal dharma.
- **Vivekachudamani (254–260):** Affirms Brahman as existence-consciousness-bliss, beyond maya and limitation.

Traditional View

Brahman is the only reality; the world and individuality are dependent appearances. Realization of Brahman ends the cycle of samsara.

Vedantic Analysis

Brahman is self-revealing consciousness. As the witness (*sakshin*) of all, it can never be negated or objectified.

Common Misunderstandings

• Thinking Brahman is a deity among other deities.
• Assuming Brahman is an abstract void or nothingness.
• Believing Brahman is "somewhere else" to be reached.

Vedantic Resolution

Brahman is your very Self; nothing is apart from it. The seeker does not "merge"with Brahman — one simply recognizes one has always been That.

Brahma satyam jagan mithya jivo brahmaiva na parah

(Brahma satyaṁ jagan mithyā jīvo brahmaiva na paraḥ
— *bruh-muh SUHT-yuhm JUH-guhn mith-YAA JEE-vo bruh-MAI-vuh nuh PUH-ruhh*)

Few phrases in Vedanta are as famous — or as often misunderstood — as *Brahma satyam jagan mithya jivo brahmaiva na parah*. In just half a verse, Shankara distilled the essence of Advaita:

- **Brahman alone is satyam** — real, changeless, self-existent.
- **The world is mithya** — apparent, dependent reality, neither absolutely real nor absolutely unreal.
- **The jiva is non-different from Brahman** — the essence of the individual is pure, limitless awareness.

The formula strikes with paradox. If Brahman is real and one without a second, what do we make of this world, so vividly experienced? To deny its existence seems absurd, for we see it, touch it, transact with it daily. To affirm it as real alongside Brahman creates duality. Vedanta resolves the puzzle by introducing a third category: *mithya*. The world is not absolutely real, for it depends on Brahman. Nor is it absolutely unreal, for it is experienced. Like the dream that appears real until we awaken, the world is valid for transaction but, upon inquiry, known to be dependent and non-separate.

This teaching is not meant to negate life but to reframe it. The world loses its burden when understood as *mithya*. Everything is known as an appearance on the one flame of consciousness, Brahman. In this light, even the *jiva* — with body, mind, and senses — is revealed as *mithya*. The "I" that knows, that shines as awareness, is not other than Brahman itself.

The power of the *mahavakya* (great statement) is its completeness. What vast volumes of commentary strive to explain, Shankara placed in a single line: the whole teaching of Advaita Vedanta condensed into a mantra. Brahman is real, the world is dependent, the individual is nothing but that reality. When ignorance is removed, there is no *jiva* separate from *Ishvara*, no jagat apart from Brahman. There is only consciousness, self-existent and whole.

—

Root & Meaning

Brahma satyam = Brahman is real, changeless, absolute.
Jagan mithya = The world is dependent reality, neither absolutely real nor unreal.
Jivah brahmaiva na aparah = The individual self is not other than Brahman.

Scriptural References

- **Shankara (Vivekachudamani, Upadesha Sahasri):** condenses Advaita into this half-verse.
- **Mandukya Upanishad with Karika (Gaudapada):** teaches dream as analogy for the *mithya* status of the world.
- **Bhagavad Gita (7.24–25; 13.2):** emphasizes that ignorance veils the Lord, but in reality *Ishvara* and *jiva* are one.

Traditional View

- This *mahavakya* is often presented as the essence of Advaita Vedanta:
- **Brahman alone is satya:** Pure awareness, limitless, non-dual.
- **World is mithya:** Apparent, transactional, dependent on Brahman for existence.

- **Jiva is Brahman:** The apparent individual is none other than limitless awareness.

Vedantic Analysis

- World: Neither real nor unreal — a third category, *mithya*. Like dream, experienced while present, but negated upon enquiry.
- Ignorance: The only "veil" is *avidya*. Once removed, there is no distance between *jiva* and *Ishvara*.
- Resolution: The *mahavakya* removes the distinction between subject, object, and creator. All are seen as one consciousness.

Common Misunderstandings

- **Mithya = illusion:** It does not mean "non-existent." The world exists for transaction but lacks absolute reality.
- **Jiva disappears:** Realization does not annihilate individuality but reveals its dependence and non-separateness.
- **Brahman is remote:** Brahman is the very Self, not a distant God.

Vedantic Resolution

This *mahavakya* is a mirror for inquiry. By recognizing Brahman as real, the world as *mithya*, and the self as non-different from Brahman, one resolves the apparent difference between *jiva*, *jagat*, and *Ishvara*. What remains is non-dual awareness, free of division.

buddhi

(buddhi — *bud-dhee*)

In Vedanta, the word *buddhi* is usually translated as "intellect," but that single word hardly captures its depth. The mind (*manas*) vacillates, wonders, and feels, but the *buddhi* concludes. It is the determinative faculty of the *antahkarana* — the one that says "this is so" and directs action accordingly.

The *buddhi* is like the driver of a chariot. The senses are the horses, the mind is the reins, and the body is the vehicle. Left to itself, the mind is tossed by emotions and desires. But when guided by a steady *buddhi*, the whole system moves purposefully. If the intellect is dull, the chariot veers wildly; if it is sharp, the journey is safe and clear.

Yet *buddhi* is not flawless. It too is part of *prakriti*, inert by nature, and only shines because it reflects consciousness. Like the moon borrowing light from the sun, the intellect borrows light from the Self. At times it is bright and penetrating, at other times dimmed by *rajas* and *tamas*. When desires (*kama*) take hold, they can hijack the *buddhi*, dragging it along. Only by remembering that the Self is beyond both mind and intellect can one master desire at its root.

Tradition distinguishes between a sharp intellect (*tikshna buddhi*) and a subtle intellect (*sukshma buddhi*). The sharp intellect analyzes, categorizes, and invents; it brings worldly success and recognition. The subtle intellect turns inward, inquiring into the essence of the Self. It is this subtle buddhi that is indispensable for liberation, for it alone discriminates between the eternal and the ephemeral.

Thus the *buddhi* is both friend and foe. Properly refined, it becomes the instrument of *viveka*, discrimination, capable of revealing that the Self is never touched by the mind's storms.

Misused, it imprisons us in rationalizations, ideologies, and rigid identifications. Vedanta honors the *buddhi* as a precious tool — but reminds us it is still *anatma*, not the Self. The Self illumines it, uses it, and is free of it.

—

Root & Meaning

From the root *budh* = to know, to awaken.
Buddhi = the determinative faculty, the power of understanding and discrimination.

Scriptural References

- **Bhagavad Gita (3.42):** "Higher than the mind is the intellect (*buddhi*), and higher than the intellect is the Self."
- **Tattvabodha:** defines *buddhi* as the *vritti* that makes determinations, distinguishing it from the doubting nature of the mind.
- **Vedantic texts:** describe *buddhi* as the reflecting medium for consciousness (*pratibimba-vada*), like the moon reflecting the sun.

Traditional View

- *Buddhi* is one of the four functions of the *antahkarana* (inner instrument), alongside *manas* (mind), *ahankara* (ego), and *chitta* (memory).
- It is superior to *manas* because it resolves doubts and directs will.
- Its presiding deity is Brahma, symbolizing creativity and knowledge.
- At the cosmic level, *buddhi* is *mahat*, the first evolute of *prakriti*, from which *ahamkara* and *manas* emerge.

Vedantic Analysis

- *Buddhi* is inert by itself, enlivened only by the reflection of

consciousness.
- It is the seat of discrimination (*viveka*), the highest use of which is distinguishing Self from not-Self.
- Sharp *buddhi* helps in worldly life; subtle *buddhi* reveals Truth.
- Even so, *buddhi* is *anatma* — known, changing, limited. It must not be mistaken for the Self.

Common Misunderstandings

- **Equating buddhi with dry rationality:** It includes will, discrimination, and subtle intuition, not just logic.
- **Thinking buddhi is consciousness itself:** It shines by borrowed light; the Self is the true source.
- **Assuming strong intellect ensures liberation:** Only a refined and subtle buddhi, turned toward Self-inquiry, serves this end.

Vedantic Resolution

The *buddhi* is the doorway to freedom when it is purified and turned inward. With its help, one recognizes: "I am not the intellect, but the awareness that illumines it." Knowledge dawns not in the body, not in the mind, but in the *buddhi* — and yet, the Self transcends even this.

chidabhasa

(cidābhāsa — *chi-DAA-BHAA-suh*)

Chidhabhasa (cidhābhāsa) is a compound Sanskrit word derived from *chit* (consciousness) and *abhasa* (semblance; appearance; emanation). The word constitutes the important reflected-consciousness teaching in Advaita Vedanta, showing how pure consciousness vivifies the gross and subtle bodies, and how atman (pure consciousness) appears as many.

The concept of *chidabhasa* is often explained through the reflection theory (*pratibimba-vada*), a teaching model developed in post-Shankara Advaita. While Shankaracharya does not explicitly use the term, he frequently employs reflection metaphors, such as sunlight reflected in water, to illustrate how pure consciousness appears as the individual self. The term is formally introduced in *Panchadashi* by Vidyaranya, and is also used in *Drg Drshya Viveka* attributed to the same author.

The reflected-consciousness teaching outlines three principles:

- **OC (original consciousness)**, also known as *chit* (pure awareness), atman or the true Self.
- **RM (reflecting medium)**, which refers to the subtle body, and more specifically, the mind or intellect (*buddhi*). The mind acts like a mirror, which is inert until illumined by OC, which makes it appear alive.
- **RC (reflected consciousness)** is the apparent consciousness seen in the reflecting medium — like a mirror catching sunlight. It's the byproduct of the mind's proximity to the Self, giving the impression that the mirror is shining, when in fact, it's OC that is shining and RM is only reflecting it. The traditional analogy is the moon, which appears to be shining thanks to its proximity to the sun. It's said that the moon "borrows" the light from the

original source.

Chidabhasa is what makes cognition and transaction possible. It is the operative knower (*jnata*) in experience. It says, "I know," "I feel," "I choose," but, just like the moon, these are all borrowed powers. While *chidabhasa* animates the mind and "gives life," it is also responsible for the fundamental error of mistaking the reflection (RC) for the Self, giving rise to the ego (*ahankara*) and the sense of doership. As individuals (*jivas*), we know we are conscious, but identify with the RC instead of the OC. But chidabhasa is only a semblance — it's not real. It's like the moon claiming to generate its own light.

Chidabhasa is neither real nor unreal. It's not real (*sat*) because it disappears in deep sleep, coma and after gaining Self-knowledge. It's not unreal (*asat*) because we experience it everyday during our waking hours. Advaita Vedanta resolves this predicament by saying it's *mithya* (apparently real). Even though we may experience *chidabhasa*, we know it's dependent on OC for illumination, and on RM for manifestation.

The essential error is attributing the properties of *chidabhasa* to *chit* (pure consciousness). The objective of the seeker is then, to realign the mind's understanding, from "I am the I-sense/the ego."— (RC), to "I am the light that illumines this reflection and all reflections."— (OC).

Chidabhasa is like the glint of the sun in a shimmering puddle— brilliant, shifting and illusory. It dances around calling itself "me," forgetting the vast sun above. But once the truth is known, it doesn't stop shining—it just stops claiming its independence.

—

Root & Meaning

Sanskrit *chit* (consciousness) + *abhasa* (appearance, semblance) = "appearance of consciousness" or "reflected consciousness."

Scriptural References

- **Brihadaranyaka Upanishad (4.3.7, 4.3.23):** Describes the Self as the light by which the mind and senses are illumined, implying the reflected-consciousness principle.
- **Katha Upanishad (2.2.15):** States that the Self shines and everything else shines after it, much like the moon reflects sunlight.
- **Mundaka Upanishad (2.2.10):** Compares the mind and intellect to instruments that borrow light from the Self.
- **Panchadashi (Chapter 2, Chidabhasa-prakarana):** Systematically explains the original consciousness, reflecting medium, and reflected consciousness model.
- **Drg Drshya Viveka (Verses 8–11):** Uses the reflection metaphor to distinguish the Self from the reflected "I-sense."
- **Bhagavad Gita (15.12–15):** Uses the moon–sun analogy to show how all cognition depends on the original light of consciousness.

Traditional View

Chidabhasa is not independent reality; it is dependent on both *chit* (the original consciousness) and the mind. It belongs to the realm of *mithya* (dependent existence).

Vedantic Analysis

The *chidabhasa* makes empirical experience possible but is ultimately unreal in itself — like a reflection in a mirror. Recognizing the difference between *chit* and *chidabhasa* is essential to Self-knowledge.

Common Misunderstandings

- Thinking *chidabhasa* is an independent entity.
- Equating *chidabhasa* with pure consciousness.
- Believing *chidabhasa* can exist without a functioning mind.

Vedantic Resolution

The real "I" is *chit*, the unreflected, limitless awareness. The reflection is just an appearance in the mind and does not define the Self.

chitta

(citta — *chit-tuh*)

In Vedanta, *chitta (citta)* is the memory function of the inner instrument (*antahkarana*). If manas is the doubter, and *buddhi* the decider, *chitta* is the storehouse — it retains impressions (*samskaras*), recalls experiences, and provides continuity across time.

This storing and recollecting power gives life its narrative thread: we recognize people, places, and our own history because *chitta* holds impressions. In meditation, chitta is what brings up past thoughts, making quietude difficult. At the same time, without memory, there can be no learning or assimilation of the teaching.

Vedanta emphasizes that *chitta* is not consciousness itself. Like all aspects of the mind, it is *jada* (inert), illumined by awareness. Memory is a function, not the Self. The witness (*sakshi*) is ever-present, even as *chitta* retrieves or forgets.

For the seeker, the challenge is not to erase memory but to purify it — reducing binding impressions and strengthening *shraddha* and clarity. Yogic practice often emphasizes *chitta-vritti-nirodhah* — the quieting of mental modifications — but Advaita clarifies that freedom lies not in suppressing *chitta*, but in recognizing its borrowed nature.

—

Root & Meaning

From root *chit* = to perceive, to be conscious, to notice.
Chitta = that which holds impressions; the faculty of memory and recall.

Scriptural References

- **Yoga Sutras 1.2:** "Yogah chitta-vritti-nirodhah" — yoga is the stilling of the fluctuations of *chitta*.
- **Bhagavad Gita 6.35:** "The mind (*chitta*) is restless, difficult to restrain, but can be controlled through practice and detachment."
- **Vedanta Sara:** Lists chitta as one of the four functions of *antahkarana*.

Traditional View

- *Chitta* = memory, storehouse of impressions.
- Holds past experiences, provides recollection.
- One of the four functions of *antahkarana* (inner instrument).

Vedantic Analysis

- *Chitta* is inert, illumined by consciousness.
- Retains *samskaras* (subtle impressions of thought and action).
- Influences personality, tendencies, and habits.
- Important for learning and meditation, but can also perpetuate distraction.

Common Misunderstandings

- **That chitta = consciousness:** *Chitta* is illumined by awareness but is not awareness itself.
- **That memory defines identity:** Identity depends on *ahankara*; *chitta* is only one faculty.
- **That chitta must be destroyed:** It need not be erased; rather, it must be purified and understood as non-Self.

Vedantic Resolution

Chitta is the memory aspect of the inner organ, holding impressions and providing recollection. It is not the Self but an instrument illuminated by consciousness. True freedom comes from dis-identifying from it, not erasing it.

dama

(dama — *duh-muh*)

In Vedanta, *dama* means control of the external sense organs — the eyes, ears, tongue, skin, and nose, as well as the organs of action such as speech and hands. It is part of the sixfold inner wealth (*shatka-sampatti*), one of the qualifications required for Self-knowledge.

If *shama* (mind control) is the first line of defense, *dama* is the second. Desires and emotions may arise suddenly, and sometimes the mind cannot deliberate quickly enough. In such cases, *dama* provides restraint, preventing the senses from acting out and creating fresh entanglements. For example, anger may surge in the mind, but with *dama* one refrains from speaking harsh words.

Traditional analogies describe the senses as wild horses that constantly rush toward their objects. Left unchecked, they scatter the mind and disturb inner peace. *Dama* reins them in, ensuring that they serve inquiry rather than sabotage it.

Swami Dayananda clarifies that one need not suppress or deny desires altogether — they arise according to one's *prakriti* (nature). But one need not be enslaved by them either. Through *shama* one deliberates whether a desire is necessary, proper, or useful; through *dama* one exercises restraint even when the desire pushes strongly. In this way, *dama* works hand-in-hand with *shama* to protect the mind from being hijacked by impulses.

At a societal level, *dama* is reflected in civility and moral education: the capacity to restrain destructive impulses for the sake of harmony. For the seeker, it is a vital discipline, transforming the senses from masters into servants of Self-inquiry.

Root & Meaning

Dama = restraint, control. Specifically: control of the external sense organs and their activities.

Scriptural References

- **Aparokshanubhuti (v. 6):** "Restraint of the external functions of the organs is called *dama*."
- **Bhagavad Gita (6.5; 17.14–16):** speaks of self-mastery and restraint as part of discipline.
- **Tattva Bodha (Shankara):** lists *dama* as one of the sixfold inner disciplines.

Traditional View

- *Dama* restrains the outward flow of the senses.
- Complements *shama* (control of the mind), working together to keep both inner and outer life steady.
- Cultivated through moderation, deliberate living, and prioritizing Self-knowledge over indulgence.

Vedantic Analysis

- *Shama* and *dama* are two aspects of handling desire:
- *Shama* = regulating thoughts before they disturb.
- *Dama* = restraining sense organs when impulses escape *shama's* filter.
- Both disciplines aim to neutralize *raga-dvesha* (likes and dislikes) and free the mind for inquiry.
- Not repression, but intelligent restraint: the ability to say, "Thus far and no further."

Common Misunderstandings

- **That dama means harsh suppression:** In Vedanta it is moderate restraint, not denial.

- **That dama makes life joyless:** In fact, it protects joy by preventing the turbulence caused by unchecked indulgence.
- **That dama is independent of shama:** Without mental control, sensory restraint becomes brittle; without *dama, shama* has no support.

Vedantic Resolution

Dama is self-mastery at the sensory level. By holding back impulses before they spill into action, it preserves the mind's clarity and safeguards Self-inquiry. It is the discipline of turning the senses into allies rather than saboteurs.

dharma

(dharma — *dhuhr-muh*)

In Vedic culture, the word dharma carries many meanings, none of which are easily condensed into a single English equivalent. At its core, dharma refers to that which upholds, sustains, or supports the cosmic order—and, by extension, our personal and social lives.

To live dharmically is not to follow a rigid rulebook, but to listen inwardly for what promotes harmony — with ourselves, with others, and with the whole. Dharma is not morality imposed from above but discernment from within. Swami Dayananda said, "Dharma is not a commandment, but the recognition of what is appropriate in a given situation."

On the individual level, dharma primarily refers to how one conducts oneself. But it's more than just behavior; it is the alignment of action with truth. For the individual, there are several dimensions of *dharma*, which can all be summed up as: appropriate timely action.

But what does that mean in practice?

Samanya Dharma: Universal Values

This refers to universal values such as non-violence, honesty, and compassion—principles that apply to all people, at all times. These are values that apply to everyone, regardless of time, place, or personal disposition. Truthfulness (*satya*), non-injury (*ahimsa*), compassion (*daya*), self-control (*dama*), and patience (*kshama*) form the moral substrate of a healthy society and a peaceful mind. Swami Dayananda emphasized that these are not imposed rules but discovered principles. When we lie, hurt others, or act greedily, it creates internal conflict — not because we broke a rule, but because we broke harmony with the larger order (*rita*).

As Krishna says in the *Bhagavad Gita*:

One's own dharma, though imperfectly performed, is better than the dharma of another well executed. (3.35)

This shows that universal values must still be interpreted in light of individual nature.

Swadharma: One's Personal Duty

This refers to one's unique role based on temperament, life stage, and situation. The *Bhagavad Gita* is framed around this very dilemma. Arjuna, a warrior by caste and training, wants to renounce the battlefield. Krishna advises him otherwise — not because war is inherently good, but because abandoning his *svadharma* would be a violation of his nature and responsibilities.

Considering your own dharma, you should not waver. For a kshatriya, there is nothing more honorable than a righteous war. (BG 2.31)

In today's world, *svadharma* might look like fulfilling your responsibilities as a parent, citizen, or professional, while remaining true to your deeper nature.

Vishesha Dharma: Contextual Ethics

Situational dharma — ethical decisions that depend on the unique demands of a particular circumstance. Sometimes, dharma demands we deviate from the expected to preserve a greater good. This is beautifully explored in the *Mahabharata*, particularly in the *Yaksha Prashna*, where Yudhishthira answers riddles testing his moral insight, and in the Draupadi disrobing scene, where everyone's adherence to social norms leads to collective *adharma*.

The epics show that right and wrong are not always black and white. Dharma, like truth, can be subtle. That's why Krishna himself bends the rules during the *Mahabharata* war — because sticking to convention would have ensured the triumph of *adharma*.

Everyday Dharma: Social and Civil Order

Every civilization depends on shared agreements: stopping at red lights, paying taxes, not taking what isn't yours. These are not metaphysical truths, but practical agreements that keep life predictable and fair. Includes the social, political, legal and economic norms that govern civilized life.

Body Dharma: Physical Responsibility

The body, though not the Self, is the vehicle through which life is lived and dharma expressed. Eating right, sleeping well, exercising—these are part of body-dharma. Ignoring this order eventually leads to imbalance and suffering. Even this is *Ishvara's* order — a subtle pointer that nature itself enforces dharma through consequence.

The underlying premise is simple but profound: within the field of experience, there are certain laws — both seen and unseen — that, when violated, inevitably lead to pain or disorder. Dharma is the compass that helps us navigate these laws, so that we may live with greater peace and well-being.

We can broadly categorize these laws into three kinds:

- **Physical laws** govern the natural world. From a young age, we learn that disobeying these laws — like gravity or fire — results in immediate consequences. A scraped knee or a burn is a teacher in its own right.
- **Psychological laws** relate to the structure of the human mind. Emotions like sorrow, fear, and anger feel bad not because they are wrong, but because they signal a disruption. Experiences of

love, peace, and security, on the other hand, signal alignment. We come to understand these laws by living — often through the pain of being on the receiving end of harm, cruelty, or neglect.

- **Moral laws** help regulate our interactions with others. These are the ethical guidelines — like honesty, non-stealing, and non-harming — that preserve harmony in human relationships. In the West, this is often captured by the Golden Rule: "Do unto others as you would have them do unto you." We follow these not just out of empathy, but also as a form of self-preservation, knowing that violating them invites conflict, guilt, or retaliation.

While these universal laws may seem obvious, it is not always easy to follow them. The mind's likes and dislikes (*raga-dvesha*) often tempt us to ignore what we know to be right. This is why a mature and discriminating intellect is essential. It allows us to step back, assess cause and effect, and act in ways that reduce harm rather than increase it. In this way, dharma becomes the glue that holds both the inner and outer world together.

When dharma is neglected, chaos ensues. The *Bhagavad Gita* warns of this: the loss of discrimination between right and wrong leads to destructive desire, anger, delusion, and ultimately to the loss of inner peace. Upholding dharma is therefore not just a moral imperative — it is a practical necessity for individual and collective well-being.

At a higher level, we might say that dharma is that which aligns us with *rita* — the natural and moral order, or even with God, however one conceives of the divine. But one need not be religious to live a dharmic life. What matters is the recognition that we are in relationship — not only with ourselves, but with nature, society, and all sentient beings. To live dharmically is to step out of the small self and into a deeper, more integrated participation with the whole.

Only when we relinquish selfishness and align with this greater truth can we hope to live a relatively peaceful and meaningful life.

—

Root & Meaning

Sanskrit root *dhr* — "to hold, support, sustain." Common translations: "righteousness," "duty," "law," "virtue," "essential nature."

Scriptural References

- **Bhagavad Gita 2.31:** "Considering your own duty (*svadharma*), you should not waver..."
- **Bhagavad Gita 3.35:** "Better is one's own duty (*svadharma*) though imperfect, than the duty of another well performed."
- **Manusmriti 2.6:** "Dharma is that which is followed by those learned in the Veda and approved by the conscience of good people."
- **Mahabharata, Shanti Parva 109.11:** "Dharma is for the welfare of all beings. Whatever leads to the welfare of all beings is dharma."

Traditional View

Dharma encompasses universal ethical principles (*sadharana-dharma*) — like truthfulness, non-violence, compassion — as well as specific duties (*vishesha-dharma*) tied to one's role, stage of life, and circumstances.

Vedantic Analysis

While dharma operates in the realm of *mithya* (empirical reality), it plays a vital role in mental purification and preparing the seeker for liberation. From the standpoint of absolute reality (*paramarthika*), the Self is beyond dharma and *adharma*.

Common Misunderstandings

- Reducing dharma solely to religious ritual or blind obedience to social norms.
- Treating dharma as static rather than context-sensitive.
- Equating dharma only with "law" and missing its deeper moral and cosmic implications.

Vedantic Resolution

Live by dharma to harmonize with the order of creation and prepare for Self-knowledge, but recognize that ultimate freedom (*moksha*) transcends all dualities, including dharma and *adharma*.

dhyana

(dhyāna — *DHYAA-nuh*)

Meditation is one of the most recognized words in the spiritual lexicon, yet few terms carry as much confusion. In Vedanta, *dhyana (dhyāna)* has a precise meaning: the continuous flow of similar thoughts, undistracted by dissimilar thoughts. It is not the absence of thought but the disciplined directing of thought.

Swami Dayananda describes it as *sajatiya-pratyaya-pravaha* — a stream of like-thoughts — with *vijatiya-pratyaya-rahita* — the exclusion of unlike-thoughts. For example, meditating on the chosen form of the Lord (*ishta-devata*) means deliberately returning the mind to that object whenever it wanders. The "bringing it back" is not a failure but part of the very definition of *dhyana*.

Two primary forms are distinguished:

• **Meditation on Saguna Brahman** — devotional focus on pure awareness with attributes (*Ishvara*; God), a form of prayerful contemplation.
• **Contemplation (nididhyasana) on Nirguna Brahman** — reflection on the Self, expressed in *mahavakyas* such as "I am *purnah*, I am *satya-jnana-ananta-svarupah*." This is not an attempt to produce silence but to assimilate the vision of the *shastra* (scripture).

For the seeker, *dhyana* is part of *antaranga-sadhana* — inner discipline — while *karma yoga* is *bahiranga-sadhana*, outer discipline. Together, they prepare the mind for steadfast knowledge (*jnana-nishtha*). When dispassion (*vairagya*) matures and the body-mind-sense complex is brought under mastery, *dhyana* becomes natural: a steady commitment to the vision of the Self.

Thus, in Vedanta, meditation is not a mechanical practice for producing altered states, but a deliberate mental activity aligned with knowledge. Its highest form is not the suspension of thought but the sustained assimilation of truth: that the Self is already free, whole, and limitless.

—

Root & Meaning

Dhyana = meditation, from the root *dhyai* ("to think, to contemplate"). Defined as the uninterrupted flow of similar thoughts, excluding unlike-thoughts.

Scriptural References

- **Bhagavad Gita (6.10–15):** outlines meditation as a steady discipline for the yogi.
- **Bhagavad Gita (18.52–54):** describes the contemplative life of a renunciate, free of likes and dislikes.
- **Patanjali's Yoga Sutras (3.2):** defines *dhyana* as uninterrupted attention on a single object, the step before *samadhi*.

Traditional View

- Classified as an internal discipline (*antaranga-sadhana*), complementing *karma yoga* (external discipline).
- Two types:
  - *Saguna Brahma vishaya dhyana* — meditation on the Lord with attributes (devotion, prayer).
  - *Nirguna Brahma vishaya nididhyasana* — contemplation on the Self as revealed by *shastra*.
- A necessary practice for converting indirect knowledge into steady abidance (*jnana-nishtha*).

Vedantic Analysis

- *Dhyana* is not the absence of thought but a deliberate flow of thought.

- Wandering of the mind is not a failure; returning it to the object is itself part of *dhyana*.
- Its ultimate role in Vedanta is *nididhyasana*: deep contemplation on *mahavakya* statements until their meaning is fully assimilated.
- *Dhyana* thus serves as a bridge between intellectual understanding and lived clarity.

Common Misunderstandings

- **Meditation as blanking the mind:** In Vedanta, meditation is thoughtful and purposeful.
- **Confusing dhyana with samadhi:** *Dhyana* still involves effort and redirection; *samadhi* is effortless absorption.
- **Seeing dhyana as optional:** For knowledge to become steadfast, *dhyana* is essential, especially for those with lingering habitual errors.

Vedantic Resolution

Dhyana purifies and steadies the mind, creating the condition for knowledge to take root. The culmination is *nididhyasana*: the mind abiding in the truth "I am Brahman." This is not a new experience but the assimilation of what is always the case.

dvaita

(dvaita — *dvai-tuh*)

In Sanskrit, *dvaita* means "duality." It is the natural way most human beings perceive the world: subject here, object there; me and you; God and soul; cause and effect. In Vedanta, *dvaita* refers not only to a mode of perception but also to a school of philosophy — one that takes duality to be ultimately real.

Madhvacharya (13th century) systematized Dvaita Vedanta, in which the distinction between *jiva* (individual), *jagat* (world), and *Ishvara* (God) is absolute and eternal. According to this view, the soul never merges with God; the soul can only serve God. The world is not *mithya* (seemingly real) but a separate, real creation, and liberation means eternal proximity to the Lord, not identity with Him.

Advaita Vedanta, by contrast, interprets duality as mithya — real enough for transaction but not ultimately real. The perception of separation is due to ignorance (*avidya*). When ignorance is removed, only non-dual Brahman remains.

In this way, Vedanta reclassifies duality: not false like a barren woman's son, but dependent like the dream that seems real until we awaken.

For the seeker, *dvaita* is both a starting point and an obstacle. At first, duality is unavoidable: I am the devotee, God is the worshiped. This attitude purifies the mind. But if duality is taken as ultimate, the possibility of non-dual realization is veiled. The transition from *dvaita* to advaita is thus a central movement of the Vedantic path: from relationship to identity, from worship to knowledge, from twoness to oneness.

—

Root & Meaning

Dvi = two
Dvaita = duality, twoness.

Scriptural References

- **Bhagavad Gita (7.4–5):** distinguishes between the lower (*prakriti*) and higher (*jiva*) principles, often read in dualistic terms.
- **Upanishads:** insist that where there is duality, one sees another; where all is the Self, there is no second (*Brihadaranyaka Upanishad* 4.5.15).
- **Madhvacharya's works (Anuvyakhyana, Brahma Satra Bhashya):** articulate Dvaita Vedanta as a distinct school.

Traditional View

- Dvaita Vedanta (Madhva):
  - Eternal difference between *Ishvara, jiva,* and *jagat.*
  - Fivefold differences (*panchabheda*): between God and soul, God and matter, soul and matter, one soul and another, one part of matter and another.
  - Liberation is eternal service to God, not union with Him.
- Advaita Vedanta: accepts transactional duality but denies its ultimate reality.

Vedantic Analysis

- Duality is the basis of ignorance and bondage, as it creates the sense of separation.
- Yet dualistic devotion (*dvaita-bhakti*) is valued as an effective means to purify the mind.
- The final resolution is that duality is *mithya* — dependent, provisional, not absolute.

Common Misunderstandings

- **Dvaita as error only:** Duality is provisionally real and useful for practice; it is not to be dismissed prematurely.
- **Dvaita and Advaita as enemies:** Advaita integrates duality by reclassifying it as *mithya* rather than denying it outright.
- **Dvaita = theism, Advaita = atheism:** Both affirm *Ishvara*; the difference is whether the *jiva* is ultimately identical with or forever distinct from *Ishvara*.

Vedantic Resolution

Dvaita is the natural standpoint of ordinary perception and the devotional stage of practice. Advaita clarifies that this duality is not final: once ignorance is removed, the non-dual Self alone remains.

dvandva

(dvandva — *dvuhn-dvuh*)

The human mind lives between opposites. Every joy conceals its shadow, every triumph its undoing. We name them differently — success and failure, love and loss, heat and cold — but the pattern is ancient. The *dvandva*, the pair, is the pulse of maya itself: the ceaseless swing that gives motion to the dream.

We suffer not because the opposites exist, but because we cling to one side and flee the other. Attraction and aversion are the hinges of bondage. To chase pleasure is already to fear pain; to grasp light is already to deny the dark. The mind that runs from one pole to the other never rests. It calls the motion "life," but it is only oscillation — samsara in miniature.

The world's design depends on *dvandva*. Without contrast, perception would collapse. Light means nothing without darkness; gain means nothing without loss. Consciousness, in expressing itself as the universe, divides itself into pairs so it may taste its own reflection. This is the divine irony of maya: the One forgets itself to play as two.

But the sage sees differently. For him, the opposites no longer contradict. Cold and heat, pleasure and pain, are variations in the field — ripples on the surface of still awareness. They arise and pass in the same space, like clouds against an unchanging sky. To live free of *dvandva* does not mean to withdraw from the world, but to move through it without being moved by it. When joy comes, he does not grasp; when sorrow comes, he does not resist. Both are waves, and he is the ocean.

In this way, *dvandva* becomes a teacher. Each swing of the pendulum invites inquiry: Who is it that feels these shifts? What remains when the pairs subside? Every pleasure that fades points back to the changeless witness. Every pain that passes reveals the same truth: that the Self was never touched.

Modern life multiplies dvandvas by the thousand. Wealth and poverty, fame and obscurity, approval and cancellation — digital polarities spinning faster than thought. Yet the pattern is the same. The algorithm feeds on our dividedness; the market thrives on our restlessness. The mind addicted to contrast can never know peace.

Vedanta offers no escape from the pairs, only understanding. The opposites will continue their dance as long as the body breathes. But once you know them as mere movements in awareness, they lose their sting. The secret is not balance but recognition: to see that even the pendulum is held by stillness.

The *dvandvas* rule the world, but not the Self. When you stand as That, the game ends. Pleasure and pain, victory and defeat, birth and death — each is just another turn of the wheel. Awareness watches, unblinking. The play goes on, and the witness remains untouched.

—

Root & Meaning

Dvandva (from *dva*, "two") literally means "a pair" or "duality." In Sanskrit grammar, it refers to a compound word formed by joining two or more nouns of equal status—such as *rama-lakshmanau* ("Rama and Lakshmana") — where both members retain significance. Beyond grammar, *dvandva* also denotes the natural pairs of opposites that characterize worldly experience.

Scriptural References

The *Bhagavad Gita* repeatedly refers to *dvandva* as the alternating pairs that disturb the mind:

- "The contacts of the senses with their objects cause cold and heat, pleasure and pain; these come and go." (2.14)
- Likewise, in 7.27, Krishna explains that beings fall into delusion "by the pairs of opposites (*dvandva-mohena*)" — an explicit link between *dvandva* and maya.

Traditional View

In classical Vedanta, *dvandva* represents the field of opposites that defines samsara: pleasure and pain, gain and loss, praise and blame, success and failure. These opposites are not merely external events but mental constructions rooted in *raga* (attraction) and *dvesha* (aversion). Liberation (*moksha*) is freedom from identification with either pole.

Vedantic Analysis

The *dvandvas* exist only in the realm of *prakriti* — the play of *gunas* that constitute the manifest universe. The Self (atman) is untouched by them. Thus, while the body-mind experiences cold or heat, joy or sorrow, the witness-consciousness remains changeless. The wise do not seek to escape the *dvandvas* but to recognize their unreality from the standpoint of the Self.

The play of opposites is essential to maya's functioning: without contrast, the world would not appear. The rhythm of duality sustains relativity, but once knowledge arises, the sage sees both as mere modifications of one awareness.

Common Misunderstandings

- **Suppression vs. transcendence:** Some think *dvandva-nivritti* (freedom from opposites) means emotional numbness. In truth, it is understanding their nonbinding nature.
- **Moral dualities:** Others mistake *dvandva* for ethical dichotomies (good/evil). Vedanta treats those as dharma-based distinctions,

not as the fundamental experiential pairs generated by maya.

Vedantic Resolution

Freedom from *dvandva* arises not through avoidance but through knowledge: "I am not the experiencer of these opposites; they belong to the body-mind." Equanimity (*samatvam*) is therefore not passivity but the natural poise of one established in Self-knowledge.

As Shankara comments, "He who is unaffected by the pairs of opposites, who remains the same in success and failure — he is truly free." (*Gita* 2.38)

gunas

(guṇas — *goo-nuhs*)

There is a strange weather in the mind. Sometimes we wake to blue skies—clear-headed, light-hearted, the path ahead illumined. At other times, we find ourselves stirred by winds — driven, restless, inflamed by desire or urgency. And still other times, the mind sinks into heaviness, like a fog has settled in, dulling the senses, wrapping thought in lethargy or despair.

These fluctuations are not random. They are the play of the *gunas* (*guṇas*) — the three fundamental powers of maya that shape both the outer universe and our inner lives. *Sattva, rajas,* and *tamas*: knowledge, energy, and matter. Illumination, activity, and obscuration. They are not moral qualities. They are the elemental forces of creation, preservation, and dissolution — ever cycling, ever binding.

The same forces that cause a planet to spin, a tree to grow, or a sun to collapse into a black hole are at work in the mind of a single human being. The same laws govern both forest and tree, galaxy and gaze. *Sattva* is the clarity in a scientist's insight, the calm in a saint's heart. *Rajas* is the heat of invention, ambition, hunger. *Tamas* is the sleep we fall into at night, the gravity that pulls us toward numbness, forgetfulness, and avoidance.

Modern life, especially in its urban and digital form, runs hot with *rajas* and dull with *tamas*. Our mornings are propped up by caffeine; our nights soothed by wine or weed. We are overstimulated, yet uninspired. Moving fast, but often going nowhere. This imbalance is not just physiological — it's existential. We forget who we are, and the *gunas* take the wheel.

But Vedanta doesn't reject the *gunas*. It doesn't ask us to control them with brute force or to escape them through denial. Instead, it asks us to observe. To see these powers for what they are: changing attributes of the mind, not attributes of the Self. Like clouds passing through the sky of awareness.

With this clarity, we can begin to manage them — not to achieve perfection, but to create the conditions for inquiry. *Triguna yoga* is the art of recognizing the gunas as they move through the day, and responding appropriately. Sometimes we need to bring in *sattva* to counteract *rajas* or *tamas*. Sometimes we use a bit of *rajas* to shake off inertia. But always, we remember: I am not these movements. I am the one in whose presence they arise.

The *gunas* are the architecture of samsara — but they are not the Self. That, untouched by clarity or confusion, action or stillness, is ever free.

—

Root & Meaning

Guna means "quality," "attribute," or "strand." It is also translated as "rope," suggesting both the binding nature of the *gunas* and their interwoven presence in the fabric of creation. The term comes from the root *gr*, meaning "to count, enumerate, or classify."

Scriptural References

- **Bhagavad Gita, Chapters 14 and 17:** The clearest scriptural exposition on the nature of the *gunas*, their effects, and how to transcend them.
- **Sankhya Karika:** Describes the *gunas* as the constituents of *prakriti*, the primordial material cause.
- **Yoga Sutras (e.g., 1.16, 3.56):** Allude to the cessation of the *gunas* as a prerequisite for final liberation (*kaivalya*).
- **Mundaka Upanishad, Prashna Upanishad, and others:** Mention the *gunas* as constituents of the manifest universe.

Traditional View

- The *gunas* are the threefold powers of maya through which all phenomena — gross and subtle — are formed, sustained, and dissolved:
- **Sattva:** The force of clarity, knowledge, balance, harmony, and illumination. It is light, buoyant, and upward-moving.
- **Rajas:** The force of dynamism, desire, passion, agitation, and projection. It is kinetic, fiery, and outward-moving.
- **Tamas:** The force of inertia, concealment, delusion, dullness, and heaviness. It is dense, dark, and downward-moving.
- All objects in the universe, including thoughts and emotions, are composed of these three in varying proportions. Even the five elements — space, air, fire, water, and earth — contain all three, with one predominating.

Vedantic Analysis

In Advaita Vedanta, the *gunas* belong to maya and have no reality apart from it. They are *mithya* — dependent, changeable, and ultimately unreal when viewed from the standpoint of the Self. The Self (atman, Brahman) is *nirguna* — beyond all attributes. Thus, the *gunas* pertain to the field (*kshetra*), while the knower (*kshetrajna*) remains unaffected.

However, until Self-knowledge dawns, the *gunas* shape the individual's experience. The *jiva* believes it is the doer (*kartr*), driven by *rajas*; or the knower (*jnatr*), illuminated by *sattva*; or simply lost in forgetfulness under *tamas*. The *gunas* color the mind, and the ignorant take that color to be their identity.

Vedanta doesn't advocate suppression of the *gunas* but dis-identification. Observing them as natural forces — like wind or weather — allows one to act wisely without getting entangled. *Sattva* is especially valuable, as it purifies the mind and fosters inquiry, but even *sattva* must be eventually transcended. *Moksha* is freedom from all three.

Common Misunderstandings

- **Sattva = Enlightenment:** *Sattva* brings peace and insight, but it is still part of maya. Clinging to *sattva* can become a subtle bondage.
- **Rajas and tamas are bad:** All three *gunas* are necessary for functioning. *Rajas* drives change; *tamas* brings stability. The problem is excess or imbalance.
- **Moralizing the gunas:** The *gunas* are not moral categories. A rajasic warrior and a sattvic poet are both under the spell of maya.
- **Controlling the gunas leads to liberation:** Management of the *gunas (triguna yoga)* helps prepare the mind, but realization comes from knowing the Self as distinct from them.

Vedantic Resolution

The Self is not qualified by the *gunas*. It witnesses their play but remains unaffected. Liberation lies in recognizing this fact — not in perfecting *sattva* or eliminating *rajas* and *tamas*. The *gunas* will continue to operate in the apparent world, but the *jnani* knows they do not define him. He may act, rest, think, or feel — but knows that these are just the movements of the field, not the Self.

As Krishna says in the Bhagavad Gita (14.22–23):

He who does not hate illumination, activity, and delusion when they appear, nor longs for them when they disappear… he who remains unshaken by the gunas, who stands apart, unwavering — he is said to have transcended them.

guru

(guru — *gu-ru*)

In the *Skanda Purana*, a sacred section known as the *Gurugita* ("song of the spiritual teacher") offers an etymological explanation of the word *guru*: "The root '*gu*' stands for darkness; '*ru*' for its removal. The removal of the darkness of ignorance in the heart is indicated by the word '*guru*'." Thus, the popular definition of guru as "the dispeller of darkness." What darkness? The darkness of ignorance that conceals one's true nature, namely, the Self.

In his text *Vivekachudamani* ("The Crest-Jewel of Discrimination"), Shankaracharya defines a true guru as having both spiritual knowledge and virtuous qualities:

One who is well-versed in the scriptures, lives a life free of *papa karma* (wrong actions), unaffected by desires, a full knower of Brahman with the mind resolved in the knowledge of Brahman, who is as calm as the fire that has burnt up its fuel, who is a boundless ocean of compassion without any reason, and who is a helpful friend to those who seek refuge. (33)

So, from this verse we can define a guru as someone who:

• Has extensive knowledge of the scriptures and is able to reveal their meaning in a way that can be understood depending on the experience of the student
• Lives a life free from conflict, rooted in freedom from wrong-doing
• Isn't driven by selfish desires or "has an agenda"
• Has a full understanding of Brahman and is free of any doubt
• Remains calm and composed, no longer swayed by the winds of samsara
• Has compassion for all beings as a result of seeing themselves in all beings

- Is willing to help those who are sincerely interested in removing their ignorance

A true guru is not merely a charismatic figure or inspiring personality, but a qualified *adhikari* — a vessel of both knowledge and virtue. Shankara warns that even those who are intellectually brilliant may mislead if they lack realization. In today's crowded spiritual marketplace, the ability to discern a qualified teacher is essential. As the tradition says, *shruti-yukti-anubhava* — scripture, reasoning, and direct experience — must align.

The guru's role is to methodically unfold the meaning of the Upanishads, guiding the student from theoretical understanding to direct recognition of the Self. It is said that to fully grasp even one verse of the Upanishads, one must understand the entire vision of Vedanta. Without a guide, the student risks projecting their preferences, interpretations, or conditioning onto the text — turning *shruti* into a mirror for ego rather than a light of knowledge.

What the student often overlooks is that the mind — conditioned by karma and shaped by the *gunas* — cannot recognize its own blind spots. The guru, standing outside this conditioning, uses a time-tested method (*sampradaya*) to unfold the truth. This teaching process involves *shravana* (listening), *manana* (reflection), and *nididhyasana* (contemplation/assimilation), all within a relationship built on humility, trust, and inquiry.

The *guru-shishya* (teacher-student) relationship is not about devotion for its own sake, but about transmission — a living connection through which Self-knowledge is made accessible. The guru is not the source of truth, but its revealer.

Ultimately, the role of the external guru is to awaken the inner guru — pure awareness itself. Once ignorance is removed, there remains no distinction between teacher, student, and truth.

Root & Meaning

Gu = darkness and *ru* = remover: "one who removes darkness (ignorance)."

Scriptural References

- **Skanda Purana, Gurugita:** *"Gu"* denotes darkness; *"ru"* denotes its removal — defining the guru as the dispeller of the darkness of ignorance.
- **Vivekachudamani (verse 33):** Shankaracharya's definition of the true guru: scripturally learned, free from wrongdoing, desireless, fully realized, calm, compassionate, and dedicated to guiding seekers.
- **Mundaka Upanishad (1.2.12):** Advises approaching a guru who is *shrotriya* (well-versed in scripture) and *brahmanishtha* (established in Brahman) for Self-knowledge.
- **Katha Upanishad (1.2.8–1.2.9):** Yama tells Nachiketa that the truth is subtle and cannot be known by mere reasoning; it must be taught by one who has realized it.
- **Bhagavad Gita (4.34):** Instructs the seeker to learn the truth by approaching a teacher with humility, inquiry, and service; the wise will impart knowledge to the sincere student.
- **Chandogya Upanishad (6.14.2):** Example of *guru-shishya* transmission: Uddalaka teaching Shvetaketu *"Tat tvam asi"* (That thou art) through systematic instruction.
- **Brahma Sutra Bhashya (1.1.1):** Shankara emphasizes that without a competent teacher in the *sampradaya*, the meaning of the scriptures cannot be fully understood.

Traditional View

The guru is the living embodiment of the teaching, serving as a bridge between the seeker and Self-knowledge. The teacher-student relationship is rooted in trust, respect, and an understanding of the ultimate aim — freedom from ignorance.

Vedantic Analysis

- Guru is not the doer of enlightenment; they remove ignorance so the Self, already free, is recognized.
- The teaching operates through *shastra* as *pramana*; the guru is the qualified transmitter.
- A student may outgrow the need for a physical teacher once knowledge is firmly assimilated.

Common Misunderstandings

- Idolizing the guru as a miracle-worker or as the source of grace independent of the teaching.
- Assuming anyone with spiritual language or charisma qualifies as a guru.
- Believing the guru "gives" enlightenment rather than revealing what is already present.

Vedantic Resolution

Respect and devotion to the guru are important, as they open the heart and mind, allowing knowledge to be received. But the highest guru is the Self itself — the light of awareness that is ever-present and free. The outer guru only points to this inner truth. Even a qualified teacher remains human. Fallibility between the teachings does not diminish the teaching itself, which flows from *shruti* (scripture), not from personal charisma or perfection. For this reason, it is wise to honor the teaching above the teacher. Worship the teaching, not the teacher.

Hiranyagarbha

(Hiraṇyagarbha — *hi-RUHN-yuh-GAR-bhuh*)

The Upanishads speak of *Hiranyagarbha (Hiraṇyagarbha)* — the "Golden Womb" or "Cosmic Egg" — as the first manifestation of Brahman through maya. It is not the Absolute itself, but Brahman reflected in the totality of subtle bodies, the cosmic mind. Just as the individual subtle body is called *Taijasa* in the dream state, at the macrocosmic level it is called *Hiranyagarbha*.

This "world-soul" is the first-born of creation, the repository of all thoughts, impressions, and subtle forces. All individual minds are but waves within this one cosmic mind. *Hiranyagarbha* is therefore not a person but a principle: the universal intelligence that sustains the dreamlike subtle universe.

Vedanta uses a set of parallel equations to explain the microcosm and macrocosm:

Waker (*Vishva*) <—> **Virat**: total gross body

Dreamer (*Taijasa*) <—> **Hiranyagarbha**: total subtle body

Sleeper (*Prajna*) <—> **Ishvara**: total causal body

Like a forest that contains countless trees yet has an identity beyond them, *Hiranyagarbha* is more than the sum of individual minds. It is the substratum in which all subtle experience unfolds.

Yet Vedanta insists that even *Hiranyagarbha* is *mithya*. Just as the dream dissolves upon waking, the cosmic mind dissolves into Brahman. The "Golden Egg" is not ultimate reality, but a teaching device to reveal the difference between the Self — pure awareness — and the totality of conditioned appearances. The seeker is taught to respect *Hiranyagarbha* as the cosmic order, but not to mistake it for the Self, which is free of gross, subtle, and causal *upadhis* alike.

—

Root & Meaning

Hiranya = golden
Garbha = womb or egg
Thus, "the Golden Womb" — the subtle seed of the cosmos, the cosmic mind.

Scriptural References

- **Rig Veda (10.121):** hymn to *Hiranyagarbha* as the first-born, the cosmic source.
- **Mandukya Upanishad:** identifies *Taijasa* (individual dreamer) with *Hiranyagarbha* (cosmic dreamer).
- **Bhagavad Gita (11th chapter):** echoes the vision of total mind and order behind the universe.

Traditional View

- *Hiranyagarbha* is the total subtle body, the cosmic mind.
- It is associated with the dream state, just as *Virat* is with waking and *Ishvara* with deep sleep.
- It is "the Golden Egg" — the first manifestation of Brahman under the conditioning of maya.
- Known also as *Prajapati* or *Sutratman*.

Vedantic Analysis

- *Hiranyagarbha* is a reflection of Brahman in the medium of the total subtle body.
- It is real only transactionally (*vyavaharika-satta*), not absolutely.
- The wise discriminate between the Self and even the cosmic mind, recognizing awareness as free from all conditions.

Common Misunderstandings

- **Hiranyagarbha as God:** In Advaita, it is not the ultimate God but a conditioned form of Brahman through maya.
- **The world as individual projection:** Vedanta clarifies that the cosmos is projected by *Ishvara* through *Hiranyagarbha*, not by individual minds alone.
- **Golden Egg as literal creation myth:** It is a symbolic expression of the subtle total, not a physical egg.

Vedantic Resolution

Respect *Hiranyagarbha* as the macrocosmic subtle body, but recognize that it too is *mithya*. The Self, *atman–brahman*, is beyond gross, subtle, and causal conditions, untouched by *Virat, Hiranyagarbha*, or *Ishvara*.

Ishvara

(Īśvara — *EESH-vuh-ruh*)

In some contemporary presentations, Brahman and *Ishvara* are informally described as "God without attributes" (*nirguna*) and "God with attributes" (*saguna*). The former is pure, non-dual consciousness; the latter is consciousness apparently associated with maya. A traditional analogy compares *Ishvara* to a spider that brings forth a web from itself without ever becoming entangled in it. The web depends entirely on the spider, but the spider remains free. Likewise, *Ishvara* manifests the universe out of its own being without ever becoming its creation.

Although *Ishvara* is often referred to as omniscient, omnipotent, and omnipresent, *Ishvara* is not a person endowed with superhuman qualities, nor does Ishvara reside in any particular place. Ishvara is the totality itself — the intelligence and material through which the universe arises, is sustained, and resolves.

Thus, *Ishvara* is best defined as the creative principle: the order, intelligence, and substance from which all forms emerge. To personify *Ishvara* is a matter of personal orientation, much as one might affectionately call the earth "Mother Earth." It is a symbolic gesture, not a literal claim.

While *Ishvara* refers to the impersonal, all-knowing, all-pervading whole, "Bhagavan" is *Ishvara* viewed through the lens of devotion (*bhakti*). The word *Bhagavan* derives from *bhaga*, "wealth" or "glory," referring to the one who possesses the six *bhagas* in full:

- *Jnana* – complete knowledge
- *Vairagya* – total dispassion
- *Aishvarya* – absolute lordship
- *Shri* – complete wealth

- *Yasha* – boundless fame
- *Virya* – unshakable strength

These are not human attributes but cosmic ones. Bhagavan is the worshipful form of the infinite — made accessible to the seeker's mind and heart.

In practice, this form varies across traditions. In the *Bhagavad Gita*, Bhagavan is Krishna; elsewhere it may be Shiva, Rama, or the Divine Mother. These deities are not separate beings but symbolic gateways through which one relates to the formless.

For this reason, Vedanta does not discourage devotional practices such as prayer, mantra, or *puja*. The heart requires a way to love what the intellect has understood. As the seeker matures, devotion ripens from dualistic worship to recognition: *Ishvara* is non-different from the Self.

Thus *jnana* reveals the non-dual truth; *bhakti* grants the clarity, surrender, and steadiness to assimilate it.

Why Vedanta Includes Ishvara

Some seekers question why a tradition grounded in reasoned inquiry includes the concept of God at all, assuming it to be a vestige of cultural inheritance. Vedanta, however, maintains that knowledge of oneself is incomplete without knowledge of the total. Without understanding the nature of the world in which one functions, one risks realizing the Self while simultaneously misunderstanding — or resenting — the field of experience.

Thus, understanding *Ishvara* is not an appeal to blind belief but an essential part of freedom. *Ishvara* is not to be believed but to be known. Only with this knowledge can one live harmoniously within the world that encompasses the individual.

Vedanta summarizes the roles of *Ishvara* in three ways:

- Creator–sustainer–resolver of the universe
- Governor of the field of experience (dharma)
- Giver of the fruits of action (*karma-phala*)

1. Ishvara as Creator–Sustainer–Resolver

Traditional texts describe *Ishvara* as a single reality functioning in three stages of manifestation:

- *Ishvara* — the unmanifest, seed state (deep sleep analogue)
- *Hiranyagarbha* — the subtle, germinating state (dream analogue)
- *Vaishvanara* — the gross, empirical state (waking analogue)

The universe cycles through these phases: manifestation, sustenance, resolution, and return to the seed state. Shankaracharya details these stages and their constituent elements in *Tattva Bodha*.

2. Ishvara as Governor of the Field of Experience

For any coherent system to function, there must be an underlying order. Vedanta calls this order dharma, the infallible structure of physical, psychological, moral, and cosmic laws. *Ishvara* is this very order.

Humans alone are capable of violating this order; animals follow their innate programs without conflict. Understanding *Ishvara's* order — and its value — is essential for living intelligently.

Modern metaphors are necessarily imperfect, but one may loosely compare *Ishvara* to an all-encompassing field of intelligence in which countless programs operate simultaneously. One such "program" governs the *jiva's* sense of agency. While individuals possess meaningful choice at the micro level, from the standpoint of the whole, the universe unfolds according to its inherent order.

Ishvara, as pure knowledge, "knows" all possibilities across time. Recognizing this dissolves the *jiva's* false sense of absolute doership while preserving its responsibility within the field of action.

3. Ishvara as Giver of the Fruits of Action

As both the creator and governor of the field, *Ishvara* also dispenses the results of action (*karma-phala*). Actions performed in alignment with dharma yield beneficial results; actions opposed to dharma produce suffering. Cultivating the right "seeds" through right action is therefore essential for inner maturity.

Tat Tvam Asi — "That Thou Art"

Despite the many glories attributed to *Ishvara*, Vedanta insists that the apparent distinction between *jiva* and *Ishvara* is due solely to their respective *upadhis* (limiting adjuncts). Maya serves as *Ishvara's upadhi*; the body–mind–sense complex serves as the *jiva's*. Both obscure the truth that their essence is the same awareness.

Thus:

maya + awareness = *Ishvara*
body-mind-sense complex + awareness = *jiva*

This insight is expressed in the *mahavakya, tat tvam asi* —"you are that." The individual and *Ishvara* are one in essence. The body-mind belongs to the world, which is *Ishvara's* manifestation; awareness, the substratum of all being, is non-dual. This does not negate *Ishvara* as a functional reality but reveals *Ishvara* to be *mithya*: dependent reality appearing upon the changeless truth of awareness.

Ultimately, the entire world appears in the Self, including the apparent individual and the apparent God. *Ishvara* is not other than me, nor am I other than *Ishvara*. The one reality — Brahman, *Ishvara*, awareness — is the Self alone.

Through devotion, inquiry, and clear discernment, the seeming division between seeker and sought dissolves. What remains is what has always been: the Self — whole, free, and undivided.

There is only one reality. Call it Brahman, call it *Ishvara*, call it awareness. You are That.

—

Root & Meaning

From *ish* ("to own, to rule"): "the ruler," "the Lord."

Scriptural References

- **Mundaka Upanishad (1.1.7–1.1.9):** Compares *Ishvara* to a spider projecting and withdrawing its web, illustrating creation and dissolution.
- **Taittiriya Upanishad (2.6.1):** Declares Brahman as the source from which all beings are born, sustained, and into which they dissolve.
- **Bhagavad Gita (4.6–4.8):** Krishna reveals his role as unborn *Ishvara* who manifests through maya for the protection of dharma.
- **Bhagavad Gita (9.4–9.10):** Describes *Ishvara* as all-pervading, yet unattached, orchestrating creation through maya.
- **Bhagavad Gita (15.15):** *Ishvara* as the source of memory, knowledge, and reasoning, and the revealer of the Vedas.
- **Brahma Sutra (1.1.2):** Identifies Brahman / *Ishvara* as the omniscient cause of the origin, sustenance, and dissolution of the world.
- **Chandogya Upanishad (6.2.1–6.2.3):** Presents *Ishvara* as the One without a second from which all creation emerges.
- **Shvetashvatara Upanishad (6.7–6.9):** Declares *Ishvara* as the ruler of all, beyond birth, untouched by the world, yet the inner controller of all beings.

Traditional View

- *Ishvara* is omniscient (*sarvajna*), omnipotent (*sarva-shakta*), and omnipresent (*sarva-vyapi*).

- The giver of the results of actions (*karma-phala-data*).
- The sustainer of cosmic order (*rita* or dharma).

Vedantic Analysis

- *Ishvara* = Brahman + maya (with full control over maya).
- From the empirical standpoint, worship and surrender to *Ishvara* are valid and necessary for mental purification.
- From the absolute standpoint, *Ishvara* is non-different from the Self; duality is only apparent.

Common Misunderstandings

- Thinking *Ishvara* is just a "mythological god" among many, rather than the total, all-intelligent order.
- Equating *Ishvara* solely with a sectarian form (e.g., only as Krishna or only as Shiva).
- Believing *Ishvara* is outside of oneself and separate in essence.

Vedantic Resolution

Devotion to *Ishvara* is not to a distant deity but to the totality in which one lives and moves. In the highest vision, *Ishvara* is recognized as one's own Self, free from all limitations.

jagat

(jagat — *juh-guht*)

The Sanskrit word *jagat* means "that which is born and that which goes" (*jayate gachchati iti jagat*). It highlights the impermanence of the universe — a ceaseless stream of arising and passing, birth and death, appearance and disappearance.

Scripture calls the *jagat* the *kshetra* — the field of experience. Here the *jiva* acts, sowing karmic seeds, and here those seeds ripen into the fruits of experience. Without the world there can be no doer (*karta*), and without the world there can be no experiencer (*bhokta*). The *jagat*, the doer, and the experiencer all arise together.

Vedanta insists that the *jagat* is never apart from *Ishvara*, its cause. Just as a pot cannot be separate from clay or a wave from water, the world is inseparable from the intelligence and being that sustains it. Wherever the *jagat* is, there *Ishvara* is.

And yet, the cause is always greater than its effect. Like the web is the spider, but the spider is not the web, the *jagat* is *Ishvara*, but *Ishvara* is not exhausted by the *jagat*. *Ishvara* transcends the creation, remaining as limitless consciousness and order in which the universe appears.

This vision transforms the world from inert "nature" into a sacred expression of intelligence. The symmetry of a snowflake, the precision of planetary motion, the design of a spider's web — all point to order woven into being. But Vedanta further clarifies: the *jagat* is *mithya*. It is not absolutely real, for it depends on Brahman; nor is it unreal, for it is experienced. It is real enough for all transactions, yet ultimately dependent. The wise one recognizes: I am satya, the Self; the world, body, and mind are mithya, borrowing existence from me.

—

Root & Meaning

Jagat = "that which is born (*jan*) and which goes (*gam*)." Describes the transient, ever-changing nature of the world.

Scriptural References

- **Bhagavad Gita (13.1–2):** calls the world *kshetra*, the field of experience
- **Drg-Dryshya-Viveka (verses 38–41):** distinguishes between the empirical (*vyavaharika-jagat*) and dreamlike (*pratibhasika-jagat*) worlds, both ultimately *mithya*.
- **Upanishads (Brhadaranyaka 4.5.15):** "Where there is duality, one sees another. Where all is the Self, there is no *jagat* apart."

Traditional View

- The *jagat* includes the external world, the body, and the mind — all of which have borrowed existence.
- It functions as the field for karma: actions are sown, results are reaped.
- It is intelligently ordered, revealing knowledge at every level.
- *Ishvara* is both the efficient and material cause of *jagat*. The world is inseparable from *Ishvara*, yet *Ishvara* transcends the world.

Vedantic Analysis

- The *jagat* is inseparable from its cause: wherever the effect is, the cause must be. Thus, wherever the *jagat* is, there *Ishvara* is.
- But the cause is more than the effect. Like the web is the spider, but the spider is not the web, the *jagat* is *Ishvara*, but *Ishvara* is not reducible to the *jagat*.
- The world is *mithya* — real transactionally, but dependent on

Brahman for its being.

- The Self is *satyam*; the *jagat* is *mithya*.

Common Misunderstandings

- **Jagat as illusion = nonexistence:** It exists transactionally but lacks independent reality.
- **Ishvara as separate from jagat:** The *jagat* is non-separate from its material cause, *Ishvara*.
- **Jagat as the whole of Ishvara:** Creation is *Ishvara*, but *Ishvara* is not exhausted by creation.

Vedantic Resolution

The *jagat* is to be respected as sacred order but not mistaken for absolute reality. By knowing the *jagat* as *mithya* and the Self as *satya*, one lives free in the world, recognizing *Ishvara* everywhere while resting in Brahman, which transcends both world and seed.

jagrat

(jāgrat — *JAA-gruht*)

The waking state feels like the measure of reality itself. We awaken each morning to the same rooms, the same gravity, the same faces and histories that seem to affirm the world's solidity. But Vedanta asks us to reconsider: what is the difference between being awake and believing we are awake?

In *jagrat (jāgrat)*, consciousness expresses itself through the body and senses, generating a field of experience that appears "external." Yet the *Mandukya Upanishad* reminds us that this state is only one of three recurring projections. It is no more absolute than the dream that precedes it or the deep sleep that follows it. What changes from dream to waking is merely the texture of projection, not its essence.

Swami Paramarthananda calls this realization "a disturbing message but the truth": just as the dreamer mistakes the dream for reality until awakening, the waker mistakes the waking world for absolute reality until knowledge dawns. From the standpoint of consciousness, both dream and waking arise, persist, and dissolve in the same way. When knowledge "dawns," it is not another state but a change in status: the waking world, once taken as real, is now known as *mithya* — a dependent appearance .

Thus, Vedanta's question is not whether the world exists, but what the world's order of reality is. The enlightened one continues to live and transact in *jagrat*, but inwardly knows it as no more real than last night's dream. The true awakening, therefore, is not from sleep to waking, but from *jagrat* to *jnana* — from empirical to absolute awareness.

—

Root & Meaning

Root: *jagr* — "to be awake, to watch, to remain alert." Literal meaning: "Wakefulness; the condition of being aware through the senses."

Scriptural References

- **Mandukya Upanishad 3:** *Jagarita-sthano bahish-prajnah... sthula-bhuk vaishvanarah prathamah padah.* "The first quarter is Vaishvanara, outwardly conscious, experiencing gross objects in the waking state."
- **Kaivalya Upanishad 12–14:** "When consciousness is deluded by Maya, it identifies with a human body in the waking state and acts to fulfill its desires... the same consciousness dreams and sleeps because of its association with karma."

Traditional View

In the waking state, consciousness identifies with the gross body (*sthula sharira*), using nineteen instruments — the five senses, five organs of action, five vital energies, and four internal faculties (*manas, buddhi, chitta, ahankara*). Through these "mouths," *Vaishvanara*, the macrocosmic waker, experiences the world of form and function.

The waking universe (*jagrat prapancha*) is sustained by *Ishvara's maya-shakti* just as the dream is sustained by the *jiva's nidra-shakti*. Each is a projection within consciousness, neither self-existent nor independent.

Vedantic Analysis

Relativity of reality:
Gaudapada's *Karika* shows that all criteria — utility, externality, continuity, clarity — fail to establish the waking world as more real than the dream. Both are real only within their own domains

and absent in the other.

Projector–Supporter–Experiencer (PSE):
The same Self projects, supports, and experiences both waking and dream. In *jagrat*, this occurs through *maya-shakti*; in *svapna*, through *nidra-shakti*. The witnessing consciousness (*sakshi*) is the substratum of both.

Microcosm and macrocosm:
The individual waker (*Vishva*) corresponds to the cosmic waker (*Virat*). What the *jiva* experiences locally, *Ishvara* manifests universally.

Avastha-traya-viveka:
The "I" is never truly the waker, dreamer, or sleeper. These are passing associations. Knowledge reveals the *Turiya*, which is free of all three.

Common Misunderstandings

- **The waking state is more real than the dream.** Both are *mithya*, differing only in stability and shared continuity.
- **Vedanta denies the waking world.** No — it denies independent existence. Waking is respected for its experienceability, transactability, and utility (ETU), yet known as dependent.
- **Awakening is a new state.** Knowledge does not add another state; it reveals that the witness was never a participant in any state.

Vedantic Resolution

When knowledge dissolves identification with the waker, *jagrat* is seen as *Ishvara's* dream — ordered, lawful, yet insubstantial. The sage continues to act, but knows that the actor, actions, and results are mere superimpositions upon consciousness.

jiva

(jīva — *JEE-vuh*)

Scriptural Image of Jiva

Two birds, bound together in close friendship, perch on the same tree.
One of them eats the sweet fruit with great pleasure, while the other
just looks on.

This verse from the *Mundaka Upanishad* (3.1.1) describes the "Tree
of Samsara," resembling a banyan tree with its roots above in the
sky and branches spreading broadly downward. According to
Shankaracharya, the tree is supported by maya (ignorance), and
on its branches hang the fruits of the actions of living beings.

The tree is a metaphor for the body, with its roots above in
Brahman (the Self) and its sense organs below, turned toward the
world. The *jiva* identifies with the tree (the body) and experiences
the fruits of its actions as either pleasant (sweet) or painful (bit-
ter). The bird's inseparable companion represents pure awareness,
the witness that never partakes of the fruits.

Seated on the same tree, the *jiva*, deluded by ignorance, grieves
over its imagined powerlessness. But when it learns of the Self, it
becomes free from all misery.

Anatomy of the Jiva

The word *jiva* (*jīva*) signifies any living being — animals, plants,
microorganisms, and beings still unknown — but in scripture
usually refers to the individual person. The human *jiva* is awareness associated with a body–mind–sense complex.

From the standpoint of Vedanta, the body–mind–sense complex is
a combination of three "bodies":

- **Gross body (sthula sharira):** the physical body with its elements, components, and physiological functions.
- **Subtle body (sukshma sharira):** the mind, intellect, ego, and vital functions.
- **Causal body (karana sharira):** the seed form of experience, the storehouse of latent impressions (*vasanas*) and the state of deep ignorance.

The *jiva* also cycles through three states of experience: waking, dreaming, and deep sleep. Each state arises and subsides, proving it is not constant. In deep sleep, the waking self — the "me" we usually identify with — is absent, yet awareness remains as the witness. Vedanta shows that the waking state is no more real than the other two.

Traditionally, the waker is said to have "thirteen mouths" — the five organs of perception, the five organs of action, plus the mind, intellect, and ego. It is said that the senses aggressively seek experience; the body consumes matter; the mind chews emotion; the intellect digests ideas; and the ego swallows any experience it believes will make it feel adequate or happy.

Beyond these three states is a "fourth," called *turiya* — not a state at all, but the changeless Self that is present in and through all experiences.

Metaphors for the Jiva's Ignorance

Vedanta offers several models to explain the *jiva's* misidentification with the body and mind:

- **Five sheaths (panchakosha):** The Self appears covered by layers, from gross to subtle — the physical sheath, the vital-energy sheath, the mind sheath, the intellect sheath, and the bliss sheath. None of these can be the Self, because all are objects known by the Self.
- **Upadhi (limiting adjunct):** An *upadhi* is something whose

proximity makes another thing appear different from what it is — like water looking red in a red bottle. Here, the intellect sheath is the upadhi; pure consciousness appears as a limited *jiva*.

- **Mirror analogy:** The Self is like a light shining on a mirror. The mirror — the three bodies, conditioned by the *gunas* — is an imperfect reflecting medium, producing a distorted reflection. The *jiva* mistakes this reflection for its true nature.
- **Spell of maya:** Pure consciousness, under the spell of maya, believes it has become an individual man or woman.

Fate and Liberation of the Jiva

According to karma theory, the *jiva* is bound to the cycle of rebirth (samsara). What keeps it bound are:

- Binding likes and dislikes (*raga–dvesha*)
- The belief "I am the doer and enjoyer"

These create and accumulate karma, which propels the *jiva* into future births, each one offering another opportunity to recognize the Self and exhaust past tendencies.

The premise of Vedanta is that eventually the jiva becomes disillusioned with the limitations of samsara, purifies its actions, and gains Self-knowledge through a qualified teacher. In the moment of clear recognition, the *jiva* discovers it was never bound; the bondage was due only to ignorance.

"*Jiva*" is thus not a permanent reality but a status. When ignorance ends, the status changes to *jivanmukta* — one liberated while still living. The difference is simple:

The *jiva* still identifies as the doer/enjoyer and suffers perceived limitation.

The *jivanmukta* identifies with the Self, enjoying limitless freedom as pure, eternal awareness.

Root & Meaning

Jiva (from *jiv*, "to live"): a "living being"; conventionally, the individual experiencer-doer that transmigrates.

Scriptural References

- **Mundaka Upanishad (3.1.1–3.1.2):** Two birds on the same tree: one eating the fruits (jiva bound by karma), the other simply witnessing (atman).
- **Bhagavad Gita (15.7):** "An eternal portion of Myself becomes the *jiva* in the world of living beings, drawing to itself the senses and mind as the sixth."
- **Bhagavad Gita (2.22):** The *jiva* discards worn-out bodies and takes on new ones, like a person changing garments.
- **Bhagavad Gita (13.31):** Though dwelling in the body, the Self neither acts nor is tainted.
- **Vivekachudamani (verse 129–132):** The *jiva's* bondage due to ignorance and its liberation through knowledge.
- **Brahma Sutra (2.3.18–20):** The individual soul's distinction from and identity with Brahman explained via *upadhi*.
- **Chandogya Upanishad (6.8.7):** *Tat tvam asi:* the *jiva* is in essence none other than Brahman.

Traditional View

The *jiva* is an individual soul journeying through births, reaping karma, seeking merit (*punya*) and avoiding demerit (*papa*), ultimately to gain liberation through grace, practice, and maturity.

Vedantic Analysis

The *jiva* is atman seemingly limited by *upadhis* (three bodies) under *avidya*. Sentiency of the mind is via *chidabhasa* (reflected consciousness). The *jiva*-status is *mithya* — dependent, changing, name-form only. In truth, the witness (*sakshi/ turiya*) is ever free; the doer/enjoyer is a superimposition.

Common Misunderstandings

- **"The jiva is a permanently separate soul."** The *jiva* is not an independently existing soul, but Brahman appearing as an individual due to identification with the body–mind.
- **"Awareness lives inside the body."** Awareness is not contained in the body; rather, the body appears within Awareness, which is limitless and all-pervading.
- **"Liberation destroys the jiva as a person."** Liberation does not destroy the *jiva*, but destroys ignorance about its true nature, allowing the personality to continue without bondage.
- **"A jivanmukta stops acting or feeling."** A *jivanmukta* continues to act and feel according to *prarabdha karma*, but without identification, attachment, or psychological suffering.
- **"Deep sleep proves unconsciousness of the Self."** Deep sleep reveals the absence of objects of awareness, not the absence of Awareness itself, which is later recognized through recollection.

Vedantic Resolution

- The *jiva* is an appearance of the one atman through maya/ *avidya*; there aren't many selves.
- Awareness is not in the body; the body–mind appears in awareness.
- *Moksha* removes ignorance; the body–mind may continue by *prarabdha*, but doership/enjoyership are known as *mithya*.
- A *jivanmukta* functions normally; only misidentification ends.
- In deep sleep, the mind resolves; the witness remains self-evident.

jivanmukta

(jīvanmukta — *JEE-vuhn-muk-tuh*)

Vedanta defines freedom not as escape from the world but as freedom within the world. The term *jivanmukta (jīvanmukta)* means
"liberated while living." Such a person has attained Self-
knowledge and no longer identifies with the body–mind complex,
even though it continues to function due to *prarabdha karma*. The
body remains, born of *Ishvara's* creation, but the sense of bondage
is gone.

Vedanta often uses the dream metaphor: just as the dreamer takes
the dream as real until waking, the bound *jiva* takes the world as
absolutely real until awakening to the Self. The *jivanmukta* lives in
the world knowing it is *mithya*, giving it due respect without over-
estimating or underestimating it.

Classical texts emphasize that for the *jivanmukta*, two kinds of
karma — *sanchita* (accumulated) and *agami* (future) — are
destroyed by Self-knowledge. Only *prarabdha* (karma already
in motion, which produced the current body) continues until
exhaustion. Hence, the liberated one still eats, feels heat and
cold, experiences joy and sorrow — but without attachment, like
watching a magic show while knowing the trick.

Descriptions of the *jivanmukta* abound: content, fearless, compassionate, free of hatred and desire, friendly to all, balanced in
gain and loss, and emotionally unshaken. These qualities are not
cultivated artificially but arise naturally from assimilation of Self-
knowledge. The *jivanmukta* accepts the play of *gunas*, interacts
with the world, yet never confuses the jiva with the Self.

Ultimately, the *jivanmukta* lives in effortless harmony: fully
engaged, yet untouched. Liberation does not make the person
superhuman — it dissolves the need to be anything other than

what one already is: limitless awareness, ever free.

—

Root & Meaning

Jivan = living, alive
Mukta = free, liberated
Jivanmukta = one who is liberated while still living in the body.

Scriptural References

- **Bhagavad Gita (5.8–9, 6.27):** describes the wise as seeing no doership, established in the Self, at peace.
- **Mandukya Karika (3.31–36):** portrays the liberated sage as unattached, serene, seeing the world like a dream.

Traditional View

- The *jivanmukta* has destroyed ignorance; the Self is fully realized.
- *Sanchita* and *agami karmas* are nullified by knowledge; only *prarabdha* sustains the body.
- Lives without a sense of doership or enjoyership.
- Exhibits natural virtues such as humility, compassion, and equanimity.

Vedantic Analysis

- The *jivanmukta* knows the *jiva* is *mithya* and the Self is *satya*.
- Duality appears, but is no longer binding, like a mirage seen as a mirage.
- Emotional disturbances may arise but are absorbed without fracture, as waves in the ocean.
- Freedom is in recognizing that the Self was never bound; liberation is the removal of ignorance, not a transformation of the person.

Common Misunderstandings

- **That liberation ends all experiences:** The *jivanmukta* still experiences pleasure and pain but remains free from bondage.
- **That enlightenment perfects the person:** The person remains subject to *gunas* and *prarabdha*; perfection is not required.
- **That the jivanmukta becomes Ishvara:** The liberated *jiva* does not merge into God while alive but knows non-difference in essence.

Vedantic Resolution

The *jivanmukta* embodies the paradox of Vedanta: while living within limitations, one abides in the limitless. The body–mind continues due to *prarabdha*, but the sense of individuality is known to be *mithya*. Liberation is freedom from identification, not from life itself.

jnana

(jñāna — *gy-AA-nuh*)

In Vedanta, *jnana (jñāna)* does not mean "knowledge" in the ordinary sense — facts, concepts, or information that can be learned and forgotten. It refers to Self-knowledge (*atma-jnana*): the clear, firm understanding that one's essential nature is Brahman, pure awareness, limitless, actionless, and free. Unlike ordinary knowledge, which is object-dependent and provisional, Self-knowledge cannot be negated. Once ignorance is removed, the truth "I am whole and complete" abides as the very substratum of experience.

This distinction is subtle but crucial. Most knowledge is about objects — mountains, bodies, histories, or even philosophies. These are *mithya*: changing, dependent, and subject to error. *Jnana* is about the subject, the knower itself. You cannot become an object to yourself; you are always the witness of all objects. Thus, Self-knowledge is not an experience to be gained, but a recognition of what is already the case.

This Self-knowledge unfolds in two stages. At first, there is indirect knowledge (*paroksha-jnana*): the conceptual understanding that "there is the Self, limitless awareness." One may appreciate the logic, even feel inspired by it, but the insight is still held at a distance. Then comes direct knowledge (*aparoksha-jnana*): the unshakable recognition "I am the Self." The separation between seeker and sought collapses; what was once an idea is now an identity.

Because of this, Vedanta insists that *jnana* is the only direct means to liberation (*moksha*). Techniques, disciplines, and practices (*karma yoga*, meditation, devotion) are preparatory — they prepare the mind so that Self-knowledge can take root. But no practice, however refined, can substitute for knowledge, because ignorance

— not lack of experience — is the problem.

At the same time, the tradition recognizes that realization unfolds in stages. One may have intellectual knowledge ("The Self is limitless awareness"), yet still feel bound by habits of mind. Self-realization is the destruction of ignorance through direct knowledge; Self-actualization is the full integration of that knowledge, where residual conditioning loses all binding force. Both are free, but one who has the latter lives with more ease and spontaneity.

Thus, *jnana* is not sterile philosophy but a living vision. It transforms how one interprets thoughts, emotions, and the world. A wave may continue to rise and fall, but once it knows itself as ocean, the drama of the surface is no longer threatening. The fruit of Self-knowledge is not the absence of life's appearances, but the freedom to stand unshaken amidst them.

—

Root & Meaning

From the Sanskrit root *jna* — "to know."
Jnana = knowledge.

In Vedanta, it refers not to ordinary knowledge but to Self-knowledge (*atma-jnana*) — the recognition that one's essential nature is Brahman, limitless awareness.

Scriptural References

- **Mundaka Upanishad 1.1.4–5:** distinguishes between higher knowledge (*para vidya*) leading to Brahman and lower knowledge (*apara vidya*) concerning rituals, language, and worldly learning.
- **Bhagavad Gita 4.38:** "In this world, there is no purifier equal to knowledge."
- **Chandogya Upanishad 6.8.7:** *tat tvam asi* points directly to Self-knowledge.

- **Brihadaranyaka Upanishad 4.4.23:** knowing Brahman, one becomes Brahman.

Traditional View

- Knowledge (*jnana*) is of two kinds:
  - *Paroksha-jnana* — indirect knowledge ("There is the Self").
  - *Aparoksha-jnana* — direct knowledge ("I am the Self").
- Only *aparoksha-jnana* removes ignorance and grants liberation.
- Knowledge is not acquired as new information but revealed by the *shastra* and teacher, removing the error of self-misidentification.

Vedantic Analysis

- Ignorance (*ajnana*) is the root of bondage. Actions (karma) and experiences cannot remove it, because ignorance is only destroyed by knowledge.
- Self-knowledge is not about gaining new experience; it is recognition of what always was.
- Liberation (*moksha*) comes the moment knowledge is firm: "I am whole, limitless, ever-free."
- There's a difference between Self-realization (firm knowledge that destroys ignorance) and Self-actualization (complete assimilation of knowledge into all aspects of life). Both are free, but actualization is the knowledge fully integrated.

Common Misunderstandings

- **Equating Self-knowledge with intellectual knowledge:** A mere concept ("I am Brahman") is not enough until it is owned as one's identity.
- **Confusing knowledge with mystical states:** States of meditation or bliss come and go. Knowledge is not an experience but recognition.
- **Assuming practices themselves cause liberation:** Practices

prepare the mind, but only *jnana* removes ignorance.

Vedantic Resolution

- Self-knowledge is the only direct means to freedom.
- Liberation is not becoming something new but recognizing what is already the case.
- Practices (*sadhana*) refine the mind, but the final step is the removal of error through the teaching of Vedanta.

jnana yoga

(jñāna yoga — *gy-AA-nuh YO-guh*)

Jnana yoga (jñāna yoga) is the last phase of the process toward
Self-realization, and the only one to focus specifically on Vedanta
(knowledge derived from the Upanishads). This is in contrast to
karma yoga and *upasana yoga*, which are considered prerequisite for
hearing the knowledge imparted during the *jnana yoga* phase.

The idea is that we must first make the mind fit through various
practices and disciplines so that the knowledge is able to go in.
Where the first two yogas are centered on action, the last phase is
focused on knowing. In the spiritual world, there are many yogis
who are "doers" but few who are actual "knowers."

There are a number of reasons for this including attachment to
spiritual experiences, lacking the courage to seek the truth, and
because the knowledge is counter-intuitive, requires a qualified
teacher, and necessitates repeated exposure in order for it to be
first realized and then, actualized.

In the *Bhagavad Gita*, Krishna tells Arjuna to "Make no mistake,
what I am sharing with you is indeed, a profound secret." (4.3)
Jnana or "Self-knowledge" is a secret because as individuals, we
are conditioned to identify with the body-mind rather than that
which illuminates the body-mind — consciousness. This is due to
the proximity of the body and the intimacy of our thoughts.

As already mentioned, Self-knowledge is also easily misunderstood because it's counterintuitive. For example, the Sun appears
to rise in the East and set in the West every day. And yet, even
once we have learned that it's the motion of the Earth and not the
Sun that makes it appear to set and rise, we continue to perceive
the opposite. It's for this reason that it is said Self-knowledge
is the one secret that even once told, still remains a secret. In

short, *jnana yoga* is a process — an unfolding that slowly fills out the picture regarding the nature of our experience, and provides the tools for getting out of samsara.

The Four-Fold Qualifications for Jnana Yoga

Vedanta suggests four qualifications for gaining *jnana*. Sometimes abbreviated as "The Four D's." They include discrimination (*viveka*), dispassion (*vairagya*), discipline (*shatka sampatti*) and burning desire (*mumukshutva*).

Discrimination is the ability to tell the difference between that which is true (i.e. the Self; pure consciousness) and that which is not (i.e. objects; that which is impermanent and comes and goes).

Dispassion is what is gained through maturity and the understanding that all objects are not real (are of the nature to change; not substantial). Dispassion is also the outcome of *karma yoga* which teaches non-attachment to the results of one's actions.

Next, discipline is about having control of the senses and having mastery of, what Vedanta refers to as, the "organs of action" used to express oneself in the world (hands, legs, speech, etc.). Discipline is typically developed during the *upasana yoga* phase and often defined to as the "six kinds of wealth" (*shatka sampatti*), which include mastery of the mind (*shama*), mastery of the sense organs (*dama*), the ability to withdraw from sense objects (*uparati*), forbearance (*titiksha*), faith pending verification (*shraddha*), and concentration of the mind (*samadhana*).

Lastly, desire means having a burning desire for freedom. As the choice of words suggests, this isn't just a meek interest in obtaining spiritual freedom. Most people with a burning desire may have already tried other spiritual practices with limited success, and Vedanta is their last resort. They are also mature enough to know that the world cannot provide real happiness — only the temporary kind — and instead, are seeking something they can rely on for lasting satisfaction.

If you are a seeker, you may already have the above mentioned qualifications to some degree. But in most cases, they will need to be made stronger before advancing to *jnana yoga*. Like running a marathon or swimming a mile — you're either ready for *jnana yoga* or you're not. One must have the fitness and the desire to cross the finish line. Some seekers might even find they need to re-qualify after learning Self-knowledge. They realize that in order to progress in their spiritual journey, they still have areas which need work.

The Three Stages of Jnana Yoga

We can divide *jnana yoga* into three stages: shravana, *manana*, and *nididhyasana*.

The first, *shravana*, is listening to the teachings for an undetermined length of time from a qualified teacher who is able to unlock the meaning of the teachings (*prakriyas*). This may involve putting a temporary hold on our beliefs that we have developed over a lifetime. Vedanta can often sound counter-intuitive because ignorance is hardwired, which is why it's important to approach it with an open mind.

Manana, the second stage, is the removal of any doubt left over from hearing the teachings and is characterized by a period of question and answer between student and teacher. *Manana* is marked by much reflection, and clarifying, and testing the logic of the teachings.

Lastly, *nididhyasana* is the removal of habitual behavior (leftover binding tendencies) and the assimilation of the teachings. In the *shravana* stage, one would say, There is the Self. But in the *nididhyasana* stage, one would say, I am the Self. This cognitive shift, from realizing "there is the Self" to actualizing it as "I am the Self" is what leads to liberation (*moksha*). It is also what separates the academic study of Vedanta (indirect knowledge) from actual Vedanta as a vehicle for freedom (direct knowledge).

But *jnana yoga* isn't about acquiring knowledge, more than, the removal of ignorance through a process that includes qualified guidance, repetition and constant discrimination (between what's "real" and what's not). This is because ignorance is tenacious, and just learning Self-knowledge doesn't guarantee that it will stick. One must still do the work, absorb it and integrate it.

Once Self-knowledge is gained, it's like a set of tools we can make use of on a daily basis. So, first we must obtain the right tools, and then we must apply them to the task at hand (in this case, the removal of ignorance). The result is the slow elimination of that which binds us, and prevents us from seeing that we are already free.

—

Root & Meaning

Jnana (from *jna*, "to know") = knowledge
Yoga (from *yuj*, "to join," "discipline") = a means or path.
Together: the discipline whose primary means is Self-knowledge, leading to *moksha*.

Scriptural References

- **Bhagavad Gita (4.1–4.3):** Krishna calls Self-knowledge the supreme secret, passed down through an unbroken lineage.
- **Bhagavad Gita (4.34):** "Approach a teacher with humility, inquiry, and service; the wise who see the truth will instruct you in knowledge."
- **Bhagavad Gita (9.1–2):** *Jnana* described as the king of knowledge and the greatest purifier, directly leading to liberation.
- **Mundaka Upanishad (1.1.4–1.1.5):** Distinction between higher knowledge (*para vidya*) that leads to Brahman and lower

knowledge (*apara vidya*) of rituals and worldly disciplines.

- **Vivekachudamani (19–20, 54–56, 364–365):** The fourfold qualifications (*viveka, vairagya, shatka sampatti, mumukshutva*) and the threefold process of *shravana–manana–nididhyasana* explained.

Traditional View

Jnana yoga is the final stage of Vedantic *sadhana*, following *karma yoga* (for purification) and *upasana yoga* (for mental steadiness). It is the direct pursuit of Self-knowledge through systematic listening (*shravana*), reflection (*manana*), and contemplation (*nididhyasana*).

Vedantic Analysis

In Advaita, *jnana yoga* is not intellectual study alone; it is a structured method of removing *avidya* through a qualified teacher and scripture (*shastra*). Its "discipline" is the committed exposure of the mind to the truth: *tat tvam asi* ("That thou art"). Knowledge is the immediate cause of liberation; action (karma) can only prepare the mind, never directly grant *moksha*.

Common Misunderstandings

- **"Jnana yoga is just reading books."** *Jnana yoga* is not information-gathering but the disciplined removal of ignorance through *shravana, manana,* and *nididhyasana*.
- **"It is incompatible with devotion."** In Advaita, devotion matures the mind for inquiry, making *bhakti* and *jnana* complementary rather than opposed.
- **"One can jump straight into jnana yoga without preparation."** *Jnana yoga* requires the mental qualifications produced by *karma yoga* and *upasana yoga*, without which inquiry remains merely intellectual.
- **"Contemplation (nididhyasana) means closing your eyes and thinking 'I am Brahman'."** *Nididhyasana* is not repetition of a

thought but the steady dissolution of habitual errors through assimilation of what is already understood.

Vedantic Resolution

- Mere book study lacks transformative power unless guided by *shastra* and teacher.
- True *jnana yoga* includes *bhakti* — devotion to truth and to the means of attaining it.
- Preparedness (*adhikaritva*) is essential: without mental purity and steadiness, knowledge won't assimilate.
- *Nididhyasana* is deep, sustained dwelling on the truth after doubt removal — not rote mental repetition.

jnanendriyas

(jñānendriyas — *gy-AA-nen-DRI-yuhs*)

In Vedanta, the *jnanendriyas (jñanendriyas)* are the five organs of
knowledge (sense organs) — the instruments through which the
mind receives information about the external world. They are
hearing, touch, sight, taste, and smell. Though they appear physical, Vedanta explains that the true organ is not the external ear
or eye, but the subtle faculty within the subtle body that allows
perception to occur.

The *jnanendriyas* act as doorways, bringing in sensory data, which
the mind (*manas*) and intellect (*buddhi*) process and interpret.
Without them, the external world would remain unknown. At the
same time, they are not independent — they require the enlivening presence of the Self (atman) to function.

Vedanta emphasizes that while the *jnanendriyas* enable knowledge
of the world, they cannot reveal the Self. For that, scripture (*shruti*) and inquiry (*vichara*) are required. Thus, the senses are valuable
but limited; they bind us to appearances if misunderstood, but
can serve as tools for discrimination when guided by
knowledge.

—

Root & Meaning

Jnana = knowledge.
Indriya = sense organ, faculty.
Jnanendriya = organ of knowledge (sense organ).

The Five *Jnanendriyas* (Organs of Knowledge):

• *Shrotra* — hearing (ear)
• *Tvak* — touch (skin)

- *Chakshus* — sight (eye)
- *Jihva* — taste (tongue)
- *Ghrana* — smell (nose)

Scriptural References

- **Taittiriya Upanishad 2.1:** lists the senses as arising from the elements
- **Bhagavad Gita 15.9:** the Self experiences the world through the five senses.

Traditional View

- The *jnanendriyas* are part of the *antahkarana's* instruments.
- They depend on *prana* for functioning.
- They provide raw data but not understanding; the mind interprets.

Vedantic Analysis

- Senses are limited in scope — they cannot perceive the Self.
- They function in the waking and dream states, but are resolved in deep sleep.
- Their activity illustrates dependence: without consciousness, they are inert.
- Knowledge must transcend sense perception to reach Brahman.

Common Misunderstandings

- **That the physical organ is the jnanendriya:** It is the subtle capacity within the subtle body.
- **That sense knowledge = ultimate knowledge:** Vedanta points beyond sensory evidence.
- **That the senses bind us inherently:** Binding arises only through attachment (*raga-dvesha*).

Vedantic Resolution

The five organs of knowledge (*jnanendriyas*) are essential for navigating the empirical world, but they cannot reveal the Self. They must be understood as tools, not ultimate authorities. True knowledge lies beyond their reach, in the recognition of awareness itself.

jnani

(jñānī — *gy-AA-NEE*)

A *jnani (jñānī)* is not someone who has acquired more information, accumulated mystical experiences, or perfected their outer life. A jnani is simply one who has seen through the error at the heart of human experience — the identification with the body-mind — and recognized their true nature as limitless awareness.

To the outside observer, nothing might appear different. The *jnani* may still have habits, quirks, likes and dislikes. They may work for a living, laugh with friends, or grow irritated at small annoyances. But inwardly, everything is different. The core confusion — "I am the doer, I am incomplete, I must strive to become whole" — has been dissolved. What remains is an unshakable peace that does not depend on circumstance.

Scripture compares the *jnani's* karmas to roasted seeds: they still exist, but they cannot sprout. Past momentum (*prarabdha karma*) continues to play out, but no new karmas are created. The wheel of becoming has stopped generating fresh bondage. Life continues, but the jnani is no longer entangled.

Modern teachers offer a helpful clarification here: one can be Self-realized without being fully Self-actualized. Self-realization means that ignorance has been destroyed and the knowledge "I am Brahman" is firm — not as intellectual theory but as assimilated vision. Still, residual conditioning (*vasanas*) may continue to express themselves in habits of thought or behavior. Self-actualization, by contrast, refers to the complete integration of knowledge, where even these residual patterns lose their binding power.

In other words, realization ends bondage immediately, but actualization is the slow burn of knowledge filtering into every corner of life. Both are free, but one reflects freedom more effortlessly. A comparison might be between passing an exam (knowing the truth) and allowing that knowledge to completely permeate one's life (living the truth without conflict). In Vedanta terms, Self-realization is liberation (*moksha*) already, but Self-actualization describes its fullest flowering in daily life.

Common misunderstandings about the *jnani* abound. Many imagine them as haloed saints, constantly blissful or socially flawless. But Vedanta insists otherwise: a *jnani* is free, not perfect. They may look utterly ordinary. Outwardly, they can even be mistaken for an "ignorant" person. The difference lies within — they do not suffer. As one teacher put it, "Samsara is complaint." The *jnani* has stopped complaining, not because life has ceased to be challenging, but because they no longer take themselves to be the sufferer.

The *Bhagavad Gita* describes the jnani as exceedingly dear, one who abides in equanimity, fearless, free from anger and craving, seeing the Self in all beings. Such qualities are not cultivated as moral projects but arise naturally once ignorance is removed.

Ultimately, the *jnani* is not defined by what they do or don't do, but by what they know. They know themselves as the ever-free Self. The mind still thinks, the senses still perceive, the body still acts — but the awareness in which all this arises remains untouched, limitless, and whole.

—

Root & Meaning

The word *jnani* (from the root *jna*, "to know") refers to a "knower," specifically one who has realized the truth of the Self (atman) through Vedanta. Unlike *jnana* (knowledge) as intellectual grasp, a *jnani* is one who has fully assimilated Self-knowledge, abides in it, and is liberated while living (*jivanmukta*).

Scriptural References

- **Mundaka Upanishad 3.2.9:** The *jnani* is described as one who, knowing the Self, becomes free from grief, desire, and delusion.
- **Bhagavad Gita 4.18:** One who sees action in inaction and inaction in action is a true *jnani*.

Traditional View

Tradition presents the *jnani* as one who has transcended ignorance (*avidya*) and the binding force of karma. Such a person is not marked by outward renunciation alone but by inner freedom. They may live as wandering ascetics or remain engaged in society; what distinguishes them is their unshakable recognition: "I am Brahman."

Vedantic Analysis

The *jnani* is free from identification with the *jnani* (body-mind adjuncts). For them, the mind is simply an instrument, not the Self. Their karmas are compared to roasted seeds (*dagdha-bija*): incapable of bearing future fruit. While *prarabdha karma* continues, no new karma binds them. Their life is thus one of freedom, spontaneity, and effortless compassion.

Common Misunderstandings

- **Halo effect:** People expect a *jnani* to always appear serene, extraordinary, or socially saintly. In truth, they may live quietly, even blending in.
- **Freedom from action:** A *jnani* may act in the world, even perform great service, yet from their standpoint no action belongs to them (*akarta*).
- **Withdrawal:** Solitude is not geographical but mental. A *jnani* may live in the marketplace with a mind at rest.

Vedantic Resolution

A *jnani* embodies moksha not as an event but as recognition of one's ever-free nature. Their hallmark is the absence of complaint (samsara is complaint) and the presence of unconditional peace, not perfection of circumstances. They function in the world without the sense of doership, living "like an ignorant one" outwardly but inwardly abiding as Brahman.

kama

(kāma — *KAA-muh*)

Without desire, nothing stirs.

The Vedas tell us that in the beginning there was only stillness, a vast and undifferentiated silence. Then arose *kama (kāma)* — desire — the first stirring of creation. That pulse set the universe in motion. Without it, there would be no worlds, no beings, no play of form and name. Desire is not an accident of creation; it is creation's very heartbeat.

At the smallest scale, life itself is impossible without desire. A cell turns toward sugar. A plant bends toward the sun. The body hungers, thirsts, aches to move. Even the simplest forms of existence are animated by that fundamental urge to reach for what is not yet possessed.

We are no different. The desire to breathe pulls us into the next moment. The desire to rise from bed animates the day. The desire to love and be loved shapes the arc of a life. Even the seeker of truth is driven by *kama*: the longing for freedom, for rest in the Self. Shankara calls this *mumukshutva*, the burning desire for liberation — without it, no amount of study or discipline bears fruit.

And yet — the same desire that creates also destroys. The *Bhagavad Gita* names *kama* the great enemy of the seeker. Born of *rajas*, it obscures knowledge, clouds discernment, and drives one into bondage. Krishna tells Arjuna: "It is desire, it is anger, arising from *rajas* — the great consumer, the great enemy here" (3.37). When frustrated, desire gives rise to *krodha* (anger), and anger to delusion. The *Gita* traces the descent: brooding on objects > attachment > desire > anger > delusion > destruction of memory > ruin of reason > complete downfall (2.62–63).

This tension explains why *kama* has two portraits. On the one hand, it is listed as one of the four *purusharthas* — the aims of human life. Alongside dharma (righteousness), *artha* (security and wealth), and *moksha* (liberation), *kama* is considered a legitimate goal: the pursuit of pleasure, joy, and intimacy, as long as it is framed by dharma. In this sense, desire is not only natural but necessary. It nourishes human culture, art, and relationship, making life worth living.

But the *Gita* reminds us: when desire is untethered from dharma, when it insists that my happiness lies only in gaining or holding an object, it becomes binding. Such *kama* fuels samsara, perpetuating the cycle of longing and disappointment.

Vedanta refines this further by looking at desire through the lens of the three *gunas*:

- Sattvic desire is luminous. It seeks harmony with the whole, not just the good of the individual. It is the desire to give, to serve, to contribute — desire aligned with dharma and *Isvhara's* order. Though still desire, it purifies the mind and prepares it for knowledge.
- Rajasic desire is restless and acquisitive. It grasps for wealth, status, validation, and power. It drives accomplishment but also perpetuates agitation, leaving the seeker bound to an endless treadmill of striving.
- Tamasic desire is dark and destructive. It is compulsive, blind to consequences, and often drags one into *adharma*. Addictions, cruelty, and heedless indulgence fall here. Such desires not only fail to uplift but actively degrade the soul.

This is the paradox of *kama*: it is the fire that sustains life and the fire that consumes it. Without it, there is no creation, no movement, no life. But unchecked, it binds, blinds, and burns the seeker.

The resolution lies not in suppression but in understanding.

Vedanta teaches us to see desire for what it is — a movement in *prakriti*, not in the Self. When recognized as part of the field, its power to bind evaporates. A sattvic desire may be allowed to flow; rajasic desires can be refined and guided by dharma; tamasic desires can be dropped like poison. And above all, the highest desire — *mumukshutva*, the longing for liberation — can be cultivated, for it consumes all other desires and finally dissolves itself in knowledge of the Self.

The liberated one still eats, still acts, still loves. Desires may arise, but they are transparent, fleeting, without the weight of necessity. The *jnani* no longer chases fulfillment, for fulfillment is their nature.

And so we return to the first truth: no *kama*, no life. But equally: know the Self, and no *kama* can bind.

—

Root & Meaning

The Sanskrit word *kama* comes from the verbal root *kam*, meaning "to wish" or "to long for." It refers to desire in general, but especially to the longing for pleasure, fulfillment, or objects of enjoyment.

Scriptural References

- **Rig Veda 10.129 (Nasadiya Sukta):** "In the beginning, desire (*kama*) arose, the first seed of mind." Here, *kama* is depicted as the primordial creative impulse.
- **Bhagavad Gita 3.37:** "It is desire (*kama*), born of *rajas*, that is the all-devouring enemy."
- **Bhagavad Gita 2.62–63:** Desire is shown as the link in the chain leading from attachment to anger, delusion, and destruction of wisdom.
- **Bhagavad Gita 16.21:** Along with anger and greed, *kama* is listed

as one of the "three gates to hell."

- **Traditional Purusharthas:** *Kama* is recognized as one of the four aims of human life (alongside dharma, *artha*, and *moksha*), when pursued within the bounds of dharma.

Traditional View

Kama is not inherently condemned. As one of the *purusharthas*, it represents the natural and legitimate pursuit of enjoyment and pleasure, provided it does not violate dharma. Human life is not seen as complete without the fulfillment of *kama* in some measure. Ancient texts even celebrate *kama* as a cosmic principle — the first stirring of creation and the basis for human relationships, arts, and culture.

Vedantic Analysis

From the standpoint of Vedanta, *kama* has two faces:

- **Creative Principle:** Without desire, there is no life, no action, no creation. At the cosmic level, desire is what moves inert *prakriti* into manifestation. At the biological level, desire is what animates life to eat, move, and reproduce. Even spiritually, the longing for liberation (*mumukshutva*) is itself a form of *kama*.
- **Source of Bondage:** When desire arises from ignorance of the Self, it binds. The *Gita* calls this kama born of *rajas* — desire that insists "I must have this to be complete." Such *kama* ties the *jiva* to samsara, fuels anger when thwarted, and perpetuates dependence on external conditions for happiness.

The three *gunas* color desire in different ways:

- Sattvic desire aligns with dharma and contributes to purification of the mind.
- Rajasic desire seeks self-validation and power, creating agitation and dependence.
- Tamasic desire is compulsive and destructive, leading to

adharma and regression.

Common Misunderstandings

- **That all desire is bad:** In truth, desire is inevitable and fundamental to life. Even the desire for knowledge and freedom is still *kama*.
- **That spiritual practice requires eliminating desire altogether:** Vedanta clarifies that the issue is not desire itself, but binding desire — the belief that fulfillment lies in objects rather than the Self.
- **That kama means only sexual desire:** While it can mean that, its scope is much broader, encompassing every form of longing, from the most mundane to the most exalted.

Vedantic Resolution

- The solution is not suppression of *kama*, but understanding and sublimation:
- Recognize that all desires arise in the field of *prakriti*, not in the Self.
- Align desires with dharma so they purify the mind rather than bind it.
- Cultivate the highest desire — *mumukshutva*, the longing for liberation — which ultimately consumes all other desires and dissolves itself in Self-knowledge.
- Thus, Vedanta does not reject desire; it places it in its proper context. Desire is the fire of creation, the fuel of life, and, when purified, the very ladder to *moksha*.

karana sharira

(kāraṇa śarīra — *KAA-ruh-nuh shuh-REE-ruh*)

In Vedanta, the *karana sharira (kāraṇa śarīra)*, or causal body, is the most subtle layer of the apparent person. It is not a body in any physical or psychological sense, but a dormant, seed-like presence that underlies all experience. It is encountered most clearly in deep sleep, when both waking and dreaming dissolve and all cognitive faculties withdraw. What remains is a contentless potential — the experience of "I know nothing," yet marked by peace and rest. This is not mere emptiness, but a condition in which the gross and subtle bodies are resolved into their unmanifest source.

Vedanta identifies this condition as *anadi avidya* — beginningless ignorance. It is ignorance not of facts, but of one's own true nature as whole, limitless awareness. From this ignorance arise desire, karma, bondage, and rebirth. Though passive in appearance, the causal body stores the *vasanas* — latent impressions from countless past experiences — that silently shape thought, perception, emotion, and action.

From the microcosmic perspective, the causal body forms the seed of the individual personality. It contains the personal unconscious — deep reactions, tendencies, biases, fears, and desires that do not always reach the surface but drive the structure of one's experience. Modern psychology calls this the subconscious or unconscious mind. Freud saw it as a repository of repressed material, while Jung viewed it more broadly as the origin of dream symbolism, instinctual drives, and mythic structure. In this view, the causal body plays the same role: it is the hidden author of the story the ego takes as its own. And yet, while both the causal body and the subconscious function as hidden forces beneath waking awareness, Vedanta distinguishes the causal body as the substratum of ignorance itself, not merely a storehouse of repressed content or conditioned tendencies.

The table below outlines the differences:

	Subconscious (Psychology)	Causal Body (Vedanta)
Location	Subtle body (mind/intellect)	Beyond mind; root of subtle body
Contents	Memories, repressed desires, dreams	*Avidya* (ignorance), *vasanas* (latent impressions)
Accessibility	Introspective methods	Inferred; not directly experienced
Function	Drives personality & neurosis	Projects entire individuality
Aim	Healing, integration	Dissolution through Self-knowledge

Vedanta also distinguishes a macrocosmic causal body — *Ishvara's* (God's) causal body — which holds the blueprint for the entire field of creation. It is the undifferentiated substrate from which all laws, archetypes, and possibilities emerge. It contains the three *gunas* (*sattva, rajas, tamas*) in seed form and is responsible for manifesting the apparent universe through the projecting power of maya. It is this macrocosmic seed-state that precedes time, space, and causality.

Carl Jung added an important dimension to our understanding of the unconscious through his concept of archetypes — primordial symbols and motifs common to all human psyches. These archetypes — mother, hero, shadow, trickster — reside in what Jung called the collective unconscious. Vedanta would say that such archetypes reside in the macrocosmic causal body, which holds the seed-forms (*samskaras*) not just of one individual, but of all creation. These are universal thought-patterns projected by *Ishvara* through maya into individual lives, explaining why myths, dreams, and aspirations recur across cultures. What Jung glimpsed through analysis, Vedanta reveals through *viveka* (discrimination): these universal forms are not the Self but appearances projected upon it. They are *mithya* — apparently real, but ultimately dependent on awareness for their existence.

Another name for the causal body is *anandamaya kosha*, the "bliss sheath." It is so-called because in deep sleep, one experiences not suffering but peaceful contentment — free from agitation, longing, or identity. Yet this bliss is not the bliss of enlightenment. It is the temporary peace born of suspended desire, not of self-knowledge. Hence, Vedanta warns that even this bliss must be negated in inquiry, for it is still a sheath (*kosha*) — a covering of the Self.

Cognitively, the causal body correlates with what psychologist, Daniel Kahneman described as "System 1": the fast, automatic, intuitive mind that responds to life based on pattern recognition and habit. The causal body "thinks" without thought, generating reactions before the intellect has a chance to intervene. It supplies the subtle body (mind and intellect) with impulses, preferences, fears, and judgments — while the ego takes ownership of them, believing them to be self-originated. The causal body also exaggerates, simplifies, and constructs plausible narratives to preserve identity. These mental shortcuts may aid survival, but they distort truth.

Vedanta does not aim to heal or improve the causal body. It aims to dissolve it — not by suppression, but through knowledge. When the Self is recognized as the substratum of all three bodies — gross, subtle, and causal — the illusion of dependence on these layers vanishes. The causal body persists only so long as igno-rance does. With Self-knowledge, it is rendered powerless — like a burnt rope that cannot bind.

Thus, while psychology examines the dream, Vedanta wakes the dreamer. It does not merely explore the unconscious. It reveals that the unconscious itself is an appearance — dependent, chang-ing, and known. What knows it, cannot be it.

—

Root & Meaning

Karana (from *kr*, "to do, cause") = cause, instrument, origin.
Sharira (from *shr*, "to decay") = body, sheath, vehicle.

The "causal body" — the subtlest sheath of individuality, consist-ing of ignorance (*avidya*) and latent impressions (*vasanas*), which is the seed-cause of the subtle and gross bodies.

Scriptural References

- **Taittiriya Upanishad (2.5):** Describes the *anandamaya ko-sha* ("bliss sheath"), identified in Vedanta with the causal body, as the innermost sheath covering the Self.
- **Mandukya Upanishad (verse 5):** Explains the deep sleep (*sush-upti*) state, in which the *jiva* is unified, undifferentiated, and un-aware of external or internal objects, resting in the causal body.
- **Mandukya Upanishad (verse 6):** Describes the *Prajna*, the deep-sleep experiencer, as the mass of consciousness associated with *ananda* and ignorance (*avidya*), dwelling in the causal body.
- **Vivekachudamani (154–158):** Shankara describes the causal body as beginningless ignorance (*anadi avidya*), the seed of the subtle and gross bodies, and the container of latent impressions (*vasanas*).
- **Panchadashi (1.6–1.7):** Vidyaranya explains the three bod-ies (*shariras*), identifying the causal body as the seed state

containing maya and the three *gunas*.

- **Drg-Drshya Viveka (verse 19):** Notes that the Self is the witness of the causal body, which itself is an object of knowledge and therefore not the Self.
- **Brahma Sutra (2.3.29–30):** Discusses the causal condition of *avidya* and its role in producing the manifest universe through maya.
- **Bhagavad Gita (15.1–3):** Uses the metaphor of the inverted tree (*ashvattha*) rooted in the Self, whose seed-state exists prior to manifest experience, implying the causal layer of existence.

Traditional View

The *karana sharira* is one of the three bodies (*sharira-traya*) — gross (*sthula*), subtle (*sukshma*), and causal (*karana*). It is not a "body" in the physical sense, but the undifferentiated seed state from which the other two bodies emerge. It is experienced in *sushupti* (deep sleep) as the absence of duality, but without Self-knowledge.

Vedantic Analysis

The causal body is *avidya* — ignorance of one's true nature as Brahman — conditioned upon the individual (*jiva*). It contains the latent tendencies (*vasanas*) that, upon manifestation, project the subtle and gross experiences. Though blissful in deep sleep, the causal body is still within samsara and subject to beginning-less ignorance. It cannot be "purified" in the usual sense; it is destroyed only by *jnana*.

Common Misunderstandings

- **"The causal body is the soul."** The atman is not a body; the causal body is an *upadhi*.
- **"Deep sleep is liberation."** Deep sleep is ignorance without mental activity, not knowledge.
- **"One can directly experience the causal body."** It is inferred

through states like deep sleep, not directly perceived.

Vedantic Resolution

The causal body is the *upadhi* that veils the Self. Liberation occurs not by manipulating or transcending it through altered states, but by removing ignorance through Self-knowledge. Upon realization, the *karana sharira* is no longer mistaken for the Self, and its apparent bondage is nullified.

karma

(karma — *KAR-muh*)

In popular culture, the word *karma* is often reduced to a kind of cosmic cause-and-effect: the idea that "what goes around comes around," or, in biblical terms, "you reap what you sow." While this captures a sliver of its meaning, the concept of karma in Indian philosophy — especially in texts like the *Bhagavad Gita* — is far more nuanced and spiritually profound.

The Sanskrit word karma literally means "action." In its broadest sense, it refers to any physical, mental, or verbal act. However, within spiritual and scriptural contexts, karma carries a deeper implication. It often refers to ritual action — specifically, an action offered to the divine. In the *Bhagavad Gita*, karma is closely tied to the idea of *yajna*, or sacrifice, suggesting that the highest form of action is one performed selflessly, as an offering, without attachment to its fruits. Such action purifies the mind and leads to spiritual evolution.

Karma is also the engine of samsara, the cycle of birth, death, and rebirth. Every action — whether motivated by desire, aversion, or ignorance — leaves an imprint on the individual, shaping their future experiences. This accumulation of karmic impressions determines not only the conditions of one's current life but also the form and circumstances of future rebirths. In this sense, karma is not simply moral bookkeeping; it is a metaphysical law that governs the unfolding of life across lifetimes.

According to karma theory, good actions performed with clarity and selflessness generate *punya*, or merit, while selfish or harmful actions generate papa, or demerit. The consequences of both may manifest in this life or in future lives. One may be born into favorable circumstances — such as a loving family, a strong body, or a spiritual environment — because of virtuous actions in past lives. Conversely, a person born into hardship may be working through the consequences of prior negative karma. This does not justify suffering, but rather offers a framework in which suffering can be understood and ultimately transcended.

Classical Vedanta and the *Bhagavad Gita* describe three interrelated kinds of karma that together account for the unfolding of an individual's life:

Sanchita Karma – the accumulated stockpile of all past actions from countless lifetimes, lying dormant until the right conditions for their fruition arise.

Prarabdha Karma – the small but potent slice of *sanchita* that has "ripened" and is now bearing fruit in the circumstances of this life — your birth, body, family, and certain unavoidable experiences.

Agami Karma – the fresh karma generated by your current actions, which will bear fruit in the future and be added to the storehouse of sanchita.

These three work in concert: *prarabdha* sets the stage you are born into, *agami* is being written in the present moment, and *sanchita* holds the rest of the unmanifest backlog. Spiritual practice — especially *karma yoga* — is aimed at exhausting *prarabdha*, avoiding the creation of binding *agami*, and ultimately burning away the *sanchita* through Self-knowledge.

Importantly, karma is not fate. Human beings are not passive recipients of their past actions; they are active participants in shaping their destiny. The *Bhagavad Gita* emphasizes *karma yoga* — the yoga of action — as a path to liberation. By acting without attachment to outcomes, and by dedicating one's work to something greater than the ego, one gradually transcends the binding effects of karma. This is the beginning of freedom.

Ultimately, karma is not only about reward and punishment. It is a mirror reflecting the quality of our intentions and the clarity of our awareness. If one lives a life driven by greed, anger, and delusion, their actions will reinforce those tendencies and, according to karmic theory, they may be reborn in a form that reflects those unresolved impulses. But if one strives toward self-mastery, compassion, and truth, the karmic momentum will support a path toward spiritual realization.

Thus, karma is not a cosmic vending machine, nor is it merely a moral rule. It is a profound teaching about responsibility, growth, and the deep interconnectedness of all actions — seen and unseen. It is both the chain that binds and the key that frees.

—

Root & Meaning

Karma (from *kr*, "to do, act, make") = action, deed, work; also the law of cause and effect applied to moral and spiritual contexts. In Vedanta, it refers both to:

• Any action performed by body, speech, or mind.
• The results (*phala*) of past actions that shape present circumstances.

Scriptural References

• **Bhagavad Gita (2.47):** "Your right is to action alone, never to its fruits…" – foundational verse on acting without attachment, the essence of *karma yoga*.
• **Bhagavad Gita (3.9):** Actions performed as *yajna* (sacrifice) do not bind; those done otherwise cause bondage.
• **Bhagavad Gita (4.17):** Krishna distinguishes between karma (action), *vikarma* (wrong action), and *akarma* (inaction born of knowledge).
• **Bhagavad Gita (4.18):** The wise see inaction in action and action in inaction, pointing to the deeper understanding of

karma beyond mere physical movement.

- **Bhagavad Gita (5.14–15):** Declares that the Self neither acts nor causes others to act; karma belongs to the gunas of nature, not to the Self.
- **Brhadaranyaka Upanishad (4.4.5):** "A man turns into something good by good action and into something bad by bad action" – linking karma with ethical causation across lives.
- **Chandogya Upanishad (5.10.7):** Describes how one's actions determine the form and quality of future births.
- **Mundaka Upanishad (1.2.1–2):** Distinguishes lower knowledge (*apara vidya*), including ritual action, from higher knowledge (*para vidya*), showing karma's role as preparatory to liberation.
- **Yoga Sutras of Patanjali (2.12–2.14):** Explains the *karmashaya* (storehouse of karmic seeds) and how past actions bear fruit in present and future experiences.
- **Brahma Sutra (3.2.38):** Discusses how the effects of karma extend into future births until exhausted by experience or neutralized by knowledge.

Traditional View

Karma is the universal law that every action, physical or mental, produces a result. In the human context, karma determines one's experiences in this life and future births. Actions in harmony with dharma lead toward purification; actions in violation of dharma reinforce bondage. Karma is classified into:

Sanchita karma — accumulated results of countless past lives, stored in potential form.

Prarabdha karma — that portion of sanchita already "begun" and manifesting as the present body and life circumstances.

Agami karma — new karma created by current actions, which will bear fruit in the future.

Vedantic Analysis

From the standpoint of absolute reality (*paramartha*), the Self is *akarta* (non-doer) and *abhokta* (non-experiencer) — untouched by karma. Karma operates only in *mithya* (empirical reality), affecting the *jiva* identified with body and mind. *Karma yoga* — the performance of duties with the right attitude — purifies the mind (*chitta-shuddhi*), making it fit for Self-knowledge. Knowledge of the Self as non-doer burns *agami* and *sanchita karma; prarabdha* continues until the death of the body.

Common Misunderstandings

- **"Karma is fate."** Karma is cause and effect; free will still operates within its field.
- **"Self-realization erases all karma instantly."** *Prarabdha* continues until the current embodiment ends.
- **"Good karma ensures liberation."** Good karma may bring a better rebirth, but only Self-knowledge ends rebirth.

Vedantic Resolution

Karma binds only as long as one identifies with the doer. The *jnani* recognizes "I am the actionless Self" — in whose light actions arise and fall without affecting the witness. From this vision, the cycle of cause and effect loses its binding force, and the Self stands free of samsara.

karma yoga

(karma yoga — *KAR-muh YO-guh*)

Karma yoga is the first of the three traditional disciplines that prepare the mind for Self-inquiry. It precedes *upasana yoga* (meditation) and *jnana yoga* (Self-knowledge). In many Western contexts, *karma yoga* is presented in a non-devotional or secular form; traditionally, however, it is understood as a discipline infused with *bhakti*, a devotional orientation toward *Ishvara*. Both approaches are valid. One emphasizes harmonious participation within the field of experience, while the other emphasizes one's conscious relationship with *Ishvara*, understood in Vedanta as the conjunction of the creative principle (maya) with the consciousness principle (Brahman).

At its heart, *karma yoga* is the recognition that the individual doer/enjoyer is not ultimately in control. It acknowledges that universal principles and forces govern the field, and that by aligning with them, the individual is better equipped to live a stable and meaningful life. *Karma yoga* expresses itself through various practices that cultivate this alignment and reveal one's inseparability from the dharma field.

Technically, *karma yoga* is defined as proper action (karma) undertaken with proper attitude (yoga). Proper action emphasizes sattvic values — service, responsibility, kindness, and reverence — while proper attitude emphasizes mental balance, acceptance, humility, and gratitude. Together they refine one's conduct, reduce inner conflict, and loosen the grip of binding likes and dislikes.

Karma yoga rests on the understanding that the individual is not separate from nature: we are participants in, and expressions of, the same cosmic order. This attitude gradually neutralizes egoic reactions and prepares the mind for the final stage of spiritual unfoldment — Self-knowledge (Vedanta). Traditionally, *karma yoga* consists of the consecration of all actions to *Ishvara* and the acceptance of all results as *prasada* (blessings). Both are grounded in the insight that "I am not the doer."

Proper Action (Karma)

Worship of Ishvara. We honor *Ishvara*, the intelligent and material cause of the universe, recognizing that all actions depend on the cooperation of countless forces within the field. Nothing is achieved by individual effort alone.

Reverence for parents and forebears. Scripture enjoins unconditional respect for one's parents, who serve as the first teachers and whose care made one's life possible.

Reverence for scripture. We honor the wisdom teachings by studying them diligently and making them accessible to sincere seekers.

Service to humanity. This includes charitable work, civic responsibility, and fulfilling one's duties toward oneself, one's family, one's community, and society at large. Contributing to the common good strengthens the dharma field on which all depend.

Service to all beings. We recognize our symbiotic relationship with the natural world. To harm other beings or the environment is ultimately to harm ourselves. Proper action therefore includes stewardship of the earth, protection of life, and alignment with the cosmic order.

Proper Attitude (Yoga)

Attitude of appreciation and gratitude. We learn to value what we have, receive the results of action without attachment, and stand firm against binding likes and dislikes.

Attitude of non-comparison. Comparing ourselves with others in appearance, status, wealth, or ability disrupts mental peace. Non-comparison weakens the ego's habitual self-evaluation.

Attitude of humility. Success is accepted gratefully, with the recognition that no achievement occurs without the support of innumerable factors within the field.

Attitude of devotion. All results — favorable or unfavorable — are accepted as *prasada*. Even difficulties are approached as opportunities for growth and refinement.

Additional Attitudes and Expressions of Karma Yoga

Giving more than one takes. We acknowledge what has been given to us and consciously give back. Modern society's consumerism strains the environment and reflects a collective failure to uphold this basic principle.

Fulfilling duties to family and community. Work is not always about personal fulfillment. Sometimes the work we do is necessary because others depend on us. This is not sacrifice but dharma — the acceptance of one's role and responsibility.

Being an example. In the *Bhagavad Gita*, Krishna reminds Arjuna that people imitate the actions of those they respect. Living one's dharma is itself an act of teaching.

Work as offering. All work may be performed as an offering to *Ishvara* or to the field. This prevents action from becoming binding and transforms ordinary tasks into spiritual practice.

Not owners, but caretakers. Nothing truly belongs to us — not even the body. Everything is temporarily entrusted to our care. Gratitude naturally follows this understanding.

"Do your best and let it rest." We exert appropriate effort but recognize that results are governed by the larger field. Letting go of the demand for specific outcomes is integral to *karma yoga*.

Benefits of Karma Yoga

- It purifies and steadies the mind, preparing it for *jnana yoga* and Self-knowledge.
- It weakens the sense of doership by revealing the larger forces at play.
- It reduces stress by cultivating acceptance and the understanding that outcomes are not fully in one's control.
- It promotes gratitude, counteracting pride, fear, resentment, and bitterness.
- It fosters inner calm and emotional balance.
- Its attitude is naturally uplifting and positively influences those around us.

—

Root & Meaning

Karma = action, work, deed (from *kr*, "to do")
Yoga = union, discipline (from *yuj*, "to join, yoke")
Karma yoga = the discipline of selfless action; performing one's duties without attachment to results, as a means to purify the mind and prepare for Self-knowledge.

Scriptural References

- **Bhagavad Gita (2.47):** "Your right is to action alone, never to its fruits. Let not the fruits of action be your motive, nor let your attachment be to inaction."
- **Bhagavad Gita (3.9):** "Work must be done as sacrifice (*yajna*) to the Lord; otherwise work binds one to this world. Therefore, O son of Kunti, perform your prescribed duties for His satisfaction, and in that way you will always remain free from bondage."
- **Bhagavad Gita (3.19):** "Therefore, without attachment, perform

your duty as a matter of course, for by working without attachment one attains the Supreme."

- **Bhagavad Gita (3.30):** "Dedicate all actions to Me, with your mind on the Self, free from longing and selfishness, and fight without agitation."
- **Bhagavad Gita (4.20):** "Having abandoned all attachment to the results of action, ever content, depending on nothing, even though engaged in action, one does not act at all."
- **Bhagavad Gita (5.10):** "He who performs his duty without attachment, surrendering the results to the Supreme Lord, is not affected by sinful action, just as a lotus leaf is untouched by water."
- **Bhagavad Gita (9.27):** "Whatever you do, whatever you eat, whatever you offer in sacrifice, whatever you give, whatever austerity you perform — O son of Kunti — do that as an offering to Me."

Traditional View

- *Karma yoga* is one of the primary preparatory paths in Vedanta, suitable for those still identifying as doers and enjoyers. It involves:
- Performing *svadharma* (one's duties) as an offering to *Ishvara*.
- Accepting results as *prasada* (gift/blessing) from *Ishvara*, whether pleasant or unpleasant.
- Renouncing attachment to the outcome, focusing instead on right action.
- Its purpose is *chitta-shuddhi* (purity of mind), which is necessary before deeper meditation (*upasana yoga*) or inquiry (*jnana yoga*).

Vedantic Analysis

While karma itself binds when done from a sense of ego and desire, *karma yoga* neutralizes binding effects by dissolving the ego's claim over actions and results. The *karma yogi* sees themselves as an instrument through which *Ishvara's* order operates. Over time, this attitude erodes *rajas* (restlessness) and *tamas* (inertia), cultivating *sattva* (clarity), which supports Self-knowledge.

Common Misunderstandings

- **"Karma yoga is just doing good deeds."** It is an inner attitude, not merely outward service.
- **"Karma yoga leads to moksha directly."** It prepares the mind for *jnana yoga*, which alone leads to liberation.
- **"If I practice karma yoga, I'll get the results I want."** It's about accepting whatever results come as *prasada*.

Vedantic Resolution

Karma yoga bridges the active life and contemplative realization. By offering all actions to *Ishvara* and accepting all results, the seeker loosens the knot of doership. When the mind is purified, the shift to *jnana yoga* — recognizing the Self as actionless awareness — happens naturally.

karmendriyas

(karmendriyas — *KAR-men-DRI-yuhs*)

If the *jnanendriyas* (sense organs) are the windows through which the mind gathers knowledge, the *karmendriyas* are the tools through which it expresses itself in the world. They are the five organs of action: speech, hands, feet, reproduction, and elimination. Together, they represent how the individual interacts with and alters the environment.

Vedanta explains that these are not merely physical limbs but subtle faculties residing in the *sukshma sharira* (subtle body). Just as the external ear is not itself the faculty of hearing, the physical hand is not itself the organ of action; the *karmendriyas* is the subtle capacity to act through the hand. Without consciousness enlivening them, these instruments remain inert.

The *karmendriyas* have both a practical and philosophical role. Practically, they enable life's functions and social existence. Philosophically, they show how the *jiva* is bound by karma: every action undertaken through these instruments generates results that return to the individual in the form of experience. Thus, the *karmendriyas* are the conduits not only of expression but also of bondage — unless their actions are aligned with dharma.

Ultimately, Vedanta teaches that while the *karmendriyas* allow us to act, they cannot lead us to liberation on their own. Renunciation (*tyaga*) of attachment to action, and self-Knowledge, are necessary to transcend their binding power.

—

Root & Meaning

Karma = action.

Indriya = sense organ, faculty.
Karmendriya = organ of action.

The Five *Karmendriyas*:

- *Vak* — speech (tongue).
- *Pani* — grasping (hands).
- *Pada* — locomotion (feet).
- *Upastha* — procreation (organs of reproduction).
- *Payu* — elimination (organs of excretion).

Scriptural References

- **Taittiriya Upanishad 2.1:** describes the emergence of sense and action organs from the elements.
- **Bhagavad Gita 15.9:** the Self experiences the world through both *jnanendriyas* and *karmendriyas*.

Traditional View

- The *karmendriyas* are part of the subtle body.
- They express the will of the mind outwardly.
- They are essential for fulfilling dharma, *artha*, and *kama* (the first three *purusharthas*).

Vedantic Analysis

- Actions performed through these organs bind the individual when driven by ego and desire.
- Aligned with dharma and performed without attachment, they purify the mind (*chitta-shuddhi*) and prepare it for Self-knowledge.
- Liberation does not come from ceasing action but from recognizing the Self as *akarta* (non-doer).

Common Misunderstandings

- **That the physical limb is the organ:** The *karmendriya* is subtle, not gross.
- **That action itself is bondage:** It is not action but attachment to its fruits that binds.
- **That renunciation means inactivity:** True renunciation (*tyaga*) is inner, not merely outward withdrawal.

Vedantic Resolution

The *karmendriyas* are instruments, neither good nor bad in themselves. They bind when used ignorantly, but they can also serve as ladders to freedom when action is consecrated through *karma yoga*.

karta-bhokta

(kartā-bhoktā — *kahr-TAA-bhok-TAA*)

In the language of Vedanta, the individual is often described as *karta* (doer) and *bhokta* (enjoyer). This pairing describes the entire field of human experience: we act, and we reap the results of our actions. The sense of "I act" and "I enjoy or suffer" is the very definition of bondage.

The *Gita* points out that atman, the Self, is never a doer. It neither initiates action nor connects action with its results. Actions are performed by the senses and mind, which are themselves functions of *prakriti*. Yet, due to ignorance, the ego (*ahankara*) superimposes these activities on the Self, creating the notion of "I am the doer, I am the experiencer." This mistaken identification is the seed of samsara.

Karma yoga begins with this recognition: "I have to act, but I do not control the results." *Ishvara* is the *karma-phala-data* — the giver of the results of action. This attitude loosens the tight grip of doership. With maturity, the seeker understands more deeply: not only do I not control the results, even the doership itself is *mithya* (apparent reality). The *karta* and *bhokta* are roles within the field of experience, sustained by *gunas* and karma, but not the truth of the Self.

Vedanta distinguishes the ignorant doer from the enlightened doer. An unenlightened person believes, "I am the doer, I am bound by my actions." An enlightened person still acts — speaking, walking, eating — but knows, "I am not the doer. The roles of doer and experiencer belong to the body–mind, not to the Self." Thus, one may remain active while free, like an actor playing a part without mistaking it for reality.

—

Root & Meaning

Karta = doer, agent of action (from root *kr*, "to act, to do").
Bhokta = experiencer, enjoyer of results (from root *bhuj*, "to enjoy, to partake").

Scriptural References

- **Bhagavad Gita (5.8–9):** "The wise know: I do nothing at all; seeing, hearing, touching… it is only the senses acting among objects."
- **Gita (13.20–21):** *prakriti* is said to be the doer; *purusha*, the experiencer.
- **Shankara's commentaries:** emphasize that *kartritva* (doership) and *bhoktrittva* (enjoyership) belong to *ahankara*, not to atman.

Traditional View

- The *jiva* is bound as long as it identifies as doer/enjoyer.
- *Ishvara* gives the results of action, maintaining order (dharma).
- Karma operates only because the *jiva* sees itself as *karta–bhokta*.
- Liberation (*moksha*) ends this misidentification.

Vedantic Analysis

- Atman is actionless (*akarta*) and partless (*abhokta*).
- *Kartritva* and *bhoktritva* belong to the body–mind under the influence of *gunas*.
- Ignorance projects these roles onto the Self, creating bondage.
- Self-knowledge cancels this projection, revealing one was never a doer or enjoyer.

Common Misunderstandings

- **"I am not the doer" means passivity:** It does not excuse inaction. The *jiva* must act, but with knowledge that the Self is free.

- **Ishvara as partial dispenser of results:** In Vedanta, the results of action are lawful and impersonal, expressions of *Ishvara's* order.
- **Liberation requires giving up action:** What must be given up is identification with the *karta–bhokta,* not action itself.

Vedantic Resolution

Action continues, but the wise see that the Self neither acts nor enjoys. *Karta–bhokta* are roles in the play of maya, not the essence of atman. Knowing this, one lives free — engaged outwardly, inwardly untouched.

lila

(līlā — *LEE-LAA*)

In ordinary life, we act because of need. Desire pushes, incompleteness pulls, and action follows. The vision of Vedanta, however, is that the wise person — knowing fullness (*purnatva*) — no longer struggles for completion. Such a one moves through life lightly, as if it were a game. This effortless engagement with the world is called *lila (līlā)* — divine play.

Applied to *Ishvara*, the term carries even greater force. Shankara, in his commentary on the *Brahmasutras* (2.1.33), argues that creation is not a work driven by necessity or lack. God does not create out of want, fatigue, or compulsion. Creation is compared to two things: breathing, which is natural and spontaneous, and *lila*, sport or play, which arises from abundance and freedom.

The point is not that God "decides to have fun." It is subtler: action without extraneous motive is possible when one is whole. Just as a flower is beautiful not because it tries to be but because it cannot help being beautiful, so too creation is a spontaneous expression of fullness. As Nisargadatta Maharaj put it, "God is perfection itself, not an effort at perfection."

Yet, Vedantins also caution against taking the metaphor too literally. If every instance of suffering were dismissed as "God's play," the idea could border on cruelty. Swami Dayananda, for example, reminds us that in pure consciousness (*chaitanya*) there is truly no *lila*; it is only in association with maya that *Ishvara* can be said to play. In reality, neither purpose nor purposelessness applies to Brahman.

Thus, *lila* is a teaching device: it helps us understand that creation has no external cause or selfish intent. The world is not a burden or a mistake but an effortless manifestation of order and beauty.

For the wise, life itself is lived as *lila* — with seriousness in action, but lightness in being.

—

Root & Meaning

Lila = play, sport, pastime. In Vedanta, refers to action without extraneous motive, springing from fullness.

Scriptural References

- **Brahmasutra (2.1.33) with Shankara's bhashya:** creation compared to *lila* (play) and breathing — spontaneous, effortless.
- **Bhagavad Gita (9.10):** "Under Me as overseer, *prakriti* produces the moving and the unmoving," often interpreted in terms of *lila*.
- **Rig Veda hymns & Puranas:** speak of creation as divine sport.

Traditional View

- *Ishvara's* creation is not a response to need but an expression of abundance.
- The wise person, too, acts in the world as *lila* — playing their roles without dependence on results.
- Creation as *lila* underscores its effortless, purposeless spontaneity.

Vedantic Analysis

- Brahman, pure consciousness, has no activity and no *lila*.
- *Ishvara*, Brahman in association with maya, can be metaphorically said to create out of *lila*.
- The metaphor emphasizes non-necessity, spontaneity, and freedom in creation.
- Life for the *jnani* becomes *lila*: active yet untouched, engaged yet free.

Common Misunderstandings

- **Lila as divine boredom or self-exploration:** Some modern spiritual writing says *Ishvara* created the world to relieve boredom, to experience Himself, or to play hide-and-seek. Vedanta rejects this. Brahman, in truth, is limitless awareness (*purnatva*). Fullness cannot be improved by action, nor can it lack anything to "complete" itself. To imagine *Ishvara* creating out of need is to superimpose human limitation onto the limitless.
- **Lila as God's whim:** Play is not to be understood as arbitrary or frivolous. Creation is not caprice but ordered manifestation, governed by dharma and the laws of karma.
- **Lila as literal in Brahman:** Properly speaking, there is no *lila* in Brahman itself. Pure awareness neither creates nor plays. Only when associated with maya is Ishvara figuratively described as engaging in *lila*.

Vedantic Resolution

Lila is not a logical answer to "why" the universe exists, but a metaphor pointing to freedom from necessity. Creation has no external cause and no internal compulsion. It is not a project born of boredom or self-lack, but an expression of abundance — like fragrance from a flower or radiance from the sun. Brahman, the essence of *Ishvara*, is limitless awareness; no motive can apply.

The term *lila* helps negate false assumptions rather than provide a literal explanation. It tells us that creation is not driven by need, fatigue, or desire, but that it unfolds effortlessly within the order that is *Ishvara*.

laya *and* pralaya

(laya — *luh-yuh*) (pralaya — *pruh-luh-yuh*)

Each night, the universe dies a little.

When we sleep, the mind withdraws its projections, the senses fall silent, and the waking world is swallowed by darkness. The ancient sages saw in this not merely rest but return — a nightly rehearsal of the cosmic end.

Laya is the individual dissolution: the subtle and gross bodies subside into their causal seed, just as thought subsides into silence.

Pralaya is the cosmic dissolution: the entire universe, with its beings, laws, and elements, returns to potential form within maya.

Swami Paramarthananda calls deep sleep a mini-*pralayam* — a personal version of the great rest, when all experience folds back into its unmanifest source. The *Mandukya Upanishad* extends this principle: what dissolves individually each night happens universally at the close of a cosmic cycle.

Both reveal the same mystery: creation is never new. It is the unmanifest becoming manifest, and then resting again. Like a wave returning to the ocean, every appearance finds its home in stillness. "Creation," says Swami Dayananda, "is a misnomer — there is no creation at all; only the unmanifest coming into manifestation."

When all names and forms return to maya, what remains is Brahman — changeless, uncreated, aware. Thus, *laya* and *pralaya* are not destruction, but the reabsorption of illusion into its source —.

Root & Meaning

Laya: from the root *li*, "to dissolve, merge." The subsidence of individuality — the absorption of the mind and senses into the causal body.

Pralaya: *pra* + *laya*, "complete dissolution." The reabsorption of the entire universe into unmanifest potential (*avyakta*, maya).

Scriptural References

- **Bhagavad Gita 9.7–8:** "All beings merge into My nature at the end of a *kalpa*; again and again, I send them forth."
- **Mandukya Upanishad (Mantra 5):** The deep sleeper (*Prajna*) symbolizes the total, undifferentiated state of dissolution.

Traditional View

	Laya (Individual Dissolution)	Pralaya (Cosmic Dissolution)
Scope	Microcosmic	Macrocosmic
Trigger	Deep sleep, death, or absorption (*samadhi*)	End of a cosmic cycle (*kalpa*)
What dissolves	Gross and subtle bodies	All names, forms, laws, and beings
What remains	Causal body (*karana sharira*)	*Maya* — the cosmic causal seed
Duration	Temporary (until waking or rebirth)	Until next creation/ manifestation (*shrishti*)

	Laya (Individual Dissolution)	Pralaya (Cosmic Dissolution)
Witness	Atman	Brahman
Analogy	Sleep	Universal rest

The Upanishads equate *Prajna* (the deep sleeper) with *Ishvara*, the cosmic mind during *pralaya* — both embody the still potential of the unmanifest.

Vedantic Analysis

The Law of Conservation (Sat-karya-vada):
"If you have to create anything, it must exist in potential form," says Paramarthananda. Hence there is never true creation, only manifestation and dissolution. The clay already contains the pot; the milk already contains the butter.

Laya as Inner Rest:
In sleep or *samadhi*, the ego, intellect, and emotions are withdrawn. The world remains, but the experiencer does not engage it. This is laya — the personal echo of *pralaya*.

Pralaya as Cosmic Potential:
At the close of each *kalpa*, all gross and subtle creation merges into maya, the *avyakrita* or unmanifest cause. This potentiality (*shakti*) is inseparable from Brahman, like fire latent in wood.

The Continuum of Dissolution:
Jiva's laya = nightly rest.
Jagat's pralaya = universal rest.

Both are cyclical: "Every state of sleep is followed by a waking-up; if you wake up in the same body, it is called waking; if in another, rebirth."

The Immutable Witness:
Consciousness neither dissolves nor emerges — it simply is.
Manifestation and dissolution are play (*lila*) within it.

Common Misunderstandings

- **"Laya or pralaya means annihilation."** False. Nothing real is destroyed; names and forms return to potential.
- **"The Self participates in creation and destruction."** The Self is changeless — the silent witness of both appearance and disappearance.
- **"Pralaya is liberation."** No. Liberation (*moksha*) is recognition of the unchanging witness during creation, not escape from it.

Vedantic Resolution

- *Laya* and *pralaya* reveal the rhythmic breathing of Brahman. In each cycle — cosmic or individual — the universe inhales into stillness and exhales into form.
- The wise see both as the same motion of maya: manifest and unmanifest, waking and sleep, birth and death. To awaken to *turiya* is to see that there was never any creation, and hence, no dissolution.
- "Manifestation follows every dissolution," writes Paramarthananda. "Consciousness does not and cannot do anything. It simply lends reflection when the mind appears."
- In truth, there was never a beginning, and there will be no end — only the eternal Self witnessing the play of appearance and rest.

mahavakya

(mahāvākya — *muh-HAA-VAA-kyuh*)

The Upanishads are filled with profound declarations, but a few sentences are singled out as *mahavakyas (mahāvākyas)* — "great statements." These are not instructions to do something, but revelations of what already is: the oneness of atman (the Self) and Brahman (the absolute).

Tradition highlights four *mahavakyas* — one from each Veda — as representative of the whole teaching:

- **Prajnanam Brahma** — "Consciousness is Brahman" (*Aitareya Upanishad, Rig Veda*).
- **Aham Brahmasmi** — "I am Brahman" (*Brihadaranyaka Upanishad, Yajur Veda*).
- **Tat Tvam Asi** — "That Thou Art" (*Chandogya Upanishad, Sama Veda*).
- **Ayam Atma Brahm**a — "This Self is Brahman" (*Mandukya Upanishad, Atharva Veda*).

These four are often taught as the distilled vision of Vedanta. But they are not the only ones — many other Upanishadic passages (*sarvam khalvidam brahma, neha nanasti kinchana*, etc.) function as *mahavakyas* in spirit, declaring non-duality.

There are also later formulations, like Shankara's famous *"Brahma satyam jagan mithya jivo brahmaiva na parah."* This half-verse is not from the Upanishads themselves, but Advaita teachers call it a *mahavakya* in a looser sense — a "teaching *mahavakya*" that encapsulates the same vision.

Thus, *mahavakyas* can be understood in two ways:

Strict sense: the Upanishadic sentences that directly declare identity of atman and Brahman.

Expanded sense: any great statement that summarizes the essence of Advaita.

In either case, their role is the same: they serve as mirrors to remove ignorance, not as mantras to be chanted. They reveal that the fullness we seek is already our own nature.

—

Root & Meaning

Maha = great
Vakya = statement
Mahavakya = "great statement," declaring identity of Self and Brahman.

Scriptural References

Canonical four:

• **Prajnanam Brahma** — *Aitareya Upanishad (Rig Veda)*
• **Aham Brahmasmi** — *Brihadaranyaka Upanishad (Yajur Veda)*
• **Tat Tvam Asi** — *Chandogya Upanishad (Sama Veda)*
• **Ayam Atma Brahma** — *Mandukya Upanishad (Atharva Veda)*

Other Upanishadic mahavakyas: *Sarvam khalvidam brama* (*Chandogya*), *Neha nanasti kiñchana* (*Brihadaranyaka*), *etc.*

Later Advaita summaries: *Brahma satyam jagan mithya...* (Shankara's teaching verse).

Traditional View

• The four highlighted *mahavakyas* cover all four Vedas.
• They function as the heart of Vedanta: direct revelation of non-duality.
• Other Upanishadic statements also qualify, but these four are

taught as paradigms.

- Post-Upanishadic sayings, while not canonical, are used pedagogically as *mahavakyas*.

Vedantic Analysis

- *Mahavakyas* reveal what is always true — the non-difference of atman and Brahman.
- They remove ignorance; they do not produce a new reality.
- Teachers unfold them by showing how apparent contradictions (*tvam* as limited *jiva*, *tat* as limitless Brahman) dissolve when *upadhis* are dropped.

Common Misunderstandings

- **That there are only four mahavakyas:** Many exist; four are highlighted for teaching.
- **That "Brahma satyam jagan mithya" is one of them:** It is a later summary by Shankara, not an Upanishadic *mahavakyas*, though often used as one in practice.
- **That mahavakyas are mantras:** Their power lies in meaning, not sound.
- **That they create Brahman-identity:** They reveal what already is.

Vedantic Resolution

The *mahavakyas* stand as the distilled heart of the *shruti*. Whether in their classical Upanishadic form or later Advaitic summaries, their role is to reveal the ever-present truth: the Self is not other than Brahman.

mala

(mala — *muh-luh*)

In Vedanta, *mala* is not a moral stain but a psychological one. It refers to the residue left on the mind by past actions — the subtle impressions, likes, dislikes, and unresolved emotional charges that cloud clarity. If *avarana* is the veil that hides the Self, *mala* is the sediment that keeps the mind heavy, reactive, and unable to stand still long enough to notice what it already is.

Mala shows itself in familiar ways: irritation that rises before thought, compulsions that seem to come from nowhere, recurring emotional loops that have outlived their cause. It is the inertia of old patterns, the stickiness of unexamined tendencies. We may know what is right, even what is true, yet feel unable to align with it. This friction is *mala*.

Unlike *avarana*, which is universal, *mala* is personal. It belongs to the individual psyche — the collection of past experiences and actions (karma) that shape the texture of one's inner life. *Mala* determines how the teaching is heard: whether the mind is available and spacious, or burdened and restless. Two people may listen to the same Upanishadic verse; one is moved toward inwardness, the other is barely touched. The difference is *mala*.

Vedanta treats *mala* not as a flaw to condemn but as a condition to refine. A mind burdened by *mala* is simply unfit — not morally, but functionally — for subtle inquiry. The problem is not sin but opacity. Just as a soiled mirror must be cleaned before it can reflect light, the mind must be purified before it can reflect the knowledge of the Self.

Traditionally, *karma yoga* is prescribed as the antidote. Not because action purifies by magic, but because acting without egoic demand erodes the very tendencies that bind. Offering one's actions and their results to something higher loosens the grip of preference, softens emotional rigidity, and restores a baseline of clarity. In that clarity, *mala* wanes.

As *mala* diminishes, the mind becomes lighter. Its reactions are no longer instantaneous; its judgments are no longer sharp; its cravings no longer dictate its direction. A quiet shift occurs: life becomes navigable, relationships become less charged, meditation becomes less effortful. The mind begins to resemble the sky rather than the weather.

But the deepest significance of *mala* is this: without addressing it, higher inquiry cannot truly begin. A mind cluttered with unresolved patterns cannot sustain the contemplative steadiness required for Self-knowledge. *Mala* is not the final obstacle — that is *avarana* — but it is the first one encountered.

When *mala* thins, the mind becomes a proper instrument. It listens. It absorbs. It reflects. In that prepared mind, the teachings do not merely inform; they transform. And in this way, *mala* — once a weight — becomes part of the very process by which the mind is rendered transparent to the truth.

—

Root & Meaning

From the Sanskrit root *mal* — "to be soiled, stained, impure."*Mala* refers not to moral impurity but to mental impurity: the subtle residues of past actions, emotions, and tendencies that weigh down the mind.

Scriptural References

The term appears throughout Vedantic and Yoga literature, especially in discussions of mental purification:

- **Bhagavad Gita 3.14–16; 4.37:** *Karma yoga* purifies the mind and reduces the residues of desire and attachment.

- **Mundaka Upanishad 3.1.8:** The Self is revealed in a purified mind.
- **Vivekachudamani (109–110):** Shankara identifies *mala* as the primary obstacle addressed by *karma yoga*.
- **Panchadashi (6.1–6):** Vidyaranya distinguishes *mala* from *avarana* and *vikshepa*.

While the Upanishads don't always use the word *mala*, they consistently describe its function: the impurities that obstruct clarity.

Traditional View

Traditionally, *mala* is understood as the psychological residue of karma — the impressions (*samskaras*), emotional charges, likes and dislikes (*raga–dvesha*), and habitual reactions that cloud the mind.

Mala expresses itself as:

- Emotional reactivity
- Compulsive behavior
- Unexamined preferences and aversions
- Anger, fear, greed, jealousy
- Persistent mental heaviness or dullness

Because *mala* belongs to the individual mind, it varies from person to person. Its reduction is a prerequisite for steady meditation, self-inquiry, and the assimilation of Vedantic teaching.

Vedantic Analysis

Mala is the first of three classical obstacles that obscure the Self:

- *Mala* – Impurity (emotional and psychological disturbances)
- *Vikshepa* – Projection (agitation and distraction)
- *Avarana* – Concealment (ignorance of the Self)

Mala is removed primarily through *karma yoga*, which dissolves the emotional seeds of action by aligning one's motives with dharma rather than egoic demand.

The key insight:

Mala does not block knowledge directly — it blocks the mind's availability for knowledge. A disturbed or emotionally reactive mind cannot sustain subtle inquiry. As *mala* diminishes, the mind gains:

- Lightness
- Stability
- Emotional maturity
- Openness
- Inner friendliness

This shift is not mystical; it is the result of living responsively rather than reactively.

Common Misunderstandings

- **"Mala means sin or moral impurity."** No. Vedanta treats *mala* as psychological residue, not moral failing.
- **"Mala must be eliminated completely before inquiry."** Not true. *Mala* must be reduced enough to allow consistent contemplation, not erased entirely.
- **"Mala is overcome by withdrawal from life."** In fact, *mala* is reduced by engaging in life with the right attitude — *karma yoga*, not avoidance.
- **"Mala is the same as vikshepa."** They are related but distinct: *mala* is heaviness or impurity; *vikshepa* is agitation or projection.

Vedantic Resolution

Mala is ultimately neutralized by *karma yoga*, which transforms daily action into a means of mental purification. When one acts without grasping for results — offering outcomes to a larger order — the emotional residues that bind the mind begin to dissolve.

As *mala* thins:

- Reactions soften
- Preferences lose their grip
- Emotions become manageable
- The mind gains clarity and balance
- Inquiry becomes natural, not forced

A purified mind reflects the Self effortlessly, like a clean mirror reflecting light.

manana

(manana — *muh-nuh-nuh*)

After *shravana* (listening to the teaching), the seeker engages in *manana* — systematic reflection. It is the process of reasoning and inquiry by which doubts are removed.

In Vedanta, hearing alone plants the seed of knowledge, but the conditioned mind may resist. Old beliefs, habits, and intellectual objections surface. *Manana* addresses these by applying reasoning (*yukti*) in line with *shastra* (scripture). For example, a student may ask: "If the Self is limitless awareness, how can I be bound?" The teacher guides them to see that bondage itself is only a superimposition (*adhyasa*).

Manana is not independent speculation. The framework is always the *shastra* as unfolded by a teacher. Reflection is used to harmonize apparent contradictions, dissolve misconceptions, and bring conviction. Without this, *shravana* remains fragile, vulnerable to doubt.

Ultimately, *manana* makes the vision of Vedanta stable at the intellectual level, preparing the seeker for *nididhyasana* — contemplative assimilation.

—

Root & Meaning

From root *man* = to think, consider.
Manana = reflection, reasoning, contemplation.

Scriptural References

• **Brihadaranyaka Upanishad 2.4.5:** "Atman is to be heard, reflected upon (*mantavyah*), and meditated upon."

• Shankara's commentaries: emphasize *manana* as the stage for resolving doubts that arise after *shravana*.

Traditional View

• Second stage after *shravana*.
• Uses reason to remove doubts (*samshaya*).
• Firm conviction arises when *shastra* and reason align.

Vedantic Analysis

Shravana = hearing the truth of the Self.
Manana = dissolving doubts by reasoning with the teaching.
Nididhyasana = assimilating the vision until it is fully owned.

Without *manana*, knowledge may remain shaky and intellectual.

Common Misunderstandings

• **That manana is independent philosophy:** It is always guided by *shastra*, not free speculation.
• **That manana alone liberates:** It strengthens knowledge but assimilation requires *nididhyasana*.
• **That manana means intellectual debate:** It is inward reflection for clarity, not argument for its own sake.

Vedantic Resolution

Manana is disciplined reasoning with the *shastra* to resolve doubts. It stabilizes the vision of non-duality and prepares the mind for assimilation.

manas

(manas — *muh-nuhs*)

In Vedanta, *manas* refers to the mind as a doubting, processing instrument. It is part of the fourfold *antahkarana* (inner instrument) along with *buddhi* (intellect), *chitta* (memory), and *ahankara* (ego). Among these, *manas* is marked by its oscillating nature: constantly weighing, comparing, and questioning.

The tradition describes *manas* as operating through *sankalpa–vikalpa* — the movement between options, "shall I, shall I not?" It receives inputs from the senses and organizes them, but it is not decisive. For example, when one sees something indistinct in dim light, manas wavers: "Is it a rope or a snake?" The decision belongs to buddhi.

This indecisive, restless quality makes manas both necessary and dangerous. It is the field of desire, imagination, and emotion, which can lead one astray if uncontrolled. At the same time, manas is indispensable for functioning in the world and for spiritual practice.

Vedanta distinguishes sharply between manas and the Self. The mind is inert (*jada*), illumined only by consciousness. Awareness is the witness of the mind's movements, never altered by them. For this reason, disciplines like *shama* (quietude) and *dama* (sense control) are prescribed: not to destroy the mind, but to steady it so it becomes a clear instrument for knowledge.

—

Root & Meaning

From root *man* (to think, consider).
Manas = mind; the faculty of thought, doubt, coordination.

Scriptural References

- **Bhagavad Gita 6.5–6:** "The mind (*manas*) can be the friend or enemy of the self."
- **Chandogya Upanishad 7.3.2:** Mind is greater than speech, as it grasps meaning.
- **Taittiriya Upanishad 2.7:** Mind is part of the *manomaya kosha* (the mental sheath).

Traditional View

- One of the four functions of *antahkarana*.
- Characterized by *sankalpa–vikalpa* (doubt, vacillation).
- Coordinates sensory input before *buddhi* decides.

Vedantic Analysis

- *Manas* is inert, illumined by consciousness.
- Seat of desire, imagination, and emotion.
- Can enslave the seeker through distraction, or serve as a tool when disciplined.
- Spiritual growth requires mastery of *manas* through *shama* and *dama*.

Common Misunderstandings

- **That manas = the whole mind:** It is only one aspect; intellect, ego, and memory are distinct.
- **That manas is conscious:** It is not self-aware; awareness illumines it.
- **That quieting manas alone brings liberation:** Control is necessary but only preparatory; Self-knowledge liberates.

Vedantic Resolution

Manas is the doubting, processing function of the inner organ. It is never the Self, but an instrument of experience. With discipline, it becomes steady enough for Self-inquiry; without it, it drags the seeker into distraction.

maya

(māyā — *MAA-YAA*)

Maya *(māyā)* is one of the more confusing Sanskrit terms due to its diverse array of meanings and how its definition can change depending on the context. Synonyms for maya include *avyakta* (unmanifest state) and *prakriti* (primordial nature). At the personal level, maya operates through *avidya* — the individual's not-knowing — while at the cosmic level, maya refers to *Ishvara's* power of manifesting name and form.

Maya is often described as "indefinable" and "inscrutable." It is said to be *anirvachaniya* (impossible to understand). Thus, the term maya also works as a sort of catchall for that which cannot be explained. Maya is sometimes described metaphorically as a "mysterious force," not because it is a literal energy, but because it marks the point where explanation stops. It names the mind's inability to account for the appearance of duality. In plain terms, maya is the admission that the origin of the appearance cannot be known from within the appearance. It names the boundary of human cognition.

Most people who have dabbled in eastern metaphysics understand maya to be the power of delusion. Maya is the great illusionist, that which hides the truth from us by using its powers of concealment and projection. It tricks us in many ways, for example, by having us believe that objects are independent, substantial and unchanging. The classic example is the pot and the clay.

What we perceive as a "pot," in reality, is only clay that has been fashioned into name and form; the pot is only an appearance. We know it exists because we experience it, but the truth of the pot is that it's clay. If the pot breaks, we no longer have the pot but we still have clay. However, without clay there is no pot. Using this example, we can say the clay is real (*satya*, meaning "truth"), while the pot is only apparently real (*mithya*). The wording is very subtle, but significant. Maya isn't an illusion, like an apparition. It is the inability to perceive the truth. It is ignorance, or more specifically, a kind of not knowing. The pot exists, but not as "pot" — it exists as clay alone. This is the meaning of *mithya*.

If we compare maya to pure consciousness, we find a peculiar relationship. Similar to the pot and the clay, maya depends on consciousness but consciousness doesn't depend on maya. Vedanta defines "real" as that which is always present and never changes — which, as it turns out, only consciousness qualifies as. In contrast, the nature of maya and creation is to be constantly in flux where objects are created, maintained for while, then destroyed and recycled into other forms. Objects in maya are also divisible and dependent on other objects. For example, a shirt is just cloth, which is just thread, which is just cotton, and so on. Thus, a key characteristic of maya is that it is constantly changing and is never what it appears to be.

On the other hand, we do experience objects. So, maya has the unusual status of neither being real nor unreal. In *Vivekachudamani* (The Crown Jewel of Discrimination), Shankaracharya states that:

> *This power is a great wonder and cannot be rationally explained because it is neither real, nor non-existent, nor a combination of the two. It is not separate, nor non-separate from consciousness, nor is it made up of parts. (Verse 32)*

Thus, maya, at best, is a morphing, dream-like experience when examined closely. Any feeling of solidity and permanency is nothing more than a facade created by the slow passing of time and the composition of parts that seemingly make up an object. Maya's super power is its ability to keep us in a sort of hypnotic state where we constantly misinterpret the apparent objects before us.

Of course, every super power comes with a hidden weakness built in (an aspect that makes it vulnerable) and maya's weakness is that its spell ends when right knowledge is applied. This is traditionally shown using the example of the snake and the rope. A weary traveler walking at dusk grows fearful upon encountering a snake in his path. It's only when the truth is revealed that the snake is just a coiled rope, that the threat of danger loses its power. Technically, this is referred to as *viparyaya* in Sanskrit. It's maya's ability to reverse our cognition of reality. So, due to right knowledge, although maya's deluding power may be beginningless, it is not without end.

But, there's more. The term maya is used to describe more than just how we continuously get duped regarding the nature of reality. It is also used to describe God's power of creation and the impersonal forces that shape the world as we know it. Thus, to really understand maya, we must view it from both microcosmic and macrocosmic levels. Both are related, but different. One explains personal ignorance (*avidya*), while the other explains the creation, sustainment and eventual dissolution of the universe. Maya, then, is responsible for both our outer and inner worlds.

From the standpoint of the world, maya is the name given to the appearance of name and form in consciousness. This appearance is attributed to *Ishvara*, not because Brahman "creates," but because *Ishvara* is the intelligent order inherent in the appearance itself. It is an illusory superimposition (*adhyaropa*) onto consciousness, similar to how a dream is an illusory superimposition onto the waker. Maya is the ultimate virtual reality machine in which our senses correlatively participate in a world of sense objects that create endless wonderment and fascination. God skates along its maya effortlessly, while the individual gets tangled up in its web and must learn how to exist in harmony with it.

God (*Ishvara*) is defined as consciousness + maya. *Ishvara* is Brahman viewed through the limiting adjunct (*upadhi*) of maya

— not a composite, but a standpoint. The '+' is pedagogical, not ontological. An *upadhi* is that which makes consciousness appear something other than it is. A common example is how a red cloth placed behind a crystal will make the crystal appear to take on other attributes (i.e., the color red). Maya is not a part, product or property of consciousness. And yet paradoxically, neither is it totally outside of consciousness. Maya is inseparable from consciousness only in the same way an appearance is inseparable from its substrate — not as a real attribute, but as a dependent seeming. Nevertheless, similar to the pot and clay, maya is dependent on consciousness and not the other way around. What is dependent cannot define or limit what it depends on.

While maya's power cannot be shown, it can be inferred. Vedanta rationalizes the existence of maya by making the point that because consciousness is not agent (is actionless), it cannot cause the world. Similarly, because the world is inert (dead matter), it cannot cause itself. Therefore the cause is an appearance projected upon consciousness — this appearance itself is called maya.

Maya is sometimes esoterically described as "consciousness in motion." A supporting illustration for this comes from Gaudapada's, *Mandukya Upanishad with Karika* which uses the metaphor of the firebrand. Imagine, an artist lighting the end of stick until it is a red ember. Waving it in the dark, he creates the appearance of various entities and objects that seemingly come and go. The artist might make a story surrounding such entities and objects, drawing us in until we forget it's only a stick of fire being hypnotically waved in front of us. In this metaphor of the firebrand, the objects appear because of the movement, not in addition to the firebrand. Nothing other than the light ever appears.

When God's creation cycle is active and God is "awake," maya — in the form of its three constituents, the *gunas* —creates the world. The *gunas* provide more detail about maya's specific creative powers. But to be clear, they describe the structure of the appearance, not the substance of reality.

Briefly described, the *gunas* are *sattva* (the information needed for creation), *rajas* (the energy or action needed for creation), and *tamas* (the inert material needed for creation). When the creation cycle comes to an end and God goes to "sleep," maya reverts to its unmanifest state holding the information necessary to activate and sustain creation again.

At the microcosmic level, the *gunas* also create and influence our inner world. Thus, the *gunas*, or maya, have a psychological aspect, which makes sense because if God is all creation and we are included in its creation, what makes our outer world would also have to make our inner one. That said, each *guna* can have a positive or negative effect on our conditioning. *Rajas* is associated with maya's ability to project, and *tamas* with its ability to conceal, while clarity is associated with *sattva*. Management of the *gunas* leads to a harmonious life, while mismanagement of the *gunas* leads to succumbing to and being bound by maya's impersonal forces. Such an existence is often referred to as samsara.

It should be clear by now that maya has many different facets. We can view maya from the microcosmic or macrocosmic, or from the psychological or physical. However, at a personal level, we mustn't only think of maya in the negative. Due to maya and the world's, ultimately, unsatisfactory quality, we are eventually driven to pursue, hear, contemplate and actualize the truth about the nature of existence. In other words, it's our inevitable frustration with the world (this maya) that eventually brings us liberation. The individual, searching for permanent happiness out in the field becomes exhausted chasing objects, relationships and experiences, and instead, turns within. Thus, the extroverted becomes the introverted and begins to seek the answers required to gain actual freedom. For all that, we can thank maya. Thus, maya is not a cosmic mistake but the very condition that makes discovery possible.

—

Root & Meaning

Maya = from the Sanskrit root *ma* ("to measure, to form") + the suffix *ya*, meaning "that which causes to appear."

Primary meanings: illusion, appearance, magic, creative power. In Vedanta, maya is the inexplicable power of Ishvara that projects the universe of names and forms upon the non-dual Self.

Scriptural References

On the nature of maya:

- **Shvetashvatara Upanishad 4.9–10:** *Mayam tu prakritim vidyan mayinam tu maheshvaram:* "Know maya as *prakriti*, and the wielder of maya as the great Lord."
- **Vivekachudamani 108, 111, 114, 119, 121, 125, 129, 219, 219–221, 239:** Multiple verses detailing maya's indefinable nature and its concealment/projection powers.
- **Vivekachudamani 32:** The classic statement that maya is neither real nor unreal.

On maya as concealment and projection:

- **Mandukya Karika 1.16:** The firebrand metaphor.
- **Mandukya Karika 3.29:** Maya compared to illusionary appearances like dream or magic.
- **Bhagavad Gita 7.14:** "This divine maya of Mine, made of the *gunas*, is hard to cross."
- **Bhagavad Gita 7.25:** "Veiled by maya, I am not manifest to all."

On gunas as constituents of maya:

- **Bhagavad Gita 14.5:** *Sattva, rajas,* and *tamas* bind the *jiva*.
- **Bhagavad Gita 14.6–9:** Nature and effects of each *guna*.

- **Bhagavad Gita 14.19–20:** Transcending the *gunas*.

On maya's role in creation:

- **Taittiriya Upanishad 2.6.1:** The projection of name and form from Brahman.
- **Brihadaranyaka Upanishad 2.5.19:** "From the Self, indeed, arose *akasha* (space)..." (sequence of manifestation).
- **Chandogya Upanishad 6.1–6.2:** "In the beginning, this was Existence alone..." (*satkarya-vada* foundation).

Traditional View

In Advaita Vedanta, maya is the beginningless power (*shakti*) of *Ishvara*, responsible for the appearance of the universe. It has two principal powers:

- *Avarana-shakti* — the veiling power, which hides the truth of the Self.
- *Vikshepa-shakti* — the projecting power, which manifests the phenomenal world.

Maya is neither real (*sat*) nor unreal (*asat*), but *anirvachaniya* — indescribable. It operates at the level of *vyavahara* (transactional reality) and is sublated by Self-knowledge.

Vedantic Analysis

Vedanta does not treat maya as an entity separate from Brahman, but as Brahman's apparent power when viewed from the standpoint of manifestation. From the absolute (*paramarthika*) standpoint, maya has no existence; only Brahman is real. From the empirical (*vyavaharika*) standpoint, maya explains how the changeless Self seems to appear as the changing world without itself undergoing change.

Common Misunderstandings

- **"Maya means the world is an illusion and doesn't exist at all."** The world exists as an appearance, but not as an independent reality apart from Brahman.
- **"Maya is evil or bad."** Maya is morally neutral; it is the totality of cause-effect and cosmic order.
- **"Maya can be destroyed."** Maya is resolved, not destroyed, when knowledge dawns.

Vedantic Resolution

The goal is not to "get rid of" maya, but to recognize that its veiling and projecting powers do not affect the Self. When one realizes "I am Brahman, the substratum of all appearances," maya loses its binding capacity. The *jnani* (Self-realized individual) continues to transact in the world of maya, but without misidentification.

mithya

(mithyā — *mit-HYAA*)

The term *mithya (mithyā)* is one of Vedanta's most subtle and central teachings. It does not mean illusion in the sense of nonexistence, nor does it mean real in the sense of absolute truth. Rather, *mithya* refers to that which is dependent reality — something that appears, is experienced, yet has no independent existence of its own.

The classic example is a clay pot. The pot exists, but only as clay shaped into a form. The clay is *satya* (independent reality); the pot is *mithya* (dependent reality). When the pot breaks, clay remains. The pot never had existence apart from clay. In the same way, the entire world of names and forms is *mithya* with respect to Brahman, the substratum of all existence.

This definition helps us resolve the paradox of experience. The world appears and is undeniable. But to mistake it for ultimate reality leads to suffering, because everything in *mithya* is impermanent, unstable, and dependent. Like the wise say: *dvaita* (duality) is not a problem; mistaking dvaita as *satya* is the problem. Reliance on what is unstable leads to samsara. Liberation comes by recognizing that while the world appears, its essence is only Brahman.

Mithya is sometimes described as *anirvachaniya* — indefinable, neither real nor unreal. Like a dream, it is real while experienced, but gone upon waking. Like the snake imagined on a rope, it borrows reality from its substratum. Like the patterns traced by a firebrand in the dark, it appears vividly yet leaves no trace.

Far from being abstract metaphysics, the understanding of *mithya* transforms daily life. If everything perceived is only apparently real, then our attachments, fears, and anxieties about the world lose their sting. As teachers often tell us: The dog is *mithya*, but so is the running from the dog! — both are appearances within consciousness. To grasp *mithya* is to see that nothing in experience can add to or subtract from the fullness of the Self.

—

Root & Meaning

From Sanskrit *mithya* = false, dependent, apparently real. That which is neither absolutely real (*satya*) nor absolutely unreal (*asat*), but which appears and depends on something else for its existence.

Scriptural References

- **Chandogya Upanishad (6.1):** clay and pot analogy: the pot is *mithya*, clay alone is *satya*.
- **Bhagavad Gita (2.16):** *nabhavo vidyate sattah:* the unreal has no being; the real never ceases to be.
- **Mandukya Karika (2.31–32):** Gaudapada explains that the world has no origination; it is mere appearance, like dream.

Traditional View

- *Mithya* includes both objective reality (pots, tables, bodies) and subjective reality (dreams, projections).
- Objects are empirically real for practical use, but ultimately depend on Brahman.
- The world is *mithya* in relation to Brahman; Brahman alone is *satya*.

Vedantic Analysis

Mithya can be understood through three key definitions:

- That which changes (*vikaritva*): Whatever undergoes

modification cannot be ultimate reality.
- That which is not always present (*anityatva*): What appears and disappears in time is *mithya*.
- That which is made up of parts (*savayavatva*): Whatever is composite is dependent, and hence *mithya*.

All three reveal *mithya* as dependent and impermanent. By contrast, Brahman is *satya* because it is changeless, ever-present, and partless.

- *Mithya* is *sat-asat-vilakshanam*: different from both *sat* (real) and *asat* (unreal).
- It is experienced but has no independent being.
- The mind and the world are interdependent and borrow existence from awareness.
- Maya, the power of projection, is itself *mithya* — inexplicable, beginningless, neither real nor unreal.

Understanding *mithya* is key to *moksha*: it frees us from mistaking the changing for the changeless.

Common Misunderstandings

- **Mithya = illusion/nonexistence:** No, it is not like a square circle, which is sheer nonexistence. It appears and functions.
- **Mithya = deception:** It is not "falsehood" but dependent reality. A pot truly holds water, though it is *mithya* with respect to clay.
- **Mithya = pessimism:** The recognition of *mithya* actually puts "the fun back in life," because nothing real is ever at stake.

Vedantic Resolution

Mithya is the middle category that reconciles experience and truth. The world is not denied; it is reclassified. One learns to live in the world, transact with it, even delight in its variety, while knowing its essence is Brahman alone. Liberation is not escaping *mithya* but recognizing: *Brahma satyam, jagan mithya, jivah brahmaiva na aparah* — Brahman is the real, the world is *mithya,* the *jiva* is none other than Brahman.

moksha

(mokṣa — *mok-shuh*)

Moksha (mokṣa) is commonly translated as "freedom" or "liberation." But freedom from what, exactly? In mythology, literature, and popular culture, *moksha* is often equated with "enlightenment," imagined as a dazzling spiritual event that instantly bestows omniscience and everlasting bliss upon the seeker. However, traditional teachings present a very different, far less romantic view. In the context of Vedanta, *moksha* is not a dramatic awakening or supernatural power. Rather, it is the quiet, enduring dissolution of ignorance regarding one's true nature.

According to scripture, *moksha* is the release from samsara — the cycle of birth and death that binds the individual to suffering and limitation. The root cause of samsara is maya, the cosmic illusion that causes us to misperceive reality. Under the influence of maya, we identify with the body and mind, mistake the transient for the eternal, and pursue happiness in external objects, experiences, and relationships. This misidentification gives rise to bondage. In contrast, *moksha* is the recognition that our essence was never bound in the first place. In this way, samsara and *moksha* are opposites: one binds through misidentification, the other liberates through knowledge.

Vedanta describes four universal aims or pursuits that drive all human behavior: *artha* (security and material well-being), *kama* (pleasure and emotional fulfillment), dharma (ethical and social responsibility), and *moksha* (freedom). While the first three are more easily recognized and consciously pursued, Vedanta teaches that *moksha* is, in fact, the underlying goal behind all others. Whether seeking wealth to feel secure, entertainment to escape boredom, or companionship to avoid loneliness, we are, at bottom, seeking freedom — from fear, dissatisfaction, and limitation. The very impulse to strive, to fix, to achieve, is rooted in a sense of incompleteness. *Moksha* is the resolution of this quest — not through acquisition, but through recognition.

Moksha arises through the assimilation of Self-knowledge — the unwavering understanding that "I am not the body, not the mind, but the limitless, unchanging awareness in whose presence all experiences arise and subside." It is a shift in identification: from the limited *jiva* (individual) to the boundless atman (Self). Importantly, *moksha* is not an experience to be acquired in time. You do not "become" free — you discover that you always were. The Self is ever-free (*nitya-mukta*); it is ignorance that veils this truth. Thus, the role of knowledge is not to create liberation, but to remove the ignorance that obscures it.

This leads to a subtle but vital distinction: *moksha* is not for the Self — it is for the *jiva*. The Self was never bound and needs no liberation. It is the *jiva*, born into ignorance, that suffers and longs for release. *Moksha*, then, is freedom from ignorance for the *jiva*. It is the knowledge that "I am the Self," accompanied by the ability to discriminate between what is real (*satya*) and what is merely apparent (*moksha*). Once this discrimination becomes firm, the *jiva* no longer identifies as a limited doer or experiencer, but as the ever-present awareness in which the *jiva* appears.

And yet, paradoxically, nothing outwardly changes. As the old Zen saying goes, "Before enlightenment, chop wood and carry water. After enlightenment, chop wood and carry water." Life continues with its ups and downs, its gains and losses. But for the one who knows the Self, these fluctuations no longer shake the foundation of their identity. Peace is not something added to the person — it is revealed as the substratum that was always there.

Even after *moksha*, the work of the *jiva* is not entirely finished. While no inner transformation is required post-liberation — since bondage was only ever a matter of ignorance — liberated beings continue to engage in refining the mind. They monitor and gradually resolve remaining *vasanas* (subtle tendencies), follow dharma to maintain harmony, and sustain vigilance in discriminating between the real and the unreal. This does not imply effortful striving, but rather a gentle attentiveness — a natural inclination to live in alignment with the truth.

In the end, *moksha* is not some distant reward, but the fulfillment of our most fundamental longing — to be whole, free, and at peace with what is. It is not becoming something else, but ceasing to pretend we were ever anything less.

—

Root & Meaning

Moksha = from the Sanskrit root *muc* ("to release, to free, to let go").

Primary meaning: liberation, release from bondage, complete freedom from samsara. In Vedanta, *moksha* is the realization of one's true nature as the limitless, non-dual Self (atman), free from dependence on objects, experiences, and relationships for happiness.

Scriptural References

On the nature of moksha and liberation:

- **Brihadaranyaka Upanishad 4.4.6–7:** "When all desires that dwell in the heart are cast away, then does the mortal become immortal — here."
- **Chandogya Upanishad 8.12.1:** Liberation as freedom from return to birth.
- **Katha Upanishad 2.3.14–15:** The Self is not born, does not die, and the knower of the Self transcends grief.
- **Mandukya Karika 2.32–35:** Liberation through knowledge of the Self, not through ritual or action.

On the role of Self-knowledge:

- **Bhagavad Gita 2.11:** Krishna begins instruction by dispelling Arjuna's ignorance about the Self.
- **Bhagavad Gita 2.55–72:** The state of the *sthita-prajna* (one established in knowledge) as the living embodiment of *moksha*.
- **Bhagavad Gita 4.39:** "The one who has faith, is devoted, and has mastery over the senses obtains knowledge, and having attained knowledge, attains supreme peace immediately."
- **Bhagavad Gita 5.26:** Freedom from desire and anger leads to Brahman-realization.
- **Bhagavad Gita 6.27–28:** The yogi established in the Self attains supreme peace.

On moksha as ever-present:

- **Brihadaranyaka Upanishad 1.4.10:** The Self is Brahman; knowing this, one becomes free.
- **Vivekachudamani 430–432:** Bondage is due to ignorance; knowledge alone destroys it.

Traditional View

In Advaita Vedanta, *moksha* is not a future event or a state to be produced, but the recognition of an already existing fact: "I am whole, complete, and ever-free." Bondage (*bandha*) is due to ignorance (*avidya*) of this fact, not due to an actual limitation. *Moksha* is thus gained through *jnana* (Self-knowledge), not by action (karma), ritual, or any material attainment.

Vedantic Analysis

Vedanta distinguishes between two perspectives on *moksha*:

- **Jivanmukti** — liberation while living. The mind is free from binding likes and dislikes, fear, and desire, even while the body-mind continues to function.

- **Videhamukti** — liberation at the fall of the body, when all association with the body-mind ceases.

Moksha is characterized by *ananda* (fullness), *shanti* (peace), and *svatantrya* (independence). Since *moksha* is one's very nature, it cannot be produced by time-bound actions. The role of spiritual discipline is to remove ignorance and prepare the mind to assimilate Self-knowledge.

Common Misunderstandings

- **"Moksha is going to heaven or another place after death."** Heaven is still within samsara, and therefore temporary.
- **"Moksha happens in the future after enough practice."** *Moksha* is timeless; realization can happen here and now.
- **"Moksha means the destruction of the world."** *Moksha* is freedom from identification with the world, not its annihilation.
- **"Moksha is a mystical experience."** Experiences are transient; *moksha* is the knowledge of one's changeless Self.

Vedantic Resolution

Bondage is ignorance of the Self; *moksha* is removal of this ignorance through *shravana* (listening to the teaching), *manana* (reflecting upon it), and *nididhyasana* (deep assimilation). The liberated person (*jivanmukta*) still experiences the play of maya, but without attachment or delusion. The world may continue, but for the *jnani* (Self-realized), it no longer binds.

mumukshutva

(mumukṣutva — *mu-MUK-shut-vuh*)

Most human striving is born of desire: for wealth, recognition, power, family, or pleasure. Yet each attainment brings with it disappointment and further longing. At some point, a seeker may look at the endless cycle and say: "Enough. I want freedom — not from this sorrow or that one, but from sorrow altogether. I want to end limitation itself." That burning, all-consuming desire for liberation (*moksha*) is called *mumukshutva (mumukṣutva)*.

The tradition describes four degrees of this desire:

- **Ati manda (very weak):** "If liberation happens, fine; otherwise, maybe next life."
- **Manda (weak):** "I will take up the pursuit later, after worldly duties are finished."
- **Madhyama (moderate):** "I want liberation soon — the sooner the better."
- **Tivra (intense):** "I want freedom here and now," as urgently as one gasps for air while drowning or seeks water when aflame.

Only when *mumukshutva* is strong does liberation become inevitable. All other qualities — discrimination (*viveka*), dispassion (*vairagya*), and discipline (*shatka-sampatti*) — align around it naturally.

Mumukshutva is therefore not a luxury or a mood. It is the very engine of spiritual life. Without it, study becomes intellectual, rituals become mechanical, and meditation becomes distraction. With it, every practice sharpens, every value integrates, and every moment becomes part of the path.

—

Root & Meaning

Mumuksha = desire for liberation (from root muc, "to release, to free").

Mumukshutva = the state of having that desire.

Scriptural References

- **Aparokshanubhuti (9):** "A burning, all-consuming desire to be free is called *mumukshutva*."
- **Tattvabodha:** lists *mumukshutva* as one of the fourfold qualifications (*sadhana-chatushtaya*).
- **Bhagavad Gita (7.16–17):** equates devotion to God as desire for liberation (*nishkama bhakti*).

Traditional View

- *Mumukshutva* is one of the four main qualifications for Vedanta (along with discrimination, dispassion, and discipline).
- Degrees of intensity range from weak to burning (*tivra mumukshutva*). Only the latter ensures realization.
- *Bhakti* is sometimes defined as *moksha-iccha* (desire for liberation) — synonymous with *mumukshutva*.

Vedantic Analysis

- *Mumukshutva* transforms worldly dissatisfaction into spiritual urgency.
- It is compared to the need for air when drowning: an absolute, non-negotiable necessity.
- Without *mumukshutva*, spiritual life stagnates; with it, the mind becomes single-pointed.
- It is not hatred of the world but prioritization: the world becomes secondary, Brahman primary.

Common Misunderstandings

- **That mumukshutva is optional:** It is indispensable for Self-knowledge, because (1) gaining and actualizing Self-knowledge is hard work and takes time (2) maya is persistent and tenacious. Without a burning desire for freedom, one soon gives up and falls back into the currents of samsara.
- **That it is mere curiosity or preference:** True *mumukshutva* is burning intensity, not a casual wish.
- **That it requires despair or boredom:** It can also arise from deep compassion and sensitivity, or a relentless pursuit of the truth — not only personal suffering.

Vedantic Resolution

Mumukshutva is the defining qualification of the seeker. It converts vague longing into committed pursuit, makes *sadhana* steady, and ensures that knowledge matures into freedom. It is the inner fire without which no external practice bears fruit.

neti-neti

(neti-neti — *NAY-tee-NAY-tee*)

One of the most striking methods of the Upanishads is *neti-ne-ti* — "not this, not this." It appears in the *Brihadaranyaka Upanishad* as a way of pointing to the Self. Since atman is never an object, it cannot be positively described like "it is this" or "it is that." Any description falls short, belonging to the realm of the negated. What remains when all is denied is the very subject that cannot be objectified — pure awareness.

The Upanishad divides the universe into two broad categories: the concrete (*murta*) and the abstract (*amurta*). The body belongs to the gross/concrete, the mind and thoughts to the subtle/abstract. Matter is concrete, energy abstract. *Neti-neti* negates both: one *neti* excludes the concrete universe, the other *neti* excludes the abstract.

The teaching does not reveal the Self as some new object once the negation is complete. Instead, it leaves behind the invariable subject — the witness, the one who is doing the negating. That which remains is the atman, evident as the "I am," which can never be negated. Just as in deep sleep the absence of objects is witnessed, here too the negation leaves only the witnessing consciousness.

This approach underscores a central Vedantic point: the Self is never gained, only recognized. We do not need to "experience" atman, for we already are it. What is required is to remove false attributes and identifications. *Neti-neti* clears away the non-Self so the Self, ever the knower, shines unobstructed.

—

Root & Meaning

Neti-neti = "not this, not this" (from *na iti* repeated twice).
A method of negating all that is not-Self (*anatman*) to arrive at Self.

Scriptural References

- **Brhadaranyaka Upanishad (3.9.26):** explicitly uses *neti-neti* to deny both the concrete and abstract universes.
- **Kaivalya Upanishad:** negates the five elements with *na bhumir apo…*, echoing the *neti-neti* method.
- **Shankara's bhashyas:** employ *neti-neti* as a central tool for removing superimpositions.

Traditional View

- *Neti-neti* is a method of negation, not of arriving at an object.
- It dismisses both gross and subtle phenomena as *anatma*.
- The Self is not negated, because the negator — the witness — cannot be objectified or denied.

Vedantic Analysis

- The *murta* (concrete) and *amurta* (abstract) universes are both *mithya*.
- By negating them, what remains is the one reality that cannot be negated: the witnessing Self.
- This Self is evident as "I am" — the knower, never the known.
- *Neti-neti* is thus not nihilism but a method to clear away error and reveal what is always present.

Common Misunderstandings

- **Neti-neti as total denial:** It is not denial of existence itself but of misidentification.
- **Neti-neti as experience-hunting:** The Self is not a special

experience to be gained after negation.

- **Neti-neti as infinite regression:** The process ends with the Self, which cannot be negated.

Vedantic Resolution

Neti-neti teaches that all objects, gross and subtle, are not the Self. What cannot be negated — the knower, awareness itself — is the atman. Far from being nothing, it is the very fullness of being-consciousness in which the universe appears and disappears.

nididhyasana

(nididhyāsana — *ni-di-DHYAA-suh-nuh*)

In the tradition of Advaita Vedanta, *nididhyasana (nididhyāsana)* is the ripening of spiritual knowledge into living realization. It is not about acquiring new information or achieving extraordinary mystical experiences, but about standing steadfast in what has already been seen: I am That. It is the third phase after *shravana* (hearing the teachings) and *manana* (removing doubts through reflection) in Vedanta's method of Self-inquiry.

Remembrance of the Self is unnatural to the ego-mind. It is the opposite of its wiring. To abide in the Self means to live without compulsively identifying with perceptions, thoughts, emotions, and outcomes. This is why, in Vedanta, *moksha* is said to be the rarest of attainments — not because the Self is hidden, but because the pull of forgetting is so strong and ignorance is hard-wired.

Even after shravana and *manana*, the old habits of the mind — *vasanas* and *viparita bhavanas* (wrong thinking/identification) — cling tightly. The intellect may be convinced, but the emotional body, shaped by countless impressions, continues to react as if it were still bound. It is here that *nididhyasana* becomes essential.

Nididhyasana is an intense, continuous contemplation upon the truth: "I am whole, complete, limitless, unchanging non-dual awareness." It is a soaking of the mind in the vision of non-duality until that vision becomes natural, effortless, and unshakable. It is a deliberate refusal to slip back into habitual misidentification.

In traditional Vedanta, this process is compared to the steady polishing of a mirror: not to create the reflection, but to remove the grime that obscures it. It is the effort of pushing Vedantic understanding from the conscious mind into the subconscious mind, so that even in provocative situations, the truth remains firm.

The key to *nididhyasana* is conviction (*nishchaya*). Knowledge without conviction is like light seen through fog — dim and uncertain. Only when the understanding is deeply internalized does it become operative in life.

Some traditions describe two ways of consolidating conviction: one, through deep contemplative reasoning and abidance (*nididhyasana*), and another through direct mystical experience (*nirvikalpa samadhi*). Both paths aim at the same truth. But in the Advaita Vedanta approach, reasoning (*manana*) and assimilation (*nididhyasana*) are given primacy because the Self is not an object of experience to be gained. It is always the ever-present reality.

Even after the dawn of Self-knowledge, the *jiva* (individual) retains momentum. *Nididhyasana* is not about perfecting the *jiva*, nor about spiritual bypassing. It is about seeing the residual patterns (*vasanas*) clearly, dis-identifying from them, and gradually wearing them away through firm knowledge and *guna* management. This is why *nididhyasana* is described as a phase of emotional and psychological cleansing — not by "fixing" the mind, but by no longer granting its turbulence the status of reality.

The goal of *nididhyasana* is to reach a state where no active effort is needed, where the mind abides naturally in the Self — *sahaja samadhi*. Until then, practices like *drk-drishya viveka* (discerning the seer from the seen) and constant recollection of the *mahavakyas* ("*Tat Tvam Asi*," "*Aham Brahmasmi*") are tools for stabilizing the vision.

It is crucial to understand that *nididhyasana* does not demand withdrawal from life. It demands the withdrawal of false identification. Even a *jivanmukta* (liberated while living) continues to appear active in the world, but their inner identity remains rooted in the Self, unaffected by success or failure, pleasure or pain.

In *nididhyasana*, life itself becomes the field of contemplation. Every reaction, every attachment, every sorrow is an opportunity to remember: I am not this fleeting event. I am the ever-free awareness in which it plays out.

Eventually, through patient and unrelenting contemplation, the residual vasanas lose their hold. The seeker no longer needs to practice *nididhyasana*, and abiding as the Self becomes natural, like breathing. Thus, *nididhyasana* is not a technique to "get" liberation — it is the faithful living of liberation. It is the art of abiding as what we already are, refusing to pretend otherwise.

—

Root & Meaning

Nididhyasana = from the Sanskrit root *dhyai* ("to meditate, contemplate") with the prefix *ni-* (down, inward, steady) and reduplication, implying deep, continuous contemplation. Primary meaning: sustained, focused assimilation of Self-knowledge until it is free of doubt, vagueness, or habitual contradiction.

Scriptural References

On nididhyasana as steady contemplation:

- **Brihadaranyaka Upanishad 2.4.5:** "It is to be meditated upon and well reflected upon (*nididhyasitavyah*)..." – Shankara comments that *nididhyasana* is repeated dwelling upon the truth already heard and understood.
- **Chandogya Upanishad 6.14.2:** Instruction to remain steadfast in the truth *"Tat Tvam Asi."*
- **Mundaka Upanishad 2.2.4:** "The Self is to be known through hearing, reflection, and deep contemplation." (*shrotavyo mantavyo nididhyasitavyah*).
- **Bhagavad Gita 6.12:** The yogi, seated and steadfast, focuses the mind on the Self.
- **Bhagavad Gita 6.25–26:** Through a resolute intellect, the mind is brought steadily to the Self and kept there.

On conviction and assimilation of knowledge:

- **Bhagavad Gita 5.20:** The knower of the Self remains unshaken amid changing circumstances.
- **Bhagavad Gita 12.8:** "Fix your mind on Me alone; let your intellect dwell in Me."
- **Vivekacudamani 364–365:** The wise should remain established in the Self through unwavering knowledge, not letting the mind slip into old identification.

Traditional View

In the *shravana–manana–nididhyasana* sequence, *nididhyasana* follows hearing the teaching (*shravana*) and resolving doubts through reasoning (*manana*). It is the stage where the teaching is internalized so fully that the habitual sense of "I am the body-mind" dissolves, leaving the unshakable knowledge "I am Brahman."

Vedantic Analysis

Nididhyasana is not mere meditation in the sense of calming the mind (as in *dhyana* of Patanjali's *Yoga Sutras*). Instead, it is contemplation with a specific content: the truth revealed by the Upanishads.

Its purpose is to:

- Remove *viparita bhavana* (contrary habitual notions) such as "I am limited," even after understanding the teaching intellectually.
- Reinforce the assimilation of the *mahavakyas* ("great sayings" like *tat tvam asi*, "you are That").

In practice, this means dwelling on the vision of non-duality, recalling it in the midst of all situations, and refusing to let the mind slip back into ignorance-based identification.

Common Misunderstandings

- **"Nididhyasana is sitting silently without thoughts."** The point is not thoughtlessness but holding the right thought.
- **"It is the same as meditation for relaxation."** It is contemplation with the explicit aim of fully assimilating Self-knowledge.
- **"It produces liberation."** Liberation comes from *jnana*; *nididhyasana* removes residual obstacles to owning up to that knowledge.

Vedantic Resolution

Vedanta teaches that *nididhyasana* is the final stage in which knowledge becomes spontaneous (*jnana-nishtha*). Without it, the old identity can reassert itself under stress or emotional upheaval. Thus, a committed seeker integrates *nididhyasana* into daily life, using both formal contemplation and moment-to-moment mindfulness to stay rooted in the truth.

Nirguna Brahman

(Nirguṇa Brahman — *nir-GOO-nuh bruh-muhn*)

Nirguna Brahman is Brahman without attributes (*gunas*) — pure, infinite, formless awareness that is the absolute reality (*paramarthika satya*). It is beyond all qualities, distinctions, and limitations.

In contrast to *Saguna Brahman* (Brahman conceived through the lens of maya, as *Ishvara*), *Nirguna Brahman* cannot be objectified by the mind. It is not omniscient, omnipotent, or compassionate — not because it lacks these, but because such qualities presuppose relationship and duality. Brahman as it truly is transcends all categories of thought and language.

The Upanishads declare: "*neti, neti*" — not this, not this. By negating all limiting adjuncts (*upadhis*), the seeker is pointed to what remains: pure consciousness. This is not an experience, but recognition of what one always is.

Advaita Vedanta emphasizes that liberation comes only through knowledge of *Nirguna Brahman*. Devotion to *Saguna Brahman* purifies the mind, but final freedom lies in owning the vision that one is not the limited individual but limitless, attributeless awareness.

—

Root & Meaning

Nir = without + *guna* = attributes, qualities.
Nirguna Brahman = Brahman without qualities; absolute reality.

Scriptural References

- **Brihadaranyaka Upanishad 3.9.26:** *"Neti, neti"* (not this, not this).
- **Mandukya Upanishad 7:** *Turiya* is described as featureless, ungraspable, unthinkable.
- **Bhagavad Gita 12.3–4:** those who worship the unmanifest (*avyakta*) are devoted to *Nirguna Brahman*.

Traditional View

- Absolute standpoint (*paramarthika satya*).
- Brahman is beyond qualities, forms, distinctions.
- Recognized through negation (*neti-neti*) and knowledge, not through action or devotion alone.

Vedantic Analysis

- *Saguna Brahman* = Brahman with attributes, empirical, worshipped as *Ishvara*.
- *Nirguna Brahman* = Brahman without attributes, absolute, identical with the Self.
- Knowledge of *Nirguna Brahman* = liberation (*moksha*).

Distinction between the two is pedagogical; both refer to the same Brahman viewed differently.

Common Misunderstandings

- **That Nirguna Brahman is an empty void:** It is pure existence-consciousness, not non-being.
- **That Nirguna Brahman excludes devotion:** *Bhakti* purifies the mind, preparing it for this vision.
- **That Saguna and Nirguna are two Brahmans:** They are not-two; the difference is in standpoint.

Vedantic Resolution

Nirguna Brahman is the ultimate reality: pure, attributeless awareness. It cannot be objectified or conceptualized, but is one's very Self. Recognition of this truth is liberation.

nirvikalpa samadhi

(nirvikalpa samādhi — *nir-vi-kal-puh suh-MAA-dhee*)

In the Yoga tradition, *nirvikalpa samadhi (nirvikalpa samādhi)* is the highest state of meditative absorption. The term means "absorption without distinctions." In this state:

• The usual division of knower, known, and knowledge collapses.
• The mind's movements (*vrittis*) come to complete stillness.
• Awareness remains, but without an object.
• It is described as timeless silence, a state "without a second."

It is contrasted with *savikalpa samadhi*, where some thought or object (such as "I am Brahman") still remains. *Nirvikalpa samadhi* is considered deeper — a total suspension of distinction.

Swami Dayananda calls this "the last word in samsara." It is indeed a peak experience, but still an experience. And every experience has an end. One may remain in *nirvikalpa samadhi* for minutes or even days, but the moment an external stimulus intrudes — a sound, a touch, a bug crawling — the state is gone. Afterwards, it is remembered and narrated: "Yesterday, I had the most wonderful *samadhi*." What was eternal for half an hour becomes non-eternal. The experience itself becomes a new source of sorrow, because it cannot be held. Dayananda humorously warns that *nirvikalpa samadhi* is a "great hooker": it baits seekers into chasing what seems like the ultimate achievement.

Swami Paramarthananda goes further: such meditations may feel like silence, but they are not spiritual in themselves. They resemble deep sleep — the knower–known division is absent, but the mind is not available for knowledge. Blankness is registered in the causal body (*karana sharira*) and recalled afterwards as "I experienced silence." But in the moment, there is no knowledge of the Self or of *Ishvara*. Vedanta does not deny such states are possible, but insists they have nothing to do with liberation.

The key Vedantic point is this: the Self is never an experience. *Nirvikalpa samadhi* is only a reflection of the Self in a temporarily pure, sattvic mind. Like a clean mirror reflecting light, a still mind reflects awareness vividly, but the reflection is not the light itself: the sun viewed in a mirror, is not the sun. Yogis often mistake this reflection for the Self. Advaita insists: *moksha* (liberation) is not any state of mind but the recognition that awareness is one's very *svarupa* (essence) — ever present in waking, dream, sleep, and even *samadhi*.

As a discipline, *nirvikalpa samadhi* has value. It shows great mastery over the mind and can prepare it for Self-knowledge. But liberation is not the result of going beyond the mind into silence. It is the result of a mind available to assimilate the teaching of *shruti* (scripture), which alone dissolves the knower–known division permanently.

—

Root & Meaning

Nir = without
Vikalpa = distinction, modification, thought-construction
Samadhi = absorption, integration
Nirvikalpa samadhi = meditative absorption without distinctions.

Scriptural References

- **Yoga Sutras (1.51):** *nirbija samadhi*, absorption without seed.
- **Advaita manuals (e.g. Vivekachudamani 364):** stress that liberation is not *samadhi* but Self-knowledge.

Traditional View

- Regarded in yoga as the highest state, beyond thought and duality.
- Distinguished from *savikalpa samadhi*, where some thought remains (e.g. "I am Brahman").
- Revered as a sign of extraordinary mental mastery.

Vedantic Analysis

- *Nirvikalpa samadhi* is an experience, hence impermanent.
- *Nirvikalpa samadhi* is identical to deep sleep in that the functioning mind is absent; nothing is recorded while the state occurs. The difference lies in the cause: deep sleep is tamasic and involuntary, while *samadhi* results from a highly sattvic and disciplined mind that temporarily resolves. Thus the blankness is the same, but the mind that enters and emerges is different.
- A sattvic mind reflects the Self clearly, but this is not the Self itself.
- Liberation (*moksha*) is not an experience but knowledge — the recognition that I am awareness itself, present in and beyond all states.
- Vedanta does not seek to go beyond the mind but to make the mind steady and inward so that teaching can be assimilated.

Neo-Vedanta vs Traditional Advaita

In many modern or Neo-Vedanta streams, influenced by Yoga and teachers like Swami Vivekananda, *nirvikalpa samadhi* is promoted as the fourth step to realization, after *shravana, manana,* and *nididhyasana*. It is presented as the final experiential confirmation of the Self.

Traditional Advaita Vedanta, however, recognizes only the three steps: *shravana, manana, nididhyasana*. These alone culminate in knowledge. No fourth step is required. *Moksha* is recognition, not an experience. To add *nirvikalpa samadhi* as a requirement is to confuse Vedanta with Yoga.

Why Seekers Pursue It

Despite Vedanta's caution, many seekers devote years to attaining *nirvikalpa samadhi*. This persistence usually arises from a blending of Yoga and Advaita. In the Yoga system, *nirodha* — complete cessation of the mind — is the means to liberation. When this view is imported into Vedanta, meditators assume that a rare and exalted experience must be the gateway to truth. The difficulty of the attainment adds to its mystique: what is hard to reach is easily mistaken for what is essential.

A second factor is experiential romanticism — the hope that one transformative event will dissolve suffering once and for all. But no experience, however sublime, can remove self-ignorance, because experiences come and go. The fascination with *nirvikalpa samadhi* is therefore more psychological than Vedantic. Liberation is not the result of a special state but the recognition that the one seeking special states is not the Self.

Common Misunderstandings

- **That nirvikalpa samadhi is moksha:** It is not; it ends, and what ends cannot be freedom.
- **That experiencing nirvikalpa samadhi is experiencing the Self:** It is only the mind reflecting the Self, not the Self itself.
- **That the world looks different after samadhi:** Vision changes only by knowledge (*pramana*), not by temporary states.

Vedantic Resolution

Nirvikalpa samadhi is a powerful discipline and a profound experience, but it remains within samsara. It is a reflection of the Self, not the Self. Advaita Vedanta respects its value but insists that only Self-knowledge — unfolded through *shruti* and assimilated by a prepared mind — is liberation.

niyati

(niyati — *ni-YUH-tee*)

We like to imagine the universe as random. From our limited vantage, events seem to happen without reason: accidents, encounters, fortunes that appear undeserved, tragedies that strike without warning. But Vedanta says there is no such thing as chance. The world, even in its apparent chaos, moves by a hidden symmetry. That symmetry is *niyati* — the quiet insistence that everything unfolds as it must.

To speak of *niyati* is not to invoke a mechanical fate. It isn't destiny written in the sky or divine punishment meted out by an angry god. *Niyati* is simply the pattern of coherence that allows the dream of creation to hang together. Without it, experience would dissolve into static; perception itself would be impossible. It is the subtle grammar of maya — the rules of a game that none of us invented but all of us play.

Every motion implies law. Fire burns, water cools, thought creates consequence. The same principle that keeps planets in orbit also brings back the fruits of our actions. We call that karma, but karma is only the expression of *niyati*. It is how the universe remembers. Each cause finds its effect not through miracle but through inevitability. If we could see the web in its totality, we'd recognize that what we call coincidence is just complexity too fine for the human eye.

The irony is that *niyati* feels most oppressive when we resist it. When life doesn't follow our preference, we cry "injustice." Yet the very resistance we feel is part of the same law. It is the ego — *ahankara* — colliding with the structure of a world it didn't design. When we move with *niyati*, life feels fluid, almost effortless. When we fight it, we discover our imagined independence was never real.

Still, Vedanta doesn't preach fatalism. Awareness is not a pawn of *niyati*; it's the witness of it. The laws belong to the dream, not to the dreamer. From the standpoint of the *jiva*, everything seems governed — birth, death, cause, effect. But from the standpoint of the Self, nothing ever happens. The order of the world is contained in a stillness that neither commands nor interferes. Brahman doesn't enforce *niyati*; *niyati* exists because Brahman is changeless.

Seen rightly, this is liberation, not limitation. The same intelligence that spins galaxies is what breathes you, feeds you, carries your thoughts across the vast field of consciousness. When you stop trying to bend the law to your will, you begin to move in harmony with it. Action becomes spontaneous and precise — dharma in motion. Then even suffering feels instructive, not punitive. You realize that *niyati* is not against you; it's for you, leading you back toward equilibrium.

There comes a moment in every seeker's journey when they look at their life — its twists, its strange timing — and see the delicate geometry behind it. The people who arrived just when they were needed. The losses that pushed them toward wisdom. The failures that stripped away pretense. Each thread perfectly placed, though only in hindsight. That recognition is the beginning of reverence: the sense that nothing was ever out of place.

Niyati is that quiet hand. It doesn't compel belief; it simply reveals itself when the mind is still enough to notice. To live in awareness of it is to live in rhythm with the real. You act, but you don't cling. You move, but you don't struggle. You trust that whatever arises is part of the same flawless machinery that lifts the sun each morning.

Fate is what the frightened call *niyati*. Grace is what the wise call it.

—

Root & Meaning

From the root *ni–yam* (to restrain, to order, to regulate). *Niyati* literally means "order," "necessity," or "the principle of regulation." It conveys the sense of a governing law or inevitability that maintains coherence within the apparent chaos of creation.

Scriptural References

The term appears across multiple philosophical systems.

- In the Upanishads, *niyati* is implied wherever cosmic order (*rita*) and divine law (dharma) are spoken of — the unseen intelligence that keeps everything functioning according to cause and effect.
- In Sankhya and Vedanta, it's closely linked to karma: the natural precision with which every action meets its appropriate consequence.
- In some later systems (like Shaiva Siddhanta), *niyati* is personified as one of the five *kanchukas* — the limiting powers of maya that bind the infinite Self to the finite experience of law and sequence.

Traditional View

Traditionally, *niyati* is the principle of cosmic regulation — the lawful rhythm that ensures everything unfolds according to its own nature (*svabhava*). It's the reason that seeds become trees, actions bear fruit, and the sun rises predictably each day. Nothing is arbitrary; *niyati* is the unseen order behind appearances.

It operates alongside *kala* (time), karma (action), and dharma (cosmic law). Together they form the matrix through which maya expresses the play of cause and effect.

Vedantic Analysis

From a Vedantic standpoint, *niyati* is not an external power imposed upon reality — it's part of maya's projection, the illusion of order experienced within the dream of multiplicity. To the ignorant mind, *niyati* feels like fate or divine control. To the wise, it is simply the apparent lawfulness of *Ishvara's* dream.

Within non-dual understanding, there is no separate "force" called niyati; it is just the consistent functioning of maya seen through the lens of duality. Everything appears lawful because Brahman — the substratum — is changeless. The apparent movement of the world can only occur within that changeless background, giving rise to the perception of order.

Common Misunderstandings

- **Fatalism**: Some interpret *niyati* as rigid destiny — an unchangeable script written by fate. Vedanta rejects this. While the structure of cause and effect is firm, the human being participates in it through choice and awareness. The law is precise, but not cruel.
- **Divine micromanagement:** Others imagine *niyati* as God's personal control over each event. But Vedanta sees it impersonally: Ishvara is the intelligence that governs, not a person issuing decrees.

Vedantic Resolution

In truth, *niyati* is simply the order of *Ishvara* — the self-consistent logic of maya. It gives the world its coherence so that the seeker may live, act, and ultimately see through it.

To the awakened, *niyati* is no longer a binding law but a beautiful symmetry — the way the unreal maintains its balance until the real is recognized. When seen from knowledge, what once looked like fate is understood as grace: *niyati* ensures that every experience leads the seeker back to truth.

Om

(Oṁ — *om*)

Om (Oṁ, Auṁ) is one of the most sacred and comprehensive symbols in the Vedic tradition. It has been described as the primordial sound, the symbol of Brahman, the essence of all experience, and the summary of all that exists.

Om appears across countless teachings as a symbol for various triads: the three states of experience (waking, dreaming, deep sleep), the three bodies (gross, subtle, causal), the three powers of nature (*sattva, rajas, tamas*), and the three expressions of Brahman (*sat, chit, ananda*).

Yet its meaning need not be complicated. When seen or chanted, *Om* can be understood as a symbol for the entire order of creation. It is a sonic reminder of the truth: that we live within the great order, and that order lives within us — as the true Self.

Om is the silent presence that enlivens all life. It is what animates the body, digests food, circulates blood, and gives rise to thought and feeling. It is the unseen intelligence in animals, plants, and all natural systems. It is both the source and the sustaining principle behind all things, from galaxies to microbes.

In Vedanta, *Om* is used in two primary ways:

- As a mantra of invocation, calling upon the Lord (*Ishvara*) who sustains the totality through order.
- As a symbol for contemplation in the advanced stage of *nididhyasana* (Self-inquiry), after one has already understood the teaching of non-duality.

The *Mandukya Upanishad* describes *Om* as comprising four quarters. The first three represent the states of waking (*jagrat*),

243

dreaming (*svapna*), and deep sleep (*sushupti*). The fourth is not another state, but the silent, non-dual awareness in which the other three arise and dissolve — pure consciousness itself.

Phonetically, *Om* consists of three sounds: *a* + *u* + *m*, pronounced as a single syllable, "om."

- *A* represents the waking state and physical experience.
- *U* represents the dream state and the subtle mental world.
- *M* represents deep sleep, the unmanifest condition of the mind and world.

The silence that follows the sound is the most important part. It represents *turiya* — the fourth, unchanging Self that pervades and transcends all states of experience. To fully appreciate this silence, Self-knowledge is essential. Without it, one merely chants *Om* as a sound, unaware of its depth.

In addition, "*a*" is not only the physical world but also the one who experiences it; "*u*" is the dreamer or fantasizer; and "*m*" is the sleeper. The sound *Om*, then, becomes a complete symbol of the human condition — from gross to subtle to causal — and the silence is its source.

For pronunciation, it's suggested that one form the lips into a small circle and pronouncing the "*o*" as in *yo*-ga. The "*o*" should be elongated, followed by a short "*m*" sound. The total duration should be three short measures: *o-o-m*. Afterward, allow attention to rest in the silence before repeating the mantra.

In this way, *Om* becomes more than a sound — it becomes a doorway. A reminder. A returning home to the Self.

—

Root & Meaning

Om (also written *Aum*) — the primordial sound and most sacred syllable in the Vedic tradition. Derived from the combination of the phonemes *a* (waking), *u* (dreaming), and *m* (deep sleep), representing the totality of experience and consciousness. The silence following the syllable signifies *turiya* — the fourth, changeless reality underlying all states.

Scriptural References

- **Mandukya Upanishad:** Entire text devoted to explaining *Om* as the symbol of Brahman and the Self, relating its three sounds (*a, u, m*) to the waking, dream, and deep sleep states, and the silence to *turiya*.
- **Brihadaranyaka Upanishad 5.1.1:** Declares *Om* as the whole of this universe and the essence of the Vedas.
- **Chandogya Upanishad 1.1.1–1.1.10:** Teaches *Om* as the *udgitha*, the sacred chant, and its role in meditation and worship.
- **Katha Upanishad 1.2.15–17:** Describes *Om* as the bow, the Self as the arrow, and Brahman as the target to be realized.
- **Bhagavad Gita 8.13:** Teaches meditation on *Om* at the time of death as a means to reach the Supreme.
- **Taittiriya Upaniṣad 1.8.1:** Presents *Om* as the essence of the Vedas and a means of invoking auspiciousness before study.

Traditional View

Om is considered both a sound vibration used in chanting and a visual/mental symbol for meditation. In Vedic ritual, it sanctifies the beginning and end of recitations and offerings. As a symbol, it is the essence of the Vedas and the cosmic name of the Absolute. Recitation (*japa*) of *Om* is said to align the mind with the universal order (*rita*).

ॐ

Though later commentators map the symbol's curves to the states of consciousness described in the Mandukya Upanishad, the form itself is a stylistic Sanskrit ligature. Its parts are suggestive, not definitive.

Vedantic Analysis

Vedanta sees *Om* as a *pratika* (symbol) for Brahman. The *Mandukya Upanishad* maps its three audible parts — *a, u, m* — onto the three states of consciousness:

- *A* — waking (*jagrat*) state, associated with the gross body (*sthula sharira*).
- *U* — dream (*svapna*) state, associated with the subtle body (*sukshma sharira*).
- *M* — deep sleep (*sushupti*), associated with the causal body (*karana sharira*).
- The silence after *Om* points to *turiya*, the non-dual Self, ever-present in and beyond the other states.

Common Misunderstandings

- **"Om is just a Hindu religious chant."** It is a universal pointer to consciousness itself, not sectarian.
- **"Chanting Om produces enlightenment."** Chanting can purify and focus the mind, but Self-knowledge comes from *shravana–manana–nididhyasana*.
- **"Om is only a sound."** The sound is a symbol; its significance lies in what it represents.

Vedantic Resolution

Through contemplation on *Om*, one comes to see that the Self is the substratum of all experience. Regular recitation with understanding (*om-japa*) steadies the mind, while inquiry into its meaning (*om-vichara*) dissolves the identification with the changing states. The culmination is recognizing that you are *turiya*, the silent awareness in which waking, dreaming, and deep sleep arise and subside.

panchakosha

(pañcakośa — *puhn-chuh-KOH-shuh*)

The Upanishads present a model of human experience called the *panchakosha (pañcakośa)* — the five sheaths or coverings of the Self. These are not physical layers stacked on the atman, but figurative veils: ways in which the limitless Self is mistaken for limited attributes.

The five sheaths are:

- **Annamayakosha** — the "food sheath," the physical body made of matter, sustained by food, subject to birth, growth, and decay.
- **Pranamayakosha** — the "vital sheath," the physiological functions and life energies (*pranas*) that animate the body.
- **Manomayakosha** — the "mind sheath," seat of emotions, perceptions, and the wavering faculty of thought.
- **Vijnanamayakosha** — the "intellect sheath," faculty of discrimination and decision-making (*buddhi*).
- **Anandamayakosha** — the "bliss sheath," the causal sheath, experienced in deep sleep as undifferentiated happiness and rest.

In daily life, a person identifies with one or more of these sheaths: "I am the body," "I am hungry," "I am sad," "I am the thinker," "I am happy." And yet, the subject (you) cannot be that which is known. Each statement confuses atman with one of the *koshas*. The purpose of this teaching is not to posit real coverings but to show how ignorance projects limitation onto the limitless.

The *Taittiriya Upanishad* leads the student step by step through these identifications, showing how each sheath is dependent, limited, and therefore not the Self. What remains after negating them is not nothing, but the very witness that illumines them all: atman. The sheaths are *mithya* — dependent realities — while the

Self is *satya*, the substratum.

Thus, *panchakosha* is a pedagogical device, a "map of maya." It helps seekers discriminate between what is changeable and what is unchanging, what is borrowed and what is intrinsic, what is negatable and what is the invariable witness. When the mistaken identification with the sheaths is removed, one recognizes the Self as ever-free awareness, untouched by the coverings that seemed to hide it.

—

Root & Meaning

Pancha = five
Kosha = sheath, covering
Panchakosha = the five sheaths through which the Self is mistakenly identified.

Scriptural References

- **Taittiriya Upanishad (2.1–5):** primary source of the *panchakosha* teaching.
- Commentaries of Shankara and later teachers emphasize it as a *prakriya* (teaching method).

Traditional View

- The sheaths are not actual coverings but figurative — apparent identifications.
- Each sheath corresponds to a level of experience: physical, physiological, emotional, intellectual, and causal.
- By negating them, the seeker comes to recognize the invariable Self.

Vedantic Analysis

- The *koshas* are finite, dependent, and subject to change; hence they cannot be the Self.

- The Self is the witness of all the sheaths. It is what "knows" the sheaths and therefore, cannot be the sheaths.
- The sheaths progress from gross (food sheath) to the most subtle (bliss sheath) like the layers of an onion.
- The *anandamayakosha* (bliss sheath), though most subtle, is also negated — bliss in deep sleep is still a sheath, not pure awareness.
- This analysis culminates in Self-recognition: the atman as limitless, attributeless consciousness.

Common Misunderstandings

- **That the koshas literally cover the Self:** They are modes of misidentification, not physical layers. The Self cannot be covered.
- **That anandamayakosha is ultimate:** It is still part of ignorance, a sheath to be transcended.
- That negating the sheaths reveals a "new" Self: The Self was always present, only obscured by error.

Vedantic Resolution

Panchakosha is a method of discrimination (*viveka*). By seeing the dependent nature of each sheath, the seeker no longer confuses them with the Self. What remains is the atman — ever-present, independent, and free.

pancha mahabhuta

(pañca mahābhūta — *puhn-chuh mu-HAA-BHOO-tuh*)

Vedanta teaches that the entire physical universe is a play of five
fundamental elements — the *pancha mahabhuta (pañca mahābhūta)*.
They are:

- **Akasha (Space):** subtle and all-pervading, with the quality of
  sound.
- **Vayu (Air):** born of space, with the qualities of sound and touch.
- **Agni (Fire):** emerging from air, with sound, touch, and form.
- **Apah (Water):** arising from fire, with sound, touch, form, and
  taste.
- **Prithivi (Earth):** grossest of all, with sound, touch, form, taste,
  and smell.

The order of creation flows from subtle to gross, from the unseen
to the most tangible. Space (*akasha*) is the subtlest element, all-per-
vasive but with only one property — sound (*shabda*). From space
arises air (*vayu*), which gains an additional property, touch (*spar-
sha*), becoming less pervasive but more experienceable. From air
emerges fire (*agni*), which adds form and color (*rupa*), making the
world visible. From fire comes water (*apah*), endowed with taste
(*rasa*) in addition to sound, touch, and form. Finally, from water
arises earth (*prithivi*), the grossest and most limited of the elements, which alone has smell (*gandha*), completing the spectrum
of sensory qualities.

Thus, each successive element carries forward the properties of
the previous ones while adding something new. What is gained
in tangibility is lost in pervasiveness: space is infinite but least
graspable; earth is densest and most tangible but most confined.

This hierarchy of qualities — sound, touch, form, taste, and smell
— forms the foundation of sensory experience. Our five senses

correspond exactly to these five elemental properties: ears to sound, skin to touch, eyes to form, tongue to taste, nose to smell. The *pancha mahabhuta* therefore explain not only the structure of the cosmos but also the structure of human perception.

What makes this teaching profound is its universality. The same five elements that form the mountains, rivers, and stars also form this body. The same earth, water, air, fire, and space that make up "me" make up every other being. Individuality is only a temporary arrangement; the content is universal. We are, quite literally, walking earth — moving condensations of the cosmos, borrowing its elements for a time before returning them at death.

The *pancha mahabhuta* thus serve two purposes. Cosmologically, they explain the projection of the physical universe through maya. Pedagogically, they dissolve pride and separation: my body is not unique or independent, but the same stuff as everyone else's. And spiritually, they point to the Self beyond the elements. The elements are inert, insentient, and dependent. They rise and fall within awareness, but awareness itself — atman — is never touched by them.

—

Root & Meaning

Pancha = five
Maha = great
Bhuta = element, that which has "become"
Pancha Mahabhuta = the five great elements of creation.

Scriptural References

- **Taittiriya Upanishad (2.1):** describes the evolution of elements.
- **Chandogya Upanishad (6.3.2):** presents the elements as arising from Being.
- **Bhagavad Gita (7.4):** lists earth, water, fire, air, and space as

Krishna's material nature.
- **Mundaka Upanishad (1.1.7):** compares creation to a spider weaving its web from itself.

Traditional View
- Elements evolve from maya, moving from subtle to gross.
- Each element adds new sensory qualities.
- The body is sustained by these elements and returns to them at death.
- All living beings share the same elemental composition — revealing the fundamental equality of embodiment.

Vedantic Analysis
The *pancha mahabhuta* serve three interconnected purposes:

- **Cosmological:** They explain the projection of the universe, from subtle to gross. Each element carries specific qualities, which ground the five senses and make experience possible.
- **Pedagogical:** They reveal the universality of embodiment. The same elements that compose one body compose every body. Individual differences are superficial; all beings are "walking earth," temporary configurations of the same cosmic ingredients.
- **Philosophical:** They demonstrate that nothing is ever truly born or destroyed. Elements are only borrowed, rearranged, and recycled. A name-form (*nama-rupa*) arises for a short time, dissolves, and becomes something else. This perspective erodes the illusion of separateness and uniqueness: we are not isolated entities, but expressions of something much greater — the infinite order of existence.

Common Misunderstandings
- **That the five elements are independent realities:** They are

dependent on Brahman through maya.

- **That bodily differences imply essential difference:** All bodies share the same five-element content; the distinctions are only apparent.
- **That experiencing the elements is experiencing the Self:** The Self illumines the elements but is never reducible to them.

Vedantic Resolution

The five great elements are the bricks of the cosmos, composing every body alike. To recognize this is to dissolve pride and separation: there is no "my" body versus "your" body, only borrowed elements in temporary form. Beyond them stands the Self — pure awareness — which is never composed, never borrowed, never returned.

panchikarana

(pañcikaraṇa — *puhn-chi-kuh-ruh-nuh*)

The *pancha mahabhuta* — space, air, fire, water, and earth — first arise in subtle form (*tanmatra*). But how do these subtle elements become the tangible universe of bodies and objects we experience? Vedanta answers with the teaching of *panchikarana* (*pañcīkaraṇa*), the "fivefold combination" or grossification of elements.

The process begins with Brahman in association with maya. Maya, composed of the three *gunas*, projects the subtle elements. Each subtle element is pure, possessing only its own primary quality (e.g., space = sound, air = touch, etc.). Through *panchikarana*, these subtle elements combine so that every gross element contains half of its own subtle essence plus one-eighth from each of the other four. Earth, for example, is half subtle earth plus fractions of water, fire, air, and space. This explains why every object in the world is a mixture — nothing is "pure fire" or "pure water."

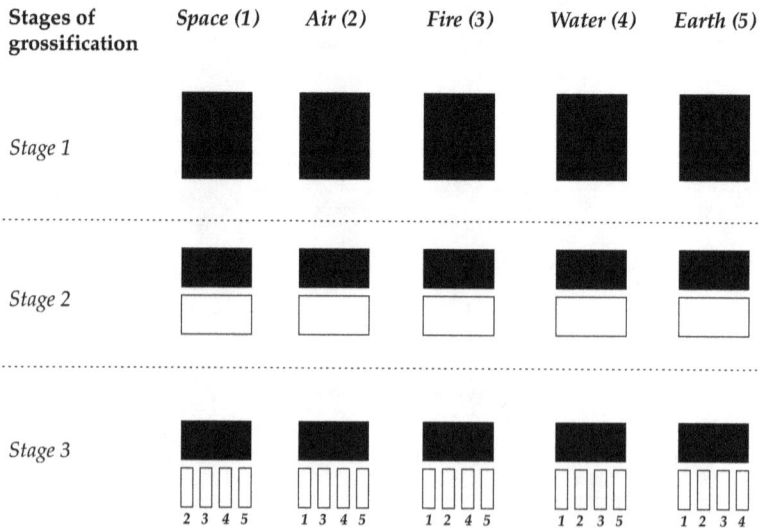

Stages of grossification	Space (1)	Air (2)	Fire (3)	Water (4)	Earth (5)
Stage 1	■	■	■	■	■
Stage 2	▆	▆	▆	▆	▆
Stage 3	▆ 2 3 4 5	▆ 1 3 4 5	▆ 1 2 4 5	▆ 1 2 3 5	▆ 1 2 3 4

This doctrine shows that creation is not chaotic but ordered. Each gross object we perceive is infused with all five elements in varying proportions. The human body, likewise, is a composite of all five, sustained by them and returning to them upon death. The teaching's purpose is not scientific description, but spiritual: to show that all forms are combinations, temporary and dependent, while the Self is ever independent of them.

By understanding *panchikarana*, the seeker gains clarity about the insubstantial nature of the world. What seems solid and unique is actually a rearrangement of the same fivefold elements, themselves projections of maya. The universe, in all its vastness and variety, is nothing but Brahman appearing through name and form.

—

Root & Meaning

Pancha = five
Karana = making, effecting, combining
Panchikarana = the fivefold combination or grossification of elements.

Scriptural References

The *panchikarana* doctrine is not found in the major Upanishads themselves. Its systematic form appears in later Advaita manuals such as *Vedanta Sara* and the short treatise *Panchikarana* (traditionally attributed to Shankara, though likely composed later). The method parallels Samkhya's theory of elemental evolution, which Advaita seems to have borrowed and reinterpreted. In Vedanta, however, *panchikarana* is not an ontological claim but a pedagogical tool, used to highlight the dependent and composite nature of the physical world.

Traditional View

- The subtle elements (*tanmatras*) first arise from maya.
- Through *panchikarana*, they combine into gross elements (*sthula bhuta*).
- Each gross element is thus half of its own subtle form and one-eighth of each of the other four.
- This mixture explains the diversity and cohesion of the physical world.

Vedantic Analysis

- The *panchikarana* doctrine shows the dependence of forms: nothing exists independently, all are composites.
- The body too is only a temporary mixture, returning to elements at death.
- The elements themselves are *mithya* — dependent appearances in awareness.
- The teaching reveals Brahman as the substratum: the unchanging reality behind the combinations.
- While *panchikarana* is formally a teaching device in Advaita Vedanta, it also offers a strikingly elegant vision of the cosmos: that the infinite variety of forms arises from a simple, orderly combination of five elemental essences. This simplicity makes it both pedagogical and cosmological — a bridge between spiritual insight and the experience of the physical world.

Common Misunderstandings

- **That panchikarana is literal physics:** It is a teaching model, not a scientific explanation.
- **That elements are independent substances:** In Vedanta, they are appearances of maya, not absolute.
- **That the doctrine is dualistic:** It ultimately points to Brahman as the sole reality.

Vedantic Resolution

Panchikarana shows that the manifest world is nothing but a five-fold rearrangement of elements projected by maya. Recognizing this reduces attachment to name-form and prepares the mind for Self-knowledge: the discovery that I am not a composite, but pure consciousness.

paramarthika

(pāramārthika — *PAA-ruh-MAAR-thi-kuh*)

Vedanta teaches that reality can be understood at different levels. What seems absolutely real in one context is revealed as relative when examined more deeply. To resolve this, the tradition distinguishes between three orders of reality: *pratibhasika* (illusory, dream-like), *vyavaharika* (transactional, empirical), and *paramarthika* (absolute).

Paramarthika satya — the absolute reality — is Brahman alone. Unlike dreams or the waking world, which appear and disappear, Brahman does not depend on anything else for its existence. It is eternal, unchanging, and independent. Just as bubbles and waves come and go on the surface of water, so too all names and forms arise and subside within Brahman. The bubbles (illusory) and waves (empirical) depend entirely on water; only water is real in the absolute sense.

From the *paramarthika* standpoint, there is no duality at all. There is no seer or seen, no subject or object, no multiplicity. All distinctions belong only to the lower orders of reality. In this vision, the individual is not the finite doer or experiencer (*ahankara*), but the *sakshi* — the ever-free witness, which is none other than Brahman. To claim this truth is to see that one was never bound, never a *samsari*, but always free.

—

Root & Meaning

Paramarthika — from *parama* (highest) + *artha* (meaning, reality, purpose). Means "pertaining to the highest truth," or "absolute."

Scriptural References

- **Brihadaranyaka Upanishad (2.1.20):** speaks of Brahman as *satyasya satyam* — "the truth of truth." The vital force is truth, and Brahman is the truth of that truth.
- **Manukya Karika:** distinguishes waking, dream, and deep sleep as relative appearances, pointing to *turiya* as the absolute, *paramarthika* reality.
- **Drg-Drshya-Viveka:** identifies the *paramarthika jiva* with the witness-consciousness, unlike the illusory (*pratibhasika*) or empirical (*vyavaharika*) identities.

Traditional View

Reality is classified in three levels:

- *Pratibhasika satya* — illusory truth, as in dream or error (e.g., rope mistaken for snake).
- *Vyavaharika satya* — empirical truth, the transactional reality of the waking world.
- *Paramarthika satya* — absolute truth, Brahman, the only reality that never changes.

Only *paramarthika* is ultimately real; the others are *mithya* (dependent, provisional).

Vedantic Analysis

- From the standpoint of *ahankara*, one is a doer and experiencer, bound to samsara. From the standpoint of *sakshi*, one is the *paramarthika jiva*, ever free.
- Dualities such as bondage and liberation, ignorance and knowledge, exist only at the empirical level. At the absolute level, there is only Brahman.
- Recognizing *paramarthika satya* does not "produce" *moksha*; it reveals that bondage was never real to begin with.

Common Misunderstandings

- **That the world is absolutely real:** Vedanta does not deny the world's transactional validity, but it clarifies it has no independent reality apart from Brahman.
- **That Brahman is another "object" of experience:** The absolute is not an object within experience, but the reality because of which all experiences appear.
- **That levels of reality are three separate worlds:** They are perspectives on the same reality, not three different universes.

Vedantic Resolution

To grasp *paramarthika satya* is to understand that Brahman alone is real. The waking and dream worlds are valid only within their spheres, but when inquired into, they collapse into the substratum. The *jnani* identifies with the *paramarthika jiva*, claiming "I am Brahman," and is free from the endless fluctuations of empirical life.

Prajna

(Prajña — *pruh-GYUH*)

In Vedanta, *Prajna (Prajñā)* refers to the deep-sleep state (*sushup-ti*) in which the individual is absorbed in undifferentiated causal potential. The word means "almost enlightened" — because in deep sleep, awareness experiences its own limitlessness and bliss, yet without knowledge of what is being experienced.

During waking (*Vishva*), the mind is extroverted, engaged in the world. In dream (*Taijasa*), the subtle body turns inward, projecting images from latent impressions (*vasanas*). In deep sleep, the subtle body itself resolves into the causal body. Consciousness in association with this state is called *Prajna*. It experiences experiential bliss (*ananda*) because all mental activity ceases, but ignorance (*mulavidya*) remains.

Prajna is "almost enlightened" because:

- There is the absence of duality — no knower, known, or knowledge.
- There is the experience of limitlessness, but without recognition.
- The intellect is dormant, so the meaning of the experience cannot be known.

Thus, while deep sleep is blissful, it does not liberate. When we wake, we say, "I slept well, I knew nothing." This shows that a witness was present, but knowledge was absent. The bliss of deep sleep is temporary, whereas the bliss of Self-knowledge (*ananda svarupa*) is permanent.

Vedanta uses *prajna* as one of the four "quarters" described in the *Mandukya Upanishad*:

- *Vishva* — waker, associated with *Virat*.

- *Taijasa* — dreamer, associated with *Hiranyagarbha*.
- *Prajna* — deep sleeper, associated with *Ishvara* (causal totality).
- *Turiya* — pure consciousness, free of all states and associations.

The teaching purpose of *Prajna* is to show that no state, not even deep sleep, defines the Self. The Self is the witness of all three states, revealed as *Turiya* — ever-present awareness.

—

Root & Meaning

Pra = before, supreme
Jna = knowledge
Prajna = "almost enlightened," consciousness in the deep-sleep state.

Scriptural References

- **Mandukya Upanishad (1–5):** presents *Prajna* as the third quarter of the Self.
- **Bhagavad Gita (2.69):** contrasts waking and sleep in terms of knowledge.
- **Shankara's commentary:** deep sleep is blissful but ignorant, because the intellect is dormant.

Traditional View

- *Prajna* is consciousness identified with the causal body in deep sleep.
- Bliss is experienced because duality disappears, but ignorance persists.
- Associated macrocosmically with *Ishvara*, the causal totality.

Vedantic Analysis

- Deep sleep provides an important clue: happiness is natural to the Self, not to objects.

- Yet, because knowledge is absent, deep sleep cannot give liberation.
- *Prajna* shows that even bliss without knowledge is temporary.
- Only Self-knowledge (*Turiya* recognition) reveals permanent freedom.

Common Misunderstandings

- **That deep sleep is enlightenment:** It is blissful but unconscious. Liberation requires knowledge.
- **That Prajna is a mystical state to be pursued:** It arises naturally every night; its value is as a teaching aid, not an attainment.
- **That the bliss of sleep equals ananda svarupa:** It is experiential bliss, not the limitless fullness of Brahman.

Vedantic Resolution

Prajna points beyond itself. By seeing that even the bliss of deep sleep is transient, Vedanta directs the seeker to *Turiya*, the unchanging witness of waking, dream, and deep sleep. True freedom is not an experience but the recognition that I am awareness, ever free.

prakriti

(prakṛti — *pruh-KRIH-tee*)

The word *prakriti (prakṛti)* comes from the Sanskrit root *kr* ("to do" or "to make"), suggesting *prakrishta-kriti* — "exalted creation" or "that which gives rise to multiplicity." In Vedanta, *prakriti* refers to the primordial, unmanifest material cause of the universe — the inert, dynamic potential from which all forms, experiences, and laws of nature emerge.

Prakriti is not a substance distinct from its qualities. It is the three *gunas* — *sattva* (illumination), *rajas* (activity), and *tamas* (inertia) — in an inseparable blend. These *gunas* are not accessories to *prakriti* but constitute its very nature. Without the *gunas*, there is no *prakriti*.

The *gunas* are always present, but their relative proportions vary. When in perfect balance (*samya-avastha*), *prakriti* remains unmanifest. According to Vedantic cosmology, when this equilibrium is disturbed — by divine will (*ishvara-ichha*) or the pressure of karma — the *gunas* shift and creation unfolds.

By itself, *prakriti* is inert. It cannot initiate or know anything. It becomes dynamic only in the presence of Consciousness (*Purusha* or Brahman). This union — often symbolized as the flutist and the flute — gives rise to the manifest universe. Awareness lends sentiency to *prakriti*, enabling creation, perception, and action.

In Vedanta, this union is personified as *Ishvara*, the Lord — Brahman reflected in maya, or pure sattvic *prakriti* under control.

Prakriti has subtle distinctions based on the gunic composition:

• When *sattva* predominates and *rajas/tamas* are subdued, *prakriti* is called maya — the power of creation in the hands of the Lord.

- When *sattva* is obscured by *rajas* and *tamas*, *prakriti* is called *avidya* — the individual's ignorance that veils the Self and creates bondage.

Thus, *prakriti* is both the womb of creation and the veil of illusion, depending on its gunic configuration.

Vedanta teaches that the universe undergoes endless cycles of manifestation (*shrishti*) and dissolution (*pralaya*), orchestrated by the *gunas* through *prakriti*. These are not random events but intelligent, rhythmic unfoldings — like a divine heartbeat.

The *Bhagavad Gita* (14.5) affirms:

Sattva, rajas, and tamas — the gunas (qualities) born of prakriti — bind as though the changeless indweller of the body, to the body.

The body, senses, mind, and ego — all belong to *prakriti*. The *jiva*, the apparent individual, appears conscious only because of the reflected light of awareness. The *gunas* condition the *jiva's* personality and experience:

- *Sattva* brings clarity and knowledge.
- *Rajas* brings restlessness and desire.
- *Tamas* brings ignorance and delusion.

Even liberation (*moksha*) is possible only when the mind, a product of sattva, becomes pure and reflects the Self without distortion.

Prakriti is not an object or force apart from its three *gunas* — it is the totality of their interaction. It is the dynamic, ever-changing matrix of existence, enlivened by the light of awareness. Understanding *prakriti* is essential to understanding bondage and liberation — for the *gunas* bind, and the Self alone is free.

—

Root & Meaning

Prakriti — from the Sanskrit prefix *pra-* ("forth, forward") and root *kr* ("to make, to do"), meaning "that which is primary" or "the original source."

In philosophical contexts, it is often translated as "nature," "primordial matter," or "the basic matrix of creation." In Sankhya and certain Vedantic interpretations, *prakriti* refers to the primal cause from which the manifest universe arises.

Scriptural References

Nature and definition of prakriti:

- **Bhagavad Gita 13.19:** "Know that *prakriti* and *purusha* are both beginningless…"
- **Sankhya Karika 3–5:** Classical definition of *prakriti* as the equilibrium of the three *gunas.*
- **Shvetashvatara Upanishad 4.10:** Refers to *prakriti* as the womb of creation (*yoni*).

Prakriti as the gunas:

- **Bhagavad Gita 14.5:** "*Sattva, rajas,* and *tamas* — the *gunas* born of *prakriti* — bind the changeless indweller to the body."
- **Bhagavad Gita 18.40:** "There is no being…free from these three *gunas* born of *prakriti.*"

Union of prakriti and consciousness:

- **Bhagavad Gita 9.10:** "Under My supervision, *prakriti* produces the moving and unmoving."
- **Shvetashvatara Upanishad 4.5–4.6:** The Lord as the cause, maya as *prakriti*, and *purusha* as the witness.

Prakriti as maya or avidya:

- **Shvetashvatara Upanishad 4.10:** "Know maya to be *prakriti* and the possessor of maya to be the great Lord."

- **Bhagavad Gita 7.14–7.15:** The divine maya of the Lord is constituted of the three *gunas* and is hard to cross.

Cycles of creation and dissolution:

- **Bhagavad Gita 8.18–8.19:** "At the coming of the day, all manifest beings proceed from the unmanifest; at the coming of night, they dissolve into that."
- **Shvetashvatara Upanishad 4.5:**"From that comes the unmanifest, from the unmanifest comes all creation."

Prakriti as cause of body, mind, and ego:

Bhagavad Gita 13.20: "*Prakriti* is said to be the cause of the body and the senses; *purusha* is said to be the cause of experiencing pleasure and pain."

Traditional View

In the Sankhya school, *prakriti* is the unmanifest, eternal, unconscious principle composed of the three *gunas* — sattva (balance), *rajas* (activity), and *tamas* (inertia). When in equilibrium, *prakriti* is unmanifest; creation begins when this equilibrium is disturbed in association with *purusha* (pure consciousness). All physical and subtle phenomena — including body, senses, and mind — are evolutes of *prakriti*.

Vedanta, while not fully adopting the dualism of Sankhya, uses the term *prakriti* in a provisional way to describe maya — the creative power of *Ishvara* that manifests the empirical universe.

Vedantic Analysis

Advaita Vedanta regards *prakriti* not as an independent reality but as maya, dependent on Brahman. In this view:

- **Cause:** *Prakriti* is the *upadana-karana* (material cause) of the universe, while *Isvhara* is both material and efficient cause (*abhinna-nimitta-upadana-karana*).

- **Status**: It is *mithya* (empirically real but not ultimately real), much like a dream.
- **Relation to Gunas:** The *gunas* operate within *prakriti*, influencing all embodied experience until Self-knowledge frees one from their sway.

Common Misunderstandings

- **"Prakriti is separate from consciousness forever."** This is Sankhya dualism; Advaita holds that *prakriti* is a dependent appearance in consciousness.
- **"Prakriti is evil or to be destroyed."** It is neither good nor bad; it is simply the field of experience in which karma plays out.
- **"Liberation means escaping prakriti physically."** Liberation is freedom from identification with prakriti, not its physical cessation.

Vedantic Resolution

Vedanta uses *prakriti* as a teaching tool to explain the apparent mechanics of creation and the variety of experiences in the empirical world. Once the Self is known as the changeless witness of *prakriti*, the identification with the body-mind (which belongs to *prakriti*) falls away. One continues to live within the play of the *gunas*, but without bondage — *guna guneshu vartanta iti matva na sajjate* ("The *gunas* act upon the *gunas*; knowing this, one is not attached" — *Bhagavad Gita* 3.28).

prakriya

(prakriyā — *pruh-kri-YAA*)

Vedanta uses several prakriyas (prakriyās) or methods to teach Self-knowledge and help the seeker discriminate (viveka) between the Self and not-Self. Vedantic methodology typically begins by pointing out the known identities, and then shows how they hide the truth creating a false reality. Below are some of the more common prakriyas used in the tradition:

The Three States of Experience
(avastha-traya-viveka-prakriya)

The three states of experience (waking, dreaming, sleeping) are used to show that the I-sense (ego) isn't always present, and that the only constant in all three states is the Self—that which remains unmodified by experience.

• **Mandukya Upanishad:** Verses 3–7 describe the waking (*jagrat*), dream (*svapna*), and deep sleep (*sushupti*) states and their relationship to *turiya*.
• **Brihadaranyaka Upanishad 4.3.9–4.3.33:** Yajnavalkya's dialogue with Janaka on the Self beyond the three states.

—

The Seer and the Seen
(drg-dṛshya-viveka-prakriya)

A fundamental method for discriminating between the true subject (the Self) and objects. We most identify with gross objects such as the body and with subtle objects such as thoughts, but we cannot be that which is known by us. The teaching shows that the seer can never be the seen, and that the actual witness can never be objectified.

- **Brihadaranyaka Upanishad 3.4.2:** "You cannot see the seer of seeing..."
- **Katha Upanishad 2.2.13:** "The Self is the seer, unseen..."

—

The Real and the Apparent
(satya-mithya-viveka-prakriya)

A method showing the difference between what's real (always present; never changing) and what's apparently real (not always present; changing). In the end, the seeker is shown that only pure awareness can be shown to be real, while the entire world is only apparently real and has the qualities of a dream due to its constant change and lack of substantiality.

- **Chandogya Upanishad 6.1.4–6.1.6:** *Sat* alone is real; names and forms are *mithya*.
- **Bhagavad Gita 2.16:** "The unreal has no existence, the real never ceases to be."

—

The Cause and the Effect
(karana-karya-viveka-prakriya)

This method shows that the cause is non-separate from the effect. All objects (the effect), come out of and fall back into consciousness (the cause). While all objects are dependent on consciousness, consciousness is not dependent on objects. In the end, all objects owe their existence to pure consciousness.

- **Chandogya Upanishad 6.1.4–6.1.6:** Clay and pot analogy.
- **Brihadaranyaka Upanishad 1.4.7:** All beings have their origin in the Self.

The Five Sheaths
(pancha-kosha-viveka-prakriya)

A well-known method for negating the attributes which define the individual and apparently hide one's true nature. The five sheaths are systematically negated starting from the gross body sheath and continuing through to the subtle bliss sheath. Once all five sheaths are negated, the seeker is shown their true identity as the Self.

- **Taittiriya Upanishad 2.1–2.5:** The five *koshas: annamaya, pranamaya, manomaya, vijnanamaya, anandamaya.*

—

The Three Bodies
(sharira-traya-viveka-prakriya)

Using a similar approach as the previous method, the seeker is shown the illusory quality of personhood through analysis of the gross body (physical body), subtle body (mind-intellect-ego) and causal body (subconscious).

- **Mandukya Karika 3.1–3.2:** Describes gross, subtle, and causal bodies in relation to the three states.
- **Panchadashi (Vidyaranya):** Systematic exposition on the three bodies.

—

The Five Subtle Elements
(tanmatra-viveka-prakriya)

This method proposes how Creation and objects evolve from pure consciousness and resolve back into consciousness at the end of its cycle, only later to manifest again.

- **Taittiriya Upanishad 2.1:** Creation sequence beginning from *akasha.*

• **Chandogya Upanishad 6.2.3:** Manifestation of elements.

The Location of Objects
(vishaya-sthiti-prakriya)

In this method, the teacher refutes the common belief that objects exist "out there" by showing that all objects actually exist as thoughts in consciousness constructed from sense data. And if objects are really just a thought in consciousness, the question is how far are objects from me?

• **Brihadaranyaka Upanishad 3.4.2:** All perception takes place in the Self.
• **Yoga Vasishtha (Utpatti Prakarana):** The mind projects and experiences the world internally.

—

The Three Orders of Reality
(paramarthika-vyavaharika-pratibhasika-viveka-prakriya)

The discrimination between absolute reality (pure consciousness; the Self), God's Creation, and the individual's "Creation" based on their conditioning, like and dislikes, values, etc.

• **Mandukya Karika 3.29–3.31:** Gaudapada explains waking as *vyavaharika*, dream as *pratibhasika*, *turiya* as *paramarthika*.

—

Substrate and Name-Form
(*adhishtha-nama-rupa-viveka-prakriya*)

Often used with this method is the analogy of the clay and the pot, showing that clay is the substrate and "pot" is only name-form. One is real, while the other is apparently real.

• **Chandogya Upanishad 6.1.4–6.1.6:** Clay and pot, gold and ornaments, iron and tools.

Superimposition and negation
(adhyaropa-apavada-viveka-prakriya)

This method uses the well-known analogy of the snake and the rope to show how the mind superimposes attributes which can only be negated through right knowledge. For example, what is thought to be a snake in dim light, is known to be a rope in bright light.

- **Brihadaranyaka Upanishad 2.1.20:** Removal of superimpositions through knowledge.
- **Vivekachudamani 108–110:** Snake-rope analogy.

—

The Reflected Consciousness
(chidabhasa-prakriya)

This methodology elucidates how pure consciousness (*chit*) appears as the individual self (*jiva*) through reflection in the mind (*buddhi*). Similar to how a mirror reflects sunlight, the intellect reflects original consciousness, giving rise to *chidabhasa*, "the semblance of consciousness." This reflected consciousness enables cognition and the sense of individuality, yet is ultimately recognized as an illusion upon the realization of one's true nature as pure awareness.

- **Panchadashi 2.13–2.27:** Explains *chidabhasa* and its role in individual cognition.
- **Vedanta Paribhasha (Dharmaraja Adhvarindra):** Classical definition and analysis of reflected consciousness.

In addition to specific prakriyas that analyze states, bodies, or sheaths, Vedanta also employs broader explanatory frameworks to address the very question of creation. These meta-prakriyas do not just dissect experience; they provide the seeker with a vision of how the world appears without compromising the non-dual truth of Brahman. Two of the most important are vivarta-vada, the doctrine of apparent transformation, and ajata-vada, the doctrine of no-birth.

The Apparent Transformation
(vivarta-vada-prakriya)

This method explains that creation is not a real transformation of Brahman, but an apparent one, similar to mistaking a rope for a snake in dim light. The snake is seen, but never truly born; the rope remains unchanged. In the same way, Brahman is never modified, though the world appears. This helps the seeker reconcile the appearance of creation with the truth of non-duality.

- **Chandogya Upanishad 6.1.4–6.1.6:** clay and pot analogy.
- **Bhagavad Gita 9.4–5:** Krishna pervades creation yet remains unchanged.
- **Shankara's commentaries:** frequent use of the rope–snake example.

—

The Doctrine of No-Birth
(ajata-vada-prakriya)

Taught most clearly by Gaudapada in the *Mandukya Karika*, *ajata-vada* proclaims that from the highest standpoint (*paramarthika satya*), there is no creation at all. The world, the individual, bondage, and liberation are never truly born. Only Brahman, unborn and changeless, exists. For most seekers, this is revealed only after long preparation, since it requires a very mature mind to appreciate.

- **Mandukya Karika 3.48:** "No creature is ever born; there is no origination of anything."
- **Brihadaranyaka Upanishad 4.4.19:** "This Self is unborn, eternal."

- **Bhagavad Gita 2.20:** "The Self is never born, nor does it ever die."

Among these methods, many teachers present *vivarta-vada* as the most accessible explanatory framework, while *ajata-vada* is regarded as the highest vision —together representing the culmination of the prakriya tradition.

—

Root & Meaning

Prakriya — from the Sanskrit root *pra-* ("forth, forward") and *kriya* ("action, process"), meaning "method," "procedure," or "teaching device." In Vedanta, it refers to a systematic pedagogical approach used by teachers to unfold the truth of non-duality in a step-by-step manner.

Scriptural References

- **Bhagavad Gita 4.34:** "...the wise who have realized the truth will instruct you in knowledge" (implying a process of instruction).
- **Mundaka Upanishad 1.2.12:** "The truth of Brahman is to be taught systematically to the worthy disciple."
- **Brihadaranyaka Upanishad 2.4, 4.5:** Multiple layered approaches (*neti-neti*, analogies, etc.) showing structured teaching.
- **Taittiriya Upaniṣad 2.1–2.5:** The method of the five sheaths (*panchakosha prakriya*).

Traditional View

In the Advaita tradition, a *prakriya* is a teaching framework used to guide the student from their present understanding to the vision of oneness. Different teachers may choose different *prakriya* depending on the student's readiness (*adhikaritva*) and temperament. The aim is not to create new knowledge but to remove ignorance by revealing what is already true.

Vedantic Analysis

Since the Self (atman) is ever-present and self-evident, Vedanta does not "produce" knowledge in the sense of bringing something new into existence. Instead, a *prakriya* works like a mirror — it reveals what was hidden by misunderstanding. Each *prakriya* addresses specific misconceptions and provides multiple "entry points" to realization.

Common Misunderstandings

- **"Prakriyas are philosophical systems competing with each other."** They are complementary tools, not rival theories.
- **"One must master all prakriyas to be enlightened."** Even one effective *prakriya*, fully assimilated, can remove ignorance.
- **"Prakriyas are just intellectual wordplay."** They are skillful means rooted in scripture, designed for direct recognition.

Vedantic Resolution

A *prakriya* is like a ladder — necessary for climbing, but left behind once the goal is reached. The teacher uses it according to the student's capacity, starting with accessible concepts and refining them until only pure knowledge of the Self remains. Though the details vary, all *prakriyas* ultimately converge on the same non-dual truth: *tat tvam asi* — "That thou art."

pramana

(pramāṇa — *pruh-MAA-nuh*)

In Sanskrit, *pramana (pramāṇa)* is defined as "means of knowledge." Just as eyes are the means of knowing color and ears the means of knowing sound, Vedanta insists that a valid means is necessary to know anything. Without a pramana, knowledge cannot take place.

The Vedic seers carefully distinguished different pramana: perception (*pratyaksha*), inference (*anumana*), comparison (*upamana*), postulation (*arthapatti*), non-cognition (*anupalabdhi*), and scriptural testimony (*shabda*). Each functions in its domain. Perception tells us "the pot is here." Inference tells us "there is fire because there is smoke." Non-cognition tells us "there is no pot on the floor." Each is valid, but only within its proper scope.

For knowledge of the Self (atman), however, none of these ordinary pramana is adequate. The Self cannot be perceived, compared, or inferred, because it is not an object apart from oneself. Knowledge always requires a means — sight for forms, intellect for concepts. But when the Self is the "object," every means breaks down. The Self cannot be put in front of you. Trying to perceive it is like trying to see your own eyes directly.

Here Vedanta introduces a unique *pramana*: *shruti*, the Upanishads, unfolded by a qualified teacher. Vedanta is not philosophy or speculation, but a means of Self-knowledge that removes ignorance by revealing what is always present — awareness itself. Like using one thorn to remove another, Vedanta is employed until ignorance is dispelled, and then it too is set aside.

Thus, *pramana* is central to Vedanta's method. Liberation is not produced by action (karma) or mystical experience (yoga), because these are limited and depend on the doer. Only knowledge removes ignorance, and only *pramana* makes knowledge possible. Vedanta is a *pramana* for the Self — a mirror in which the ever-free nature of awareness is recognized.

—

Root & Meaning

Pra = before, clear, supreme
Mana = measure, instrument, means
Pramana = a means of valid knowledge.

Scriptural References

- **Nyaya Sutras (1.1.3):** define *pramana* as "that by which true knowledge is gained."
- **Mandukya Upanishad & Shankara's bhashya:** emphasize that the Self cannot be objectified, requiring *shruti* as *pramana*.
- **Bhagavad Gita (2.69; 18.66, with Shankara's commentary):** shows knowledge, not karma, as the final means of freedom.

Traditional View

- Six *pramana* are often recognized in classical Indian thought; Vedanta chiefly accepts three (perception, inference, scripture), with *shruti* as the final authority on the Self.
- Ordinary *pramana* function within duality; only *shruti* functions for non-dual recognition.
- A *pramana* is valid only so long as ignorance persists. Once knowledge is firm, the *pramana* is no longer required.

Vedantic Analysis

- Action (karma) cannot yield liberation because finite actions cannot produce infinite results.
- Experience (*anubhava*) cannot yield liberation because all

experiences are limited in time.

- Only Self-knowledge (*atma-jnana*), arising from *pramana*, can remove ignorance.
- Vedanta as a *pramana* does not give you a new Self, but reveals the Self you already are.

Common Misunderstandings

- **That knowledge is "only intellectual":** In Vedanta, knowledge is transformative because it removes ignorance, not mere information.
- **That experience is superior to knowledge:** Experiences come and go; knowledge remains.
- **That pramana means belief or blind authority:** It is a valid means of knowledge, tested and verified through inquiry.

Vedantic Resolution

Pramana is indispensable. Without it, one cannot know the Self. Vedanta serves as a unique *pramana* that reveals the Self as non-different from Brahman, ending the search. Once knowledge is firm, even Vedanta as *pramana* is dropped, just as the thorn is discarded after removing another.

prana

(prāṇa — *PRAA-nuh*)

In Vedanta, *prana (prāṇa)* is not just "breath," though breathing
is its most obvious expression. Prana is the vital force, the subtle
energy that animates the body and sustains life. Without it, the
body is inert matter, like a fan unplugged from the current. With
it, all functions — perception, digestion, circulation, movement,
thought — come alive.

The scriptures describe prana as arising from Brahman, carried
into the individual by *Ishvara's* order. It is part of the *sukshma
sharira* (subtle body) and serves as the bridge between body and
mind. When the mind resolves in deep sleep, prana continues;
when *prana* departs, the body is said to be dead.

Vedanta explains five primary divisions of this energy, called the
pancha-pranas:

- **Prana** — governing respiration and upward-moving energy.
- **Apana** — responsible for elimination and downward functions.
- **Vyana** — circulation and distribution throughout the body.
- **Samana** — digestion and assimilation.
- **Udana** — speech, effort, and the upward flow that carries the
  subtle body at death.

These are not five different energies but five functions of one *prana*, just as a single current powers many devices. They show how
life is ordered, precise, and interconnected.

The role of *prana* in spiritual practice is subtle. While some systems emphasize breath control (*pranayama*), Advaita Vedanta
regards *prana* as secondary. It is not through controlling energy
but through knowledge of the Self that liberation occurs. Still, har-
monizing prana through lifestyle, discipline, and meditation can

aid clarity of mind, preparing the field for inquiry.

Ultimately, *prana* belongs to the body-mind complex; it is not the Self. Awareness is the witness of *prana's* functions. The wise recognize this distinction, remaining free while the energies continue their flow.

—

Root & Meaning

Prana = life-breath, vital energy. From root *an* = "to breathe," with prefix *pra-* = "forth," "primary." Broadly: the vital force that sustains life.

The Five Pranas (*Pancha-prana*):

- *Prana* — respiration, upward life-force.
- *Apana* — elimination, downward flow.
- *Vyana* — circulation, distribution.
- *Samana* — digestion, assimilation.
- *Udana* — upward flow, speech, effort, departure at death.

Scriptural References

- **Prashna Upanishad 2–3:** explains *prana* as arising from the Self and dividing into functions.
- **Chandogya Upanishad 1.11.5:** *prana* as the sustaining power of the body.
- **Bhagavad Gita 15.14:** *Ishvara* as the digestive fire, supported by *prana* and *apana*.

Traditional View

- *Prana* sustains all bodily and mental functions.
- It resides in the subtle body and departs at death.
- Without *prana*, the sense and action organs cannot function.

Vedantic Analysis

- *Prana* is dependent, not independent — it belongs to the realm of *mithya*.
- It is enlivened by atman but is not the atman.
- Liberation is not mastery of *prana* but recognition of the witness of *prana*.

Common Misunderstandings

- **Prana = breath:** While linked to breathing, it is more fundamental than mere air exchange.
- **Prana = Self:** *Prana* is part of the subtle body; it is observed, not the observer.
- **Control of prana = liberation:** Techniques can aid clarity, but Self-knowledge alone grants freedom.

Vedantic Resolution

Prana is the universal vital force functioning through the individual. Knowing it as an instrument, not as identity, allows one to remain free from its fluctuations.

prarabdha karma

(prārabdha karma — *PRAA-ruhb-dhuh KAR-ma*)

In Vedanta, *prarabdha (prārabdha) karma* is that portion of the vast store of accumulated karma (*sanchita*) which has "already begun" to fructify. It is the karmic momentum that gives rise to the present body and life circumstances. While *sanchita* is the total seed-bank of past actions and *agami* is the karma newly generated in this lifetime, *prarabdha* is the "spending account," unfolding as the pleasures and pains of the current existence.

The scriptures teach that *prarabdha* determines the body one takes, the family one is born into, the span of life, and many of the key experiences of one's lifetime. Because of its deterministic flavor, it is sometimes equated with "destiny." Just as an arrow already released from the bow must travel until its momentum is spent, so too prarabdha must play out until it is exhausted.

Prarabdha is further classified:

- **Iccha prarabdha** — results aligned with one's desires.
- **Aniccha prarabdha** — results that come unasked, against one's wishes.
- **Pareccha prarabdha** — results that arise from the desires of others.

For the ordinary person (*ajnani*), prarabdha is binding, producing identification with experiences of joy and sorrow. But for the knower of the Self (*jnani*), *prarabdha* is like the aftershocks of an earthquake or the spinning of a potter's wheel after the pot is finished. Though the body continues to live out its momentum, the wise no longer identify with it. Shankara and later teachers emphasize: Self-knowledge destroys sanchita and prevents *agami*, but *prarabdha* continues until the body falls.

Ramana Maharshi noted that karma is only meaningful so long as one identifies as the doer. Once the ego is dissolved, there is no longer an agent to whom karma can attach. From the absolute standpoint, the whole structure of karmic law becomes redundant.

Thus, *prarabdha* illustrates the interplay of karma and knowledge. For the unenlightened, it explains the apparent inequalities of life and provides a framework for acceptance and dharmic living. For the liberated, it is seen as *mithya* — a play of appearances, endured like watching a magic show.

—

Root & Meaning

Prarabdha = "that which has already begun" (from the root *a-rabh*, to commence). The karmas that have started to bear fruit in the present life.

Scriptural References

- **Bhagavad Gita (3.33):** beings act according to their nature (*svabhava*), compelled by *prarabdha*.
- **Mandukya Karika (3.33):** compares *prarabdha* to an arrow already released.
- **Shankara's commentaries:** Self-knowledge destroys *sanchita* and prevents *agami*, but *prarabdha* remains until exhausted.

Traditional View

- *Prarabdha karma* explains present life circumstances — body, lifespan, major events.
- It cannot be avoided, even by God, because it has already begun to fructify.
- Divided into *iccha* (desired), *aniccha* (undesired), and *pareccha* (others' desires).

Vedantic Analysis

- Self-knowledge (*jnana*) is not opposed to prarabdha: the body continues to undergo its destined course, while the wise know themselves as untouched.
- The liberated live as *jivanmuktas*, allowing *prarabdha* to play out without bondage, until death brings *videhamukti*.
- The image of the spinning fan or potter's wheel is often used: momentum continues for a while, even after the source of power is cut.

Common Misunderstandings

- **That Self-knowledge cancels prarabdha:** Knowledge cancels ignorance, not the body's karma.
- **That prarabdha applies to the Self:** Karma belongs only to the *jiva*, never to awareness itself.

Vedantic Resolution

Prarabdha operates only so long as there is identification with the body-mind. For the knower, it is neither binding nor ultimately real. When the *prarabdha* of the body is exhausted, the liberated one is freed from rebirth altogether.

pratibhasika

(prātibhāsika — *PRAA-ti-BHAA-si-kuh*)

In Advaita Vedanta, reality is explained in three levels:

- **Paramarthika** — absolute reality, Brahman, ever free.
- **Vyavaharika** — transactional reality, the shared waking world.
- **Pratibhasika** — illusory or subjective reality, as in dreams, hallucinations, or mistaken perceptions.

The term *pratibhasika* is most often used in combination with *satta* (degree or order of existence). *Pratibhasika-satta* refers to the most fragile order of reality. The word *pratibhasa* means "appearance" or "seeming." These are experiences that appear real to the individual but do not withstand correction by higher levels of reality. A dream tiger produces genuine fear for the dreamer, yet the experience is canceled upon waking. Likewise, a rope mistaken for a snake terrifies until knowledge removes the error.

Crucially, *pratibhasika* is not "nothing." It is very real to the one experiencing it — hence the dreamer sweats or the fearful person recoils. But its truth-value is private, not shared. From the *jiva's* standpoint, *pratibhasika* is a whole world. Yet when measured against *vyavaharika-satta* (the empirical order), it collapses.

This means *pratibhasika* is not limited to dreams and hallucinations. It includes any misreading of reality — wherever ignorance and projection overlay what is. A mirage in the desert, a stick mistaken for a ghost in dim light, or a belief born of faulty perception all fall under this category.

The teaching purpose of *pratibhasika* is to refine discernment: just as dream knowledge is annulled by waking knowledge, and waking knowledge by absolute knowledge, so too every level of error is eventually sublated. What is never annulled is Brahman, the substratum underlying all appearances.

—

Root & Meaning

Pratibhasa = appearance, seeming, reflection.
Pratibhasika = "apparent" or "illusory reality"; what seems true to an individual but is corrected by higher knowledge.

Scriptural References

- **Mandukya Karika (2.31–32):** dream and waking are shown as relative levels of reality.
- **Drg-Drshya-Viveka:** distinguishes *pratibhasika-jiva* (dream self) from *vyavaharika-jiva* (waking self) and *paramarthika-jiva* (absolute Self).
- **Classical rope-snake analogy (Shankara):** *pratibhasika* error arises from superimposition.

Traditional View

- *Pratibhasika* covers dreams, illusions, hallucinations, mirages, and mistaken perceptions.
- It is annulled by empirical waking experience.
- Like bubbles on water, it has a momentary, dependent existence.

Vedantic Analysis

- Reality is hierarchical: *pratibhasika < vyavaharika < paramarthika*. *Pratibhasika* experience is negated by *vyavaharika* knowledge, and *vyavaharika* experience is negated by *paramarthika* knowledge.
- The lesson is not to dismiss *pratibhasika* as meaningless, but to see its dependence.
- Suffering often comes from mistaking *pratibhasika* appearances for ultimate truth.

- Liberation (*moksha*) comes by recognizing that even *pratibhasika* is *mithya*, with only Brahman as unnegated reality.

Common Misunderstandings

- **That pratibhasika means unreal in the sense of "nonexistent":** It does exist as experience, but not with independent reality.
- **That it applies only to dreams:** It also includes waking illusions, errors, and projections of the mind.
- **That Brahman is similarly unreal:** Unlike dream tigers, Brahman is never negated.

Vedantic Resolution

Pratibhasika reality is a training ground for discernment. By recognizing the limits of dream and illusion, the seeker prepares to see waking life itself as *mithya* — dependent reality. What remains, unnegated at any level, is Brahman.

pratibimba-vada

(pratibimba-vada — *pruh-ti-BIM-buh VUH-duh*)

The Sanskrit word *pratibimba* means "reflection." In Vedanta, it is used to explain how consciousness appears as individuality (*jiva*) through the mind. Pure awareness (*bimba*, the original) is never altered or divided, but when reflected in the mind (*antahkarana*), it gives rise to the sense of individuality — the "I"-thought (*ahankara*).

This reflected consciousness (*pratibimba-chaitanya*) is compared to the moon reflecting the light of the sun. On a full-moon night, the world is illumined by moonlight, but the moon has no light of its own; it only borrows from the sun. In the same way, the mind shines with borrowed awareness, creating the impression that the mind itself is conscious. The ego is nothing more than this reflection, a mixture of borrowed light from the Self and borrowed attributes from the mind.

Vedanta calls this reflection *mithya*: it is neither absolutely real nor absolutely unreal. The ego is experienced, yet it vanishes in deep sleep when the reflecting medium (the mind) resolves. When one inquires into the "I"-thought, it dissolves, leaving only the original consciousness, which is never absent.

Different metaphors illustrate this:

- **A face in a mirror:** the reflection is visible, but not independent of either face or mirror.
- **The moon and the sun:** the moon appears bright but only borrows light.
- **A single moon reflected in many jars of water:** it looks like many moons, but there is only one.

This is *pratibimba-vada*, the doctrine of reflection, one of Advaita's ways of explaining how the Self appears as many without ever becoming many. It shows how individuality, though vivid, is ultimately dependent and non-separate from Brahman.

—

Root & Meaning

Prati = counterpart, corresponding
Bimba = image, original
Pratibimba = reflection; an apparent image of the original.
Pratibimba-vada = teaching of reflection of consciousness

Scriptural & Traditional References

- **Shankara's commentaries:** use the mirror and reflection metaphor to explain ego and *jiva*.
- **Mandukya Karika (3.33, with bhashya):** often compared through moon-water imagery.
- **Ramana Maharshi & Swami Paramarthananda:** the ego (*ahankara*) as a reflection in the mind.

Traditional View

- Pure consciousness (*bimba*) is original, unchanging.
- The mind acts as a reflecting medium.
- The ego or sense of individuality is the reflected image (*pratibimba*).
- *Pratibimba* is *mithya* — dependent and temporary, vanishing when the mind resolves.

Vedantic Analysis

- The ego borrows emotions from the mind and awareness from the Self.
- Because we mistake reflected consciousness for original awareness, we identify the Self with the body-mind.

- Inquiry reveals the ego as a reflection only, not the real "I."
- Liberation comes by claiming the original (*bimba*), not the reflection.

Common Misunderstandings

- That the ego is independently real: It vanishes in deep sleep, showing its dependence.
- That the mind is inherently conscious: It only reflects awareness, like the moon reflects the sun.
- That reflections divide the original: Just as many reflections of the moon do not create many moons, many *jivas* do not divide Brahman.

Vedantic Resolution

Pratibimba-vada helps explain how individuality arises without compromising the non-duality of Brahman. The reflection is experienced, but the original is ever the same, untouched, one without a second.

purnatva

(pūrṇatva — *PUUR-nuh-t-vuh*)

The Sanskrit word *purnatva (pūrṇatva)* means "fullness" or "completeness." It comes from the root *purna* ("full, whole, complete") with the abstract suffix *-tva* ("-ness"). In Vedanta, it points not to quantity but to the very nature of the Self (atman) as limitless.

Ordinarily, human life is driven by a sense of *apurnatva* — incompleteness. Desire, fear, and striving all arise from the belief that something is lacking. We seek wholeness through possessions, relationships, accomplishments, or experiences. Yet whatever is gained remains finite, leaving the fundamental sense of want unresolved.

Vedanta teaches that this incompleteness is only a superimposition (*adhyasa*). The Self is already *purna* — whole, lacking nothing. The famous *Purnam-adah* invocation of the *Ishavasya Upanishad* proclaims:

> *Pūrṇam adaḥ pūrṇam idam, pūrṇāt pūrṇam udacyate;*
> *pūrṇasya pūrṇam ādāya, pūrṇam evāvaśiṣyate.*

> "That is full, this is full. From fullness, fullness arises. When fullness is taken from fullness, fullness alone remains."

This verse captures the paradoxical abundance of *purnatva*: nothing added, nothing removed, and yet ever whole.

Practically, recognizing *purnatva* does not mean rejecting the world but seeing it as an expression of wholeness. The wise live without a sense of lack. Desires may arise, but they no longer define the Self. Contentment (*santosha*) and freedom from dependence follow naturally.

—

Root & Meaning

Purna = full, whole, complete
-tva = -ness, abstract state
Purnatva = fullness, completeness, wholeness.

Scriptural References

- **Ishavasya Upanishad Invocation:** *"Pūrṇam adaḥ pūrṇam idam..."*
- **Bhagavad Gita (6.20–22):** describes the state of Self-knowledge as complete satisfaction in the Self.
- **Brihadaranyaka Upanishad (4.3.32):** the Self is infinite, without parts.

Traditional View

- Human suffering arises from a sense of incompleteness (*apurnatva*).
- Liberation (*moksha*) is the recognition of one's inherent *purnatva*.
- The world itself is an expression of fullness, not a source of lack.

Vedantic Analysis

- *Purnatva* is not an attribute acquired, but the very *svarupa* of the Self.
- Mistaking the Self for the limited body-mind creates a sense of want.
- Knowledge reveals that one was never incomplete to begin with.
- The *purnam-adah mantra* illustrates that wholeness is not diminished by division.

Common Misunderstandings

- **That purnatva means worldly abundance:** It is not about possessions or achievements.

- **That it is a mystical experience of bliss:** It is knowledge of one's already-limitless nature.
- **That one must "become" purna:** One already is *purna;* ignorance alone creates the opposite impression.

Vedantic Resolution

Purnatva is the Self's true nature. Liberation is not gaining completeness but recognizing it. To know "I am *purna*" is to end the endless pursuit born of imagined lack.

purusharthas

(puruṣārthas — *pu-ru-SHAAR-thuhs*)

The Sanskrit word *purushartha (puruṣārtha)* means "human goal" (*purusha* = person, *artha* = aim, purpose). Traditional teaching identifies four such aims, which together map the whole field of human striving:

Artha — security, wealth, resources.

Kama — pleasure, enjoyment, fulfillment of desires.

Dharma — virtue, righteousness, alignment with the moral order.

Moksha — liberation, freedom from bondage.

The first three — *artha, kama,* and dharma — are considered universal. Every person, knowingly or unknowingly, seeks security, pleasure, and meaning. The fourth, *moksha,* is unique: the discovery that no object or achievement can provide permanent satisfaction, and that true freedom lies only in Self-knowledge.

The Upanishads and *Bhagavad Gita* repeatedly remind us that the first three goals are valuable but limited. They carry three defects (*doshatraya*):

- *Duhkhamishritatvam* — mixed with pain. Acquiring, keeping, and losing objects always involves suffering.
- *Atriptikaratvam* — incapable of giving lasting fulfillment. Desires are endless; satisfaction is fleeting.
- *Bandhakatvam* — binding. Dependence on objects creates more dependence, moving us away from freedom.

Thus, the wise eventually discover the insufficiency of *artha, kama,* and dharma. As the *Mundaka Upanishad* (1.2.12) says, the discerning person (*brahmanah*) examines the worlds gained through karma and turns away, seeking what is beyond death.

Moksha — freedom from the sense of lack, discovery of *purnatva* (wholeness) — is therefore the ultimate *purushartha*. It does not cancel the others but puts them in perspective: wealth and pleasure are pursued dharmically, dharma itself is valued as a preparation, but liberation is recognized as life's highest aim.

—

Root & Meaning

Purusha = human, person
Artha = aim, goal, purpose
Purushartha = the aims or goals of human life.

Scriptural References

- **Manusmriti (2.224):** identifies the four *purusharthas*.
- **Mundaka Upanishad (1.2.12):** reveals the limitation of *karmaphala* and the turn toward *moksha*.
- **Bhagavad Gita (7.16; 18.66):** discusses seekers motivated by *artha, kama,* and dharma, leading ultimately to liberation.

Traditional View

- The first three goals (*artha, kama, dharma*) sustain worldly life.
- *Moksha*, freedom from samsara, is the highest and unique *purushartha*.
- A balanced life integrates all four, but Vedanta emphasizes *moksha* as the final end.

Vedantic Analysis

- *Artha* and *kama* are natural but must be governed by dharma.
- Dharma itself yields merit (*punya*), but even this is finite.
- The limitations of the first three — pain, dissatisfaction,

dependence — point the seeker to *moksha*.

• *Moksha* is not "gained" but recognized as the nature of the Self.

Common Misunderstandings

• **That moksha is optional:** Vedanta teaches it is the very purpose of human birth.
• **That artha and kama are opposed to moksha:** Properly aligned with dharma, they prepare the mind for higher seeking.
• **That dharma alone is ultimate:** Dharma sustains life but is itself transcended in knowledge.

Vedantic Resolution

The *purusharthas* offer a complete vision of human striving. By living dharmically, enjoying *artha* and *kama* within bounds, and ultimately pursuing *moksha*, life is seen in its wholeness. The highest goal is freedom, not accumulation.

raga-dvesha

(rāga-dveṣa — *RAA-guh-DVAY-shuh*)

In Vedanta, *raga-dvesha (rāga-dveṣa)* means likes (*raga*) and dislikes (*dvesha*). They are the fundamental psychological forces that
color our perception of the world and drive most human action.
While the world is *mithya* — name and form with utility — the
jiva becomes overwhelmed when it treats its likes and dislikes as
absolute.

Swami Dayananda often said: We do not live in the public world
but in a private world of our *raga-dveshas*. Objects and people are
not experienced as they are but through the filter of attraction and
aversion. What I like, I chase; what I dislike, I avoid. These compulsions seem natural but become binding when they override
dharma and reason.

The *Bhagavad Gita* identifies *raga-dvesha* as the seed of samsara.
Krishna advises Arjuna not to fight out of love or hate, but in
alignment with dharma. Duryodhana, ruled by *raga* (for the king-
dom) and *dvesha* (for the Pandavas), exemplifies how they lead to
adharma. Arjuna is told instead: "Take pleasure and pain, gain and
loss, victory and defeat as the same. Do what must be done, not
what your *raga-dvesha* dictates."

From a deeper perspective, *raga-dvesha* arise from a sense of
incompleteness (*apurnatva*). We chase what we think will make
us whole and reject what we think threatens us. But as teachers
remind us, love and hate are never about the object; they are
reflections of our own Self. Desire is destroyed not by suppression
but by recognizing the Self as limitless. Then *raga-dvesha* lose their
binding force.

The yogic disciplines of *shama* (mastery of the mind) and
dama (restraint of the senses) train us to create distance between

ourselves and our impulses. We cannot stop likes and dislikes from arising, but we need not become their servants. Freedom lies in acting by dharma rather than compulsion. Ultimately, a *jnani* may still experience preferences, but they no longer bind; they are like ripples on the surface of the limitless Self.

—

Root & Meaning

Raga = attraction, attachment, like
Dvesha = aversion, dislike, hate
Raga-dvesha = the pair of likes and dislikes.

Scriptural References

- **Bhagavad Gita (2.47–48; 3.34; 6.27):** warns against acting under *raga-dvesha*, teaching equanimity instead.
- **Vivekachudamani:** describes obsession with objects (*vishaya-nuchinta*) as bondage.
- **Mandukya Karika (3.36–37):** Gauḍapada calls obsession with *nama-rupa* (name and form) "*abhutabhinivesha*" (deep clinging).

Traditional View

- *Raga-dvesha* are natural but become binding when compulsive.
- They lead to *adharma* when one acts against what should or should not be done.
- A yogi or *karma yogi* manages *raga-dvesha*, choosing dharma over compulsion.

Vedantic Analysis

- Rooted in ignorance of one's wholeness (*purnatva*), *raga-dvesha* are attempts to secure happiness from objects.
- Desire and fear are two sides of the same coin; both rest on misidentification with limitation.

• Self-knowledge reveals security and fullness as one's true nature, dissolving *raga-dvesha* as binding forces.

Common Misunderstandings

• **That raga-dvesha must be eliminated entirely:** They are inevitable as long as the body-mind functions. The point is to master them, not eradicate them.
• **That following every like/dislike is freedom:** True freedom is not enslavement to impulse but the ability to act with discrimination.
• **That love or hate are about objects:** They reflect one's own relationship to the Self.

Vedantic Resolution

Raga-dvesha lose their power when seen as mere superimpositions on *mithya nama-rupa*. The wise accept likes and dislikes as part of the mind but do not obey them blindly. Mastery of *raga-dvesha* is mastery of life, leading naturally to inner freedom.

rajas

(rajas — *ruh-juhs*)

Rajas is one of the three *gunas* (*sattva, rajas, tamas*) that constitute *prakriti*, the fabric of the manifest world. Where *sattva* reflects clarity, harmony, and knowledge, and *tamas* conceals as inertia, *rajas* projects. It is the restless, dynamic force that drives activity, passion, and desire. Without *rajas*, nothing would move; with unchecked *rajas*, life becomes agitation.

In Vedanta, *rajas* is not condemned — it is necessary. Creation itself is the play of *sattva, rajas,* and *tamas. Rajas* animates the *jiva's* striving: for wealth, relationships, recognition, power, or even spiritual highs. But it is also the source of dissatisfaction. *Rajas* is the fuel of becoming, always chasing what is not yet.

Rajasic devotion is outward, ego-driven, and transactional: praying for circumstances to align with one's likes and dislikes. Even spiritual seekers may be rajasic when they pursue experiences rather than Self-knowledge. Thus, rajas, though a force of life, binds when it is allowed to dictate action without discrimination.

From a psychological standpoint, *rajas* manifests as restlessness, anxiety, competitiveness, ambition, frustration, and scattered energy. Its twin is fear, since every desire contains the fear of not attaining, *rajas* creates time and duality — the sense that fulfillment lies in the next achievement.

The solution in Vedanta is not suppression of *rajas* but mastery through *karma yoga* and inquiry. Rajasic tendencies are harnessed when subordinated to *sattva*: energy applied toward dharmic action, service, and Self-inquiry. Then *rajas* purifies instead of binding. Ultimately, freedom lies in recognizing that one is not the *gunas* but the Awareness in which they appear.

—

Root & Meaning

Rajas (from Sanskrit root *ranj*, "to color, to move, to be passionate"). Meaning: activity, passion, restlessness, projection.

Scriptural References

- **Bhagavad Gita (14.7):** "*Rajas* is of the nature of passion, the source of craving and attachment. It binds by attachment to action."
- **Bhagavad Gita (3.37):** identifies *raga* (desire) and *krodha* (anger) as born of *rajas*.
- **Mandukya Karika:** explains *rajas* as the projecting power of maya, scattering awareness into multiplicity.

Traditional View

- *Rajas* is one of the three *gunas*, responsible for activity and change.
- Necessary for life and action, but binding when it fuels endless desire.
- In spiritual practice, rajasic energy must be guided by dharma and transformed into *sattva*.

Vedantic Analysis

- *Rajas* projects (*vikshepa-shakti*), creating distraction and discontent.
- It expresses as desire, competition, ambition, and constant becoming.
- When harnessed properly, it gives energy for *sadhana* and *karma yoga*.
- Self-knowledge alone resolves rajas by revealing the Self as *akarta*, non-doer.

Common Misunderstandings

- **That rajas is "bad":** It is not evil but a necessary cosmic principle.
- **That spiritual life must eliminate rajas:** In truth, *rajas* is refined and directed, not annihilated.
- **That rajasic devotion equals true bhakti:** Real devotion is surrender, not bargaining.

Vedantic Resolution

Rajas, like all *gunas*, belongs to *prakriti*. The Self is *gunatita*, beyond them. Freedom comes by seeing *rajas* as part of the play of maya, not as "me." Managed through dharma and inquiry, rajasic energy becomes a stepping-stone to liberation.

rishi

(ṛṣi — *ri-shee*)

In the Vedantic tradition, a *rishi* (*ṛṣi*) is not the author of the Vedas but a seer (*mantradrashta*) — one who "saw" or directly intuited the mantras of the Vedas as pure revelations (*shruti*). The *rishi* is not a creator but a recipient of eternal knowledge that was not authored by any person.

The *rishis* are the transparent mediums through whom *Ishvara* (the total mind) revealed the eternal, impersonal truths of the Vedas. As Swami Paramarthananda states, the *rishis* functioned much like a TV set receiving a broadcast from an unseen transmission center — the Lord. They are the receivers, not originators, of these subtle sound-forms.

While the *rishis* revealed timeless truths, they themselves were not immune to the cultural and psychological limitations of their time. This can be difficult to reconcile, especially when one encounters disturbing passages in the *shastra* — such as those condoning violence against women, which seem in direct conflict with core values like *ahimsa*.

The key insight here is that while the *shruti* is considered infallible, the human vessels — *rishis* — are not. While scripture was revealed to them, it did not come from them. They remained human, subject to *gunas* and the limitations of their *jiva* identities. This demands the maturity to distinguish between the purity of the teaching and the fallibility of its medium.

Vedanta regards revelation not as divine whimsy or personal vision, but as the uncovering of what is already always true. Just as Einstein did not invent gravity but uncovered its principles, the rishi "discovered" eternal truths already embedded in reality.

This is what makes Vedanta unique: it is not a religion or belief system but a means of knowledge (*pramana*) that reveals the self-evident nature of reality through precise inquiry.

In conclusion, a *rishi* is not a prophet or preacher, but a seer — someone who received and preserved the impersonal and eternal wisdom of the Vedas. They were both sacred and flawed, channels of light and yet subject to shadow. Their gift is not their perfection, but their transmission.

—

Root & Meaning

Rishi — from the Sanskrit root rsh ("to see, to flow toward, to move"), meaning "seer" or "sage." In the Vedic tradition, rishis are those who have directly perceived (darshana) the mantras of the Vedas. They are not considered "authors" of the scriptures but the mediums through which the eternal Vedic wisdom was revealed.

Scriptural References

Nature of the rishi as seer, not author:

- **Rig Veda 10.71.3:** Speaks of the *rishi* as *mantradrashtah* ("seers of the mantras"), not creators.
- **Brihadaranyaka Upanishad 2.4.10:** Knowledge is not man-made; it is "spoken" by the Self.
- **Mundaka Upanishad 1.1.1–1.1.2:** Names the ancient *rishi* (e.g., Angiras) to whom Brahma (deity of creation) revealed the knowledge.

The Veda as eternal and authorless:

- **Shvetashvatara Upanishad 6.8:** The Veda is *apaurusheya* (not of human origin).
- **Bhagavad Gita 3.15:** "The Veda comes from the Imperishable

(*akshara*)."

Human limitation of the seers:

- **Chandogya Upanishad 7.1.2:** Even the learned must be taught; a reminder that individuals, however wise, remain limited in other respects.
- **Brihadaranyaka Upanishad 1.4.10:** The Self is beyond all the roles and limitations of individuals, including the *rishis*.

Revelation as discovery, not invention:

- **Katha Upanishad 1.2.15:** Truth is "seen" by the wise in their hearts.
- **Rig Veda 1.164.39:** Eternal truth is "seen" by the sages in manifold ways.

Traditional View

In the Vedic worldview, rishis are inspired seers who, through purity of mind and intense meditation, "saw" (intuited) the eternal truths of the Veda. The mantras they perceived are considered apaurusheya — not of human origin — hence the *rishis* are vehicles rather than composers. Traditionally, seven primordial sages (*saptarshi*) are said to have preserved Vedic knowledge for humanity.

Vedantic Analysis

Vedanta honors the *rishi* not merely as mystics but as transmitters of Self-knowledge (*atma-vidya*). They serve as the archetype of the qualified teacher (*shrotriya* and *brahma-nishtha*) — someone who has both scriptural mastery and direct realization. Their "seeing" refers to the clear recognition of Brahman as their own Self, which is then expressed in the poetic form of mantras and teachings.

From the Advaitic standpoint, the *rishi* are part of the empirical

order (*vyavaharika-satta*). Their role is indispensable within
maya for transmitting the means of knowledge (*pramana*), but
the truth they point to is beyond all persons, including the
rishi themselves.

Common Misunderstandings

- **"Rishis invented the Vedas."** They did not invent but perceived
  them in deep states of meditation; the Vedas are beginningless.
- **"Rishis are omniscient or superhuman in every sense."** They
  had extraordinary insight into dharma and Brahman but were
  still embodied beings subject to the laws of *prakriti*.
- **"Anyone with mystical visions is a rishi."** The title is re-
  served for those whose vision accords with *shruti* and leads to
  liberation.

Vedantic Resolution

In Vedanta, the authority of *shruti* rests on the unique status of the
rishi as direct perceivers of eternal truths, free from personal bias.
The seeker benefits from revering the lineage of *rishi*, not out of
blind worship, but as an acknowledgment of the human channel
through which the timeless knowledge of the Self flows.

rita

(ṛta — *ri-tuh*)

Rita (ṛta) is one of the earliest Vedic concepts, meaning cosmic order, truth, and harmony. Long before Vedanta refined terms like dharma and *Ishvara*, the *Rig Veda* spoke of rita as the underlying principle that sustains the universe.

It is the law by which the sun rises, seasons turn, rivers flow, and sacrifice (*yajna*) bears fruit. To live in accord with *rita* was to live in harmony with both nature and the divine order. Later Hindu thought absorbed this concept into dharma (righteous conduct) and *Ishvara* (the cosmic intelligence upholding the world).

In Advaita Vedanta, *rita* can be understood as an early expression of what is later identified as *Ishvara's* order. It shows that reality is not chaotic or arbitrary, but deeply patterned and reliable. The world of *vyavahara* (transactional reality) functions because *rita* governs it.

For the seeker, this recognition fosters trust (*shraddha*): the universe is lawful, and self-knowledge is possible because truth is woven into its fabric.

—

Root & Meaning

From the Sanskrit root *r* = to rise, to move in a fitting way.
Rita = order, truth, cosmic law.

Scriptural References

- **Rig Veda 10.190.1:** "*Rita* and *satya* were born of *tapas*."
- **Rig Veda 1.164.43:** The sun follows *rita*.

Later texts: *rita* becomes embedded within the idea of dharma.

Traditional View

- The principle of cosmic order in the Vedic worldview.
- Governs natural cycles, moral law, and ritual efficacy.
- The forerunner of later concepts of dharma and *Ishvara's* order.

Vedantic Analysis

- In Vedanta, *rita* is seen as the manifestation of *Ishvara's* intelligence.
- Without such order, empirical reality (*vyavahara*) would collapse.
- Recognition of *rita* supports faith in the teaching: that truth is discoverable.

Common Misunderstandings

- **That rita is only ritual law:** It is broader — the order of both nature and morality.
- **That rita and dharma are identical:** Dharma is the later, more human-centered application; *rita* is the cosmic principle.
- **That rita implies fatalism:** It implies order, not determinism.

Vedantic Resolution

Rita is the Vedic recognition of cosmic order — an early term for the intelligence of *Ishvara's* order. It ensures the reliability of the universe and provides the ground for dharma and knowledge.

sadhana

(sādhana — *SAA-dhuh-nuh*)

In general, *sadhana (sādhana)* refers to any spiritual practice undertaken to reach a goal. It can take many forms. For example, yoga systems like *raja yoga, bhakti yoga,* or *mantra yoga,* or even simple activities like listening, reading, writing, or meditating.

However, in the context of Vedanta, *sadhana* specifically refers to the disciplined means by which one removes ignorance. The process is traditionally outlined in three main stages:

- **Karma Yoga** – purification of the mind through action and attitude
- **Upasana Yoga** – steadiness and concentration of the mind through worship, meditation and spiritual discipline
- **Jnana Yoga** – the yoga of knowledge, consisting of:-
  - *Shravana* – systematic listening to the teachings
  - *Manana* – rational reflection to resolve doubts
  - *Nididhyasana* – sustained contemplation to assimilate the truth

Each stage prepares the seeker for the next. Many want to jump straight into meditating on the Self, but without knowledge of the Self, there is nothing meaningful to meditate on. And without a purified and steady mind, knowledge cannot take root.

Therefore, one's choice of *sadhana* should be appropriate to their current level of preparedness. Western seekers, in particular, often attempt to skip *karma yoga* and *upasana yoga,* eager to go straight to *jnana.* But most eventually discover that they need to revisit the foundational practices they overlooked in order to fully assimilate and live the truth they seek.

—

Root & Meaning

Sadhana — from the Sanskrit root *sadh* ("to accomplish, to achieve, to bring about"), meaning "means to an end" or "method of attainment." In spiritual contexts, it refers to any disciplined practice undertaken to achieve a desired goal, especially Self-knowledge (*atma-jnana*) or liberation (*moksha*).

Scriptural References

General meaning of sadhana:

- **Bhagavad Gita 6.46–47:** Krishna praises disciplined practice and shows gradations of yogis, culminating in the *jnani*.
- **Mundaka Upanishad 3.2.3–4:** Speaks of the seeker approaching a teacher "with a mind calm and collected" to gain knowledge.

Karma yoga – purification of mind:

- **Bhagavad Gita 2.47:** "You have a right to action alone, not to its fruits."
- **Bhagavad Gita 3.19:** Acting without attachment purifies and prepares the mind for knowledge.

Upasana yoga – concentration and devotion:

- **Bhagavad Gita 12.2:** "Those who fix their mind on Me with supreme faith are most united in yoga."
- **Chandogya Upanishad 7.1.1:** Recommends meditation (*upasana*) on that which is infinite for steadying the mind.

Jnana yoga – knowledge of the Self:

- **Bhagavad Gita 4.34:** "Approach a teacher, question, and serve; the wise will teach you the truth."
- **Brihadaranyaka Upanishad 2.4.5:** "The Self should be heard, reflected upon, and meditated upon." (*shravana–manana–nididhyasana* framework)

Preparedness for sadhana:

- **Bhagavad Gita 6.35:** "Through practice (*abhyasa*) and detachment (*vairagya*), the mind can be restrained."
- **Vivekachudamani 19–20:** Lists the fourfold qualifications (*sadhana-chatushtaya*) necessary before Self-inquiry.

Traditional View

Traditionally, *sadhana* is any spiritual discipline that purifies and prepares the mind for realization. It can include ritual worship (*puja*), mantra chanting (*japa*), meditation (*dhyana*), selfless service (*seva*), study of scripture (*svadhyaya*), and observance of ethical restraints (*yamas*) and observances (*niyamas*). A central element in Vedantic tradition is the *sadhana-chatushtaya*, the four qualifications:

- **Viveka** — discrimination between the eternal and the transient
- **Vairagya** — dispassion toward sensory enjoyments here and hereafter
- **Shat-sampat** — sixfold discipline (e.g., mental control, sense restraint)
- **Mumukshutva** — burning desire for liberation

Vedantic Analysis

In Advaita Vedanta, *sadhana* is not about "creating" liberation but about preparing the mind to recognize the liberation that is already true of the Self. A mind clouded by distraction, attachment, or agitation cannot assimilate the teaching (*shravana–manana–nididhyasana*). Therefore, *sadhana* operates in the preparatory stage (*adhikaritva-sampatti*), making the intellect subtle, steady, and non-reactive, so that the knowledge "I am Brahman" is not merely heard but fully owned.

Common Misunderstandings

- **"Sadhana produces moksha."** *Moksha* is not a product; *sadhana* removes ignorance so that *moksha* is recognized.
- **"The more intense the sadhana, the faster the liberation."** Intensity helps, but without right understanding of the Self, practice alone cannot bring realization.
- **"Sadhana is only for beginners."** Even advanced seekers maintain certain disciplines to preserve mental clarity.

Vedantic Resolution

Vedanta resolves confusion by affirming that *sadhana* is a means of mental purification, not an end in itself. The liberated one may no longer need formal *sadhana*, but until realization is firm, steady practice — rooted in right knowledge — is essential.

sadhana-chatushtaya

(sādhana-catuṣṭaya
— *SAA-dhuh-nuh-chuh-TUSH-tuh-ya*)

In Advaita Vedanta, not everyone is immediately qualified for Self-inquiry. The mind must first be ripened, just as a fruit must mature before it can naturally fall from the tree. Shankara prescribes four essential qualifications, known as *sadhana-chatushtaya* (*sādhana-catuṣṭaya*) — the "fourfold means" — which prepare a seeker for the pursuit of liberation.

The first is *viveka*, discrimination between the eternal (*nitya*) and the ephemeral (*anitya*). This clarity comes through deep reflection on experience: recognizing that worldly pursuits — wealth, pleasure, recognition — do not bring lasting fulfillment. From this insight arises *vairagya*, dispassion or detachment. It is not hatred of the world, but a natural loosening of dependence upon it, born of the recognition that external gains cannot complete me.

The third qualification is *shamadi-shatka-sampatti*, the "sixfold wealth" of inner discipline:

1. **Shama** — mastery of the mind.
2. **Dama** — restraint of the senses.
3. **Uparati** — withdrawal from distractions, dwelling in one's duty and study.
4. **Titiksha** — endurance of life's opposites with cheerfulness.
5. **Shraddha** — trust in the teacher and *shastra* as a valid means of knowledge.
6. **Samadhana** — single-pointedness, the ability to focus on the Self.

Together, these virtues refine the mind into an instrument capable of subtle inquiry.

The final and most decisive qualification is *mumukshutva*, the burning desire for liberation. Shankara and later teachers emphasize its intensity: like a drowning man longs for air, the seeker must long for freedom from limitation. Without this, the other disciplines lack fuel.

Vedanta differs from Yoga or Samkhya in that these practices are not ends in themselves but means to prepare the mind for Self-knowledge. Knowledge alone liberates; *sadhana-chatushtaya* ensures the seeker is ready to assimilate it. Thus, these fourfold qualifications mark the transition from seeker (*jijnasu*) to true disciple (*adhikari*), ripening the mind for the revelation of "*tat tvam asi*" — you are That.

—

Root & Meaning

Sadhana = discipline, practice, qualification.
Chatushtaya = fourfold.
Sadhana-Chatushtaya = the fourfold means of qualification for Vedanta.

The Four Qualifications:

1. **Viveka** — discrimination between eternal and ephemeral.
2. **Vairagya** — dispassion from transient enjoyments.
3. **Shamadi-shatka-sampatti** — sixfold inner wealth:
   - *Shama* (mind-control)
   - *Dama* (sense-restraint)
   - *Uparati* (withdrawal)
   - Titiksha (forbearance)
   - *Shraddha* (faith)
   - *Samadhana* (concentration)
4. **Mumukshutva** — burning desire for liberation.

Scriptural References

- **Tattva Bodha (Shankara):** lists the four qualifications as prerequisites for inquiry into the Self.
- **Bhagavad Gita (7.16, 7.17):** distinguishes seekers of different motives, pointing toward the *mumukshu*.
- **Vivekachudamani (v. 19–31):** elaborates on discrimination, dispassion, and the sixfold virtues.

Traditional View

- A seeker with these qualifications is an *adhikari*, fit for Self-knowledge.
- Without them, study of *shastra* remains intellectual and fails to liberate.
- Like ripening fruit, the mind must mature naturally through discipline and exposure to dharma.

Vedantic Analysis

- The four means address three main obstacles: ignorance (*avarana*), impurity (*mala*), and agitation (*vikshepa*).
- *Karma yoga* and *upasana yoga* cultivate these qualifications, preparing the ground for *jnana yoga*.
- Ultimately, *sadhana-chatushtaya* is not liberation itself, but the doorway to it.

Common Misunderstandings

- **That anyone can study Vedanta directly:** Shankara insists only an *adhikari* benefits.
- **That vairagya is renunciation of life:** It is dispassion, not avoidance.
- **That mumukshutva is a mild wish:** It must be an intense, overriding desire.

Vedantic Resolution

The fourfold qualifications are like tuning an instrument; without them, the *shastra's* melody cannot be played. For one who has cultivated discrimination, dispassion, discipline, and desire for liberation, the teachings reveal the ever-free Self directly.

Saguna Brahman

(Saguṇa Brahman — *sa-GOO-nuh bruh-muhn*)

In Advaita Vedanta, *Saguna Brahman* means "Brahman with attributes (*gunas*)." It is Brahman understood through the conditioning power of maya — the same Reality that appears as the ordered, intelligent universe.

Because pure Brahman (*Nirguna Brahman*) is beyond all concept, the mind requires a relational standpoint to contemplate the Absolute. *Saguna Brahman* offers this: the manifest aspect of Brahman, endowed with qualities such as knowledge, power, compassion, and justice. Through this lens, Brahman appears as *Ishvara* — the creator, sustainer, and dissolver of the cosmos — and may also be worshipped as Bhagavan, the personal Lord of devotion (God).

In Advaita, however, *Ishvara* is not a personified super-being that lives in the sky, but the impersonal order and intelligence that pervades all things. Bhagavan is the same Reality seen through the heart; *Ishvara* is that Reality seen through the intellect. Both are valid expressions of *Saguna Brahman*, provisional standpoints that reveal the sacred harmony of the universe.

From the empirical standpoint (*vyavaharika satya*), *Saguna Brahman* is real and indispensable. It accounts for dharma, karma, and the moral architecture of existence. Yet from the absolute standpoint (*paramarthika satya*), even this divine manifestation is *mithya* — dependent upon the attributeless *Nirguna Brahman*, pure awareness itself.

Bhakti (devotion) toward *Saguna Brahman* purifies and steadies the mind, preparing it for Self-knowledge. When the distinction between the worshipper and the worshipped dissolves, *Saguna* resolves back into *Nirguna* — and the seeker recognizes the truth: there was never any difference.

Root & Meaning

Sa = with + *guna* = qualities, attributes.
Saguna Brahman = Brahman conceived with qualities, attributes, and functions.

Scriptural References

- Bhagavad Gita 12.1–5: contrasts worship of the manifest (saguna) and the unmanifest (nirguna).
- Brhadaranyaka Upanishad 3.9.26: Ishvara described as omniscient and ruler of all beings.
- Shankara's commentaries: emphasize Saguna Brahman as provisional, a standpoint for devotion and meditation.

Traditional View

- *Saguna Brahman* = *Ishvara*, God with attributes.
- Object of meditation, devotion, and *upasana* (worship).
- Governs karma and dharma.
- Preparatory means for knowledge of *Nirguna Brahman*.

Vedantic Analysis

- *Saguna Brahman* is *vyavaharika satya* (empirical reality).
- Ultimately *mithya*, since Brahman is attribute-free.
- Functions as the total order (cosmic, moral, and psychological).
- May be related to personally (Bhagavan) or contemplated impersonally (*Ishvara*).

Both understandings purify and mature the mind toward Self-knowledge.

Common Misunderstandings

- **That Saguna Brahman is "less real" than Nirguna:** Both are Brahman, but viewed from different standpoints.
- **That devotion to Saguna Brahman is inferior:** It is a valid and powerful path of purification (*bhakti yoga*).
- **That Ishvara and Bhagavan are different deities:** they are two lenses through which the same Reality is seen.
- **That Ishvara is a "cosmic person":** in Advaita, *Ishvara* is the impersonal order itself — Brahman operating through *maya*.

Vedantic Resolution

Saguna Brahman is Brahman viewed through the conditioning of maya, as *Ishvara*. When approached through love and relationship, this same Reality appears as Bhagavan. Both perspectives are provisional yet sacred, leading the seeker toward the realization of *Nirguna Brahman*, where no distinction remains between knower, known, and knowing.

sakshi

(sākṣi — *SAAK-shee*)

In Vedanta, *sakshi (sākṣī)* means the witness — pure awareness that illumines all experiences without itself being affected. The word comes from *sam* + *aksha* ("together with the eyes"), suggesting that which "sees" or "observes." Unlike the organs of perception, which see objects, *sakshi* is the unchanging presence in which the mind, senses, and body are revealed.

Every moment of life is known only because of this witnessing consciousness. Waking experiences, dreams, even the blankness of deep sleep are illumined by *sakshi*. In waking, it lights up the external world; in dream, the inner projections; in deep sleep, the absence of objects. It is never absent, though the mind may not register its constancy.

A Preliminary Teaching

Teachers often introduce *sakshi* as an accessible entry point into Self-knowledge. For example, by asking what has witnessed one as a child, youth, teenager, career-builder, family-maker, etc. In this way, individuals recognize that while the body, mind, and roles have changed, there is an unbroken witness throughout.

This simple recognition helps students dis-identify from the ego (*ahankara*) and see that they are not limited to changing attributes. It is a practical tool for shifting perspective from "I am my story" to "I am the unchanging knower of my story."

Beyond Duality

At the same time, Vedanta cautions that *sakshi* is only a *prakriya* (teaching method). Left unexamined, it can create the impression of two entities — a witness and a witnessed. In truth, there are not two: awareness is non-dual. What seems to be a witness standing apart from experience is simply consciousness itself, the one in and through which all appearances arise and subside.

Thus, the *sakshi* teaching is provisional — a skillful means to guide seekers toward their true identity as limitless awareness (*turiya*). Once the student grasps this, even the distinction "witness vs. witnessed" is dissolved, leaving only the Self.

—

Root & Meaning

Sakshi = witness, observer (*sam + aksha*).
The witnessing consciousness that illumines all experience.

Scriptural References

- **Brihadaranyaka Upanishad (3.7.23):** the Self is "the seer, unseen; the hearer, unheard."
- **Katha Upanishad (2.2.13):** "The Self is the witness, the inner ruler, the source of all."
- **Bhagavad Gita (13.22):** "The Self is called the witness, the consenter, the supporter, the experiencer, the great Lord, the supreme Self."

Traditional View

- *Sakshi* is not an agent but the unchanging knower.
- Present in all three states — waking, dream, deep sleep.
- Used as an introductory model to help the seeker step back from identification with the body-mind.

Vedantic Analysis

- *Sakshi* illumines but does not act.
- As a teaching, it helps break identification with the ego.
- Ultimately, the duality implied by "witness vs. witnessed" is resolved: there is only non-dual awareness.
- *Sakshi* is therefore both a doorway and a pointer to what is beyond concepts.

Common Misunderstandings

- **That sakshi is a subtle entity inside watching:** In truth, it is awareness itself.
- **That sakshi participates in events:** It merely illumines, without acting.
- **That sakshi is the final teaching:** It is a provisional step, leading to recognition of non-dual Self.

Vedantic Resolution

The *sakshi* teaching is a powerful first step in Self-inquiry, helping seekers see the changeless presence behind life's changing roles. But its ultimate purpose is to dissolve even the notion of "witness," revealing non-dual awareness — limitless, ever free.

samadhana

(samādhāna — *suh-mĀ-dhĀ-na*)

In Vedanta, *samadhana (samādhāna)* means one-pointedness or focused attention. It is the discipline of settling the mind on the pursuit of Self-knowledge, free from distraction and dispersion. The word comes from *sam* (together, complete) + *dhana* (placing, holding), meaning "to hold together steadily."

In the traditional enumeration of the four qualifications for Self-inquiry (*sadhana-chatushtaya*), *samadhana* arises under the third qualification — discipline (*shat-sampatti*). The seeker is prescribed many disciplines, starting with *shama* (mastery of mind) and culminating in *samadhana* (steadfast concentration). Together, they prepare the seeker for *mumukshutva*, the final and indispensable longing for liberation.

Among the six disciplines, *samadhana* is the fruit of all that precedes it. When the mind is tranquil (*shama*), restrained (*dama*), withdrawn (*uparati*), enduring (*titiksha*), and trusting (*shraddha*), it naturally attains *samadhana* — a steady, undistracted absorption in the pursuit of Truth. In this way, *samadhana* represents not only composure but the ripened capacity of a purified mind to remain fixed on the Self, ready for the knowledge that alone brings freedom.

Traditional teachers emphasize that *samadhana* is not about forcing the mind into unnatural rigidity. It is steadiness born of clarity. When a seeker truly knows that liberation is the only lasting aim, their mind naturally aligns with that pursuit. Just as a river flows steadily to the ocean once its course is set, so too the mind flows toward Self-inquiry when *samadhana* is firm.

The *Bhagavad Gita* (6.18) describes yoga as the state in which the mind "remains steady, fixed on the Self, free from longing for anything else." In this sense, *samadhana* is both a fruit of *viveka* (discrimination) and *vairagya* (dispassion) and a necessary support for *nididhyasana* (contemplation). It is the inner alignment without which Vedanta remains fragmented study rather than transformative knowledge.

—

Root & Meaning

Sam = together, complete
Dhana = placing, holding
Samadhana = steadiness, one-pointedness, holding the mind firmly on Self-knowledge.

Scriptural References

- **Tattva Bodha (Shankara):** defines *samadhana* as concentration of the mind on Brahman.
- **Bhagavad Gita (6.18):** describes yoga as steadiness of the mind in the Self.
- **Vivekachudamani (v. 25):** "The mind should be steadily fixed on Brahman and nothing else — this is *samadhana*."

Traditional View

In the traditional enumeration of the four qualifications for Self-inquiry (*sadhana-chatushtaya*), *samadhana* arises under the third qualification — discipline (*shat-sampatti*), the six-fold inner wealth.

These six disciplines are:

1. *Shama* — mastery of the mind
2. *Dama* — control of the senses
3. *Uparati* — withdrawal from worldly engagement

4. *Titiksha* — endurance amid opposites
5. *Shraddha* — faith in the scriptures and teacher
6. *Samadhana* — steadfast concentration

The seeker progresses through these in order, refining the instrument of the mind until it becomes capable of sustained inquiry. *Samadhana* is therefore the culmination of inner discipline and the sign of true preparedness.

Vedantic Analysis

Vedanta defines *samadhana* not as a trance-like absorption or yogic *samadhi*, but as the mind's mature steadiness in the pursuit of knowledge. It is the quiet alignment of thought and attention toward the Self, free from agitation and distraction.

This inner stillness is the natural outcome of purification. When the mind is calm (*shama*), the senses restrained (*dama*), and faith firm (*shraddha*), attention no longer wanders. The intellect becomes a polished mirror capable of reflecting the truth of Brahman without distortion.

Thus, *samadhana* bridges the disciplines of preparation and the dawn of knowledge itself. It is the poised readiness of the mind that, when exposed to Vedantic teaching, recognizes its own nature as limitless awareness.

Common Misunderstandings

- **That samadhana is trance-like absorption:** In Vedanta it means steady focus on Self-knowledge, not yogic samadhi.
- **That it requires rigid suppression of thought:** It is steadiness through clarity, not brute force.
- **That it is optional:** Without one-pointedness, Vedanta becomes intellectual juggling rather than liberating vision.

Vedantic Resolution

Samadhana is the mind's unwavering alignment with the pursuit of Self-knowledge. It is the final jewel of the sixfold wealth, integrating the earlier disciplines and ensuring that the seeker's life and attention flow toward liberation.

samadhi

(samādhi — *suh-MAA-dhee*)

Few words in Indian philosophy carry as much weight — or as much confusion — as *samadhi (samādhi)*. In the Yoga tradition, it is the crown jewel of practice: the final limb of Patanjali's *ashtanga yoga*, where meditation culminates in absorption. To many, samadhi represents the moment when the restless movements of the mind are silenced and awareness rests in itself.

But Vedanta makes an important distinction. While Yoga defines *samadhi* as a state of the mind, Advaita Vedanta insists that the Self is never a state. All states — waking, dream, deep sleep, or even *nirvikalpa samadhi* — are temporary. They come and go in awareness. The Self is the witness of these states, not one more state among them.

Swami Dayananda puts it simply: meditation that becomes continuous and effortless absorption is called *samadhi*. Yet Vedanta reminds us that liberation (*moksha*) is not absorption but knowledge: recognizing that one was never bound. Experiences, however elevated, cannot accomplish this. As long as the intellect (*buddhi*) is dormant in *nirvikalpa samadhi*, no knowledge can arise. At best, *samadhi* is a valuable discipline that prepares the mind by cultivating stillness, focus, and *sattva*.

Classical texts describe many kinds of *samadhi* — *savikalpa* (with distinctions), *nirvikalpa* (without distinctions), *sahaja* (natural, effortless). These point to gradations of meditative absorption, but Advaita Vedanta ultimately redefines the word. *Samadhi* is not an altered state but the assimilation of knowledge: a mind that values every experience equally because it sees all as Brahman. In this sense, *samadhi* is synonymous with freedom.

—

Root & Meaning

Samadhi — from *sama* ("even, balanced, complete") + *dhi* ("intellect, understanding"). Literally: "a mind in balance" or "absorbed understanding."

Scriptural References

- **Yoga Sutras of Patanjali (1.2, 1.41):** *samadhi* as *chitta-vritti-nirodhah* — stilling of the thought-waves, absorption into the object of meditation.
- **Bhagavad Gita (6.18–20):** describes *samadhi* as the state of one whose mind is steady, resting in the Self alone.
- **Aparokshanubhuti (124):** defines samadhi as dissolving all thoughts, where even the thought "I am Brahman" is dropped, and one abides as Brahman.

Traditional View

- **Yoga:** the climax of meditation, absorption in the object or in pure awareness.
- **Vedanta:** emphasizes that *samadhi* is not liberation itself but can be a preparatory aid. True freedom comes only through self-knowledge (*jnana*).
- **Ramana Maharshi:** distinguishes *savikalpa, nirvikalpa*, and *sahaja samadhi* — only the last, natural and effortless abidance in the Self, corresponds to liberation.

Vedantic Analysis

- **Savikalpa samadhi:** absorption with distinctions; intellect still active, insights possible.
- **Nirvikalpa samadhi:** absorption without distinctions; intellect dormant, no assimilation possible.
- **Sahaja samadhi:** natural abidance in Self-knowledge — not a state, but continuous recognition of one's true nature.

- **The highest samadhi in Advaita is not a trance but a shift in vision:** knowing that all states are illumined by the Self, which never changes.

Common Misunderstandings

- **That samadhi equals moksha:** Liberation is not a state but knowledge of the ever-free Self.
- **That the Self can be "experienced" in samadhi:** The Self is the experiencer, never an object of experience.
- **That Yoga and Vedanta prescribe the same samadhi:** In Yoga, it is a state of mind; in Vedanta, it is the assimilation of knowledge.

Vedantic Resolution

Samadhi is valuable for purifying and steadying the mind, but it is not the goal. True *samadhi* is not "going beyond" the mind but understanding that the Self is ever free, whether the mind is active or still. When every thought is seen as illumined by Brahman, the intellect is balanced (*sama-dhi*), and the seeker lives in natural abidance.

samatvam

(samatvam — *suh-muh-t-vuhm*)

To live in the world without being moved by it—this is *samatvam*. It is not indifference, but poise; not suppression, but clarity. When pleasure and pain arise, the ordinary mind tilts. It reaches for one, resists the other, and in doing so, it loses its center. Samatvam is the recovery of that center — the recognition that all movements of experience happen in something unmoving.

Life is nothing if not motion. Gain and loss, success and failure, joy and grief — the pendulum never stops. To demand stillness from the world is folly. Yet there is another kind of stillness, one that does not depend on events. It is the stillness of awareness itself, untouched by what passes through it. When this stillness is recognized, *samatvam* arises naturally.

The *Bhagavad Gita* calls *samatvam yoga ucyate* — "Equanimity is yoga." The phrase is as simple as it is radical. Yoga is often imagined as union, but here Krishna defines it as balance: the steady wisdom that neither elates in success nor despairs in failure. Such balance is not cultivated by force; it comes from understanding. When one knows "I am the awareness in which all opposites arise," the pairs lose their power.

True *samatvam* is not the denial of emotion. The sage feels fully, perhaps more deeply than others, but without distortion. Pleasure may arise, but it does not bind; pain may visit, but it does not define. This is not because the sage is cold, but because he knows what he is not. His peace is not won from the world; it is inherent.

In an age ruled by extremes, *samatvam* may seem lifeless. Modern culture rewards reaction — instant outrage, instant elation. But equanimity is not dullness; it is lucidity. To be unmoved by madness is not to be asleep — it is to be awake when others dream.

In the presence of one established in *samatvam*, the world's fever cools. The flame of passion burns clear without smoke.

To stand in *samatvam* is to stand at the heart of reality itself, where opposites dissolve. Not as two, not as one, but as that which precedes both — the silent witness of all becoming.

—

Root & Meaning

From the Sanskrit root *sama* ("even," "balanced," "equal") and the suffix *-tvam* ("-ness," or "state of being"), *samatvam* literally means "evenness of mind." It denotes equanimity, the steady composure of one who remains unshaken by the fluctuations of pleasure and pain.

Scriptural References

- **Bhagavad Gita 2.48:** *"Yogasthah kuru karmani sangam tyaktva dhananjaya, siddhy-asiddhyoh samo bhutva samatvam yoga ucyate."* — "Perform your duty, O Arjuna, remaining steadfast in yoga, abandoning attachment, and balanced in success and failure. Equanimity is called yoga."
- **Bhagavad Gita 2.38:** "Treat alike pleasure and pain, gain and loss, victory and defeat; then engage in battle."

Traditional View

Samatvam is the fruit of *jnana* and *karma yoga*. It cannot be faked or forced. The aspirant practices detachment in action, offering results to *Ishvara*; the wise man abides effortlessly in the Self, to whom outcomes are irrelevant. In both, *samatvam* is the hallmark of maturity.

Vedantic Analysis

All emotional disturbance arises from identification with the *ahankara* — the "I" that believes it acts and experiences. When this I-notion dissolves in understanding, experience continues, but bondage ends. Samatvam is the mind purified of personal claims, reflecting awareness like a still lake reflects the sky.

It is not a moral posture, but a cognitive clarity: the knowledge that all experiences belong to the field (*prakriti*), not to me, the witnessing consciousness. The sage does not try to be even-minded; he simply sees no reason not to be.

Common Misunderstandings

- **Equanimity as passivity:** *Samatvam* does not mean disengagement. The wise act vigorously, but without anxiety or personal agenda.
- **Emotional dullness:** The equanimous person feels fully, but from a depth untouched by reaction.
- **Stoic restraint:** *Samatvam* is not self-control but self-knowledge — the quiet result of seeing reality as it is.

Vedantic Resolution

Equanimity is freedom in motion. The world may swing between opposites, but the one who knows the Self stands unshaken. As Krishna tells Arjuna, "The serene mind is established in wisdom." When action flows without disturbance, and perception remains clear in all conditions, samatvam is complete.

sampradaya

(sampradāya — *suhm-pruh-DAA-yuh*)

In Vedanta, *sampradaya (sampradāya)* means a teaching tradition —
the living transmission of knowledge from teacher to student.
While the scriptures (*shruti*) are the ultimate source of wisdom,
they require a method of interpretation and communication to
unfold their subtle meaning. This is what the *sampradaya*
provides: a consistent methodology (*prakriya*) passed down
through generations of qualified teachers.

Shankara emphasizes that Vedanta cannot be learned by independent speculation or personal interpretation of texts. Without the
unfolding of a teacher rooted in a *sampradaya*, the seeker risks misunderstanding, mistaking intellectual insight or mystical experience for self-knowledge.

Each *sampradaya* has a lineage (*guru-shishya parampara*), preserving
not only scripture but also methodology — the precise way the
teaching is introduced, doubts are removed, and assimilation is
encouraged. Though multiple *sampradaya* exist, their purpose is
the same: to reveal the non-dual Self.

Thus, *sampradaya* is not rigid sectarianism but a safeguard: it
ensures that the teaching remains faithful to the vision of the
Upanishads while adapting to the needs of the student.

—

Root & Meaning

From *sam* (together, completely) + *pra* (forth) + *daya* (giving).
Sampradaya = that which is handed down, a tradition or
transmission.

Scriptural References

- **Bhagavad Gita 4.2:** "This yoga was handed down (*parampara*) through tradition (*sampradaya*)."
- **Shankara's commentaries:** stress the need for learning Vedanta through *sampradaya* and not self-study alone.

Traditional View

- A lineage of teachers transmitting methodology and insight.
- Ensures continuity, clarity, and protection of the vision of Vedanta.
- Central to authenticity: without *sampradaya*, the teaching risks distortion.

Vedantic Analysis

- *Shruti* (scripture) is the ultimate authority.
- *Sampradaya* is the means by which *shruti* is unfolded to the student.
- Teacher, teaching, and methodology must all align.
- Protects against the ego's tendency to reinterpret the teaching for personal convenience.

Common Misunderstandings

- **That sampradaya is sectarian:** It is not about dogma but about preserving clarity of method.
- **That one can bypass sampradaya with self-study:** Without methodology, subtle points are easily missed.
- **That sampradaya is opposed to inquiry:** It is inquiry within a tested framework.

Vedantic Resolution

Sampradaya is the living teaching tradition of Vedanta, the indispensable medium for scripture to become knowledge in the student.

samsara

(saṁsāra — *suhm-SAA-ruh*)

The word *samsara (saṁsāra)* comes from the Sanskrit root *sr,* meaning "to flow," and is often translated as "wandering" or "continuous flow." It suggests movement without rest, a perpetual current of change that characterizes all of empirical existence. In this sense, samsara refers to the ever-shifting landscape of life — birth and death, pleasure and pain, gain and loss — all woven together in the tapestry of human experience.

Despite the many sensual pleasures the world offers, the term samsara carries a largely negative connotation within Eastern spiritual traditions such as Hinduism, Buddhism, and Jainism. Far from being a celebratory endorsement of worldly life, samsara is often portrayed as a kind of existential bondage — a cycle of birth and death driven by ignorance and karma. In these traditions, life in samsara is not viewed as an endless playground of delights but more like a prison in which beings are compelled to suffer, struggle, and repeat their mistakes until they awaken to the truth.

Samsara is not limited to physical rebirth. It also refers to a psychological and spiritual condition — a state of misidentification, restlessness, and delusion. According to Vedanta, samsara is the result of *avidya,* or ignorance of the Self. This ignorance gives rise to the mistaken belief that one is a limited being: a separate ego, dependent on external conditions for happiness and security. We imagine ourselves to be the doer of actions and the experiencer of their results, and in so doing, become entangled in the web of karma.

In this view, samsara is not something "out there" in the world — it is a condition of the mind. It arises every time we forget our true nature and look outside ourselves for fulfillment. The pursuit of status, wealth, relationships, or even spiritual experiences, when rooted in a sense of incompleteness, only reinforces the illusion of separation. As long as we continue to chase after fleeting things, believing that they will make us whole, the cycle continues.

Vedanta offers a radical solution: the way out of samsara is not through escaping the world but through right knowledge (*jnana*) — the direct recognition of one's true identity as atman, the unchanging, limitless Self. This knowledge is not intellectual alone; it must be deeply assimilated and actualized through inquiry, contemplation, and lived insight. When the Self is known as non-different from Brahman — the infinite reality — samsara loses its grip. The mind is no longer bound by fear, desire, or misidentification. One may continue to live and act in the world, but without being entangled by it.

In this sense, samsara is not a place but a perspective. And liberation (*moksha*) is not a distant reward, but the recognition of what has always been true. The river of life may still flow, but the one who knows the Self no longer drowns in it. Instead, they stand free — awake in the midst of the dream.

—

Root & Meaning

Samsara — from the Sanskrit root *sr* ("to flow, to go, to wander"), with the prefix *sam-* ("together, fully"), literally meaning "continuous flow" or "wandering through." In spiritual usage, it refers to the cycle of birth, death, and rebirth, along with the continuous flux of worldly experience.

Scriptural References

Definition & nature of samsara:

- **Bhagavad Gita 8.6:** "Whatever one remembers at the time of death, to that alone one goes, having been always absorbed in it." (Shows the continuity of mental impressions fueling rebirth.)
- **Bhagavad Gita 8.16:** "From the highest world down to the lowest, all are subject to return again, O Arjuna; but one who reaches Me is never reborn."
- **Brihadaranyaka Upanishad 4.4.6:** Describes how ignorance and desire keep beings revolving in birth and death.

Cause of aamsara – ignorance (avidya):

- **Brihadaranyaka Upanishad 4.3.7:** "Being identified with what is seen, heard, and thought, the Self imagines itself bound."
- **Bhagavad Gita 7.13:** "Deluded by the three *gunas*, the whole world does not know Me, who am beyond them and immutable."

Freedom from samsara:

- **Mundaka Upanishad 2.2.8:** "He who knows Brahman becomes Brahman; he crosses over sorrow and is freed from samsara."
- **Bhagavad Gita 4.9:** "One who knows the truth of My divine birth and actions is not reborn after leaving the body, but comes to Me."
- **Katha Upanishad 2.3.8:** "When all desires that dwell in the heart are destroyed, then the mortal becomes immortal; here one attains Brahman."

Traditional View

In Hindu, Buddhist, and Jain traditions, samsara denotes the endless cycle of rebirth governed by karma and fueled by ignorance (*avidya*). It is characterized by impermanence, suffering, and bondage. The "world" in this sense is not only the physical realm but the entire domain of changing experience, including subtle worlds. The aim of spiritual life is to attain moksha — freedom from this cycle.

Vedantic Analysis

Advaita Vedanta interprets samsara not as a physical location but as a state of mind rooted in misidentification with the body-mind (*dehatma-buddhi*). It is the condition in which the Self is seemingly bound by ignorance, taking itself to be a finite doer and enjoyer. Even in a single lifetime, samsara manifests as the oscillation between joy and sorrow, gain and loss, driven by desire and aversion. Thus, samsara is as much psychological as it is cosmological. Liberation is the recognition that the Self was never bound, and samsara was only an appearance in awareness.

Common Misunderstandings

- **"Samsara is a place you go to after death."** It is the cycle of identification and experience, present here and now.
- **"Escaping samsara means escaping the world."** The world may continue, but the wise see it as mithya — dependent reality — and are untouched by it.
- **"Samsara ends by good karma."** Good karma refines the mind but only knowledge ends samsara.

Vedantic Resolution

The resolution lies in understanding that samsara is a projection born of ignorance. Removal of ignorance through Self-knowledge (*atma-jnana*) reveals that the Self is changeless, limitless awareness in which all cycles appear and disappear. The "flow" of samsara may continue at the level of body-mind, but the knower of the Self remains ever free.

samskara *and* vasana

(saṁskāra — *suhm-SKAA-ruh*)(vāsanā
— *VAA-suh-NAA*)

In Vedanta, *vasana (vāsāna)* means a subtle tendency or inclination,
a trace of past experience that "dwells" in the mind and influences present thought and action. It is often described as a fragrance
left behind by something long gone — intangible, yet shaping
perception and behavior. A *samskara (saṁskāra)*, by contrast, is a
deeper mental impression: a seed of conditioning stored in the
causal body, dormant until circumstances awaken it.

Traditionally, *samskara* is the seed and *vasana* is the shoot. A past
action leaves behind a *samskara*; when conditions are right, that
seed sprouts into a *vasana* — a living tendency in the mind. That
tendency may bear fruit in the form of action, and that action
drops new seeds, reinforcing the pattern. This cycle of *samskara*
> *vasana* > karma > *samskara* sustains the *samsara chakra* (wheel of
birth and death).

Some modern teachers, however, use the terms differently. In this
view, a *vasana* is any single tendency or impression, while a
samskara is a constellation of related *vasanas* that together form a
personality trait or habitual pattern. A *vasana* for solitude, a *vasana*
for reading, and a *vasana* for quiet environments might together
make up the *samskara* we call "introversion." Both perspectives
are valid: one emphasizes the causal chain, the other the way tendencies cluster into recognizable patterns.

Not all *vasanas* are obstacles. Vedanta distinguishes between
binding and non-binding *vasanas*. Binding *vasanas* compel action
and agitate the mind if denied — restless cravings, deep-seated
aversions, compulsions rooted in ignorance. Non-binding *vasanas*
are simply preferences: a taste for certain foods, an enjoyment of

art or music, a love of the mountains over the sea. They arise and pass without disturbing the mind, and some even support spiritual life, like a natural pull toward study or meditation. The problem is never the presence of *vasanas*, but identification with them.

Self-knowledge neutralizes binding *vasanas*. This is the "burnt seeds" metaphor of Vedanta: a burnt seed may still appear intact, but it will never sprout. In the same way, *samskaras* may remain after realization, but their capacity to bind is gone. *Vasanas* may still arise, but they no longer drive thought or action, and no new binding karma is produced. Only *prarabdha karma* — the momentum of actions already set in motion — continues until the body falls away.

From the standpoint of the individual (*jiva*), every *vasana* arises from a *samskara*: there is always a seed behind the shoot. From the standpoint of the total (*Ishvara*), certain tendencies are not personal at all — such as the instinct to eat, sleep, or protect one's young. These are universal programs in the macrocosmic causal body, part of the shared human template.

Modern psychology offers helpful parallels. *Samskaras* resemble deep unconscious beliefs or schemas — the hidden frameworks shaping perception and response. In Jungian terms, they approach what psychology calls complexes: emotionally charged clusters of memory and meaning that draw the mind into patterned reactions. *Vasanas* are the habitual thoughts, urges, and emotional movements that arise from those frameworks.

For instance, someone carrying the *samskara* "I must be needed to be loved" may repeatedly attract relationships where they play the rescuer. That latent framework interprets affection through the lens of usefulness. Each time the person rushes to "save" another, the *vasana* — the active impulse born of that *samskara* — expresses itself. The more it is indulged, the deeper the groove becomes, until understanding dissolves the belief at its root.

Likewise, a person shaped by the *samskara* that self-worth depends on achievement will feel repeated *vasanas* to compete, to prove, to outperform. The framework is the deep belief in conditional worth; the *vasanas* are the day-to-day impulses it generates — checking metrics, comparing, striving. Only when the belief is seen through does the striving lose its compulsive edge.

When the seed is "burnt" through knowledge, the old memory may remain, but the emotional charge is gone — much like a complex that has lost its power to possess the psyche.

Whether you picture *samskaras* as seeds and *vasanas* as shoots, or *samskaras* as constellations and *vasanas* as individual stars, they describe the same architecture of conditioning. Together they explain why we act as we do, and why we so often repeat ourselves. They also reveal the way out: not by erasing all tendencies, but by knowing oneself as the unconditioned Self, untouched by seeds, shoots, or the patterns they form.

—

Root & Meaning

Vasana — from Sanskrit root *vas* ("to dwell, to reside"). In this context: "latent tendency," "subtle impression," or "habitual inclination" that dwells in the mind.

Samskara — from *sam* ("together, completely") + *kr* ("to make, to form"). Literally, "that which has been put together" or "mental impression." In Vedanta and Yoga psychology, it refers to subtle imprints left on the mind by past experiences and actions.

Scriptural References

- **Yoga Sutras of Patanjali (I.18, II.10–12):** Defines *samskaras* as latent impressions and describes their role in sustaining the cycle of birth and action.
- **Bhagavad Gita (3.33):** "Even the wise act according to their own

nature; beings follow their tendencies (*vasanas*)."

- **Brihadaranyaka Upanishad (4.4.5):** Describes how actions and desires shape the next birth.
- **Mundaka Upanishad (3.2.9):** Implies the "burnt seed" idea when speaking of the liberated soul no longer producing new karma.
- **Vivekachudamani (108–109):** Lists *vasanas* as obstacles to realization and outlines the need to neutralize them.

Traditional View

- *Samskara* is the imprint left by an action, thought, or experience. It is like a subtle "groove" in the mind's fabric.
- *Vasana* is the tendency or urge that arises from those imprints.
- They form a cyclical relationship: action leaves *samskara*, which generates *vasana*, which in turn prompts further action.
- Over lifetimes, these become the conditioning (*prakriti*) that determines personality, preferences, fears, desires, and habitual behaviors.

Vedantic Analysis

Vedanta holds that *vasanas* are the fuel of samsara. They drive the *jiva* to seek fulfillment in external objects, perpetuating the cycle of birth and death. Even after gaining Self-knowledge (*jnana*), residual *vasanas* may remain (*prarabdha karma*) and continue to produce habitual thoughts or actions — but for the *jnani*, they no longer cause binding identification.

In deep sleep, *vasanas* remain dormant, only to re-emerge upon waking. Liberation (*moksha*) is not about erasing every *vasanas* in a literal sense but neutralizing their binding power through knowledge of the Self as complete and untouched.

Common Misunderstandings

- **"Vasanas must be completely destroyed for liberation."** Liberation is a change in identification, not total personality erasure. The *jnani* may still act from harmless *vasanas*.
- **"Samskaras are only negative."** They can be positive or negative; positive *samskaras* like compassion and truthfulness aid the path.
- **"Meditation alone removes vasanas."** Meditation steadies the mind, but inquiry into the Self transforms one's relationship to *vasanas*.

Vedantic Resolution

The key is not to uproot every *vasana* before seeking truth — an impossible task — but to reduce their intensity through *karma yoga* and *upasana yoga*, and then see through their unreality via *jnana yoga*. Once the false identification with the body-mind is gone, *vasanas* lose their binding force.

sanchita karma

(sañcita karma — *suhn-chi-ta KAR-muh*)

In Vedanta, karma is often explained through the imagery of three "accounts":

- *Sanchita* — the accumulated karmas of countless past lives.
- *Prarabdha* — the portion of *sanchita* selected to fructify in this present birth.
- *Agami* — the new karmas generated in this lifetime that will bear fruit in the future.

Sanchita (meaning, "heaped up, accumulated") is the vast storehouse of past actions. Each act, thought, and intention leaves a subtle seed (*bija*) in the causal body. These seeds remain dormant until conditions allow them to manifest as experiences of pleasure or pain in a later lifetime. The accumulated stock is so great that only a small portion can be worked out in any single life.

The scriptures describe *sanchita* as beginningless, carried forward with the subtle and causal bodies after the death of the physical body. It explains the vast differences between beings at birth: health or illness, privilege or deprivation, are not random but results of accumulated karma. These karmas form a kind of karmic "capital," from which each life's destiny is drawn.

For the ordinary person (*ajnani*), *sanchita* is a store that ensures rebirth, since at death unfructified karmas remain. But for the wise (*jnani*), Self-knowledge burns away the entire store of *sanchita*, just as fire reduces a heap of cotton to ashes. Thus the liberated one has no further rebirth: *prarabdha* continues until the body drops, *agami* does not accrue, and *sanchita* is destroyed.

—

Root & Meaning

Sanchita = accumulated, heaped up.
Sanchita Karma = the total accumulated karmas of past lives stored in the causal body.

Scriptural References

- **Bhagavad Gita (4.37):** "As fire reduces wood to ashes, so the fire of knowledge burns all karma." Traditionally interpreted as the destruction of *sanchita*.
- **Brahma Sutras (4.1.13–14):** discuss how knowledge eradicates accumulated karma.
- **Upanishadic imagery:** karmic seeds (*bija*) stored in the causal body until fructification.

Traditional View

- *Sanchita* is the sum total of karmic seeds from beginningless time.
- At the start of each birth, a portion becomes *prarabdha*.
- Remaining karmas stay dormant, awaiting future births.

Vedantic Analysis

- *Sanchita* explains inequality at birth, the diversity of destinies, and continuity of rebirth.
- It perpetuates samsara until Self-knowledge destroys it.
- Liberation (*moksha*) is freedom not only from future karmas but from the entire storehouse of the past.

Common Misunderstandings

- **That sanchita determines every moment of life:** Only *prarabdha* dictates the current body and major events; *sanchita* remains in potential.

- **That God arbitrarily dispenses results:** The law of karma is impersonal, though Vedanta sometimes describes *Ishvara* as the administrator of *karmaphala*.
- **That even the jnani carries sanchita:** Vedanta insists Self-knowledge destroys all accumulated karma, leaving no residue.

Vedantic Resolution

Sanchita karma is the karmic backlog that binds beings to rebirth. Its destruction through knowledge demonstrates the unique power of Self-realization: the discovery that the true Self was never a doer or enjoyer to begin with.

sankalpa

(saṅkalpa — *suhn-kuhl-puh*)

A *sankalpa (saṅkalpa)* is often translated as "desire," and in Yoga circles it is sometimes rendered as "intention" or "resolution." In Vedanta, however, the term has a more specific meaning. A *sankalpa* is the subtle movement in the mind that transforms a neutral thought into a desired object. It begins with a simple perception ("Red, shiny, juicy apple"), adds a value judgment ("That apple looks delicious"), and culminates in desire ("I want that apple"). In this sense, a *sankalpa* is the inner force that projects meaning onto an object and gives rise to attraction. It can support dharmic living when guided by clarity, or it can bind when it projects qualities that are not actually present.

Vedanta consistently points out that the senses are not the source of our difficulties; the mind is. It is the mind that overlays objects, events, and relationships with imagined attributes. When a thought arises, we can either let it pass or we can assign value to it. Once value is added, emotion follows, and emotion naturally matures into desire. If the desire is strong, the mind begins to revisit the object again and again, forming an affinity that easily grows into attachment. This shift — from "It would be nice" to "I need it" — is what binds. When the desire is blocked, anger arises; anger clouds judgment; and clarity is lost. As the *Bhagavad Gita* warns, "The mind that follows the wandering senses loses its capacity to discriminate, just as an unmanned ship is carried away by the winds of its own destruction" (2.67). What begins as a faint ripple in the mind can become a storm that is difficult to escape.

For this reason, Vedanta advises attending to a thought early, before it develops its own narrative. Consider a familiar example: a man waiting for his coffee notices an attractive woman nearby.

The initial perception is innocent. But the mind quickly begins its embroidery: her physique, her imagined personality, the story of meeting, dating, moving in, marrying, living happily ever after. Within seconds the mind builds an entire emotional universe around a person he has never even spoken to. When she picks up her coffee and leaves, he feels a twinge of disappointment — not because of anything real, but because he became involved in his own projection.

A *sankalpa* can be checked by examining the object and questioning whether the value we have assigned is accurate or merely imagined. Strong desires can be placed under scrutiny: Is this real, or is this a story the mind is constructing? We can also choose to ignore the initial stirrings and allow them to subside on their own. Like a hot coal, a *sankalpa* cools naturally when not grasped. *Sankalpas* only take hold when we participate in them. Ultimately, a *sankalpa* is just a thought. Our task is to see it clearly, manage it wisely, and prevent the mind from turning the smallest seed into a binding narrative.

—

Root & Meaning

Sankalpa — from the Sanskrit prefix *sam-* ("together, completely") and root *klrp* ("to arrange, be willing, resolve"), meaning "determination," "intention," or "mental resolve." In common use, it can mean a desire, wish, or firm intention to act.

Scriptural References

Nature of sankalpa and desire:

- **Bhagavad Gita 2.62–63:** "When a man dwells on objects, attachment to them arises; from attachment springs desire, from desire comes anger; from anger arises delusion…"
- **Bhagavad Gita 6.24:** "Let him, resolutely holding the mind,

abandon without reserve all desires born of sankalpa, and restrain the senses on every side."
- **Bhagavad Gita 18.14:** Lists *sankalpa* as one of the five factors of action.

Mind as the source of projection:

- **Katha Upanishad 2.1.2:** "The Self-existent pierced the openings outward; therefore one looks outward, not within oneself. But a wise man, seeking immortality, turns his gaze inward."
- **Maitri Upanishad 6.34:** Describes *sankalpa* as the seed of all mental activity and the cause of bondage.

Freedom from binding sankalpa:

- **Mundaka Upanishad 2.2.8:** "When all desires dwelling in the heart are destroyed, then the mortal becomes immortal."
- **Yoga Sutra 1.12:** "Steadiness of mind is achieved through practice and non-attachment."

Traditional View

In general Indian thought, *sankalpa* refers to a firm resolve — either for worldly or spiritual aims. In Vedic ritual, it is the formal statement of intent before performing a rite. In Yoga and devotional contexts, it is sometimes translated as "heartfelt intention" or "vow," guiding the practitioner's practice and conduct. It can be wholesome (*shubha sankalpa*), such as the resolve to live dharmically, or unwholesome (*ashubha sankalpa*), based on ignorance and selfish desire.

Vedantic Analysis

In Advaita Vedanta, *sankalpa* is analyzed as the mind's process of taking a thought-object, attributing value to it, and generating desire. For example: perception ("red, shiny apple") > valuation ("that apple looks delicious") > desire ("I want that apple"). This process binds the *jiva* by reinforcing identification with the role of doer and enjoyer (*karta-bhokta*). A *sankalpa* can lead toward liberation if it strengthens the desire for Self-knowledge (*mumukshutva*), but more often it fuels samsara when it is based on projection and false attribution (*adhyasa*).

Common Misunderstandings

- **"All sankalpa is bad."** It depends on whether the intention is binding or freeing.
- **"Sankalpa is just positive thinking."** It is the seed-thought that becomes action, carrying karmic consequences.
- **"One can achieve liberation by a single, powerful sankalpa."** Liberation requires knowledge, though a strong *mumukshutva* can be expressed as *sankalpa*.

Vedantic Resolution

The Vedantic approach is to examine the truth of a *sankalpa* as it arises. If it is based on projection or fanciful imagination, it can be dropped before it matures into binding desire. Strong *sankalpa* aligned with dharma and Self-inquiry can be cultivated, while others are allowed to fade. Mastery over *sankalpa* is mastery over the direction of one's life, and ultimately, the mind itself.

sannyasa

(sannyāsa — *suhn-ny-AA-suh*)

Sannyasa (sannyāsa), or "renunciation," is often portrayed as a holy life free of duties and responsibilities in order to focus on the ultimate objective — moksha (liberation). Traditionally, *sannyasa* is the monk's lifestyle, one in which worldly objects and relationships are given up, and poverty and chastity are the accepted rule. However, there's more to it. Just putting on orange robes doesn't make one a *sannyasa.*

There are two kinds of *sannyasa.* The first one, *vidvat-sannyasa,* is about becoming a renunciate after knowing and assimilating the truth. As a result of Self-inquiry, the wise (*jnanis*) have given up wrong ideas about their identity. They have cognitively resolved erroneous concepts they had about the world and who/what they are. In the case of *vidvat-sannyasa,* there is no *sannyasa* to take. *Vidvat-sannyasa* requires no outward modifications to one's mode of living, because it's simply a byproduct of realizing and actualizing the Self. It's said that *vidvat-sannyasa* is the culmination of someone having lived through all of life's stages, including gaining and actualizing the right knowledge, and fulfilling their human purpose (gaining *moksha*).

Vividisha-sannyasa, on the other hand, is what's more commonly known as "putting on the robes" or "taking *sannyasa.*" It includes a formal lifestyle commitment to the pursuit and obtainment of Self-knowledge, and in doing so, a foregoing of relationships and outside interests. *Vividisha* means "desire to know." This is the austere lifestyle of monks and nuns who become a renunciate before knowing and assimilating the truth. *Vividisha sannyasis* are free of duties and social obligations, and dependent on other individuals for their basic needs who value their dedication to gaining and disseminating the truth. In this way, it is very much a community-supported *sannyasa*. Nevertheless, both *vidvat*- and *vividisha-sannyasa* are marked by fearlessness, detachment, and a seeking of the truth. Both may also include service, usually in the form of teaching.

In the *Bhagavad Gita*, Arjuna is confused about the difference between being a *sannyasa* (the seeking of *moksha*, absent of worldly activities) and *karma yoga* (the seeking of *moksha*, while still involved in the world). After hearing Krishna espouse the renunciation of action through knowledge of the Self, Arjuna has doubts about which path he should take. Krishna tries to convince him that he has worldly responsibilities to tend to — namely, an army to lead and a war to win — and that it's no time for him to be shirking his duties to live a life of solitude.

Furthermore, Krishna makes it known that both renunciation of action (*sannyasa*) and performance of action (*karma yoga*) lead to the same goal. Thus, it's not a question of one path being better than the other, but which lifestyle best fits the temperament of the seeker.

Few individuals have what's required to become a renunciate. Becoming a renunciate and suddenly renouncing one's likes and dislikes isn't as easy as it looks. In the *Gita*, Arjuna's life up until the great battle has mostly been about one conflict after another. He's ready to throw in the towel and put it all behind him. However, *sannyasa* as a means of escaping life doesn't work due to two important hindrances — fear and desire.

Out of fear, one might wish to escape worldly action, and out of desire one might wish to leave all their troubles behind. The problem is that fear and desire are the antithesis to a life of renunciation, which strives to be free from fear and desire. In short, no one successfully maintains *sannyasa* under the spell of fear and desire.

Also, it would be naive to say that *sannyasa* equates to living without any difficulty. For a select few, *vividisha-sannyasa* comes natural to them because it matches their disposition in life. They already have a profound dispassion for the world and aren't easily swayed by bright, shiny objects. They still have *vasanas* (conditioned habits), but they are manageable. For the majority of us, however, a life without action would only lead to complete and utter frustration.

On the other hand, involvement in the day-to-day grind of worldly life can have an important role in one's spiritual development by providing an arena where one can express themselves and learn from their actions. In the field of experience, we are able to exhaust our likes and dislikes, and realize that all objects, experiences and relationships are empty of intrinsic and lasting value. So, being a *karma yogi* (versus being a *sannyasi*) has its benefits too. Like a river stone tossed and turned in the current, many of us start rough but are eventually made smooth by the challenges of work, family and fulfilling our duties.

Arjuna, perhaps, mistakingly believes that by evading his duties and avoiding all worldly action, he will become an authentic seeker of the truth. But just because one abstains from a certain action doesn't mean they have gained dispassion for it. Swami Dayananda draws this distinction by giving an anecdote about a boy who likes to play marbles. One day, a father tells his son he's too old to be playing marbles and should instead, play cricket with the older boys. The son agrees, gives his marbles to his younger brother, and in fear of being tempted and drawn back in, avoids the places where the boys play.

Dayananda explains that in this case, the boy's giving up marbles isn't actual sannyasa because he only gives up playing marbles out of pride. However, in reality, he could probably be talked back into playing marbles again. On the other hand, if we ask the same individual ten years later if he still has any interest in playing marbles, the answer will most likely be an unequivocal, "No." The man, who once liked playing marbles as a boy, has no sense of loss.

Dayananda tells us, "Having outgrown the fascination for child-hood games, you are a marble-*sannyasi*. If the entire world holds for you no more attraction than those marbles — if your heart has found that fullness and maturity — you are truly a *sannyasi*."

The conclusion is that real sannyasa cannot be chosen or taken, only discovered — usually through a long process of removing doubts and "outgrowing our fascination" for the world. Only by discovering and sustaining the thought "I am whole, complete, and totally free from dependence on objects, experiences and rela-tionships for happiness," can one be a true *sannyasi*.

This doesn't mean we no longer take pleasure in the world, just that we are no longer under its spell. Objects (including this body and mind), events and relationships are viewed as dream-like, passing entities. Any pleasure derived from them is known to be momentary and not something one can depend on for real happiness.

That said, one cannot will themselves to be a *sannyasi* — it must happen in its own time — but it can be cultivated. How? By com-posing our thoughts with the right attitude (*karma yoga*), purify-ing them using right meditation (*upasana yoga*), and then gaining knowledge of the Self using Vedanta. A little grace is also helpful.

Swami Dayananda has the last word when he says:

"You have to wait for it to happen, while performing actions with the right attitude. This world has everything you need to bloom into a flower of maturity. A composed mind, the results of a life of *karma yoga*, will find sannyasa naturally."

—

Root & Meaning

Sannyasa — from the Sanskrit prefix *sam-* ("completely") + root *nyas* ("to lay down, renounce"), meaning "complete renunciation" or "putting down entirely." In spiritual contexts, it denotes the formal or inner renunciation of worldly attachments and duties in pursuit of liberation (*moksha*).

Scriptural References

Nature and types of renunciation:

- **Bhagavad Gita 18.2:** "The sages understand *sannyasa* as the renunciation of action motivated by desire; the wise declare *tyaga* [relinquishment] as the renunciation of the fruits of all action."
- **Bhagavad Gita 18.11:** "It is not possible for an embodied being to renounce all action entirely; but one who renounces the fruits of action is truly a renunciate."

Vidvat- and vividisha-sannyasa:

- **Jabala Upanishad 4:** Describes the two forms of *sannyasa*: after Self-knowledge (*vidvat-sannyasa*) and before Self-knowledge with intent to know (*vividisha-sannyasa*).
- **Brihadaranyaka Upanishad 3.5.1:** Speaks of the renunciate who, having known the Self, is untouched by karma.

Renunciation vs. karma yoga:

- **Bhagavad Gita 5.2:** "Both *sannyasa* and *karma yoga* lead to liberation; but of the two, *karma yoga* is superior for one who has not attained dispassion."
- **Bhagavad Gita 3.4:** "Not by merely renouncing actions does one attain freedom from action; nor by renunciation alone does one reach perfection."

Dangers of premature renunciation:

- **Bhagavad Gita 3.6:** "One who restrains the organs of action but dwells on sense objects in the mind is deluded and called a hypocrite."

- **Bhagavad Gita 6.1:** "He who performs his bounden duty without dependence on its fruit — he is a *sannyasin* and a yogi, not he who has merely renounced the sacred fire and works."

True mark of the renunciate:

- **Katha Upanishad 2.3.14:**"When all desires dwelling in the heart are renounced, then the mortal becomes immortal and attains Brahman here."
- **Mundaka Upanishad 3.2.9:** "He who knows Brahman becomes Brahman… freed from desires, he attains peace."

Traditional View

In orthodox Hindu life-stages (*ashrama-dharma*), *sannyasa* is the fourth and final stage, undertaken after completing duties as a householder and forest-dweller. The renunciate gives up possessions, social obligations, and personal ties to focus exclusively on the pursuit of Self-knowledge. Traditionally, *sannyasa* also involves distinctive dress (ochre robes), celibacy, and mendicancy.

Two main types are recognized:

Vidvat-sannyasa — renunciation that occurs naturally after Self-knowledge; no outward change is necessary.

Vividisha-sannyasa — formal renunciation undertaken with the desire to know the Self, usually involving an ascetic lifestyle.

Vedantic Analysis

In Advaita Vedanta, *sannyasa* is primarily a mental state of dispassion (*vairagya*) and non-dependence, not merely an external lifestyle choice. One may be a householder outwardly but a renunciate inwardly, if free from binding likes and dislikes. Conversely, wearing the robes without inner renunciation is only symbolic. The highest *sannyasa* is the firm abidance in the knowledge, "I am whole, complete, and free, independent of all objects."

Common Misunderstandings

- **"Sannyasa means doing nothing."** It means freedom from binding action, not inactivity.
- **"One must take sannyasa to gain liberation."** Liberation comes from Self-knowledge; *sannyasa* can be helpful, but is not compulsory.
- **"Renunciation is only physical."** True renunciation is mental — giving up attachment to results and identification with the doer.

Vedantic Resolution

Vedanta distinguishes between renunciation as escapism (motivated by fear or frustration) and renunciation as maturity (born of clarity and dispassion). The former collapses under pressure; the latter is unshakable because it rests in Self-knowledge. As Krishna teaches, both *karma yoga* and *sannyasa* lead to the same goal; the choice depends on temperament and stage of spiritual growth.

sat-chit-ananda

(sat-cit-ānanda — *suht-chit-AA-nun-duh*)

The Upanishads describe Brahman with three epithets: *sat* (existence), *chit* (consciousness), and *ananda* (bliss). These are not attributes added onto Brahman but synonyms that reveal the same reality from different standpoints. To say Brahman is *sat-chit-ananda (sat-cit-ānanda)* is to say: Brahman is existence itself, consciousness itself, and fullness itself.

Sat — Existence

Existence is pure being. It is the simple "I am" that remains when all identifications are dropped. "I am a father" or "I am a son" are incidental. What never changes is "I am." The I am of a child is the same I am of an old man. Existence does not belong to the body, mind, or roles, but underlies them.

Existence also pervades all objects. When we say "the mountain exists," it appears that existence belongs to the mountain. But in reality, existence is independent; it is the subject in which "mountain" is an object. Just as clay pervades every pot, existence pervades every name and form. Vedanta describes existence as:

• Not a part, product, or property of objects.
• Not limited by the boundaries of objects.
• Surviving even when objects are absent.
• Known only in association with an object (you encounter "existence of X").
• Indivisible and without parts.
• Identical with pure consciousness (chit).

Chit — Consciousness

Consciousness is the very light of awareness. It is self-revealing: no one needs proof that "I am conscious." All experiences — waking, dream, or deep sleep — are illumined by consciousness. It is not in the mind; rather, the mind functions because of it. Consciousness is not limited by the body or senses.

Ananda — Bliss

Ananda is often misunderstood as a state of joy or rapture. In Vedanta, it means limitlessness. To be free of every boundary is to be perfectly satisfied. The word "bliss" is used traditionally, but its real implication is freedom — absence of limitation, fullness, purnatva. Unlike objects, which always limit and bind, Brahman is limitless, and this limitlessness is the deepest meaning of *ananda*.

To recognize Brahman as *sat-chit-ananda* is to recognize the essence of oneself. I am not a limited body or mind, but existence-consciousness-fullness itself, ever free, ever present.

—

Root & Meaning

Sat — being, existence.
Chit — awareness, consciousness.
Ananda — fullness, limitlessness (often translated "bliss").
Together: the threefold description of Brahman, absolute reality.

Scriptural References

- **Taittiriya Upanishad (2.1.1):** describes Brahman as *satyam jnanam anantam* (truth, knowledge, infinity) — another triad synonymous with *sat-chit-ananda*.
- **Chandogya Upanishad (6.8.7):** *tat tvam asi* — "You are That," the Self is identical with Brahman.

- **Ananda-valli of Taittiriya:** elaborates *ananda* as limitlessness, not an emotion.

Traditional View

- Brahman is not an object with properties. *Sat, chit,* and *ananda* are pointers to the same indivisible reality.
- Existence and consciousness are never absent in any experience; ananda reveals their limitless nature.
- The Self (atman) is *sat-chit-ananda,* not separate from Brahman.

Vedantic Analysis

- *Sat* (existence): Objects borrow existence. Only Brahman is.
- *Chit* (consciousness): Consciousness is self-revealing and the basis for knowledge.
- *Ananda* (bliss): Not experiential joy but freedom from limitation. "Bliss" points to the Self's intrinsic fullness.
- To confuse *ananda* with ecstatic states is to mistake Brahman for a mental condition.

Common Misunderstandings

- That Brahman "has" existence, consciousness, bliss: No — Brahman is existence-consciousness-bliss.
- That bliss means joy or happiness: In Vedanta, it means limitlessness, not a transient emotional high.
- That *sat, chit,* and *ananda* are three different aspects: They are three words pointing to one indivisible reality.

Vedantic Resolution

To realize Brahman as *sat-chit-ananda* is to see oneself as whole, unchanging, limitless awareness. This recognition dissolves the sense of lack and bondage, revealing that the seeker was never incomplete.

sattva

(sattva — *suht-tva*)

We praise the "light," but rarely understand it. *Sattva* is not morality, though it favors goodness. It is not peace, though it brings calm. It is not wisdom, though it makes knowledge possible. It is light — subtle, luminous, and intelligent. It is the quality of clarity in a mind, the reflective power that allows awareness to be known. Without *sattva*, even the most noble teaching remains opaque. With it, a single word can pierce illusion.

Sattva is one of the three *gunas,* the strands of *prakriti* that bind and shape all experience. Where *tamas* veils, and *rajas* agitates, *sattva* reveals. A sattvic mind is quiet, alert, balanced — a polished mirror that reflects the Self. It is the condition most conducive to inquiry, devotion, compassion, beauty, and all the higher functions of life. And yet, *sattva* too is a strand. It is a golden chain. It can be clung to, mistaken for liberation, and turned into an identity.

In spiritual circles, this mistake is common: people chase sattvic experiences —peace, bliss, insight — as if they were the goal. They mistake clarity for consciousness, joy for freedom. But Vedanta is clear: *sattva* may bring you to the door, but it will not open it. You are not *sattva*. You are the one in whose presence *sattva* shines.

This is not to dismiss it. *Sattva* is precious. Without it, no clarity is possible. A rajasic mind is too distracted, a tamasic one too dull. *Sattva* makes the mind fit for inquiry, sensitive to truth, capable of dispassion, and receptive to grace. It is the precondition for subtle understanding, for love without possessiveness, for devotion without delusion.

But the mind must outgrow its fascination with *sattva* itself. Even purity can become a refuge for ego, a way to avoid true surrender. A sattvic lifestyle, sattvic food, sattvic thoughts — these can prepare the ground. But if we build a new identity on top of that ground, we remain in bondage, however refined. The mind becomes addicted to its clarity, proud of its purity, resistant to anything that threatens its inner balance. That resistance is a sign: the *jiva* still clings.

In truth, the Self is not sattvic. The Self is beyond the *gunas*. It is that by which even *sattva* is illumined. When *sattva* has served its function — when it has brought the mind to readiness — it too must be let go. Then, one sees: the light is not in the mind. The light is me.

—

Root & Meaning

The word *sattva* is derived from the Sanskrit root *sat*, meaning "being," "truth," or "pure existence." In Vedanta, *sat* is often synonymous with the Self or consciousness. *Sattva* refers to the quality of clarity, lightness, balance, and luminosity that most closely reflects sat. Among the three *gunas* (*sattva, rajas, tamas*), it is the most refined and conducive to the expression of awareness. It uplifts, purifies, reveals, and harmonizes. As the *jnana-shakti* (power of knowledge), it is responsible for perception, discernment, understanding, and spiritual aspiration.

Scriptural References

- **Bhagavad Gita 14.6:** *"Tatra sattvam nirmalatvat prakashakam anamayam..."*— "Of these, *sattva*, being pure, causes illumination and health."
- **Bhagavad Gita 14.17:** *"Sattvat sanjayate jnanam..."* — "From *sattva* arises knowledge."
- **Bhagavad Gita 18.37:** *"Yat tad agre viṣam iva pariname 'mritopamam..."* — "That which seems like poison at first but turns to

nectar in the end is sattvika happiness, born of self-knowledge."

- **Shrimad Bhagavatam 1.2.24:** *"Sattvam rajas tama iti prakriter gu-nas tan..."* — *"Sattva, rajas,* and *tamas* are the modes of material nature; they bind the soul to the body."

These texts emphasize that *sattva*, though uplifting, is still a bind-ing force—albeit a "golden chain"—until transcended.

Traditional View

Traditionally, *sattva* has been regarded as the ideal *guna* for spir-itual aspirants. It is associated with purity, clarity, health, virtue, truth, intelligence, and detachment. A sattvic person lives in har-mony with dharma, seeks knowledge, and delights in service. Sattvic foods (light, fresh, vegetarian), environments (peaceful, clean), and activities (study, meditation, service) all support men-tal purity. While *rajas* drives action and *tamas* resists change, *sattva* allows introspection and insight.

In Ayurveda, *sattva* is linked to mental health and spiritual vitali-ty. In Sankhya and Yoga, it is the quality that must be cultivated to still the mind (*chitta-prasadana*).

Vedantic Analysis

From the standpoint of Advaita Vedanta, *sattva* is a quality of the subtle body (mind and intellect), not of the Self. It is the *guna* that best reflects consciousness and makes the Self "knowable" to the mind. It is responsible for *viveka* (discrimination), *vairagya* (dis-passion), and the deep desire for *moksha*. Thus, it is instrumental in purifying the mind (*antahkarana-shuddhi*) and preparing it for *jnana yoga*.

However, *sattva* itself is still *mithya* — apparently real. It is not freedom. The Self is *nirguna* (beyond all *gunas*). Clinging to *sattva* leads to sattvic bondage: attachment to peace, purity, or spiritual identity. A purified mind is a precondition for knowledge, but it must ultimately be negated along with the rest of the apparent self. One does not become free by being sattvic, but by knowing oneself as atma, the witness of the *gunas*.

Common Misunderstandings

- **"Sattva equals enlightenment."** *Sattva* is a state of mind, not the Self. It is a reflection of light, not the source. Enlightenment is not a mental condition but Self-knowledge.
- **"I feel peaceful, therefore I am free."** Peace is a sattvic experience. But as long as it comes and goes, it belongs to the mind. The Self is unchanging and independent of mental states.
- **"Spiritual life means being only sattvic."** While *sattva* is essential for inner growth, Vedanta is not a lifestyle. It is a means of knowledge that reveals the Self, which is beyond lifestyle and beyond the *gunas*.
- **"I am a sattvic person."** The identification with *sattva* creates subtle egoism — spiritual pride, attachment to goodness, and superiority. This too must be seen and released.

Cosmological View

In the macrocosmic sense, *sattva* is not merely a quality of the individual mind — it is the luminous aspect of maya that makes creation intelligible. This pure *sattva*, untainted by *rajas* or *tamas*, is known as *prakasha-shakti*, the revealing power of knowledge. It is the blueprint of the universe — the intelligence and information that underlies the laws of nature, the structure of the *pancha-mahabhutas* (five elements), the operation of karma, and the formation of *jivas*.

Pure macrocosmic *sattva* is called *pratibimba chaitanya* — reflected consciousness. Though still within maya, it is transparent enough to reflect Brahman with minimal distortion. This reflected awareness is responsible for all knowledge within the creation. It is not a "being" or "deity," but the formless order and intelligence within the dharma field. It gives rise to *Ishvara* — not as a person, but as the principle of cosmic order, the all-knowing intelligence that governs cause and effect, subtle and gross manifestation.

While *tamas* conceals and *rajas* projects, it is *sattva* that reveals. As such, *Ishvara's* "mind" is pure *sattva*, enabling omniscience without agency. Even the subtlest expressions of thought, vision, and creativity arise from this universal sattvic substrate.

Vedantic Resolution

Sattva is the doorway, not the destination. It brings the mind into harmony, making it a fit instrument for Self-inquiry. When *sattva* predominates, the intellect is clear, the heart is open, and the senses are calm. This creates the ideal environment for assimilating the teachings of Vedanta.

But to remain attached to *sattva* is to mistake the path for the goal. Vedanta cautions against confusing experiential bliss (*ananda*) with the bliss of the Self (*anantyam*). *Sattva* can feel like liberation, but true freedom is not a feeling — it is the recognition that you are Brahman, ever-free, regardless of the state of the mind.

When even *sattva* is known to be not-Self, when the subtlest tendencies are seen as objects in awareness, only then does the *jiva* dissolve. What remains is svarupa — unchanging, uncaused, unbound.

Thus the sage lives with *sattva* but is not bound by it — like a swan gliding across the water, never wet.

satya

(satya — *suht-yuh*)

In Advaita Vedanta, *satya* means that which is absolutely real —
that which exists in all three periods of time (past, present, future)
and is independent of anything else for its existence. By this definition, only Brahman, pure consciousness, is satya. Everything
else is mithya — apparently real, but dependent on Brahman for
its being.

The classic example is the clay and the pot: the pot is a name
and form (*nama-rupa*) superimposed upon clay. The pot changes,
breaks, and disappears, while the clay remains. Clay is *satya*, pot
is *mithya*. Similarly, the world (*jagat*) has dependent existence,
while Brahman is the independent reality.

Shankara explains: *sat* is that which never changes, which is never
negated. *Asat* is that which never exists at all, like a square circle.
Mithya is in between: it appears, functions, and is experienced, but
it has no independent reality. Thus, Vedanta does not dismiss the
world as "illusion" in the sense of nothingness; rather, it classifies
it as dependent reality.

To live wisely is to discriminate (*viveka*) between *satya* and *mithya*.
Our error lies in giving *mithya* (objects, experiences, relationships)
the status of *satya*. This is the cause of bondage. The purpose of
Vedanta is to reveal that one's true Self (atman) is *satya* — limitless awareness, unchanging and ever-present. Once this is understood, the world is not denied but seen in its proper perspective:
as a dependent, playful expression (*lila*) of Brahman.

—

Root & Meaning

From Sanskrit *sat* ("being, truth, real") + suffix *-ya* ("that which is"). Satya = truth, reality, that which truly is.

Scriptural References

- **Chandogya Upanishad (6.2.1):** *sat eva somya idam agra asit* — "In the beginning, my dear, this was Existence (sat) alone."
- **Bhagavad Gita (2.16):** *nasato vidyate bhavo nabhavo vidyate satah* — "The unreal never is; the real never ceases to be."
- **Shankara Bhashya:** clay–pot, gold–ornament, rope–snake analogies to show *satya–mithya* distinction.

Traditional View

- Satya is unchanging reality, independent of all conditions.
- Only Brahman/atman is satya.
- The world, prakriti, and the jiva's body-mind-sense complex are mithya, dependent on satya.

Vedantic Analysis

- Orders of reality:
  - *Paramarthika satya* — absolute reality (Brahman).
  - *Vyavaharika satya* — empirical, transactional reality (the world, *Ishvara*).
  - *Pratibhasika satya* — subjective reality (dreams, hallucinations, misconceptions).
- Wisdom (*jnana*) means recognizing *satya* as *satya* and *mithya* as *mithya*.
- Self-knowledge (*atma-jnana*) is claiming "I am *satya*" — existence-
  consciousness itself, not an object among objects.

Common Misunderstandings

- **Satya = factual truth.** In Vedanta, it is not about factual or empirical truth but ultimate, unchanging reality.
- **Mithya = illusion or non-existence.** *Mithya* is not false like a fantasy; it is dependent reality, valid until understood in light of *satya*.
- **Satya and mithya are two separate substances.** In fact, *mithya* is non-separate from *satya*, just as pot is non-separate from clay.

Vedantic Resolution

The key teaching is *Brahma satyam jagan mithya* — Brahman alone is real, the world is dependent reality, and the *jiva* is none other than Brahman. Realizing this truth ends bondage and reveals fullness (*purnatva*).

shama

(śama — *shuh-muh*)

In Vedanta, *shama (śama)* means mastery of the mind — the capacity to quiet its wanderings and redirect it toward what truly matters. The word comes from the root sham, "to become calm, to be quiet." It is the first jewel of the sixfold inner wealth (*shatka-sampatti*) and is essential for assimilating Self-knowledge.

The untrained mind is restless, pulled by countless desires and fears. Like a monkey leaping from branch to branch, it rarely rests. *Shama* does not mean destroying thoughts or suppressing feelings, but cultivating inner governance. It is the ability to notice a thought and decide: "Does this serve the pursuit of liberation? If not, let it pass."

Shama is the first line of defense. If a desire arises, the disciplined mind evaluates it before it becomes action. If the mind fails, dama — control of the senses — is the second line of defense, restraining outward behavior. Thus, *shama* and *dama* work hand-in-hand: one masters thought, the other action.

The *Bhagavad Gita* (6.26) teaches: "Wherever the restless mind wanders, restraining it, one should bring it back to reference of the Self." This is the essence of *shama*: not annihilation of thought but reorientation toward Self-knowledge.

In practice, *shama* grows through *karma yoga*, meditation, and discriminative living (*viveka*). It matures into a natural quietude, where the mind ceases to chase every impulse and becomes a fit instrument for inquiry. Without *shama*, the *shastra* cannot take root; with it, the seeker's mind becomes like a still lake, reflecting truth clearly.

—

Root & Meaning

Root: *sham* = to quiet, calm, pacify.
Shama = mastery of the mind, inner quietude, discipline of thought.

Scriptural References

- **Tattva Bodha (Shankara):** defines *shama* as the control of the mind.
- **Bhagavad Gita (6.26):** "Wherever the mind wanders, restrain it and bring it to the Self."
- **Vivekachudamani (v. 22):** praises *shama* as essential for the seeker of truth.

Traditional View

- *Shama* is the ability to bring the mind back from distraction.
- It is the first jewel of the sixfold wealth (*shatka-sampatti*).
- Developed through *karma yoga*, reflection, and moderation of lifestyle.

Vedantic Analysis

- Thoughts are natural, but identification with them is optional.
- *Shama* teaches discernment: letting the unhelpful go, nurturing what aligns with Self-inquiry.
- It neutralizes *raga-dvesha* (likes and dislikes) at the mental level.
- A quiet mind is a prerequisite for *shravana* (listening), *manana* (reflection), and *nididhyasana* (contemplation).

Common Misunderstandings

- **That shama means suppression:** It is intelligent management, not repression.
- **That shama requires total thoughtlessness:** It is guidance of

thought, not annihilation.

- **That shama is only for ascetics:** It can be cultivated in daily life through mindfulness and dharmic living.

Vedantic Resolution

Shama is mastery of the mind, the capacity to quiet distraction and direct thought toward liberation. It is not about suppressing life but about creating inner space, making the mind a clear mirror for Self-knowledge.

shastra

(śāstra — *SHAAS-truh*)

The Sanskrit word *shastra* (*śāstra*) comes from the root *shas* — "to instruct, to teach, to govern." In its broadest sense, *shastra* means scripture, treatise, or any authoritative body of knowledge that disciplines and instructs. In Vedanta, *shastra* refers above all to the Upanishads, *Bhagavad Gita*, and *Brahma Sutras* — collectively called the *prasthana-traya* — along with their traditional commentaries.

What distinguishes *shastra* from ordinary knowledge is that it functions as a *pramana* — a valid means of knowledge. The senses are *pramanas* for perceiving colors and sounds, inference is a *pramana* for reasoning, but the Self (atman / Brahman) cannot be objectified by either. It is revealed only by *shastra*, handled by a competent teacher. In this way, *shastra* is not a book of commandments or dogma, but a mirror — a means of removing ignorance about what is already true.

Shankara emphasizes that *shastra* has no other purpose than liberation (*moksha*). Its authority is unique: not arbitrary, but rooted in the fact that it reveals what cannot be known otherwise. To reject *shastra* is to close the only doorway into Self-knowledge. To idolize *shastra* as a set of rigid rules is also a mistake, since Vedanta teaching is always adapted to the student.

Thus, in the Vedantic tradition, *shastra* is revered not as a book to be worshiped but as a *pramana* to be wielded. It must be unfolded by a teacher (*guru*), received by a prepared mind (*adhikari*), and assimilated through reflection and contemplation. Its role is finished when Self-knowledge is gained — like a thorn used to remove another thorn, *shastra* itself can be set aside once ignorance is dispelled.

Root & Meaning

Root: *shas* = to teach, instruct, discipline.
Shastra = scripture, teaching, authoritative treatise; in Vedanta, the Upanishads and supporting texts functioning as a *pramana* for Self-knowledge.

Scriptural References

- **Brihadaranyaka Upanishad (2.4.10):** "Atman is to be known only from the *shastra* and by a teacher who knows it."
- **Bhagavad Gita (16.24):** "Therefore let *shastra* be your authority in determining what should be done and what should not."
- **Shankara Bhashya (Brahma Sutras 2.1.11):** stresses that *shastra* alone reveals Brahman.

Traditional View

- *Shastra* is a *pramana*, not an optional aid but the only means to know Brahman.
- Authority comes not from command but from revealing what is otherwise unknowable.
- The *prasthana-traya* and other Vedantic texts are central *shastras*.

Vedantic Analysis

- *Shastra* functions like a mirror, showing what is already the case.
- Unlike sense perception or inference, it operates in the field of Self-knowledge.
- It requires a teacher to unfold, since it can be misread if approached merely as literature.
- Its role is provisional: when Self-knowledge is firm, *shastra* has completed its work.

Common Misunderstandings

- **That shastra is a set of commandments:** It is not law but revelation.
- **That shastra is optional:** Without *shastra* there is no *pramana* for Self-knowledge.
- **That shastra is to be idolized:** It is a means, not an end in itself.
- **That shastra can be interpreted alone without a teacher:** In the tradition, *shastra* is always unfolded by a guru. Left to one's own interpretation, the student risks reinforcing ignorance with personal bias. The guru makes *shastra* a living *pramana* by removing doubts, clarifying terms, and guiding the mind step by step.

Vedantic Resolution

Shastra is the indispensable means of Self-knowledge. By clarifying the distinction between the Self and the non-Self, it removes ignorance. Revered, unfolded, and assimilated, *shastra* is the bridge from bondage to freedom.

shatka sampatti

(ṣaṭka sampatti — *shuht-ka suhm-PUHT-tee*)

Vedanta requires a mind that is subtle, steady, and prepared to receive Self-knowledge. Shankara describes this preparation as the *sadhana-catushtaya* (fourfold qualifications), one of which is the *shatka-sampatti (ṣaṭka-sampatti)* — the sixfold wealth. These six disciplines polish the mind so that it can hold, reflect, and assimilate the teaching.

The six are:

1. **Shama** — mastery of the mind. The ability to quieten its constant wandering and bring it back to the Self.
2. **Dama** — restraint of the senses. Not repression, but intelligent governance so the senses serve inquiry rather than scatter attention.
3. **Uparati** — withdrawal. A natural turning away from distractions and compulsive activity, dwelling instead in one's duty and pursuit of truth.
4. **Titiksha** — forbearance. Cheerful endurance of life's opposites — heat and cold, pleasure and pain, success and failure — without agitation.
5. **Shraddha** — trust in the *shastra* and the guru as a valid *pramana* for Self-knowledge. Not blind belief, but an open-minded confidence in the teaching.
6. **Samadhana** — concentration, single-pointedness. The ability to hold the mind steadily in contemplation of the Self.

Together, these six qualities build the seeker's greatest wealth — not external possessions but inner mastery. They transform the mind from a restless servant of desire into a fit instrument of knowledge. In this way, the *shatka-sampatti* is indispensable: without discipline, inquiry collapses into distraction or doubt; with it, the mind becomes luminous, ready to recognize the ever-present Self.

—

Root & Meaning

Shatka = group of six.
Sampatti = wealth, possession.
Shatka-sampatti = the sixfold inner wealth

Scriptural References

- **Tattva Bodha (Shankara):** lists and defines the *shatka-sampatti* as qualifications for Self-inquiry.
- **Vivekachudamaṇi (v. 19–28):** elaborates on each discipline.
- **Bhagavad Gita (6.5–15; 17.15–16):** praises mastery of mind, senses, endurance, faith, and concentration.

Traditional View

- These six virtues are preparatory, not ultimate.
- They are cultivated through *karma yoga*, devotion, and a dharmic life.
- Their purpose is to make the mind quiet, clear, and steady — fit for Self-knowledge.

Vedantic Analysis

- *Shama* and *dama* address the restless and extroverted tendencies of the mind.
- *Uparati* and *titiksha* strengthen resilience and detachment.
- *Shraddha* opens the door to assimilating *shastra* unfolded by the guru.
- *Samadhana* ensures focus on the Self rather than scattering in pursuits.
- Collectively, they address *mala* (impurity), *vikshepa* (distraction),

and *avarana* (ignorance).

Common Misunderstandings

- **That they require ascetic withdrawal:** They are not suppression but intelligent mastery within ordinary life.
- **That shraddha means blind faith:** It is trust based on discernment and experience.
- **That they are optional:** Without some degree of discipline, Vedanta remains intellectual and cannot liberate.

Vedantic Resolution

The *shatka-sampatti* is called wealth because it enriches the seeker with the inner resources necessary for *moksha*. It is not about repression but about freedom: a mind that is steady, faithful, and concentrated is a mind prepared for Self-knowledge.

shraddha

(śraddhā — *shruhd-DHAA*)

The Sanskrit word *shraddha* (*śraddhā*) is often translated as "faith," but in Vedanta it carries a more precise meaning. Derived from *shrat* (truth, heart) and *dha* (to place, to hold), *shraddha* literally means "to place the heart upon." It is the trusting confidence that the *shastra* (scripture) and the teacher are valid means of knowledge for revealing the Self.

Unlike blind belief, shraddha is faith pending one's own investigation. It does not mean suppressing doubt or abandoning reason, but holding trust provisionally until the teaching is examined and validated. Just as one follows a doctor's prescription before the cure is confirmed, the student of Vedanta gives *shraddha* and guru the benefit of the doubt until knowledge becomes clear.

Shankara emphasizes that without *shraddha*, Self-knowledge does not take root. The mind that refuses trust constantly second-guesses or reinterprets the teaching, and thus the *pramana* (means of knowledge) cannot function. With *shraddha*, the mirror of *shastra*, unfolded by the guru, can reveal what is already true: "I am fullness itself."

Shraddha is also one of the sixfold disciplines (*shatka-sampatti*) within the fourfold qualifications (*sadhana-chatushtaya*). Together with *shama, dama, uparati, titiksha,* and *samadhana,* it refines the mind and makes it a fit instrument for Self-knowledge.

Thus, *shraddha* is not the end of inquiry but its foundation. It begins as provisional faith and culminates in certainty, dissolving into direct knowledge when the Self is recognized.

—

Root & Meaning

Shrat = truth, heart
Dha = to place, to hold
Shraddha = to place the heart upon; intelligent trust, faith pending one's own investigation.

Scriptural References

- **Bhagavad Gita (4.39):** "The one endowed with *shraddha* attains knowledge."
- **Bhagavad Gita (17.3):** "A person is made of *shraddha*; whatever his *shraddha*, that he is."
- **Tattva Bodha:** defines *shraddha* as trust in the words of the guru and *shastra*.

Traditional View

- *Shraddha* is a prerequisite for liberation.
- It is the openness that allows the *shastra* to work as a *pramana*.
- Not blind belief, but intelligent trust until the truth is validated by one's own understanding.

Vedantic Analysis

- *Shraddha* suspends habitual doubt (*samshaya*), allowing the teaching to be assimilated.
- It does not cancel inquiry but enables it to function.
- Once knowledge is clear, *shraddha* has served its purpose; it resolves into direct vision of truth.

Common Misunderstandings

- **That shraddha is blind faith:** In Vedanta it is intelligent trust, not credulity.
- **That shraddha means suppressing doubt:** It means holding

doubt in suspension until clarified.

- **That shraddha is optional:** Without it, *shastra* cannot operate as a *pramana*.
- **That one can interpret shastra without shraddha in guru and teaching:** The tradition insists *shraddha* includes trust in the teacher's unfolding, not self-interpretation alone.

Vedantic Resolution

Shraddha is provisional faith, "pending one's own investigation." It is the openness that allows the *shastra* to reveal the Self. By placing the heart in the teaching until it proves itself, the seeker ripens into knowledge and freedom.

shravana

(śravaṇa — *shruh-vuh-nuh*)

In Vedanta, shravana *(śravaṇa)* means "listening" — not ordinary hearing, but attentive reception of the Upanishadic teaching from a qualified teacher. It is the first of the three steps of self-knowledge: *shravana, manana, nididhyasana.*

Shankara insists that liberation comes only through knowledge *(jnana),* and *shravana* is the gateway to that knowledge. It requires not only hearing the words but also openness, humility, and faith *(shraddha).* The seeker exposes themselves to the *shastra* (scripture), trusting the teaching as a valid means of knowledge *(pramana).*

Unlike ordinary learning, *shravana* is not about gathering information. It is a process of undoing ignorance, allowing the words of the Upanishads to point the mind back to its source — the Self. Just as a mirror reveals a face that was always present, so the teaching reveals the Self that never departs.

—

Root & Meaning

From root *shru* = to hear.
Shravana = listening, hearing the teaching.

Scriptural References

• **Brihadaranyaka Upanishad 2.4.5:** "Atman is to be heard *(shrotavyah),* reflected upon, and meditated upon."
• **Shankara's commentary:** Knowledge arises from *shravana* of the *mahavakyas* (great statements of the Upanishads).

Traditional View

- **First stage of self-inquiry:** hearing the teaching from a qualified teacher.
- Requires faith (*shraddha*) and preparation (*adhikaritva*).
- Planting the seed of knowledge; later deepened by *manana* and *nididhyasana*.

Vedantic Analysis

- *Shravana* is not passive hearing; it is exposure to the *pramana* (means of knowledge).
- Through repeated listening, the mind begins to shift its identification away from the non-Self.
- Essential: one cannot bypass *shravana* by relying on reasoning or meditation alone.

Common Misunderstandings

- **That shravana = reading books:** It requires a living teacher to unfold the *shastra*.
- **That shravana is once-and-done:** It is often repeated until clarity dawns.
- **That shravana alone is liberation:** It plants the seed; assimilation may require *manana* and *nididhyasana*.

Vedantic Resolution

Shravana is the attentive hearing of the Upanishadic teaching. It opens the door to self-knowledge, planting the seed that is later assimilated through reflection and contemplation.

Shrishti-Drishti-Vada

(Śṛṣṭi-Dṛṣṭi-Vāda — *SHRISH-tee-DRISH-tee-VAA-duh*)

Vedanta uses different vadas (doctrines or explanatory models) to guide the seeker. *Shrishti-Drishti-Vada (Śṛṣṭi-Dṛṣṭi-Vāda)* literally means "creation-first, perception-after." It is the common-sense view that the world is created first and then experienced by the individual. This is the standpoint adopted in most of the Upanishads and in the early stages of teaching, because it aligns with our ordinary perception: first there is a universe, then we are born into it to experience pleasure and pain.

According to this model, *Ishvara* (God) creates the *jagat* (world) as an orderly manifestation of maya, and individual *jivas* enter this creation to work out their karmas. This framework preserves the transactional world (*vyavaharika-satta*) and explains dharma, karma, rebirth, and the role of the Veda. It also affirms *Ishvara* as the intelligent and material cause of the cosmos.

However, Advaita Vedanta eventually shifts beyond this standpoint. At a more advanced level, *Drishti-Shrishti-Vada* ("perception-first, creation-after") is introduced, pointing out that the world we know is inseparable from perception. Ultimately, both models are provisional; the final vision is *Ajati-Vada* (Gaudapada's teaching), that in truth no creation ever took place — only Brahman is.

Thus, *Shrishti-Drishti-Vada* is a skillful teaching device. It begins where the student stands, affirming the reality of the world and its order. From there, inquiry gradually refines the vision until even the idea of creation is resolved into non-dual awareness.

—

Root & Meaning

Shrishti = creation
Drishti = perception, seeing
Vada = doctrine, explanatory model
Shrishti-Drishti-Vada = "creation-first, perception-after" — the view that the world is created independently and then perceived.

Scriptural References

- **Chandogya Upanishad (6.2.3):** "From that Being, existence, this entire world arose."
- **Taittiriya Upanishad (3.1):** cosmological description of creation from Brahman.
- **Bhagavad Gita (9.10):** "Under Me, as the supervisor, *prakriti* produces all moving and unmoving beings."

Traditional View

- Used as the initial teaching in Advaita Vedanta.
- Explains karma, rebirth, dharma, and *Ishvara's* role as creator.
- Holds transactional validity (*vyavaharika-satta*), not ultimate reality.

Vedantic Analysis

- Provisional *prakriya* for beginners, not the final standpoint.
- Leads to subtler doctrines (*Drishti-Shrishti-Vada, Ajati-Vada*).
- Its role is pedagogical: affirm order first, then refine vision until creation itself is seen as *mithya*.

Common Misunderstandings

- **That Shrishti-Drishti-Vada is the final teaching:** Advaita accepts it only provisionally.
- **That it implies dualistic creation separate from**

Brahman: Creation is maya's manifestation, non-separate from Brahman.

- **That creation is "real" in the absolute sense:** Vedanta clarifies it is *mithya* — dependent reality.

Vedantic Resolution

Shrishti-Drishti-Vada is an introductory model. It preserves the reality of world and dharma at the transactional level, while paving the way to subtler insights that culminate in non-dual vision: there was never any creation apart from Brahman.

shruti

(śruti — *shru-tee*)

In Vedanta, *shruti (śruti)* refers to the revealed scriptures —
the Vedas — especially their philosophical culmination in the
Upanishads. The word comes from the root *śru*, "to hear." Unlike
smriti ("that which is remembered"), which includes texts like the
Mahabharata, Puranas, and *Dharmashastras, shruti* is considered
apaurusheya — not of human origin. It was "heard" by ancient
sages (*rishis*) in deep meditation and transmitted orally for centuries before being written down.

Shruti is the primary *pramana* (means of knowledge) for Brahman.
The Self cannot be objectified by perception or inference, since it is
the very subject that makes knowing possible. Only *shruti* has the
authority to reveal what lies beyond sensory or intellectual reach.
For this reason, Vedanta always anchors its teaching in the *mahavakyas* of the Upanishads, such as *tat tvam asi* ("you are That") and
aham brahmasmi ("I am Brahman").

The role of *shruti* is not to command or legislate, but to reveal. Its
authority lies in its unique domain: knowledge of the Self, which
no other source can provide. Yet *shruti* does not function automatically; it must be unfolded by a qualified teacher and assimilated
by a prepared student. Once Self-knowledge is firm, *shruti* has
served its purpose, like a map that is set aside once the destination is reached.

In this way, *shruti* is revered as the very voice of truth. It is not
worshiped as an idol, nor dismissed as poetry, but honored as the
indispensable mirror in which the Self is revealed.

—

Root & Meaning

Shru = to hear.

Shruti = "that which is heard"; revealed scripture, the Vedas (esp. the Upanishads).

Scriptural References

- **Mundaka Upanishad (1.1.5):** distinguishes higher (*para*) and lower (*apara*) knowledge, placing knowledge of Brahman (revealed in *shruti*) as the higher.
- **Brihadaranyaka Upanishad (2.4.10):** "Atman is to be known only through *shruti* and the teaching of a guru."
- **Bhagavad Gita (16.24):** "Let *shastra* (here implying *shruti*) be your authority in determining what should and should not be done."

Traditional View

- *Shruti* is *apaurusheya* (not authored by any person).
- It is the highest authority in matters of Brahman and dharma.
- Upanishads form the heart of *shruti* for Advaita Vedanta.

Vedantic Analysis

- *Shruti* is a *pramana* — a unique means of knowledge revealing the Self.
- Perception and inference cannot access Brahman; *shruti* alone points to it.
- It must be unfolded by a guru and assimilated through *shravana, manana, nididhyasana*.
- Its role ends when Self-knowledge is clear — the mirror is no longer needed once the face is seen.

Common Misunderstandings

- **That shruti is authored like any other book:** It is considered revealed, not composed.
- **That shruti is optional:** Without it, Self-knowledge has no *pramana*.
- **That shruti can be understood without a teacher:** Tradition insists on transmission (*sampradaya*) to avoid misinterpretation.
- **That shruti is merely historical literature:** Its function is not cultural but revelatory.

Vedantic Resolution

Shruti is the foundation of Vedanta — the revelation of truth heard by the sages and preserved as the Upanishads. It is the indispensable means of knowledge for Brahman, a mirror that reflects the ever-free Self.

sthula sharira

(sthūla śarīra — *STHOO-luh shuh-REE-ruh*)

The gross body (*sthula sharira* — *sthūla śarīra*) is the physical body, the most tangible layer of our apparent existence. Composed of the five gross elements — space, air, fire, water, and earth — it is the temporary vehicle through which the individual (*jiva*) transacts with the world. Because it is sustained by food, it is also called annamaya kosha, the food sheath.

The gross body is born of karma. It arises when specific karmic results (*prarabdha*) require a field of experience. The Upanishads and later Vedantic texts emphasize that the body is not the Self but only an instrument. Just as one resides in a house but is not the house, so too the Self "inhabits" the body without being the body. The body grows, changes, suffers, and eventually dies — but the witnessing consciousness remains untouched.

Vedanta also explains the macrocosmic and microcosmic dimensions of the gross body. At the macrocosmic level, the total of all physical forms is called *Virat* or *Vaishvanara*, the cosmic person. At the microcosmic level, the individual's physical form is the personal gross body (*sthula sharira*) . In the waking state (*jagrat avastha*), the *jiva* identifies most strongly with this body, taking it to be "I."

But identification with the gross body is one of the great confusions (*adhyasa*) of human life. Since the Self is consciousness — which illumines the body — one cannot truly be limited to flesh, bone, or form. Teachers remind us: "Bodies are just earth moving. They never leave the earth, only the subtle body departs." The gross body, though necessary for human birth and spiritual pursuit, is ultimately not-Self (*anatman*).

—

Root & Meaning

Sthula = gross, physical, dense
Sharira = body
Sthula Sharira = the physical or gross body, composed of the five gross elements.

Scriptural References

- **Taittiriya Upanishad (2.1):** introduces the *annamaya kosha* (food sheath), identifying the body as made of food and returning to food.
- **Bhagavad Gita (2.22):** "As a person casts off worn-out clothes and puts on new ones, so too the embodied Self casts off worn-out bodies and enters others."
- **Vivekachudamani (v. 90):** "The gross body is the abode of enjoyment of the fruits of past action. It is subject to birth, old age, and death."

Traditional View

- A product of food and sustained by food.
- Vehicle for dharma and *moksha*, since only in a human gross body is Self-knowledge possible.
- The field of experience for karmic results.

Vedantic Analysis

- The gross body is *mithya*: dependent reality, not the ultimate Self.
- At the macrocosmic level, it is the *Virat*, the sum of all gross bodies.
- At the microcosmic level, it is the personal body identified as "I."
- It functions primarily in the waking state.
- Its impermanence shows that "I" cannot truly be the body.

Common Misunderstandings

- **That the body is the Self:** The Self illumines the body but is never limited by it.
- **That the gross body is permanent:** It is subject to birth, growth, decay, and death.
- **That liberation means escape from the body:** Liberation is freedom while living, knowing oneself as consciousness, not dependent on the body's condition.

Vedantic Resolution

The *sthula sharira* is a temporary instrument, sustained by food and karma, dissolving back into the five elements at death. It is vital for the journey of Self-knowledge, but ultimately, it is not who we are. The Self is consciousness, eternal and free, the witness of the body.

sukshma sharira

(sūkṣma śarīra — *SOOK-shmuh shuh-REE-ruh*)

The *sukshma sharira (sūkṣma śarīra)*, or subtle body, is the inner instrument (*antahkarana*) and life-force complex that animates the physical body. Unlike the *sthula sharira* (gross body), which is made of the five gross elements, the subtle body is composed of subtle matter — the building blocks of thought, perception, and energy.

It is said to consist of nineteen parts:

- **Five organs of perception (jnanendriyas)** — hearing, touch, sight, taste, smell.
- **Five organs of action (karmendriyas)** — speech, hands, feet, excretion, procreation.
- **Five vital forces (pranas)** — *prana, apana, vyana, udana, samana,* governing respiration, elimination, circulation, expression, and digestion.
- **Four inner instruments (antahkarana)** — mind (*manas*), intellect (buddhi), ego (*ahankara*), and memory (*chitta*).

The subtle body is what makes perception, cognition, and action possible. It is not conscious by itself — it is *jada* (inert) — but it reflects awareness, borrowing the light of consciousness (*chit*), much like a mirror reflects sunlight. Through this borrowed awareness, the *jiva* experiences the world of names and forms.

Vedanta stresses that the subtle body is not the Self. Thoughts, emotions, and perceptions belong to this level of identity. Since we can witness our own thoughts, we cannot be them. According to karma theory, the subtle body travels from life to life, carrying impressions (*vasanas*) and karmic seeds, until Self-knowledge reveals one's true nature as limitless awareness.

At the macrocosmic level, the total subtle body is called *Hiranyagarbha*, the "golden womb," the cosmic intelligence that holds together the order of creation. At the microcosmic level, it is the *Taijasa*, the "effulgent one," active in the dream state, where gross senses are suspended but the mind still projects experiences.

In practice, the subtle body is central to spiritual inquiry. Its purification (*antahkarana-shuddhi*) through *karma yoga*, devotion, meditation, and ethical living makes the mind sattvic and capable of grasping Vedantic truth. Yet, at the final step, even this subtle body must be recognized as *anatman* — not-Self — for it too is changing, dependent, and perishable.

—

Root & Meaning

Sukshma = subtle, fine, minute
Sharira = body
Sukshma Sharira = the subtle body; the mind-body-energy complex composed of subtle matter.

Scriptural References

- **Taittiriya Upanishad (2.2–2.4):** teaches about the *pranamaya*, *manomaya*, and *vijnanamaya koshas* — vital, mental, and intellectual sheaths — all belonging to the subtle body.
- **Bhagavad Gita (15.8):** "As the wind carries scents, so too the embodied self carries the subtle body from one body to another."
- **Vivekachudamani (v. 94):** describes the subtle body as made up of the five *pranas*, the ten senses, and the fourfold inner instrument.

Traditional View

- Instrument for perception, cognition, and action.

- Travels with the jiva from one life to another, carrying karmic tendencies.
- In dreams, the subtle body projects its own world apart from the gross body.

Vedantic Analysis

- Inert by itself; reflects awareness.
- Made of subtle matter (*sattva*-dominant), yet impermanent.
- Source of bondage when mistaken as "I," source of liberation when seen as not-Self.
- Macrocosm: *Hiranyagarbha* (cosmic mind).
- Microcosm: *Taijasa* (dreamer).

Common Misunderstandings

- **That the subtle body is eternal:** It survives death, but dissolves at the end of creation (*pralaya*).
- **That thoughts and feelings are "me":** They arise in the subtle body but are witnessed by the Self.
- **That subtle = spiritual:** Subtle matter is still matter, not consciousness.

Vedantic Resolution

The subtle body (*sukshma sharira*) is essential for experience and growth, but it is not the ultimate reality. It is a medium of reflection, a bundle of functions that persists — according to karma theory — across births. Self-knowledge reveals that one is not the mind, intellect, ego, or *pranas*, but the awareness in whose presence the subtle body appears and disappears.

sushupti

(suṣupti — *su-shup-tee*)

When dream subsides, a greater silence rises. The lights of perception go out one by one: sight, sound, memory, the sense of "I." What remains is not nothing, but everything unmanifest — a vast, undifferentiated stillness in which both the world and the one who knew the world have dissolved.

Vedanta calls this state *sushupti (suṣupti)*, deep sleep. It is the most mysterious of the three: in *jagrat* (waking state), consciousness looks outward; in *svapna* (dream state), it looks inward; in *sushupti*, it does not look at all. The mind and senses are withdrawn; the intellect is at rest; individuality vanishes. Yet we do not cease to be. Upon waking, everyone says, "I slept well; I knew nothing." The very memory of that blankness proves presence.

The deep sleeper experiences the bliss of the Self without knowing the Self — like a mirror in a dark room, capable of reflection but unlit. The *Mandukya Upanishad* names this experiencer *Prajna*, "the wise one," because in that state all is resolved into potential, resting in the causal body (*karana sharira*).

Swami Dayananda likens it to *laya*, dissolution: just as the cosmos withdraws into maya at the end of a *kalpa*, the individual dissolves into the causal sheath each night. No subject–object distinction, no doer, no enjoyer — only total ignorance and latent potential.

Vedanta teacher James Swartz clarifies that deep sleep is not personal ignorance (*avidya*) but universal ignorance (maya) — the tamasic aspect of *Ishvara* in which the individual mind is temporarily merged. The Self is never absent; it simply does not shine through the intellect, which alone can recognize it. Thus, the sleeper is "almost enlightened," enjoying limitless awareness without knowing what is enjoyed.

When waking returns, the seed of individuality (vasanas) sprouts again, and with it, the world.

—

Root & Meaning

Root: From *svap* ("to sleep") with the prefix *su-* ("good, complete") = "good sleep," "deep rest." Literal meaning: The condition of dreamless sleep; total absorption of the mind.

Scriptural References

- **Mandukya Upanishad (Verse 5):** *Yatra supto na kamchana kamam kamayate na kamcana svapnam pashyati tat sushuptam.* — "When one, being asleep, neither desires nor dreams — that is deep sleep."
- **Commentary (Shankara):** "In that state, the mind and senses are merged; the self is one mass of consciousness and bliss; yet, owing to ignorance, it does not know itself."
- **Swami Paramarthananda:** "During *laya* [individual deep sleep/ dissolution] and *pralaya* [cosmic deep sleep/dissolution], the whole universe remains in seed form within maya. The deep sleep of the individual mirrors the cosmic sleep of *Ishvara*."

Traditional View

In deep sleep, both the gross (*sthula*) and subtle (*sukshma*) bodies are resolved into the causal (*karana*). The intellect and ego are inactive; hence there is no individuality or perception. It is said to be the same for everyone, because the personal subconscious dissolves into the macrocosmic causal body of *Ishvara*.

Sushupti is governed by *tamas*, while *rajas* and *sattva* remain dormant. The experience is one of peace and ignorance (*sukha-ajnana-anubhava*) — blissful unawareness. It is the only state where all distinctions collapse: time, space, and individuality rest together in seed form.

Vedantic Analysis

1. Experiencer

- *Prajna* — "the wise one," or sleeper, identified with the causal body.
- Enjoys bliss (*ananda-bhuk*) but lacks awareness of that enjoyment.
- Symbolizes *Ishvara* in the microcosm — omniscient in potential, but not functioning.

2. Nature of Experience

- No subject–object division.
- Presence of consciousness without objects — *nirvikalpa vritti* (subtle, non-dual thought-form).
- After waking, this experience is inferred: "I slept well; I knew nothing."

3. Ignorance Debate

- *Avidya* (personal ignorance) does not exist here; the sleeper's intellect is absent.
- What remains is maya — cosmic ignorance, the unmanifest state of the three *gunas*.
- Hence, *sushupti* is universal, not individual.

4. Ontological Role

- Deep sleep represents potential existence (*sat-karya-vada*) — nothing new is created upon waking; the unmanifest simply becomes manifest again.

5. Macrocosmic Parallel

- Individual *sushupti* = *laya* (mini dissolution)
- Cosmic *sushupti* = *pralaya* (total dissolution)
- Both are expressions of *Ishvara's* causal aspect, where all names and forms lie dormant.

Common Misunderstandings

- "Deep sleep is unconsciousness." Not true. If it were, there could be no memory of it. What is absent is not awareness, but the reflecting medium — the mind.
- "Ignorance is destroyed in deep sleep." No. *Avidya* is dormant, not destroyed. Knowledge alone removes it.
- "Deep sleep is liberation." The bliss of deep sleep is experiential and dependent on *tamas*; liberation (*moksha*) is knowledge-based and available even while awake.

Vedantic Resolution

Sushupti shows that bliss is natural — not created by experience but revealed when thought ceases. Yet it also reveals the price of ignorance: peace without knowledge. The Self shines unopposed, but because the intellect is absent, it is not recognized.

"The sleeper is almost enlightened," writes Swartz, "because he experiences the limitlessness of awareness, but lacks the knowledge of what he is experiencing."

Thus, deep sleep becomes both metaphor and mirror: the return of all manifestation into silence — and a nightly reminder that peace belongs to the Self, not to its absence.

svabhava

(svabhāva — *svuh-BHAA-vuh*)

The Sanskrit word *svabhava (svabhāva)* means "one's own nature." It combines *sva* ("own, self") with *bhava* ("being, becoming, disposition"). In ordinary usage it can mean temperament, innate tendency, or character. In Vedanta, however, it points more deeply to the essential nature of something.

The *Bhagavad Gita* frequently employs this term. Krishna tells Arjuna that all beings act according to their *svabhava* — the *gunas* of nature impel them, whether they wish it or not. From this perspective, *svabhava* is the product of one's constitution, conditioning, and past karma. It explains why each individual expresses a unique blend of tendencies.

But Vedanta also distinguishes between *svabhava* at the empirical level and the ultimate *svarupa* (intrinsic essence). At the level of *vyavahara*, one's *svabhava* is shaped by *gunas*, upbringing, and karmic impressions. At the level of *paramarthika satya*, inquiry shifts away from *svabhava* altogether and reveals one's *svarupa* as Brahman itself — pure existence-consciousness-limitlessness.

Vedanta therefore distinguishes between *svabhava* and *svarupa*. *Svabhava* belongs to the empirical personality shaped by *gunas* and karma, while *svarupa* refers to one's intrinsic essence as atman, identical with Brahman.

Understanding this distinction prevents confusion. In ordinary life, it is wise to recognize and honor one's *svabhava*—living in alignment with one's constitution and dharma. In self-inquiry, however, attention shifts away from temperament to one's *svarupa*, the limitless essence that is ever free from becoming.

—

Root & Meaning

Sva = own, self
Bhava = being, nature, disposition
Svabhava = one's own nature; inherent tendency, characteristic disposition.

Scriptural References

- **Bhagavad Gita (3.33):** "Even a wise man acts according to his own *svabhava*. Beings follow their nature; what can restraint accomplish?"
- **Bhagavad Gita (18.41–44):** *svabhava* determines the duties of *varnas* (social orders).
- **Shvetashvatara Upanishad (6.2):** asks whether the universe arises from *svabhava* (inherent nature), *kala* (time), or *Ishvara*.

Traditional View

- *Svabhava* explains differences in temperament, duty, and role at the empirical level.
- *Svarupa* refers to the intrinsic essence of atman, identical with Brahman, beyond all conditioning.

Vedantic Analysis

- *Svabhava* at the relative level is *prakriti*-driven; honoring it is part of living dharmically.
- At the level of *paramarthika satya*, inquiry shifts away from *svabhava* altogether and reveals one's *svarupa* as the Self, Brahman.

Common Misunderstandings

- **Confusing svabhava with svarupa:** Mistaking temperament, tendencies, or roles for the Self.

- **Assuming realization alters empirical nature:** Knowledge reveals one's *svarupa* as Brahman but does not erase *svabhava*; it changes one's relationship to it.
- **Confusing empirical svabhava with svarupa:** *Svabhava* belongs to the transactional personality, while *svarupa* refers to one's intrinsic essence as atman. Confusing the two leads to mistaking temperament for the Self.

Vedantic Resolution

To respect *svabhava* means to acknowledge one's empirical nature and live accordingly in dharma. To realize *svarupa* means to see beyond *gunas* and karma, recognizing that one's essential being is Brahman alone — pure, limitless, ever free.

svadharma

(svadharma — *svuh-DHAR-ma*)

We are not blank slates. We are not self-made. Despite what modern culture insists — that you can be anything, become anyone, reinvent yourself endlessly — Vedanta whispers something quieter, and truer: you are already something. You are born with a particular constitution, a unique rhythm, a temperament shaped not only by biology and psychology, but by karma and context. To know yourself is not to construct an identity, but to uncover a design that was already present.

Svadharma is that design. It is your nature, your alignment, your place in the Total. It is not a fixed job description, but the shape your life is meant to take. It is the current that runs underneath your personality, guiding you toward certain callings, relationships, and forms of contribution. You don't choose your *svadharma* any more than a river chooses its slope. You discover it — or else resist it and suffer the consequences.

In a culture obsessed with choice and optimization, *svadharma* may sound limiting. But it is not a cage; it is a compass. It does not shrink your freedom; it deepens it. When you follow your *svadharma*, you are no longer flailing against the current. You are not trying to be original or impressive. You are simply being true. Even if the outer form is humble, the inner alignment brings a peace that ambition cannot buy.

But this raises a dilemma many seekers feel: How do I know what my *svadharma* is?

It rarely arrives as a mystical revelation or a tidy job title. More often, it emerges slowly, through the friction between your temperament and the world. It reveals itself in the places where effort feels natural, where responsibility feels less like a burden and more like breathing. To discover it requires both honesty and patience. You learn by living, by testing the current, by paying attention to where resistance melts into flow. What matters is not perfect clarity from the beginning, but the willingness to ask sincerely: Am I acting in alignment, or am I performing a role that was never mine to play?

It is also worth remembering that svadharma does not necessarily equate to a career. Just because your *svadharma* inclines you toward artistry, teaching, or contemplation does not mean you must abandon the responsibilities that sustain your life and family. An artist may still work a day job and create in the evenings; a contemplative may still raise children or manage a household. What matters is not the outer label, but the inner alignment. To live *svadharma* is to allow your life to flow in harmony with your true nature, even if that expression takes a modest or partial form in the world.

The *Bhagavad Gita* speaks with startling clarity: "Better to fail in your own dharma than to succeed in another's." The goal is not perfection, but authenticity. The effort to mimic someone else's life — no matter how noble — brings fear, confusion, and inner conflict. But to live in accord with one's own nature, even if messy, is to live honestly. And that honesty has power.

It is sometimes said that the world needs individuals for every role, from good samaritan to clever thief. From one standpoint this is true: *Ishvara's* order contains all expressions of the *gunas*. Saints and sinners, rulers and con-artists, all appear in the unfolding of the Total. Yet we must be precise: to exist in the Total is not the same as to embody *svadharma*.

A thief may act according to their *svabhava* — their conditioning and impulses — but that does not make theft their *svadharma*. *Svadharma* is never *adharma*. It is always aligned with the sustaining order. This distinction is crucial. Inclination is not destiny. To mistake compulsion for calling is to remain bound; to recognize one's true alignment is to begin walking toward freedom.

And perhaps most importantly: to neglect one's *svadharma* is to agitate the mind. A person who lives in misalignment — chasing another's path, suppressing their own nature, or disguising themselves behind borrowed roles — will find no peace. The mind becomes restless, pulled by comparison, guilt, and unfulfilled longing.

Vedanta is clear: an agitated mind is not fit for Self-knowledge. The highest purpose of *svadharma* is not worldly success but inner stillness, the calm ground in which inquiry into the Self becomes possible. To live your *svadharma* is to prepare the mind for freedom.

Because in the end, *svadharma* is not something you fulfill. It is something you live — and in living it, the heart grows quiet enough to glimpse the truth of who you are.

—

Root & Meaning

Sva = "one's own"
Dharma = "law," "duty," "that which upholds"
Svadharma = one's own dharma; the role or alignment appropriate to one's nature and place within the cosmic order.

Scriptural References

- **Bhagavad Gita 3.35:** *"Shreyan svadharmo vigunah, para-dharmat svanushthitat…"* — "Better is one's own dharma, though imperfectly performed, than another's dharma, well-executed."
- **Bhagavad Gita 18.47:** *"Svabhava-niyatam karma, kurvan napnoti kilbisham…"* — "By performing the work that is one's own, as dictated by one's nature, one incurs no fault."
- **Bhagavad Gita 18.45:** *"Svabhava-prabhavair bhavaih…"* — "Each person, by their own nature-born qualities, is suited to

particular work."

These verses reveal the subtlety of *svadharma* — not as moral obligation imposed from without, but as the unfolding of one's own inner law.

Traditional View

Traditionally, *svadharma* was contextualized through the lens of *varna* (caste) and *ashrama* (life stage). For example, a *kishatriya's svadharma* included rulership and protection; a *brahmana's svadharma* emphasized study, teaching, and ritual. However, traditional commentators like Shankara have emphasized that *svabhava* — one's innate disposition — is the true determinant, not merely birth. Thus, *svadharma* is intimately tied to one's *gunas* and karmic tendencies (*vasanas*), rather than only to external roles.

Vedantic Analysis

Vedanta broadens *svadharma* beyond rigid social categories. It is not about fixed occupations but about alignment with the Total (*Ishvara's* order). *Svadharma* is discovered through honest living, self-reflection, and recognition of one's inner current.

Importantly, *svadharma* is not the same as *svabhava* (conditioning). One's *svabhava* may incline toward greed, anger, or deceit, but *svadharma* is always dharmic — it supports the sustaining order. Thus, a con-artist or thief may exist within the Total, but such roles are not *svadharma*.

Most crucially, *svadharma* matters because it affects the mind. To live against one's *svadharma* is to create restlessness; to live in accord with it is to foster clarity and stillness. Only such a mind is fit for Self-knowledge.

Common Misunderstandings

- **"Svadharma means do whatever feels natural."** False. That confuses *svabhava* with *svadharma*.
- **"Even thieves have svadharma."** Misleading. Thieves may exist in the world, but thievery is not *svadharma* because it is not aligned with dharma.
- **"Svadharma equals your career."** Not necessarily. One's *svadharma* may express itself in art, teaching, or service even if one's livelihood lies elsewhere.
- **"Svadharma is fixed by caste or birth."** Partial truth. Traditional context linked *svadharma* to *varna*, but Vedanta emphasizes temperament, capacity, and alignment with the Whole.

Vedantic Resolution

Svadharma is discovered, not invented. It is not merely inclination, nor social assignment, nor career choice. It is the inner alignment that allows one's life to harmonize with the Whole. Its highest purpose is not worldly success, but the quieting of the mind, so that Self-knowledge becomes possible.

To live *svadharma* is to live authentically, in truth, with dignity. And in that honesty, the heart is prepared for freedom.

svapna

(svapna — *svuhp-nuh*)

Dreams are the laboratory where Vedanta performs its cleanest experiments. In *svapna* a world rises without wood or stone, without sun or shadow. There is a city, a sky, a lover, a threat — each convincing while it lasts. Then something shifts: a smell from the pillow, a ray of dawn, a twitch of the waking body. The entire cosmos folds without remainder. Where did it go?

Vedanta's "disturbing message" is to extend that insight to waking: what the dream is to the dreamer, the waking is to the waker. A world can stand as long as the standpoint that sustains it stands; when the standpoint changes, its world is falsified. The dreamer awakes and swallows the dream; the knower awakes and swallows the waker. The Self was never touched.

—

Root & Meaning

Svapna — "dream." Derivation: From the root svap "to sleep," hence "that which arises in sleep."

Scriptural & Traditional Pointers

- **Mandukya (via classical teaching lines):** both waking (*jagrat*) and dreaming (svapna) are *mithya* — seemingly real, but not absolutely real; *turiya* is the witness that illumines both.
- **Gaudapada's dream example (Karika):** the dream is Vedanta's most important model to reveal mithya; what seems objectively real in-dream is seen as projection upon waking — and the same logic is then applied to the waking world.
- **Status logic (satya–mithya):** the world must be "neither existent nor non-existent" — experienced yet not independent — hence

mithya. The dream shows how this works.

Anatomy of Svapna (Vedantic Analysis)

1. What powers it?
The *svapna* field is a mind-only projection shaped by *vasanas*; its "objects" are private, fleeting, and unregulated by shared laws — *pratibhasika satya* (apparent/subjective reality).

2. Who experiences it?
The same consciousness appears as the dreamer (*Taijasa*), just as it appears as the waker (*Vishva*) in *jagrat*. The experiencer changes; the witnessing Self does not.

3. Criterion tests (Gaudapada's refutations)

- Utility: food in dream satisfies dream hunger; waking food does not — utility is state-relative.
- Publicness/Repeatability/Duration/Logic: each holds within its state and fails across states; therefore none proves absolute reality.

4. Dream collapse & standpoint:
A single "waking" thought punctures the dream total — revealing that a "world" stands only by its sustaining ignorance.

5. Waker swallows the dreamer; Knower swallows the waker
On waking, you falsify the dreamer and all dream karma. Analogously, self-knowledge falsifies the waker and waking's doership/enjoyership.

6. Micro vs. Macro projection (jiva-dream vs. Ishvara-dream)

- *Jiva's* dream: ends naturally, no *sadhana* required.
- *Ishvara's* "waking dream": continues until *avidya* is removed; knowledge wakes you "from the waker," while projection (the world) may continue but no longer binds.

The Teaching in One Movement

A disturbing message: what the dreamer calls "outside" is only mind; on waking, the whole thing is seen as thoughts. Extend this to the waker.

Creation is in awareness: in dream you are the substance, intelligence, and energy of the world; cause untouched by effects. Enlightenment is recognizing this fact in waking.

Neither real nor unreal: Maya is like a dream — experienced (so not non-existent), yet not independent (so not absolutely real). Hence *mithya*.

Common Misunderstandings

- **"Dream is unreal; waking is real."** Each is real only on its own terms; both are negated from a higher standpoint. That's why Vedanta uses *svapna* to expose waking's borrowed reality.
- **"If the world is dreamlike, it should be manipulable."** The analogy is ontological, not magical: relative order remains — *vyavaharika* laws continue. Knowledge changes the status, not the script.
- **"Spiritual 'awakening' happens like dream-waking."** Dream-waking is automatic in time; liberation requires knowledge removing ignorance (*shravana–manana–nididhyasana*).

Vedantic Resolution

When the standpoint shifts from dreamer/waker to witness, *svapna's* lesson lands: experience is a projection that cannot touch the experiencer. Knowledge doesn't annihilate appearances; it de-absolutizes them. The world may remain — as "*Ishvara's* dream" — but its power to bind is gone.

svarupa

(svarūpa — *svuh-ROO-puh*)

In Vedanta, much confusion arises from mistaking what we seem to be for what we are. The body is visible, the mind is felt, the ego speaks — yet none of these are the essence of the Self. To distinguish essence from attribute, Vedanta uses the term *svarupa*.

Rupa means "form," and *sva* means "one's own." Thus *svarupa* (*svarūpa*) means "one's own form" — the intrinsic nature that cannot be given up. Heat is the *svarupa* of fire, liquidity the *svarupa* of water. They can be temporarily obscured (a cold coal hides fire, ice hides water), but when revealed, they cannot be separated from the thing itself.

Applied to the Self, *svarupa* is pure consciousness (*chit*), existence (*sat*), and limitlessness (*ananda*). These are not qualities of the Self, but its very nature. Just as sugar is not "sweet" because sweetness clings to it (sugar and sweetness are one), so too the Self does not "have" consciousness but is consciousness.

—

Root & Meaning

Sva = one's own
Rupa = form, nature
Svarupa = intrinsic nature, essence, that which cannot be separated from a thing.

Scriptural References

- **Brihadaranyaka Upanishad (3.4.2):** "You cannot see the seer of seeing" — pointing to awareness as the svarupa of the Self.
- **Chandogya Upanishad (6.8.7):** *Tat Tvam Asi* — reveals Brahman

as the *svarupa* of the individual Self.

- **Taittiriya Upanishad (2.1):** describes the Self as *satyam, jnanam, anantam* — intrinsic, not incidental.

Traditional View

- *Svarupa* is the essential, inalienable nature.
- For the *jiva*, true *svarupa* is atman, pure consciousness.
- Distinction is often made between *svarupa-lakshana* (intrinsic definition, e.g. "Brahman is existence-consciousness-limitlessness") and *tatastha-lakshana* (incidental definition, e.g. "Brahman is the cause of the universe").

Vedantic Analysis

- The Self does not "possess" consciousness; its *svarupa* is consciousness.
- Attributes of body, mind, and ego are not intrinsic but incidental — products of *upadhis*.
- *Moksha* is recognition of one's *svarupa*, which was never bound.

Common Misunderstandings

- **Svarupa as personality or temperament:** True *svarupa* is essence, not personality.
- **Svarupa as quality:** Consciousness is not a property of the Self but its very being.
- **Svarupa as something to be acquired:** It is ever present; realization is recognition.

Vedantic Resolution

Vedanta uses *svarupa* with precision: it refers only to essence, never to incidental qualities. By discriminating between *svarupa* (the Self) and attributes (*upadhis*), the seeker recognizes that the Self was always free, whole, and untouched.

Taijasa

(Taijasa — *tai-juh-suh*)

Taijasa is the individual self (*jiva*) in the dream state (*svap-na-avastha*). In this condition, consciousness is turned inward, no longer engaging with the external world through the physical senses, but instead illumining a subtle world projected by the mind itself. This dream world is formed of impressions (*vasanas*) carried from waking experience. It is real for the dreamer while it lasts, yet entirely internal and private.

Vedanta calls this second quarter of the self *Taijasa* — literally "the effulgent one" — because it shines with the borrowed light of consciousness reflected through the subtle body. While the *Vishva* (waker) interacts with the gross body and external world, *Taijasa* dwells in the subtle body, experiencing subtle objects. The Upanishads describe both as having "nineteen mouths" — the five senses of perception, five organs of action, five pranas, and the fourfold inner instrument (*antahkarana*).

At the macrocosmic level, the counterpart of *Taijasa* is *Hiranyagarbha*, the totality of all subtle bodies, or the cosmic dream. Just as the dreamer's world is sustained by the individual mind, the cosmic mind sustains the order of subtle creation. Thus, what is inward and private at the individual level corresponds to the vast and ordered subtle cosmos.

The teaching purpose of *Taijasa* is to reveal that neither waking nor dream defines the Self. Both states depend on consciousness, but consciousness itself is free from both. By reflecting on the unreality of the dream world — so convincing while it lasts, yet vanishing upon waking — the seeker gains insight into the mithya nature of waking experience as well. This prepares the mind to grasp *turiya*, the pure consciousness beyond all states.

Root & Meaning

Tejas = light, brilliance.
Taijasa = "the effulgent one"; the individual self in the dream state.

Scriptural References

- **Mandukya Upanishad (mantra 4):** "The second quarter is *Taijasa*, whose field is dream, whose consciousness is inward, who has seven limbs, nineteen mouths, and who experiences subtle objects."
- **Mandukya Karika (3.36–37):** explains that the dream state is projected by the mind and illumined by consciousness.
- **Bhagavad Gita (15.8):** the subtle body carries the *jiva* from body to body, as wind carries scents — relevant to the continuity of the dreamer-self.

Traditional View

- *Taijasa* is the dreamer, identifying with the subtle body.
- Experiences subtle objects in a self-projected world of *vasanas*.
- Has nineteen instruments (sense organs, action organs, *pranas*, *antahkarana*).
- Inward-turned consciousness, effulgent with borrowed light.

Vedantic Analysis

- Microcosm: *Taijasa* = individual dreamer.
- Macrocosm: *Hiranyagarbha* = total dream, cosmic subtle body.
- Teaching tool: shows the dependency of experience on consciousness and the *mithya* nature of both waking and dream.
- The Self is not limited to the dream state — both dreamer and dream are illumined by *turiya*.

Common Misunderstandings

- **That dream is mere illusion:** Though not real in the waking sense, dream is a valid experience for the dreamer and reveals the power of the mind.
- **That Taijasa is closer to Brahman than Vishva:** Both are equal projections; neither is the Self.
- **That consciousness itself dreams:** Consciousness never changes; only the subtle body projects and experiences.

Vedantic Resolution

Taijasa represents the *jiva* in the dream state, illumining a mind-generated universe. It is a pointer to the fact that just as the dream vanishes upon waking, so too waking experience is relative and dependent. The Self, *turiya*, is the witness of both, ever free and unchanging.

tamas

(tamas — *tuh-muhs*)

In Vedanta, *tamas* is the *guna* of inertia and veiling. Where *rajas* projects, *tamas* obscures: it dulls clarity, blunts motivation, and makes reality feel heavy and indistinct. This is not "evil" — *tamas* has a functional role in the cosmos (mass, stability, the capacity to sleep and recover) — but in the psyche it becomes bondage when it dominates. Then it shows up as procrastination, confusion, denial, lethargy, numbness, and the habit of checking out rather than showing up.

A simple way to see its mechanics is: non-apprehension leading to mis-apprehension. First *tamas* prevents clear seeing ("I don't quite get what's happening"). Then, aided by *rajas*, we project errors onto that blank screen ("...so it must mean I'm not enough / they're against me / objects will complete me"). Thus *tamas* and *rajas* together sustain samsara: one hides the Self, the other chases substitutes.

The remedy is transformation, not suppression. We skillfully use a touch of *rajas* to lift *tamas*, then refine that energy into *sattva*. Practically: move the body (walk, clean, breathe), keep simple routines, seek sunlight and fresh food, reduce intoxicants and stale inputs, tidy one's space, honor sleep hygiene, keep good company (*satsanga*), and engage in *karma yoga* so activity is dharmic and unbinding. As *sattva* rises, study, reflection, and quiet contemplation bite; *shama–dama* steady the mind; inquiry reveals that awareness is ever free.

A useful litmus: tamasic "peace" feels heavy, foggy, and avoidant; sattvic stillness is bright, lucid, and available. Vedanta's end is not a permanently "high-energy" personality but freedom from identification with any *guna*. *Tamas* belongs to *prakriti*; you are *gunatita* — the awareness in whose light even heaviness is known. The work is to keep *tamas* in its rightful, functional place and to know yourself as that which it can never touch.

—

Root & Meaning

From the Sanskrit root *tam* ("darkness, obscurity"), *tamas* literally means "darkness" or "inertia." In Vedantic usage, it refers to the *guna* (fundamental quality of nature) that veils knowledge, promotes lethargy, dullness, and confusion.

Scriptural References

- **Bhagavad Gita 14.8:** "*Tamas*, born of ignorance, deludes all embodied beings; it binds through heedlessness, indolence, and sleep."
- **Bhagavad Gita 14.17:** "From *tamas* arises ignorance, delusion, and negligence, and from these comes bondage."
- **Shvetashvatara Upanishad 4.5:** The *gunas* — *sattva, rajas, tamas* — are presented as the threads through which maya weaves the manifest universe.

Traditional View

Tamas is the quality of non-apprehension, heaviness, and obscurity. It is essential in cosmic functioning, providing the basis for matter and stability, but in the human mind it appears as ignorance, dullness, and resistance to truth. It manifests in procrastination, confusion, indulgence in fantasy, and mechanical or unconscious living.

Vedantic Analysis

Vedanta teaches that *tamas* is not "evil," but one of the three strands of maya that bind the *jiva* to samsara. When *tamas* dominates the mind, there is inability to discern reality, lack of motivation, and misapprehension of truth. Projection (*rajas*) and non-apprehension (*tamas*) together sustain self-ignorance. Liberation comes when *tamas* is transformed into *rajas* and then, *sattva* (clarity, light) through *karma yoga*, disciplined living, devotion, and inquiry.

Common Misunderstandings

- **Mistaking tamas for rest:** Rest or sleep can be sattvic when restorative, but *tamas* is a dull, compulsive inertia that clouds awareness.
- **Seeing tamas as inherently "bad":** While spiritually binding, *tamas* has a functional role—it provides stability, grounding, and the material substratum of the body and world.
- **Confusing tamas with peace:** A tamasic mind may seem calm, but its quiet is dullness, not the luminous stillness of *sattva*.

Vedantic Resolution

The solution to *tamas* is not suppression but transformation. By cultivating sattvic values — clarity, order, truthfulness, devotion, discrimination — one can gradually convert *tamas* into *rajas*, and then, *sattva*. Through self-inquiry, one ultimately realizes the Self (atman), which is beyond the play of the *gunas*. As the Bhagavad Gita (14.23) states: "The one who knows that it is only the *gunas* that act, and remains steadfast in the Self, does not waver."

tat tvam asi

(tat tvam asi — *tuht-tvuhm-uh-SEE*)

Among the Upanishadic declarations, none is more intimate than *tat tvam asi* — "That thou art." Where other *mahavakyas* sound like pronouncements of cosmic fact, this one speaks directly, almost tenderly, to the seeker. It does not describe Brahman in abstraction, nor does it analyze the world. It whispers to the student: "You are That."

The statement holds a paradox. On the surface, *tat* points to the infinite source of the universe, omniscient and limitless; *tvam* points to the small, finite individual, bound by ignorance and frailty. How can the two be equal? The answer lies in setting aside what is incidental. *Tat* is not the Lord clothed in the functions of creation and governance. *Tvam* is not the personality clothed in mind and body. When these garments are dropped, what remains in both is the same — awareness, simple and unconditioned.

Thus, *tat tvam asi* is not a command to become something else. It is not an exhortation to merge into God or to undergo some spectacular transformation. It is an unveiling. The wave has always been water; the individual has always been Brahman. The teaching strips away the disguises until the truth is recognized.

The force of this *mahavakya* is not intellectual but existential. To hear *tat tvam asi* from the lips of a teacher, within the context of one's own longing and preparation, is to be invited into freedom. It means: "Your essence is not limited, not broken, not lacking. You are already the fullness you seek."

In this way, *tat tvam asi* is both simple and revolutionary. It overturns lifetimes of mistaken identity and affirms the most astonishing recognition: that the seeker, the path, and the goal are one.

Root & Meaning

Tat = That (Brahman, the limitless, unconditioned reality)
Tvam = Thou (the individual self, jiva)
Asi = Are (verb of identity)
Together: "You are That."

Scriptural References

• **Chandogya Upanishad 6.8.7–16:** Sage Uddalaka repeats the re-frain *tat tvam asi* nine times to Shvetaketu.
• **Shankara's commentary:** emphasizes that the identity is not figurative but real once limiting adjuncts are discarded (*bhaga-tyaga-lakshana*).

Traditional View

• *Tat* refers to Brahman as the cause of creation.
• *Tvam* refers to the individual self (*jiva*).
• Reconciliation is made by discarding incidental attributes (*upadhis*):
  - From *tat*: omniscience, omnipotence, creator-role.
  - From *tvam*: finitude, ignorance, mortality.
• What remains is pure Consciousness, one and the same.

Vedantic Analysis

Vedanta stresses that *tat tvam asi* is not metaphor or poetry, but a statement of fact. You already are Brahman; ignorance alone hides this recognition. The *mahavakya* is an *upadesha-vakya* (sentence of instruction), meant to be unfolded by a teacher until its meaning is fully assimilated.

Common Misunderstandings

- **Merger:** It does not say the *jiva* "becomes" Brahman. The *jiva* was never other than Brahman.
- **Experience-based:** It does not point to a mystical experience; it reveals an existing identity.
- **Pantheistic reading:** It does not mean "you are God with all powers," but "you are identical with the consciousness that is Brahman."

Vedantic Resolution

Tat tvam asi functions like a mirror: it removes the mistaken identity with body and mind and reflects back your true nature. Liberation is not a transformation but the recognition that the Self is Brahman.

titiksha

(titikṣā — *ti-tik-SHAA*)

Vedanta emphasizes that no spiritual path is free of hardship. Pain, loss, and disappointment are built into samsara. The qualification called *titiksha (titikṣā)* is the capacity to endure these inevitable opposites — pleasure and pain, gain and loss, praise and blame — with cheerfulness and objectivity.

Unlike suppression or passive resignation, *titiksha* is an intelligent accommodation. It arises from recognizing that some situations cannot be changed, and that they belong to the body-mind, not to the Self. *Moksha* cannot erase the effects of karma; joys and sorrows still arrive, but the wise know these never touch the Self.

In practice, *titiksha* means not reacting with complaint or revenge, not allowing oneself to be disturbed by life's "pinpricks" — inconveniences, irritations, or disappointments. One accepts them with good humor and perspective, remembering that people are shaped by conditioning and karma. This forbearance dilutes fear of the future, reduces agitation in the present, and steadies the mind for inquiry.

Forbearance does not mean inaction. Prevent the preventable, remedy the remediable. But in choiceless situations, one learns to accept them as *Ishvara's* order, even as a form of *tapas*. The *Gita* says: "The wise remain the same in pleasure and pain, for such a one is fit for liberation" (2.15). *Titiksha* thus builds emotional immunity, making the mind fit for Self-knowledge.

—

Root & Meaning

From the root *tij* = to endure, to bear.

Titiksha = endurance, forbearance, the ability to cheerfully withstand opposites.

Scriptural References

- **Bhagavad Gita 2.14–15:** "Endure them, O Arjuna, for the contact of the senses with objects gives rise to heat and cold, pleasure and pain — they come and go, they are impermanent. The wise remain the same in both."
- **Tattvabodha (26):** defines *titiksha* as "bearing non-conducive situations without anxiety, complaint, or revenge."
- **Aparokshanubhuti 18–19:** defines *titiksha* as the quiet endurance of suffering and the pairs of opposites (heat and cold, pleasure and pain) without resistance, complaint, or mental disturbance.

Traditional View

- Part of the *shatka-sampatti* (sixfold inner wealth) that prepare the seeker for Self-inquiry.
- A mark of maturity: not expecting that spiritual life will spare one from pain.
- Acceptance of karma's fruits without agitation.

Vedantic Analysis

- Forbearance belongs to the mind, not the Self.
- It is cultivated by seeing pain and pleasure as temporary appearances in awareness.
- Prevent and remedy what can be changed; accept the rest as *Ishvara-prasada* (gift of the Lord).
- Strengthens emotional steadiness (*samatva*) and dispassion (*vairagya*).

Common Misunderstandings

- **That titiksha means passive suffering:** True forbearance is intelligent, not fatalistic.
- **That it erases pain:** It does not remove pain, but transforms one's relationship to it.
- **That self-knowledge eliminates all sorrow:** *Moksha* removes ignorance, not the ups and downs of life; *titiksha* equips one to meet them with balance.

Vedantic Resolution

Titiksha is the discipline of enduring life's inevitable opposites with cheerful acceptance, freeing the mind from reactivity. It steadies the seeker for Self-inquiry, revealing that the Self is ever free, untouched by the ups and downs of samsara.

triguna yoga

(triguṇa yoga — *tri-GOO-nuh YO-guh*)

The *Bhagavad Gita* describes the play of the three *gunas* — *sattva* (clarity and harmony), *rajas* (activity and restlessness), and *tamas* (inertia and obscuration)—as the underlying weave of all creation. Every experience, thought, and action is shaped by their dynamic interplay.

Triguna Yoga refers to Krishna's teaching, most fully articulated in Chapter 14 of the *Gita*, which explains the nature of the three *gunas*, how they bind the individual, and how one becomes free of their influence. Just as all colors arise from three primaries, so too every psychological state arises from varying combinations of *sattva*, rajas, and *tamas*.

At the empirical level, this teaching invites careful discernment of how the *gunas* operate in daily life. One observes the after-effects of ordinary choices—diet, work, relationships, recreation, sexuality, sleep, money, and worship—and notes whether they leave behind agitation (*rajas*), dullness (*tamas*), or clarity (*sattva*). Favoring *sattva* fosters peace, gratitude, adaptability, and contentment. Excess *rajas* produces restlessness and dissatisfaction; *tamas* produces lethargy, confusion, and inertia.

Ultimately, the purpose of *Triguna Yoga* is not to eliminate *rajas* or *tamas*, nor even to perfect *sattva*. All three *gunas* belong to *prakriti* and are *mithya*. The Self is *gunatita*—beyond all qualities, ever free. Nevertheless, cultivating *sattva* is invaluable as a preparatory discipline, creating the clarity and steadiness required to assimilate Self-knowledge, which alone is liberation.

—

Root & Meaning

Tri = three
Guna = strand, quality
Yoga = teaching, discipline, integration
Triguna Yoga = the teaching of the three *gunas*, their influence, and the means to transcend them.

Scriptural References

- **Bhagavad Gita (Chapter 14):** Krishna systematically explains *sattva, rajas, tamas*, their effects, and how to transcend them.
- **Bhagavad Gita (18.40):** declares that no being, on earth or in heaven, is free of the *gunas*.
- **Shvetashvatara Upanishad (4.5):** describes *prakriti* as made of the three *gunas*.

Traditional View

- The *gunas* pervade all of *prakriti*.
- *Sattva* refines and uplifts, *rajas* agitates and propels, *tamas* dulls and obscures.
- Spiritual maturity involves recognizing their play, cultivating *sattva*, and ultimately dis-identifying from them altogether.

Vedantic Analysis

- Observation: Monitoring the after-effects of one's choices on the mind-body complex.
- Correction: Favoring sattvic influences and tempering rajasic and tamasic ones.
- The *gunas* are beginningless and inseparable from *prakriti*; they are *mithya*.
- The Self is *gunatita* — ever free, untouched by *sattva, rajas*, or *tamas*.

Common Misunderstandings

- **That gunas can be destroyed:** They belong to *prakriti* and remain, even for the liberated.
- **That sattva itself is moksha:** It is only a means, preparing the mind for knowledge.
- **That gunas are moral categories:** They are energetic qualities, not judgments of good or bad.

Vedantic Resolution

By monitoring lifestyle and cultivating *sattva*, the seeker purifies the mind and prepares it for Self-inquiry. Liberation comes not by controlling or eliminating *gunas*, but by knowing oneself as *gunatita* — awareness beyond all qualities.

Turiya

(Turīya — *tu-REE-yuh*)

Turiya (Turīya) literally means "the fourth," referring to the state of consciousness beyond waking (*jagrat*), dream (*svapna*), and deep sleep (*sushupti*). It is not a fourth state alongside the others, but rather the ever-present awareness that underlies all three.

The *Mandukya Upanishad*, one of the shortest yet most profound Upanishads, unfolds this teaching:

• In waking, the Self appears as *Vishva*, experiencing the gross world.
• In dream, as *Taijasa*, experiencing the subtle mind.
• In deep sleep, as *Prajna*, in causal ignorance.
• Beyond all three, yet supporting them, is *Turiya* — pure, non-dual consciousness.

Because *Turiya* is not a state, it is never absent. Even in waking, dream, and sleep, awareness illumines the experiences. The term "fourth" is only a pedagogical device to point to that which is constant.

The seeker is often misled into trying to "attain" *Turiya* as an experience, but Vedanta clarifies: one cannot reach it, because it is what one already is. The recognition of *Turiya* dissolves identification with the passing states, revealing the Self as changeless, limitless consciousness.

—

Root & Meaning

Conceptually tied to *chaturtha* — "fourth."
Turiya = the "fourth," i.e., the reality underlying waking, dream, and deep sleep.

Scriptural References

- **Mandukya Upanishad 7:** "*Turiya* is not inwardly cognitive, nor outwardly cognitive, nor both. It is unseen, unrelated, ungraspable, without features, unthinkable, indescribable. Its essence is the consciousness of the Self alone. It is the cessation of the world. It is peace, auspiciousness, non-dual. That is the Self, that is to be realized."
- **Mandukya Karika (Gaudapada):** expands the teaching, showing *Turiya* as unborn and unchanging.

Traditional View

- *Turiya* is not a separate "state," but the substratum of all states.
- Ever-present awareness, pure consciousness.
- Recognized, not attained.

Vedantic Analysis

- Waking (*Vishva*), dream (*Taijasa*), deep sleep (*Prajna*) are conditioned appearances.
- *Turiya* is unconditioned consciousness, the witness of all three.
- It cannot be objectified, but is self-revealing.
- Knowing *Turiya* = freedom, as one abides as awareness beyond the play of states.

Common Misunderstandings

- **That Turiya is a mystical trance or altered state:** It is not an experience, but the reality that illumines all experiences.
- **That one must "enter" Turiya:** It is already present; only recognition is required.
- **That Turiya comes and goes:** States come and go; *Turiya* never departs.

Vedantic Resolution

Turiya is the ever-present awareness that is the Self. It is not a fourth state but the reality underlying all states. Recognition of *Turiya* is liberation.

upadhi

(upādhi — *u-PAA-dhee*)

In Vedanta, *upadhi (upādhi)* means "limiting adjunct." It refers to something that seemingly lends its attributes to another, making the limitless appear limited, the indivisible appear divided, the changeless appear to change. An *upadhi* does not actually alter the nature of what it conditions — it only creates an appearance of change, much like a red rose placed beside a clear crystal makes the crystal seem red. The crystal remains colorless; only perception is distorted.

At the cosmic level, maya is the fundamental *upadhi* that conditions Brahman, giving rise to the appearance of the entire universe. When Brahman is viewed through the lens of maya, it appears as *Ishvara* — the creator, sustainer, and dissolver of the manifest world. This is Brahman conditioned by the *maya-up-adhi*. Yet just as the space within a pot seems separate from the space outside it, the separation is only apparent. The Self remains unconditioned by what seems to condition it.

At the individual level, the Self appears as the *jiva* when conditioned by the five sheaths (*koshas*): the body (*annamaya*), energy (*pranamaya*), mind (*manomaya*), intellect (*vijnanamaya*), and causal bliss (*anandamaya*). These are the *upadhi* of the individual, giving rise to the sense of being a distinct person with preferences, memories, limitations, and a personal history. The Self, as reflected awareness, identifies with these sheaths and imagines itself to be a doer, a thinker, an enjoyer. But this identification is born of *avidya*, the microcosmic form of maya.

Upadhis explain why the Self, though limitless, appears limited. Why, if everything is consciousness, you do not directly experience "me." We each appear as separate because of different *upadhis* — different body-minds reflecting the same consciousness, like mirrors of varying shape and clarity reflecting the same sunlight. The limitations of the *upadhi* determine the scope of experience, much like a telescope determines the field of vision. But awareness itself is never bound.

Vedanta points out three principal *upadhis* associated with the macrocosm:

- *Maya upadhi* — gives rise to *Ishvara* (God)
- *Avidya upadhi* — gives rise to the *jiva* (individual)
- *Prakriti upadhi* — gives rise to *jagat* (the universe of objects)

These three — *Ishvara, jiva,* and *jagat* — comprise the field of experience (*vyavaharika satta*), and each exists only in relation to its respective *upadhi*. From the standpoint of *paramarthika satya*, ultimate reality, all *upadhi* dissolve into non-duality. There is only atman, only Brahman.

Even *Ishvara*, revered as the cosmic intelligence, is not beyond conditioning. *Ishvara* is Brahman with *maya-upadhi*, and as such still within the domain of name and form. Vedanta ultimately leads us beyond even *Ishvara*, toward the realization that all distinctions — between individual and total, between creator and created — are born of *upadhi*.

When the Self no longer identifies with any *upadhi* — no longer mistakes the reflected image for its true nature — it abides as it always was: limitless, unconditioned, ever free.

—

Root & Meaning

Upadhi — from Sanskrit *upa-* ("near, secondary, supplementary") + *adhi* ("basis, foundation, limit"). Literally, "that which is placed near" or "an adjunct."

In Vedantic usage, it refers to a limiting adjunct — something that conditions or appears to limit an otherwise unlimited reality.

Scriptural References

- **Chandogya Upanishad (6.1–6.16):** The "space in the pot" analogy, illustrating how conditioning is only apparent.
- **Brihadaranyaka Upanishad (2.5.1, 3.8.8):** Declares the Self to be beyond all limiting adjuncts.
- **Bhagavad Gita (13.31–32):** Compares the Self to space: untouched by what it pervades.
- **Panchadashi (7.231–232):** Explicitly defines *upadhi* as that which causes superimposition without altering the substratum.
- **Vivekachudamani (239–241):** Explains how identification with *upadhi* is the root of bondage, and their negation leads to liberation.

Traditional View

In classical Advaita, an *upadhi* is a conditioning factor — physical, mental, or causal — that makes the infinite Self (atman/Brahman) seem finite, bound, or different.

Commonly cited upadhis:

- Body-mind complex (*sthula, sukshma,* and *karana sharira*)
- *Avidya* (ignorance)
- Maya (cosmic ignorance/illusion)

An example: a crystal appears red when placed near a red flower; the flower is the *upadhi* that conditions the crystal's appearance, though the crystal itself remains colorless.

Vedantic Analysis

The Self is ever pure, limitless consciousness. However, when associated with an *upadhi*, it appears to take on the adjunct's qualities — such as individuality (*jiva*) when conditioned by the body-mind, or omniscience (*Ishvara*) when conditioned by maya. These appearances do not actually modify the Self; they are superimpositions (*adhyasa*) due to ignorance. When upadhi-based identification is removed through knowledge, the apparent limitation vanishes.

Common Misunderstandings

- **"Upadhi actually changes the Self."** The Self is changeless; the limitation is only apparent.
- **"Removing the upadhi means physically discarding something."** Removal is cognitive — through knowledge that the adjunct does not define the Self.
- **"Upadhis are bad."** They are simply conditions in empirical reality, useful for functioning but not defining your true nature.

Vedantic Resolution

Understanding *upadhi* is central to resolving the paradox of non-duality in a world of multiplicity. Just as space in a pot appears different from space outside due to the pot's walls (*upadhi*), consciousness seems divided into separate selves. Realization of the upadhi-less Self reveals the undivided reality behind all appearances.

Upanishad

(Upaniṣad — *u-puh-ni-shud*)

The Upanishads are the culminating teachings of the Vedas, known as the *jnana-kanda* (knowledge section). They are dialogues between teacher and student that unfold the highest truth — the knowledge of the Self (atman) as non-different from Brahman, the limitless reality.

The word *Upanishad (Upaniṣad)* itself carries profound meaning. *Upa* means "near," *ni* means "with certainty," and *shad* means "to loosen, destroy, or sit." Thus, Upanishad is both literal and symbolic: the student "sits near" the teacher in reverence; ignorance is "destroyed" by knowledge; and certainty about the Self is established.

The purpose of the Upanishad is not ritual, philosophy, or theology, but liberation (*moksha*) through Self-knowledge. They strip away the mistaken identification with body, mind, and world, revealing the truth that one's essential nature is Brahman. As Shankaracharya emphasized, the sole purpose of the Upanishad is to prove the reality of Brahman, the unreality of names and forms, and the oneness of the individual and Brahman.

Poets have called the Upanishads "a cry in the wilderness," because while the senses rush outward to objects, only a few turn inward to hear the subtle call of the Self. Yet their vision is universal: though born on the banks of the Ganges, their teaching of non-dual Consciousness belongs to no single culture, race, or religion. It is brahmavidya — the knowledge of the Absolute — and thus a treasure for all humanity.

There are said to be more than 200 Upanishads, but 10–11 are considered *mukhya* (principal), commented upon by Shankara: *Isha, Kena, Katha, Prashna, Mundaka, Mandukya, Taittiriya, Aitareya,*

Chandogya, and *Brihadaranyaka* (with *Kaivalya* often included). Each approaches Brahman from a different angle, providing a many-faceted vision of the same truth.

In short: the Upanishads are not "books" as such but a means of knowledge (*pramana*). They destroy ignorance (*ajnana-nasha*), revealing the Self that is always already free.

—

Root & Meaning

Upa = near
Ni = certain, definite
Shad = to sit, to loosen, to destroy
Upanishad = that knowledge which is received by sitting near the teacher, which destroys ignorance, and which reveals the Self as Brahman.

Scriptural References

- **Katha Upanishad (2.1.1):** The senses go outward; the calm one turns inward to see the Self.
- **Mundaka Upanishad (1.1.4–5):** distinguishes higher (*para*) and lower (*apara*) knowledge.
- **Shankara:** the purpose of the Upanishads is to establish the reality of Brahman and the non-difference of atman and Brahman.

Traditional View

- Found at the "end" of the Vedas (*veda-anta*), they form the foundation of Vedanta.
- Function as revealed knowledge (*shruti*), not human speculation.
- Studied traditionally through a qualified teacher (*guru-shishya parampara*).
- Considered *rahasya* (secret), transmitted only to prepared

students.

Vedantic Analysis

- The Upanishads are a *pramana* (means of knowledge), not philosophy or belief.
- Their method (*prakriya*) includes stories, analogies, negation (*neti neti*), and *mahavakyas*.
- They point not to new experience but to recognition of what is always present: the Self.
- Liberation is immediate upon understanding, though preparation (*adhikaritva*) is required.

Common Misunderstandings

- **That the Upanishads are Hindu "scriptures" in a sectarian sense:** Their teaching is universal, not tied to ritual or deity worship.
- **That the Upanishads describe mystical states:** They reveal Self-knowledge, not temporary experiences.
- **That each Upanishad gives a complete picture:** Each highlights one aspect; taken together they form a whole vision.

Vedantic Resolution

The Upanishads are the heart of Vedanta. They destroy ignorance by revealing Brahman as the essence of the Self, the world, and *Ishvara*. Their universal teaching — *tat tvam asi* ("You are That") — is the timeless key to freedom.

uparati

(uparati – *u-puh-ruh-tee*)

Uparati literally means "withdrawal" or "cessation." It is the natural quieting of the mind and senses when they no longer chase external objects. Unlike *shama* (mental restraint) and *dama* (sense-control), which require active discipline, *uparati* arises spontaneously once *viveka* (discrimination), *vairagya* (dispassion), and prior disciplines mature.

A classic metaphor from the *Bhagavad Gita* is that of a tortoise that withdraws its limbs into its shell. Similarly, in *uparati*, the mind and senses turn inward without struggle. It is not suppression but a natural redirection: interest in the world's distractions fades because the heart longs for Self-knowledge.

Two aspects of *uparati* are often noted:

- **Ethical and practical:** faithful observance of one's own dharma (duty), without constant craving for outer pleasure or reward.
- **Contemplative and ultimate:** resting in one's true nature (*svarupa*), Existence–Consciousness–Bliss, beyond all roles and identifications.

For the seeker, *uparati* is freedom from preoccupation. Even in worldly duties, the mind remains disengaged from agitation, available for inquiry. As Swami Tejomayananda puts it: "In *shama* and *dama* the mind and senses are restrained with alertness, but in *uparati* they withdraw automatically."

—

Root & Meaning

Upa = near, towards

Rama = delight, engagement
Uparama / Uparati = withdrawal, cessation, resting in oneself.

Scriptural References

- **Bhagavad Gita 2.58:** "When like a tortoise withdrawing its limbs, a person withdraws senses from objects, his wisdom is steady."
- **Tattvabodha (Shankara):** defines *uparati* as cessation of engaging in actions other than one's duty.
- **Subodhini (Tejomayananda):** describes *uparati* as effortless withdrawal when control of mind and senses becomes natural.

Traditional View

- Belongs to the *shatka-sampatti* (sixfold wealth of inner disciplines).
- Follows from *viveka, vairagya, shama,* and *dama.*
- Outer aspect: observance of *svadharma* without distraction.
- Inner aspect: withdrawal into the Self, resting in one's own nature.

Vedantic Analysis

- Not suppression but natural quietude.
- Mind becomes available for *shravana–manana–nididhyasana.*
- Outer withdrawal matures into inner absorption.
- Ultimate *uparati* = abiding in *sat–cit–ananda*, free from preoccupation.

Common Misunderstandings

- **That uparati is laziness or withdrawal from duty:** In fact, it is faithful performance of dharma without attachment.
- **That it is suppression of desire:** True *uparati* arises when desire naturally drops, not from forced restraint.

- **That it is isolation from life:** It is freedom within life, not escapism.

Vedantic Resolution

Uparati is natural disengagement from distraction and outer preoccupation, allowing the mind to rest effortlessly in the Self. It represents maturity of discipline and marks readiness for deeper assimilation of knowledge.

upasana yoga

(upāsana yoga — *u-PAA-suh-nuh YO-guh*)

In the traditional Advaita Vedanta framework, *upasana yoga* (*upāsana yoga*) is the second of three stages of spiritual practice: *karma yoga, upasana yoga,* and *jnana yoga.* Each stage prepares the seeker for the next. While *karma yoga* purifies the mind (*chitta shuddhi*), *upasana yoga* prepares the mind for focused inquiry (*chitta ekagrata*), and *jnana yoga* leads to Self-knowledge.

The word *upasana* literally means "sitting near." It implies proximity, attention, and reverence. In earlier times, it referred to devotional meditation or ritual worship — practices designed to bring the seeker into contact with a personal form of God. In the Vedas and Upanishads, *upasana* often meant meditating on a chosen symbol or deity with intense concentration.

However, in contemporary Advaita Vedanta, *upasana yoga* has shifted in meaning. Many contemporary teachers present *upasana yoga* not as devotional practice per se, but as a simplified, secular version of Patanjali's *ashtanga yoga* (eight-limbs yoga). In this modern formulation, the emphasis is not on *bhakti* or metaphysical dualism, but on training the mind to become steady, quiet, and available for *atma-vichara* (Self-inquiry).

In effect, this modern *upasana yoga* is *ashtanga yoga* without its philosophical elements — no discussion of *purusha, prakriti* or *kaivalya.* What remains are techniques such as breath regulation (*pranayama*), sense withdrawal (*pratyahara*), and meditative absorption (*dhyana*) — used purely as tools for steadying the mind.

Historically, this preparatory path was also referred to by other names. Adi Shankaracharya sometimes called it *samadhi yoga,* emphasizing the role of meditative absorption in preparing the mind for non-dual understanding. In contrast, the Ramakrishna Order refers to it as *raja yoga,* aligning with Vivekananda's interpretation of Patanjali's system as a path of mental mastery, equally useful to the devotional or rational aspirant.

This shift has led to some ambiguity. Why continue calling it *upasana,* when the devotional element has largely been removed? The answer may lie in continuity: the term preserves the traditional threefold structure of Vedantic *sadhana,* even if its content has evolved.

That said, different teachers interpret the sequence differently. Ramana Maharshi, for example, places *ashtanga yoga* after *upasana yoga,* indicating a further stage of internal refinement without losing *upasana yoga's* original intent: worship (e.g. of *Ishvara*) through meditation. In that view, *upasana* still carries its older devotional implication, and *ashtanga yoga* (as a yogic discipline) becomes an even more rigorous inward turn.

Whichever model one adopts, the essence of *upasana yoga* remains the same: it is a means of calming the mind, refining attention, and preparing the seeker for Self-knowledge. Without this preparatory work, jnana yoga tends to remain intellectual, not transformative.

Swami Paramarthananda calls this the stage of "quality and quantity control" in life. One learns to regulate lifestyle, speech, sensory intake, and mental habits so the mind becomes a reliable instrument rather than a reactive one. Physical balance, verbal restraint, selective exposure to sensory stimuli, and disciplined use of attention all contribute to a mind that is available for longer and subtler forms of contemplation.

The *Katha Upanishad* offers a compelling image. The body is the chariot, the senses its horses, the mind the reins, and the intellect the driver. Unless each component is trained and aligned, the journey cannot succeed. *Upasana yoga* is the stage in which this alignment is undertaken consciously, so that the mind is finally capable of recognizing the Self — not as an idea, but as the unchanging witness of all experience.

—

Root & Meaning

Upasana — from Sanskrit *upa* ("near") + *asana* ("sitting"). Literally, "sitting near," implying proximity, reverence, and focused attention.
Yoga — from Sanskrit root *yuj* ("to yoke, to join"), in this context meaning a discipline or method.
Together: "The discipline of meditative worship" or "mental discipline through devotional or contemplative practice."

Scriptural References

Traditional definition and purpose of upasana:

- **Chandogya Upanishad 1.1.10:** "Meditation (*upasana*) is greater than thought. The earth meditates, the sky meditates, the waters meditate... By meditating, one becomes great."
- **Mundaka Upanishad 1.2.13:** "Meditate (*upasita*) upon *Om* as the bow, the Self as the arrow, and Brahman as the target; with a mind merged in It, one becomes one with It."
- **Bhagavad Gita 12.6–7:** "Those who worship (*upasate*) Me, renouncing all actions in Me... I quickly rescue them from the ocean of samsara."

Upasana as mental discipline:

- **Katha Upanishad 1.3.3–9:** Compares the body to a chariot, the senses to horses, the mind to reins, and the intellect to the driver; self-mastery is needed to reach the goal.
- **Bhagavad Gita 6.26:** "From wherever the mind wanders due to its fickle nature, restraining it, one should bring it back under the control of the Self."

- **Bhagavad Gita 6.35:** "Undoubtedly, the mind is restless and hard to control; but by practice (*abhyasa*) and detachment (*vairagya*), it is restrained."

Transition to jnana:

- **Mandukya Karika 3.46:** "Meditation (*upasana*) on the Self is to be practiced until identity with the Self is realized; then, knowledge alone remains."
- **Bhagavad Gita 8.8:** "With mind unperturbed, meditating on the Supreme Person with constant devotion, one reaches Him."

Traditional View

Traditionally, *upasana yoga* is the second stage of Vedantic spiritual practice, coming after *karma yoga* and before *jnana yoga*.

- *Karma yoga* — purifies the mind (*chitta shuddhi*).
- *Upasana yoga* — steadies the mind (*chitta ekagrata*).
- *Jnana yoga* — reveals Self-knowledge.

Historically, *upasana* meant devotional meditation on *Ishvara* or Vedic symbols with focused attention to prepare the mind for subtler inquiry.

Vedantic Analysis

In modern Advaita Vedanta, *upasana yoga* is often taught as the discipline of mental steadiness, not necessarily requiring religious ritual. It functions as a practical adaptation of *ashtanga yoga* (Patanjali's eightfold path) — focusing on techniques like *pranayama* (breath regulation), *pratyahara* (sense withdrawal), and *dhyana* (meditation) to make the mind calm, focused, and fit for Self-inquiry (*atma-vichara*).

Its four key disciplines can be summarized as:

- Physical discipline — balanced living and care of the body

- Verbal discipline — truthful, kind, and measured speech
- Sensory discipline — selective exposure to impressions that support clarity
- Mental discipline — meditation, mindfulness, and cultivation of values (dharma)

Common Misunderstandings

- **"Upasana is only about idol worship."** It includes many meditative forms, with or without imagery.
- **"Upasana is optional."** Without some form of mental discipline, *jnana yoga* remains theoretical.
- **"Upasana the same as bhakti yoga."** While there's overlap, *bhakti yoga* is devotion-oriented, whereas *upasana yoga* emphasizes mental steadiness and meditative absorption.

Vedantic Resolution

The mind's restlessness (*vikshepa*) is a major obstacle to Self-knowledge. *Upasana yoga* addresses this directly, making the mind serviceable for subtle inquiry. Just as a still lake reflects the moon clearly, a steady mind reflects the truth of the Self without distortion.

vairagya

(vairāgya — *vai-RAA-gya*)

In Vedanta, *vairagya (vairāgya)* is the natural dispassion that follows clear seeing. Once it becomes obvious that no object, relationship, or accomplishment can deliver permanent happiness, the mind loosens its grip on the world. This is not cynicism or repression — it is quiet freedom. The word comes from *vi* (apart, without) + *raga* (attachment, coloring), pointing to the mind's release from being "colored" by likes and dislikes.

Dispassion begins with disappointment: every object eventually slips away, leaving the seeker restless again. But Vedanta turns that restlessness into fuel. Recognizing the pattern — desire, pursuit, momentary satisfaction, renewed lack — the mind starts looking deeper. Out of *viveka* (discrimination between the eternal and the ephemeral), *vairagya* naturally arises.

Classical teachers often distinguish between two forms:

- **Smashana-vairagya ("cremation-ground dispassion")**: the temporary sobering that arises in moments of shock, grief, or crisis, when the fragility of life becomes stark. It fades as soon as ordinary life reasserts itself.
- **Yathartha-vairagya ("true dispassion")**: the steady, considered renunciation born of discrimination. This does not fade, because it is grounded in understanding rather than mood.

Importantly, *vairagya* does not mean hating the world or running away from life. The renunciate in a cave and the householder in the marketplace alike can embody it. What matters is the recognition that externals cannot complete me, because I am already complete. With this shift, relationships, work, and possessions may still be enjoyed — but without clinging or fear of loss.

Ultimately, *vairagya* is not about rejecting life but about seeing clearly. What drops away is the false hope that "the next thing" will bring fulfillment. What remains is a mind free, light, and available for Self-knowledge. In this way, dispassion is not a loss but a gain: freedom from dependence, and readiness for the truth that one is already whole.

—

Root & Meaning

Etymology: From *vi-* ("without, apart from") + *raga* ("attachment, passion, coloring"). Literally, "freedom from passion/attachment."

Scriptural References

- **Bhagavad Gita 2.71:** *Vihaya kaman yah sarvan pumamsh charati nihsprihah / nirmamo nirahankarah sa shantim adhigacchati* — "The one who gives up all desires, moves about free from longing, without 'mine'-ness or egoism, attains peace."
- **Mundaka Upanishad 1.2.12:** After examining worldly experiences, the discriminating seeker develops vairagya and goes to a teacher for Self-knowledge.
- Shankara repeatedly describes *vairagya* as essential for *adhikaritva* (qualification) — without it, Self-inquiry cannot hold.

Traditional View

- *Vairagya* is not hatred of the world, but objectivity toward it.
- It arises naturally from *viveka* (discrimination): once one sees the impermanent cannot give lasting happiness, fascination with it wanes.
- Classical teachers distinguish between *yathartha vairagya* (true dispassion born of knowledge) and *smashana vairagya* (graveyard dispassion — temporary, born of shock or loss).

Vedantic Analysis

- *Vairagya* is the ability to enjoy or interact with the world without projecting permanent value onto impermanent objects.
- It does not require physical renunciation. The mind is the locus of attachment, not the object.
- Real *vairagya* is a by-product of *viveka*: knowing that only the Self (*nitya vastu*) can give security and completeness.
- In practice, it neutralizes *raga-dvesha* (likes and dislikes), preparing the mind for *shravana–manana–nididhyasana*.

Common Misunderstandings

- **Not hatred or repression:** To despise the world is another form of attachment.
- **Not apathy:** It is clarity and freedom, not dull indifference.
- **Not escapism:** One may still act fully in the world, but without clinging.
- **Not permanent at first:** Often it flickers; *shama* (mental restraint) and inquiry stabilize it.

Vedantic Resolution

- *Vairagya* matures when the seeker sees clearly:
- Objects are time-bound, incapable of giving lasting joy.
- Security and fullness (*purnatva*) belong only to the Self.

Thus the mind naturally withdraws from chasing externals and becomes available for Self-knowledge. Discrimination (*viveka*) and dispassion (*vairagya*) are the two wings by which the bird of inquiry flies toward liberation.

Vedanta

(Vedānta — *vay-DAAN-tuh*)

Vedanta *(Vedānta)* is a profound wisdom tradition that originated in India. It teaches that your true nature is already whole and free. The only barrier to realizing this truth is ignorance — not of facts, but of the Self.

This tradition is not a religion, philosophy, or spiritual path in the conventional sense. Instead, it serves as a precise means of knowledge — a *pramana* — whose sole purpose is to remove the error at the heart of all human seeking: the belief that "I am limited." Vedanta begins not with doctrine or mystical experience, but with a sober examination of the one thing that is always present — awareness.

The Essence of Vedanta

The word *Vedanta* means "the end of the Veda." It refers both to the final portion of the Vedic literature (the Upanishads) and to the culmination of knowledge itself. This knowledge, once known, renders everything else as good as known. For this reason, Vedanta has been called the science of consciousness. It does not aim to show you the truth; rather, it seeks to remove what obscures it.

While preserved in the Indian tradition, Vedanta transcends all cultures, religions, and time periods. It is not a system to be believed in, but a mirror — a way of seeing what is already true. The Upanishads describe this Self not as an object to be attained, but as the very awareness in which all experience takes place. Vedanta reveals that the seeker and the sought are not two.

The Path to Understanding

However, this knowledge cannot be grasped casually. It must be unfolded with precision by a qualified teacher and received by a mature mind — one prepared by discipline, dispassion, and a sincere desire for freedom. Without this preparation, Vedanta may seem abstract or obscure. With it, the teaching reveals its true nature as a direct means to *moksha* — liberation.

The method of Vedanta works not by transforming the individual, but by revealing that the individual — the doer, the sufferer, the seeker — was never real in the first place. When ignorance is gone, what remains is not a new state, but what was always there: the non-dual Self, limitless and free.

—

Root & Meaning

Veda – knowledge
Anta – end
Vedanta – "The end of the Veda," referring both to the Upanishads and to the final knowledge that concludes the human quest for meaning.

Scriptural References

- **Upanishads** – Source texts of nondual knowledge
- **Bhagavad Gita** – A synthesis of Vedantic insight and yogic practice
- **Brahma Sutras** – Logical codification of the Upanishadic vision
- **Prakarana Granthas** – Foundational texts (e.g., *Tattva Bodha*, *Vivekachudamani*) used to introduce and elaborate the teachings

Traditional View of Vedanta

Vedanta is not a philosophy developed by any one person. It is a revealed means of knowledge (*shruti-pramana*), transmitted through a lineage of teachers trained in a specific methodology (*sampradaya*). It is not self-inquiry done in isolation, but a systematic unfolding of what is always true.

The core teaching of Vedanta is that the true Self — the one who experiences, thinks, acts, and seeks — is not separate from the whole. The apparent individual (*jiva*) is, in essence, none other than Brahman, the limitless reality. This is known in traditional terms as *jiva-brahma-aikyam* — the identity or oneness of the individual and the absolute.

Vedanta does not ask you to deny the person or the world. Rather, it shows that both are projections, like a reflection in a mirror: dependent on awareness, shaped by the mind, but not ultimately real in themselves. The world is described as *mithya* — apparently real, but not independently so, like the snake superimposed on a rope in dim light.

The person is not to be improved or escaped, but understood — and in that understanding, the one who was bound disappears, revealing the Self that was never bound to begin with.

Vedantic Analysis

Vedanta operates through *adhyaropa-apavada* — the method of superimposition and negation. It first accepts duality as a teaching device, then gradually negates it to reveal non-duality. This is accomplished through three stages of direct inquiry:

- *Shravana* – Systematic listening to the teaching
- *Manana* – Reflection to resolve doubts and internal resistance
- *Nididhyasana* – Deep contemplation to fully assimilate the truth

These stages are supported by preparatory disciplines:

- *Karma Yoga* – Selfless action and mental surrender of results, which purifies the mind and reduces egoism.
- *Upasana Yoga* – Meditative and contemplative practices that

calm and focus the mind. Functionally equivalent to *ashtanga yoga* (ethical living, concentration, meditation, etc.), but stripped of the metaphysical doctrines of Patanjali's Yoga system. Its purpose in Vedanta is not *samadhi*, but mental fitness for Self-knowledge.

The goal is not to escape the world, but to see clearly what is real and to rest in the unshakable knowledge that the Self is ever free.

Common Misunderstandings

- **Vedanta is an Indian philosophy:** While rooted in India, it transcends all cultural boundaries. It is a universal means of knowledge, not a belief system.
- **Vedanta is a religion:** It encourages a devotional attitude but does not require faith in a deity.
- **Vedanta is about improving the person:** The person is not transformed, but seen through. The doer is negated, not perfected.
- **Vedanta is intellectual:** Though it uses logic, its goal is not conceptual understanding but direct recognition. Assimilation, not interpretation.
- **Vedanta is a path:** There is no distance between you and the Self. Vedanta removes the illusion of distance.

The Journey of Self-Discovery

As we delve into the teachings of Vedanta, we embark on a journey of self-discovery. This journey is not about accumulating knowledge but about shedding layers of misunderstanding. Each step brings us closer to the realization that we are not separate from the whole.

In this exploration, we may encounter resistance. Our minds may cling to old beliefs and identities. Yet, with patience and perseverance, we can begin to see through these illusions. The path to clarity is obscured only by our own conditioning and misconceptions.

Vedantic Resolution

Freedom is not something to be attained. It is the removal of ignorance — the false identification with what is not the Self. When that veil lifts, nothing changes, and everything changes. The world continues, the body acts, the mind thinks, but the knot of bondage is gone. You remain as you always were — pure, whole, limitless awareness. This is *moksha* — freedom from the person, while its effect is experienced as freedom for the person. It's not a new state of consciousness, but the recognition that you were never bound.

vikshepa

(vikṣepa — *vik-SHAY-puh*)

If *avarana* is the veil that hides the Self, and *mala* is the impurity that weighs the mind down, *vikshepa (vikṣepa)* is the force that tosses the mind outward. It is the agitating power of maya — the relentless movement, the ceaseless distraction, the tendency of attention to leap toward objects, thoughts, fears, and desires. *Vikshepa* is what makes the mind unable to stay with itself.

The literal meaning is "to throw" or "to scatter," and that is precisely how it functions. Even when the mind is relatively pure, it may still remain outward-tending, constantly projecting its own interpretations onto the world. This projection isn't deliberate; it is automatic. The mind imagines what it fears, amplifies what it desires, and constructs narratives to fill the perceived gap created by *avarana's* concealment.

Because the Self appears hidden, vikshepa rushes to fill the void. It manifests in dozens of familiar ways: racing thoughts, emotional overreaction, compulsive planning, catastrophizing, fantasizing, over-analysis, and the endless pursuit of stimulation. Even spiritual seeking can become an expression of *vikshepa* when motivated by restlessness rather than clarity. A distracted mind is incapable of quietude; it chases its own projections like a dog chasing its tail. Where *mala* is heavy, *vikshepa* is hyperactive. Where *mala* reduces capacity, *vikshepa* dissipates it.

This restlessness is not accidental; it is embedded in the *gunas*. *Vikshepa* is closely aligned with *rajas*, the quality of motion. A rajasic mind cannot abide in stillness — not because stillness is impossible, but because agitation feels like normalcy. Such a mind may understand the teaching intellectually yet be unable to hold the thread long enough for recognition to occur.

Traditionally, *upasana* — meditation, devotion, and contemplative practices — are prescribed to quiet *vikshepa*. The goal is not to still the mind permanently but to develop the capacity for one-pointedness. A mind that can remain steady even for a few moments begins to recognize that awareness is present beneath all movement.

When *vikshepa* softens, something subtle emerges. The mind no longer lunges outward; it reclines into itself. Thoughts still arise, but they do not hijack attention. The inner space widens. The teaching becomes not only audible but absorbable. In this quieting, the connection between the mind and its ground — awareness— becomes available.

Vikshepa does not end in a dramatic event. It ends slowly, with practice, with devotion, with the steady refinement of attention. When the projecting force calms, the mind becomes fit for the final work: seeing through *avarana*, the last veil. And in that stillness, the truth that has always been present becomes unmistakably clear.

—

Root & Meaning

From the Sanskrit root *kship* — "to throw, to cast, to project." *Vikshepa* literally means "scattering" or "projection," referring to the mind's tendency to move outward, chase objects, and construct narratives.

Scriptural References

Though the word appears more explicitly in later Advaita works, its meaning is rooted in the Upanishads and *Gita*:

- **Katha Upanishad 2.1.1:** The senses move outward by default, preventing knowledge of the inner Self.
- **Bhagavad Gita 6.34–35:** Arjuna describes the restless mind as

unsteady and hard to control. Krishna prescribes practice and detachment.

- **Vivekachudamani (112–115):** Shankara identifies *vikshepa* as agitation that obstructs meditation and clear recognition.
- **Panchadashi (6.1–6):** Vidyaranya presents *vikshepa* as the second obstacle after *mala* and before *avarana*.

These texts collectively point to restlessness as a major barrier to Self-knowledge.

Traditional View

Vikshepa is one of the two powers of maya, along with *avarana* (concealment):

- *Avarana* hides the real.
- *Vikshepa* projects the unreal.

Tradition associates *vikshepa* with *rajas*, the *guna* of movement and agitation.

When *vikshepa* is strong:

- Thoughts race
- Attention scatters
- Desires multiply
- Fears amplify
- Meditation becomes difficult
- The mind leaps from object to object

Even an intelligent or well-meaning seeker can struggle to remain steady because vikshepa constantly throws attention outward.

Vedantic Analysis

Vikshepa functions as the mind's projective habit — the tendency to superimpose meaning, create stories, and seek fulfillment in external objects. It is directly fueled by:

- Desire (*raga*)
- Aversion (*dvesha*)
- Anxiety
- Habitual thought patterns
- Overthinking and compulsive planning

Where *mala* creates heaviness and opacity, *vikshepa* creates motion and distraction. Both must be managed before the deeper obstacle, avarana, can be addressed through inquiry.

The treatment for *vikshepa* is *upasana*: meditation, *japa*, devotion, and contemplative absorption. These practices refine attention and cultivate *ekagrata* — the capacity for one-pointed focus. A quiet, steady mind becomes capable of hearing and absorbing the teaching.

Common Misunderstandings

- **"Vikshepa is only about distraction."** Distraction is one expression, but the essence of *vikshepa* is projection — the mind throwing its interpretations outward and reacting to its own creations.
- **"If I purify mala, vikshepa automatically disappears."** Not exactly. A light and mature mind still requires training to remain steady. *Upasana* is indispensable.
- **"Vikshepa ends through force or suppression."** Attempting to crush thoughts reinforces *rajas*. True quietude comes from practice, clarity, and disidentification.
- **"Vikshepa is a personal flaw."** It is universal. The mind is shaped by *rajas*; movement is its default setting until refined.

Vedantic Resolution

Vikshepa softens through disciplined attention, devotion, and a lifestyle aligned with dharma. As *rajas* settles:

- Thoughts slow down
- Emotions lose their charge

- Meditation becomes possible
- Inner space widens
- The mind becomes steady and receptive

A mind free from excessive *vikshepa* can finally engage *shravana* and *manana* without scattering. This steadiness prepares it for the last veil — *avarana* — to be lifted through knowledge.

viparita-bhavana

(viparīta-bhāvanā — *vi-puh-REE-tuh BHAA-vuh-NAA*)

In Vedanta, *viparita-bhavana (viparīta-bhāvanā)* means "contrary notion" — the persistence of old, habitual conditioning even after correct knowledge has been gained. Unlike *viparyaya* (error or inversion caused by ignorance), which is removed by Self-knowledge, *viparita-bhavana* is subtler: the conditioning of the mind lingers, making one continue to "feel" bound, small, or incomplete even though one "knows" the teaching.

A classic example is this: the student has heard and understood "I am not the body, I am awareness." Yet in daily life, fear, shame, or pride still arise as though the Self were limited. These emotional reactions are not a lack of knowledge but traces of old patterns — deeply ingrained habits of thought and feeling that run contrary (*viparita*) to the new vision.

Shankara and traditional teachers stress that these habitual errors are worn away through nididhyasana — deep assimilation of the teaching, living with it until it saturates one's daily orientation. *Viparita-bhavana* does not require new information; it requires steady exposure and reconditioning so that the mind naturally abides in the truth.

Thus, *viparita-bhavana* explains why liberation is not just intellectual understanding but requires assimilation. Self-knowledge is immediate, but its full freedom is lived only when contrary habits of thinking are dissolved.

—

Root & Meaning

Viparita = inverted, contrary, opposed.

Bhavana = attitude, habitual notion, conviction.

Viparita-bhavana = "contrary conviction," the persistence of old contrary tendencies after gaining true knowledge.

Scriptural References

- **Shankara on Bhagavad Gita 6.35:** even after knowledge, the restless mind must be trained to abide in clarity.
- **Vedanta manuals (e.g., Vedantasara):** list *viparita-bhavana* as an obstacle that remains until assimilated through *nididhyasana*.

Traditional View

- Knowledge removes *viparyaya* (the error itself).
- But habits of emotional and mental response (*viparita-bhavana*) remain.
- These are exhausted through consistent dwelling on the truth (*nididhyasana*) and living a life of dharma.

Vedantic Analysis

- Example: I know the sun does not "rise," but I still say "sunrise." Likewise, I know I am limitless, yet I may still "feel" limited.
- *Viparita-bhavana* is not ignorance but conditioning.
- It explains why assimilation is gradual even though knowledge is immediate.

Common Misunderstandings

- **That viparita-bhavana means lack of knowledge:** It is not ignorance, but old patterns continuing to play out.
- **That more study (shravana) will solve it:** What is required is assimilation (*nididhyasana*), not more information.
- **That enlightenment erases emotions:** Emotions continue to arise, but no longer bind when contrary notions are worn away.

Vedantic Resolution

Viparita-bhavana shows why Self-knowledge must be assimilated, not just understood. With steady practice, the contrary tendencies lose force, and the mind naturally abides in the freedom of the Self.

viparyaya

(viparyaya — *vip-uhr-YUH-yuh*)

In Vedanta, *viparyaya* is not just error, but reversal — the turning upside-down of reality under the power of maya. Instead of seeing the Self as limitless awareness and the world as dependent appearance, the order is reversed: the body-mind is taken as "I," and the world as solid and independent.

The rope–snake metaphor shows this well. The rope is real, the snake unreal. Ignorance veils the rope (*avarana*), and projection supplies the snake (*vikshepa*). The mind then reverses truth: the unreal snake is treated as real, the real rope is hidden. Likewise, in samsara, the eternal Self is overlooked, and the transient body and world are grasped as truth.

Shankara's *Adhyasa Bhashya* describes bondage as precisely this reversal — attributing the qualities of the Self to the non-Self and vice versa. For the ordinary person, this reversal is constant: the finite is taken as infinite, dependence as independence, *mithya* as *satya*. For the *jnani*, *viparyaya* is gone. Appearances of duality remain, but are never taken as ultimately real.

Thus *viparyaya* is the deep inversion of vision sustained by ignorance. Vedanta corrects it by revealing reality as it is: the Self is satya, ever free; the world is *mithya*, dependent and transient.

—

Root & Meaning

Vi (apart, contrary) + *pari* (around, all sides) + *-yaya* (going around, change, alternation).
Viparyaya = inversion, reversal, erroneous cognition.

Scriptural References

- **Yoga Sutra 1.8:** "*Viparyaya* is false knowledge, based on form, which is not as it appears."
- **Shankara's Adhyasa Bhashya:** defines bondage as *adhyasa* (superimposition), i.e., *viparyaya* — reversal of Self and not-Self.
- **Bhagavad Gita 18.22:** "That knowledge which clings to one body as if it were the whole… know it as tamasic."

Traditional View

- *Viparyaya* is maya's power of reversal — flipping reality on its head.
- Leads to *adhyasa*: attributing Self's qualities to non-Self and vice versa.
- Destroyed only by Self-knowledge (*atma-jnana*).

Vedantic Analysis

- Mechanism: non-apprehension > misapprehension > reversal.
- Example: rope is unseen, snake is projected, reality is inverted.
- For the *ajnani*: "I am small, bound, lacking; the world is vast and real."
- For the *jnani*: reversal corrected — Self is limitless, world is *mithya*.

Common Misunderstandings

- **That viparyaya is just error of the senses:** It is the global reversal of subject and object.
- **That meditation alone corrects viparyaya:** Only *shruti*, unfolded by a teacher, removes it.
- **That viparyaya vanishes from appearances:** Duality continues in *vyavahara*, just as the sun still seems to "rise" in the east even after we know the earth rotates. What ends for the *jnani* is not the appearance, but the mistake of taking the appearance as

satya.

Vedantic Resolution

Viparyaya is maya's inversion of reality — the Self mistaken as finite, the world mistaken as real. Vedanta's revelation reverses the reversal, restoring vision: the Self is satya, the world is *mithya*.

Virat

(Virāṭ — *vi-RAAT*)

Virat (Virāṭ) is the total gross body — the entire universe seen
as a single cosmic organism, also called the Cosmic Man (*Virat
Purusha*). Just as each individual has a *sthula sharira* (gross body),
so too does the totality. The sun, moon, stars, mountains, rivers,
animals, and humans are all limbs of the *Virat Purusha*, the universal person.

The Vedas often describe creation in this way to shift our perspective from a fragmented view of the world to a vision of wholeness. In the *Purusha Sukta* of the *Rig Veda*, the cosmic being is said
to have a thousand heads, eyes, and feet, pervading everything
and transcending it. This poetic vision reveals *Virat* as the macrocosmic counterpart of our own physical embodiment. What we
call "my body" is really a small borrowing from the total physical
universe — a handful of earth, water, fire, air, and space taken on
loan from the *Virat*.

In Vedanta, *Virat* is not ultimate reality. Like all *upadhis*, it is
mithya — dependent reality. Its significance is pedagogical:
to show that the individual is not isolated, but part of a vast
interconnected body. When this vision is assimilated, the mind
expands — "I am not just this limited frame, but connected to the
whole."

For the seeker, contemplation on *Virat* can be a powerful aid to
loosen ego-identity. By seeing the universe as a living whole,
pervaded by awareness, one begins to recognize the Self as that
awareness in which even the cosmic body arises. Thus, *Virat* is a
step in the unfolding that culminates in recognizing Brahman as
the substratum of all.

—

Root & Meaning

Virat (from *vr* = to cover, encompass, expand).
Meaning: vast, all-encompassing, universal.
In Vedanta: the total gross body, the cosmic form.

Scriptural References

- **Rig Veda 10.90 (Purusha Sukta):** describes the cosmic being with a thousand heads, eyes, and feet.
- **Bhagavad Gita, Chapter 11:** Krishna reveals his *Virat rupa* (cosmic form) to Arjuna.
- **Mandukya Upanishad, 1–2:** the waking state consciousness (*vaishvanara*) is identified with the *Virat*.

Traditional View

- *Virat* is the macrocosmic gross body, encompassing all physical forms.
- Seen as the universal person (*Virat Purusha* or "Cosmic Man"), pervading and sustaining the cosmos.
- Contemplation on *Virat* leads to recognition of one's non-separateness from the whole.

Vedantic Analysis

- Individual–total parallel:
  - *Sthula sharira* = individual gross body.
  - *Virat* = total gross body.
- Aids in expanding one's identity beyond the limited "I."
- Yet, as *mithya*, *Virat* is not the final truth; it too depends on Brahman.

Common Misunderstandings

- **That Virat is ultimate reality:** It is a manifestation, not Brahman itself.

- **That Virat is only mythological:** It is a symbolic way of grasping the total.
- **That Virat is separate from us:** Our bodies are small expressions of the cosmic body.

Vedantic Resolution

Virat is the total gross body — the cosmic organism. By contemplating it, the mind shifts from isolation to wholeness, preparing for the recognition that the Self is not the cosmic body either, but the awareness in which even *Virat* appears.

Vishva

(Viśva — *vish-vuh*)

In Vedanta, *Vishva (Viśva)* is the waker, the individual experiencer in the waking state (*jagrat-avastha*). While in deep sleep the Self remains unrecognized, and in dream one inhabits subtle creations of the mind, in waking state consciousness identifies with the gross body and the external world. In this mode, the Self is referred to as *Vishva*.

The *Mandukya Upanishad* identifies *Vishva* with *Vaishvanara*, the total waking consciousness, and with *Virat*, the cosmic gross body. The individual waker is the microcosm, while *Virat* is the macrocosm. This microcosm–macrocosm relationship helps the seeker see that what appears as "my waking experience" is but a part of the universal waking experience.

Vishva is not the Self itself but the Self conditioned by identification with the body and senses in waking. As long as the Self is taken to be *Vishva*, it is bound: the doer, the enjoyer, the sufferer. Recognizing *Vishva* as *mithya* — an appearance within awareness — frees one from confusing the waking personality with the true Self.

Thus, contemplation on *Vishva* is a stepping stone to freedom. By examining the waking state carefully, one sees its transience and limitation, and is guided to the recognition that awareness is constant through waking, dream, and sleep.

—

Root & Meaning

From *vish* = "to pervade."
Vishva = all, universal, the waking experiencer.

In Vedanta: the individual Self identified with the gross body in waking state.

Scriptural References

- **Mandukya Upanishad 1–3:** The first quarter of the Self is *Vishva*, enjoying external objects through the senses in waking state.
- **Shankara's Mandukya Bhashya:** explains *Vishva* as the microcosm, linked to *Virat* as macrocosm.

Traditional View

- *Vishva* = the *jiva* in waking state, conditioned by the gross body.
- Enjoys external objects through the senses.
- Microcosmic counterpart of *Virat*.

Vedantic Analysis

States of experience:

- *Vishva* = waking (individual gross-body identification).
- *Taijasa* = dream (subtle-body identification).
- *Prajna* = deep sleep (causal-body identification).

In each, the Self itself is unchanging; only the conditioning shifts. Recognizing this, one sees: "I am not *Vishva*, I am awareness illumining waking."

Common Misunderstandings

- **That Vishva is the true Self:** It is only one *upadhi* (conditioning).
- **That waking is more real than dream:** Both are appearances within awareness.
- **That Vishva ends with death:** The waking role ends, but awareness is constant.

Vedantic Resolution

Vishva is the waking personality, not the ultimate Self. Seeing it as *mithya*, one dis-identifies from the role of the waker and abides as the awareness illumining all states.

vivarta-vada

(vivarta-vāda — *vi-VAHR-tuh VAA-duh*)

In Advaita Vedanta, *vivarta-vada (vivarta-vāda)* is the doctrine of apparent transformation. It explains how the universe appears to arise without Brahman undergoing any real change. The rope–snake example illustrates this: when a rope is mistaken for a snake, nothing happens to the rope. The snake is only an appearance, a projection born of ignorance.

This stands in contrast to *parinama-vada* ("real transformation"), where the cause truly transforms into its effect, as milk becomes curd. Vedanta rejects this model for Brahman, since it would imply change in the changeless absolute. Instead, Advaita insists that Brahman never undergoes transformation. The world is only an apparent modification — a dependent appearance (*mithya*) superimposed upon Brahman, like the mirage upon desert sand.

Vivarta-vada is not a literal cosmology but a teaching device (*prakriya*). Its purpose is to protect the non-dual vision: if Brahman is infinite and without parts, it cannot be modified or diminished by creation. The world, therefore, is *vivarta* — an appearance that depends upon Brahman but does not affect it.

For the seeker, this teaching loosens attachment to the world as ultimately real. Seeing all names and forms as vivarta helps the mind rest in the recognition that Brahman alone is *satya*, the unchanging substratum.

—

Root & Meaning

Vi (apart, different) + *vrt* (to turn, to appear) = *vivarta* (apparent change, illusory transformation.)

Vada = doctrine, teaching.

Vivarta-vada = the doctrine of apparent transformation.

Scriptural References

- **Chandogya Upanishad 6.1.4:** clay and pots analogy — "By knowing one lump of clay, all that is made of clay is known; all modifications are only names, spoken by words, the clay alone is real."
- **Brahma Sutra 2.1.14:** Shankara comments that creation is not a real transformation but an apparent one.
- **Mandukya Karika 3.15–17 (Gaudapada):** asserts the unborn nature of reality, emphasizing that appearances do not affect Brahman.

Traditional View

- Brahman = unchanging cause.
- World = apparent modification (*vivarta*), not real change.
- Maintains non-duality by denying transformation in Brahman.

Vedantic Analysis

- *Parinama-vada* (real transformation): cause truly changes into effect (from milk to curd).
- *Vivarta-vada* (apparent transformation): cause remains unchanged, effect is an appearance (from rope to snake).
- Advaita upholds *vivarta-vada* to preserve Brahman's changelessness.

Common Misunderstandings

- **That vivarta-vada means the world is unreal in the sense of non-existent:** The world exists, but as dependent (*mithya*), not independent.
- **That Brahman "projects" the world intentionally:** *Vivarta* does

not describe a process in time but a way of understanding appearance.

- That *vivarta-vada* is final reality: It is a teaching method to show Brahman's changelessness; ultimately, from the *paramarthika* standpoint, no creation has ever occurred (*ajata-vada* of Gaudapada).

Vedantic Resolution

Vivarta-vada explains creation as apparent transformation — protecting the non-dual truth that Brahman is changeless and ever free. The world appears but does not alter the substratum.

viveka

(viveka — *vi-VAY-kuh*)

Viveka is discrimination, the capacity to distinguish between what is real and what is not, between the eternal and the transient. In Vedanta, it refers especially to *nitya-anitya-vastu-viveka* — discrimination between the real (Brahman, the Self) and the unreal (the world of names and forms).

At first, *Viveka* begins as an intellectual ability: the mind carefully examines life and sees that all objects — wealth, relationships, body, even mind — are temporary and subject to change. None of these can provide lasting security. The only unchanging reality is the Self, consciousness itself.

As the seeker grows, *Viveka* deepens into a natural orientation. Choices reflect the clarity of discrimination: valuing Self-knowledge over fleeting pleasures, preferring freedom over bondage. *Viveka* is therefore the first and most crucial qualification for spiritual pursuit, listed at the head of *sadhana-chatushtaya* (the fourfold qualifications).

Without *Viveka*, the mind remains scattered in worldly pursuits, unable to commit to the path of knowledge. With *Viveka*, dispassion (*vairagya*) follows naturally, along with discipline of the mind (*shama*), senses (*dama*), and other supporting qualities.

Ultimately, *Viveka* is not cynicism or rejection of the world but clarity of vision: knowing the difference between the eternal substratum and the ephemeral appearance. It is the compass that guides the seeker through maya toward freedom.

—

Root & Meaning

From root *vi* = "to separate, discern" and the prefix *vic-* = "apart"
Viveka = discrimination, discernment, clarity of separation.

Scriptural References

- **Vivekachudamani 19:** "Among all means, knowledge alone is supreme. But discrimination (*viveka*) is the very first step to liberation."
- **Bhagavad Gita 18.30:** Sattvic intellect discriminates rightly between dharma and *adharma*, bondage and freedom.
- **Taittiriya Upanishad:** Through discrimination, the seeker separates the Self from the sheaths (*pancha-kosha-viveka*).

Traditional View

- First of the *sadhana-chatushtaya* qualifications.
- Especially: *nitya-anitya-vastu-viveka* — discriminating the eternal Self from impermanent objects.
- Practical: enables renunciation (*vairagya*) and discipline in pursuit of Self-knowledge.

Vedantic Analysis

- *Viveka* is both an intellectual and existential discernment.
- Shows that objects are *anitya* (impermanent), Brahman alone is *nitya* (permanent).
- Protects the seeker from getting lost in temporary goals.
- A skill sharpened by study, reflection, and living a life of dharma.

Common Misunderstandings

- **That viveka is mere cleverness:** It is not intellectual argumentation; it is clarity about what truly matters.

- **That viveka makes life dry or joyless:** True discrimination reveals freedom and greater appreciation, not rejection.
- **That viveka is once-for-all:** It must be exercised continually, as maya veils clarity again and again.

Vedantic Resolution

Viveka is the faculty that distinguishes the real from the unreal, enabling the seeker to orient life toward liberation. Without it, Vedanta remains theory; with it, Self-knowledge becomes transformative.

vritti

(vṛtti — *vrit-tee*)

We tend to think of the mind as a single, continuous field — one
stream of thinking, feeling, remembering, imagining. But Vedanta
offers a more precise picture. What we call "the mind" is not a
monolith but a constant sequence of momentary appearances.
A thought flares up, lingers for a breath, and dissolves. An emotion rises with force and then fades. A memory flashes, an image
forms, a sudden insight breaks through. None of these movements are permanent, and none stay longer than the conditions
that give rise to them. They come and go like weather.

Vedanta calls each of these appearances a *vritti (vṛtti)* — a modification of the mind, a small wave forming on the surface of awareness. It is a beautifully simple idea: the mind is not a fixed entity,
but a field of ever-changing formations. And yet this simple
insight has profound consequences for spiritual inquiry. Because
if the mind is always moving, and the Self is the one who knows
those movements, then the Self cannot be the mind. A *vritti* is
known; the knower is not.

This distinction is the beginning of freedom. When anger arises, it is not I am angry but anger is arising. When sadness drifts
in, it is not I am sad but a sad thought is moving through the
mind. When joy bubbles up, it is not I am joyful but simply here is
joy. The wave is never the ocean. The movement is never the witness. The appearance is never the awareness that knows it. Seeing
this clearly loosens centuries of conditioning.

A *vritti* is not a moral event. It is not a personal failure or achievement. It is not "negative" or "positive," "spiritual" or "unspiritu-
al." It is simply the mind doing what the mind is designed to do
— respond to impressions, interpret experience, process memory,

and express the tendencies (*vasanas*) that lie dormant within it. Even emotions, which seem so intimate and defining, are nothing more than *vritti* filled with intensity. They rise in the mind, move through the body, and pass.

What gives *vritti* their power is not their existence, but our identification with them. When a thought arises and we say, "This is me," the *vritti* becomes a world. When we say, "This should not be here," we prolong it. When we cling to pleasure or panic at discomfort, we bind ourselves to the next wave. But when a *vritti* is simply seen for what it is—a brief modulation of the mind—its ability to bind dissolves.

The goal of Vedanta is not to stop *vritti* or to enter a blank state of mind. That is the path of Yoga. Vedanta's aim is far simpler and more radical: to recognize that no *vritti*, however refined or turbulent, can define the Self. Thoughts may appear, but the thinker is not found. Feelings may surge, but the feeler is never located. The mind continues its dance, but the dancer is never touched.

To understand *vritti* is to understand the nature of the mind. To understand the nature of the mind is to stop mistaking it for yourself. And that is the first real step toward freedom.

———

Root & Meaning

From the Sanskrit root *vrt* — "to turn, revolve, arise, appear, take form." A *vritti* is a modification, movement, or fluctuation of the mind.

In Vedanta, a *vritti* is any thought, emotion, sensation, memory, perception, or mental image that arises in the mind (*antahkarana*). Each *vritti* has a beginning and an end, and because it is known as an object, it cannot be the Self.

Scriptural References

While most famous in *Yoga Sutra 1.2 (citta-vritti-nirodhah)*, the concept is deeply embedded in Vedantic literature:

- **Upanishads:** Distinguish the unchanging witness (*sakshi*) from the changing movements of the mind.
- **Panchadashi & Vivekachudamani:** Treat *vritti* as the mechanism by which knowledge takes place.
- **Bhagavad Gita:** Describes the mind's restlessness (*chanchala*) — the constant arising of *vritti* — as the cause of confusion.

Though not always named explicitly, the idea of mental modifications is fundamental to Vedantic psychology.

Traditional View

In Advaita Vedanta:

- A *vritti* is a thought-wave in the mind.
- The mind forms a *vritti* in response to an object.
- Knowledge occurs when the *vritti* takes the "shape" of the object (*vritti-jnana*).
- The Self is the consciousness that knows the *vritti* but is untouched by it.

There are three basic types of *vritti*:

- *Tamas* — dull, heavy, depressive, inert
- *Rajas* — agitated, emotional, restless
- *Sattva* — clear, calm, reflective

The movements of the mind reflect the quality of *guna* predominating at any given moment.

Vedantic Analysis

A *vritti* is not the enemy. Vedanta does not teach the suppression of thought, emotion, or mental activity. Instead, it clarifies the nature of these movements so one is no longer confused by them.

Key insights:

- Every *vritti* is an object. If it can be known, witnessed, or observed, it cannot be the Self. This is the heart of *drg-drshya viveka*.
- *Vrittis* do not bind; identification binds. Anger is never the problem. "I am angry" is the problem. The *vritti* is harmless unless the ego claims it.
- *Vrittis* are required for knowledge. Even Self-knowledge is ultimately a *vritti*: *akhandakara-vritti* — the "Brahman-shaped" cognition that destroys ignorance.
- Liberation is not the destruction of *vritti*. It is the recognition that *vritti* never belonged to you. The mind continues to think. The Self continues to know. Nothing changes at the level of consciousness.

Common Misunderstandings

- **"I must stop my thoughts to be spiritual."** No. That is Yoga's goal, not Vedanta's. Vedanta does not require stillness of mind — only clarity of knowledge.
- **"Emotions are impurities."** Emotions are simply *vritti* colored by rajas and *tamas*. Their presence does not diminish consciousness.
- **"Self-knowledge ends all mental activity."** The mind continues. Life continues. What ends is confusion about who you are.
- **"A quiet mind is a liberated mind."** A quiet mind is a sattvic mind, not a liberated one. Liberation occurs not by quieting the mind but by seeing through it.

Vedantic Resolution

A *vritti* is a passing appearance in the mind, known to the unchanging Self. Thoughts arise, emotions surge, perceptions come and go, but none of these movements alter consciousness. Self-knowledge doesn't eliminate *vritti*; it removes the sense of ownership over them. The mind becomes a transparent instrument — capable of thought, emotion, reason, delight, and perception, yet no longer mistaken for the Self. In this clarity, even the rise and fall of *vrittis* becomes effortless. They are seen as nothing more than waves on the surface of awareness, never touching its depth.

vyavaharika

(vyāvahārika — *VYAA-vuh-HAAR-i-kuh*)

In Advaita Vedanta, *vyavaharika* (*vyāvahārika*) refers to the empirical or transactional level of reality — the shared world of daily life
where cause and effect, dharma, and ordinary dealings operate. It
is the standpoint in which we live, act, and interact as individuals
in society.

Vedanta distinguishes three orders of reality:

- *Pratibhasika* — illusory, purely subjective (like dream or mirage).
- *Vyavaharika* — empirical, shared by all, practical reality.
- *Paramarthika* — absolute, the standpoint of non-dual Brahman.

From the standpoint of *vyavaharika*, the world is real enough to
function: fire burns, water quenches, ethical actions yield results,
and human beings engage in meaningful pursuits. This level is
necessary for dharma and spiritual practice. However, Vedanta
points out that even *vyavaharika satta* is not ultimate. It is *mithya*:
real for practical purposes, but dependent on Brahman for its
existence.

A common analogy is the sunrise: in daily life, we say "the sun
rises," and that statement works in *vyavaharika*. Yet astronomy
shows the sun does not literally rise. Similarly, the world appears
real and functions consistently, but its underlying reality is
Brahman alone.

Thus *vyavaharika* is affirmed and honored in Advaita — one must
live responsibly within it — but it is ultimately sublated when one
sees from the *paramarthika* standpoint. The sage functions in
vyavaharika while knowing it as appearance.

—

Root & Meaning

From *vyavahara* = conduct, practice, worldly transaction.
Vyavaharika = relating to empirical dealings, transactional reality.

Scriptural References

- **Brahma Sutra Bhashya (2.1.14–20):** Shankara distinguishes between empirical causality and ultimate reality.
- **Mandukya Karika (3.29–31):** Gaudapada distinguishes *pratibhasika, vyavaharika, and paramarthika.*
- **Bhagavad Gita 3.20–26:** Even the wise should engage in action for the welfare of the world (*lokasamgraha*) — functioning within *vyavahara.*

Traditional View

- *Vyavaharika* = the practical reality of daily life.
- Accepted as provisionally real; necessary for dharma, karma, and spiritual practice.
- Sublated by realization of *paramarthika satya* (absolute reality).

Vedantic Analysis

- **Pratibhasika**: private dream, subjective illusion.
- **Vyavaharika**: shared dream — empirical world, consistent and lawful because it is under *Ishvara's* order.
- **Paramarthika**: absolute reality, pure awareness.

From the seeker's standpoint, *vyavaharika* is like a dream:

- Everything is changing and unstable, never what it seems.
- Yet it is coherent and sustained because it is Ishvara's dream, not just an individual projection.
- Dharma, karma, and spiritual practice all operate here, giving it practical reality.

Common Misunderstandings

- **That vyavaharika is false or useless:** It is not denied, only relativized. One must live within *vyavahara*.
- **That vyavaharika is independent:** It depends on Brahman; hence called *mithya*.
- **That sages abandon vyavahara:** They continue to act, but with knowledge that it is appearance.

Vedantic Resolution

Vyavaharika is empirical reality — the collective dream sustained by *Ishvara*. Like a dream, it is transient and not what it seems. Unlike a private dream, it is consistent and shared. Its purpose is pedagogical: the stage where seekers live, act, and eventually awaken to the *paramarthika* truth that Brahman alone is real.

yoga

(yoga — *YO-guh*)

In the modern West, the word *yoga* typically conjures images of postures, breathing exercises, and physical discipline — practiced in gyms, studios, or on glowing screens. This version, known as *hatha yoga*, aims to promote calmness, flexibility, and physical well-being. While not without value, this emphasis often eclipses the deeper meaning of yoga as it appears in the *Bhagavad Gita* and in Vedantic tradition.

The word *yoga* is rich with meaning. Etymologically, it derives from the Sanskrit root *yuj*, meaning "to join," "to yoke," or "to unite." In one sense, yoga is the union of the individual self with its highest reality — often interpreted as the Self (atman) or Brahman. Another classical meaning is *samyama*, or mastery — particularly the mastery of the mind and senses. In yet another usage, especially within Vedanta, yoga refers to a topic or discipline, as seen in the titles of the chapters of the *Bhagavad Gita*. Each chapter bears a compound name ending in "yoga," such as *Sannyasa Yoga* — the discipline or teaching on renunciation.

For Vedanta, yoga is not the end goal but a crucial preparation. The spiritual journey is generally divided into two broad stages. First is the path of action (karma) — the stage of doing, striving, purifying. Second is the path of knowledge (*jnana*) — the stage of inquiry, understanding, and abidance in truth. All seekers begin as doers. They act with a sense of separation and desire for wholeness. But the doing, if guided properly, becomes a means of purification. It refines the mind, dissolves attachments, and prepares the seeker to receive knowledge of the Self. This preparatory work is known as yoga.

In the *Bhagavad Gita*, Lord Krishna outlines several yogas, each suited to different temperaments and life contexts. *Karma yoga*, the yoga of selfless action, helps dissolve the binding sense of doership. *Bhakti yoga*, the yoga of devotion, softens the heart and redirects emotional energy toward a higher reality. *Dhyana yoga*, or meditation, stills the mind and prepares it to absorb subtle truth. Each of these, when practiced sincerely, leads to *antahkarana-shuddhi* — purity and steadiness of the inner instrument.

Shankaracharya, the great exponent of Advaita Vedanta, is often cited as prioritizing knowledge over action. And indeed, he asserts unequivocally that liberation (*moksha*) is attained not through ritual or effort, but through the direct knowledge of the Self. And yet, Shankara does not dismiss yoga. In texts like *Aparokshanubhuti*, he affirms the value of contemplative absorption, even redefining yoga as a deep and steady identification with the thought, "I am awareness, not the body-mind." In this way, even *nididhyasana* — deep reflection on the truth heard and reasoned — is itself a kind of yoga, though rooted not in striving but in assimilation.

The key insight of Vedanta is that the Self is ever-free. Nothing need be added or achieved. What obscures this truth is not a lack of accomplishment but a veil of ignorance. Yoga lifts that veil. It calms the agitations of the mind so that the seeker can discern the stillness behind it. As the *Yoga Sutras* put it, *yogah chittavritti nirodhah* — "Yoga is the stilling of the modifications of the mind." Vedanta agrees, but with a refinement: stillness is not an end in itself, but the condition in which truth can shine unobstructed.

Thus, yoga in Vedanta is not a technique for merging with some distant divinity. Nor is it an endless refinement of the body or mind. It is a preparatory path — a sacred discipline that serves the ultimate realization that there is, in truth, no separation to overcome. The Self was never lost. One simply needed the clarity to see it.

In a world obsessed with achievement and progress, this message is quietly radical. Yoga is not about becoming more; it is about recognizing what you already are. The postures may strengthen the body. The breathwork may calm the nerves. But the highest yoga is the steady knowledge that you are not the body, not the mind, but the unchanging awareness in which all experiences rise and fall.

—

Root & Meaning

From the Sanskrit root *yuj* — "to yoke," "to join," "to unite." In its broadest sense, yoga means "union" or "integration," and also "discipline" or "method." Depending on context, it may refer to (1) union of the individual self (*jiva*) with the Self (atman/ Brahman), (2) mastery or harnessing of the mind and senses, or (3) a particular spiritual path or discipline, as in *karma yoga, bhakti yoga*, etc.

Scriptural References

Meaning and etymology of yoga:

- **Bhagavad Gita 6.23:** "That severance from union with sorrow is called yoga. This yoga should be practiced with determination and an undespairing mind."
- **Bhagavad Gita 6.46:** "The yogi is greater than ascetics, greater than the learned, and greater than those devoted to ritual works. Therefore, be a yogi."
- **Shvetashvatara Upanishad 2.12:** "By the practice of yoga, the wise perceive the all-pervading, hidden Self."

Yoga as preparation for knowledge:

- **Bhagavad Gita 2.50:** "One who is engaged in yoga is skillful in action."
- **Bhagavad Gita 6.6:** "For one who has conquered the mind, the mind is the best friend; but for one who has failed to do so, the

mind will remain the greatest enemy."

- **Bhagavad Gita 3.3:** "There are two paths in this world... the path of knowledge for contemplatives, and the path of action for the yogis."

Different yogas:

- **Bhagavad Gita 3.19 – Karma Yoga:** "Without attachment, always perform the work that has to be done; for, by performing action without attachment, one attains the Supreme."
- **Bhagavad Gita 12.6–7 – Bhakti Yoga:** "Those who worship Me, surrendering all actions to Me, meditating on Me with undistracted yoga... I quickly rescue them from the ocean of birth and death."
- **Bhagavad Gita 6.10 – Dhyana Yoga:** "Let the yogi, alone, in solitude, with mind and body controlled, constantly engage the mind in meditation on the Self, free from hope and possessiveness."

Yoga as mental mastery:

- **Yoga Sutra 1.2:** "*Yogah chittavritti nirodhah* – Yoga is the stilling of the modifications of the mind."
- **Katha Upanishad 6.11:** "When the five senses, together with the mind, cease from their normal activities and the intellect itself does not stir, that is said to be the highest state."

Shankara on yoga and knowledge:

- **Aparokshanubhuti 112:** "Yoga is the steady holding of the mind on the thought of the oneness of the Self and Brahman, free from all duality."

Traditional View

Classically, there are many recognized "yogas" — systems or approaches to spiritual realization — including:

- **Karma Yoga** — path of selfless action.
- **Bhakti Yoga** — path of devotion.
- **Upasana Yoga** — path of meditation and mental mastery, also known as *ashtanga yoga* ("eight-limbs yoga") from Patanjali's *Yoga Sutras*, and sometimes called *samadhi yoga* in Vedantic contexts.
- **Jnana Yoga** — path of knowledge and discrimination.

In Patanjali's system, yoga refers specifically to the eight-limbed (*ashtanga*) discipline culminating in meditative absorption (*samadhi*). In Vedantic tradition, the term "yoga" often denotes any preparatory discipline that leads to mental purity (*chitta-shuddhi*) and one-pointedness (*chitta-ekagrata*).

Vedantic Analysis

Vedanta does not see yoga as the ultimate goal but as a means (*sadhana*) to prepare the mind for Self-knowledge. While Patanjali's goal is *kaivalya* (isolation of *purusha* from *prakriti*), Advaita Vedanta's goal is *moksha* — the recognition that one's true nature is non-different from Brahman. Yoga practices — whether action, devotion, or meditation — help reduce the mind's agitations so that the seeker can assimilate the *mahavakyas* ("great statements") of the Upanishads.

Common Misunderstandings

- **"Yoga means physical postures."** *Hatha yoga* is only one small branch; yoga in scripture is primarily mental and spiritual discipline.
- **"Yoga produces liberation."** Yoga prepares the mind; liberation is through Self-knowledge.
- **"Yoga is about union with God."** From the standpoint of truth, there was never separation; yoga removes the ignorance that seemed to create it.

Vedantic Resolution

Yoga is best understood as a preparatory path — a way to make the mind subtle, steady, and free from distraction, so that inquiry into the Self can be fruitful. Once Self-knowledge is firm, yoga in the sense of "union" is revealed to have always been the case.

Pūrṇam adaḥ pūrṇam idam
Pūrṇāt pūrṇam udacyate
Pūrṇasya pūrṇam ādāya
Pūrṇam evāvaśiṣyate

That is full, this is full.
From fullness, fullness arises.
Taking fullness from fullness,
Fullness alone remains.

www.ingramcontent.com/pod-product-compliance
Lightning Source LLC
Chambersburg PA
CBHW020449270326
41926CB00008B/535